D1242955

Lough Neagh

COUNTY

Ballyscullen

PARISH of

GRANGE

UPPER

LONDON-SHILLIN

Artrea

DERRY

BARONY

Ballinderry

Parish

COUNTY

Parish

NCANNON

OF

Parish

ONE LAND-WEST

COUNTY OF ARMAGH

BARONY

Scago Parish

Tartaraghan

Moyntaghs

Duneane

Parish

COUNTY

Drummaul   Parish

ANTRIM

Parish

Muckam Grange

LOWE
KILLEAD
OF
Paris
MASSARE

LOUGH

Crumlin
Parish

Glenavy Pa

UPPER

Ballinderry

ANTRIM
Paris

MASSAREEN

Aghagallon
Parish

COUNTY OF DOWN

Shankill
Parish

NEAGH

NOTE

EXPLANATION

To the Right Honourable
JOHN O'NEILL
Map of
LOUGH NEAGH
and Country adjacent
Taken from Actual Survey

Lough Neagh

an atlas of the natural, built and cultural heritage

edited by

William Burke
Liam Campbell
William Roulston

Ulster Historical Foundation

FRONTISPIECE

Map of Lough Neagh by [James Lendrick?],
assisted by James Williamson and dedicated to
the Right Hon. John O'Neill, 1785
(PRONI, D604/1).

PUBLIC RECORD OFFICE OF NORTHERN IRELAND

This project has been supported by National Lottery Heritage Fund
under their Landscape Partnership programme.

Published 2022
by Ulster Historical Foundation
www.booksireland.org.uk
www.ancestryireland.com

ISBN 978-1-913993-13-9

Printed by GPS Colour Graphics Ltd
Design and production by Dunbar Design

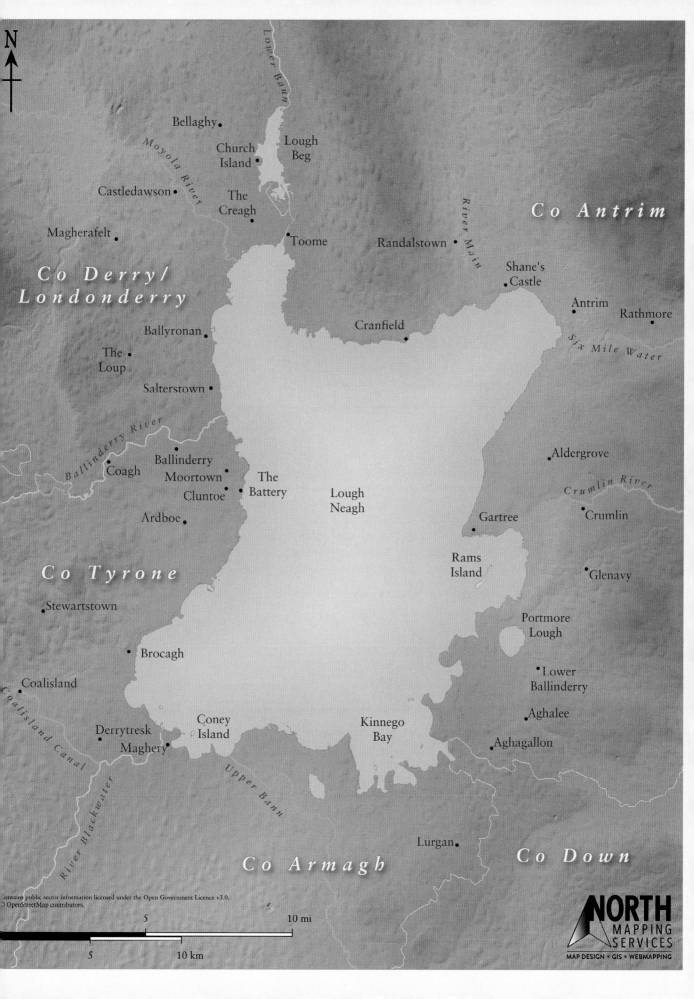

N

Co Antrim

Co Derry/
Londonderry

Co Tyrone

Co Armagh

Co Down

Lower Bann

Moyola River

Bellaghy

Church
Island

Lough
Beg

Castledawson

The
Creagh

Magherafelt

Toome

River Main

Randalstown

Shane's
Castle

Antrim

Rathmore

Ballyronan

Cranfield

Six Mile Water

The
Loup

Salterstown

Ballinderry River

Coagh

Ballinderry
Moortown
Cluntoe

The
Battery

Lough
Neagh

Aldergrove

Crumlin River

Crumlin

Gartree

Ardboe

Rams
Island

Glenavy

Stewartstown

Portmore
Lough

Brocagh

Lower
Ballinderry

Coalisland

Coalisland Canal

Derrytresk
Maghery

Coney
Island

Kinnego
Bay

Aghalee

Aghagallon

River Blackwater

Upper Bann

Lurgan

Contains public sector information licensed under the Open Government Licence v3.0.
© OpenStreetMap contributors.

5

10 mi

5

10 km

NORTH
MAPPING
SERVICES
MAP DESIGN • GIS • WEBMAPPING

Contents

NATURAL HERITAGE / GEOLOGY / ECOLOGY

BUILT HERITAGE / ARCHAEOLOGY / HISTORY

ABBREVIATIONS

AFM	*Annals of the Kingdom of Ireland by the Four Masters,* ed. John O'Donovan (7 vols, Dublin, 1848–51)
BL	British Library
CSPI	*Calendar of the State Papers Relating to Ireland, 1509–1670* (24 vols, London, 1860–1912)
DH	Drapers' Hall, London
JRSAI	*Journal of the Royal Society of Antiquaries of Ireland*
LNFCS	Lough Neagh Fishermen's Co-operative Society Ltd
NISMR	Northern Ireland Sites and Monuments Record
NLI	National Library of Ireland
OSM	*Ordnance Survey Memoirs of Ireland*, ed. Angélique Day and Patrick McWilliams (40 vols, Belfast, 1990–98)
PRIA	*Proceedings of the Royal Irish Academy*
PRONI	Public Record Office of Northern Ireland
TCD	Trinity College Dublin
TNA	The National Archives, London
UJA	*Ulster Journal of Archaeology*

Contributors

SHARON ARBUTHNOT
Department of Anglo-Saxon, Norse and Celtic, University of Cambridge

MIKE BAILLIE
Emeritus Professor, School of Natural and Built Environment,
Queen's University Belfast

KIERAN BREEN
Lough Neagh Heritage Boats

WILLIAM BURKE
Lough Neagh Partnership

SEAMUS BURNS
Area Manager, Royal Society for the Protection of Birds

LIAM CAMPBELL
Mellon Centre for Migration Studies

PAT CLOSE
Manager, Lough Neagh Fishermen's Co-operative Society Ltd

J. ANDREW G. COOPER
Professor of Coastal Studies, Ulster University

CONOR CORR
Lough Neagh Rescue

GERRY DARBY
Strategic Manager, Lough Neagh Partnership

BOB DAVIDSON
Retired Northern Ireland Environment Agency scientist

BARRY DEVLIN
Musician and author

DANIEL J. DONNELLY
Author and geographer

DEREK EVANS
Senior Fisheries Scientist, Agri-Food and Biosciences Institute

SEBASTIAN GRAHAM
Mill historian and Ulster Architectural Heritage

PAT GRIMES
Author and local historian

AILISH HANNA
Geordie Hanna Society

PETER HARPER
Shoreline Environmental Officer, Lough Neagh Partnership

RODDY HEGARTY
Cardinal Tomás Ó Fiaich Memorial Library and Archive, Armagh

DAVID JEWSON
Retired freshwater scientist, Ulster University

CONOR JORDAN
Chair, Lough Neagh Partnership

EIMEAR KEARNEY
Tourism and Marketing Officer, Lough Neagh Partnership

CIARA LAVERTY
Ranger, Lough Neagh Partnership

PATRICIA LYSAGHT
Professor Emerita of European Ethnology, University College Dublin

ANNALEIGH MARGEY
Department of Humanities, Dundalk Institute of Technology

THOMAS McERLEAN
Archaeologist and author

JOHN McKENNA
Retired scientist, Ulster University

CORMAC McSPARRON
Centre for Community Archaeology, Queen's University Belfast

GERARD McVEIGH
Lough Neagh Rescue

RUAIRÍ Ó BAOILL
Centre for Community Archaeology, Queen's University Belfast

JAMES O'NEILL
Author, historian and archaeologist

MALACHY Ó NÉILL
Director of Regional Engagement, Ulster University

JONATHAN PILCHER
Professor Emeritus, School of Geography, Archaeology and Palaeoecology, Queen's University Belfast

RORY J. QUINN
Reader, School of Geography and Environmental Sciences, Ulster University

WILLIAM ROULSTON
Ulster Historical Foundation

KATHARINE SIMMS
Former Senior Lecturer in Medieval History, Trinity College Dublin

PHILIP SMITH
Historic Environment Division, Department for Communities

SIOBHAN THOMPSON
Former Natural Heritage Officer, Lough Neagh Partnership

RÓISÍN WHITE
Local historian and author

Editors' Preface

The genesis for this publication came about in response to the delivery of a suite of built, cultural and natural heritage projects developed and delivered by the Lough Neagh Partnership as part of their National Lottery Heritage Fund Landscape Partnership Scheme. Early on in the scheme it became evident that the broad scope of projects were, in combination, producing a great deal of data and new information on the lough's heritage assets. Therefore, rather than have this sitting on some dusty shelf, we believed it should be shared with the people, communities and stakeholders that value the region.

When we first started to research the content for the book it became noticeably clear that the lough to many living outside its environs was considered a peripheral, liminal and amphibious space. However, we believe this to be an underestimation of the region and despite the slightly pejorative implications of the terms Lough Neagh is actually a central space providing a personal (and community) sense of belonging and identification which contributes to creating and forging deep relationships and a commonality with the landscape. In response to this, we believed that the book would provide a more structured narrative of this special place, remarkable for its sheer scale, its wildlife and the relationship that local people have with it, if it had contributions from a range of other writers and academics who have a more thorough disciplinary understanding of the lough's heritage. In doing so, the relevance of the book would cater to a wider local readership as well as contributing a better understanding of place-based regional heritage analysis and landscape development.

At a macro level, it is the scale and geography that makes Lough Neagh such a unique heritage feature. This cascades downwards to incorporate the natural environment, archaeology, historical structures and communities, all embracing a diversity of manifestations of interactions between the people of the lough and the natural and built environment. We have used this as the foundation for the book, dividing it into three thematic areas: Natural Heritage / Geology / Ecology; Built Heritage / Archaeology / History; and Cultural Heritage / Folklore / Community / Place. Much of the content of these themes reflect the extent to which the lough is a physically dynamic natural evolving system. It is also dynamic in terms of changing ecologies, the expansion and contraction of flora and fauna, the growth and decline of economic opportunities, the presence or absence of pollution, the variations in population pressure and the consequent relationships of the lough with urban environments.

The morphologies of Lough Neagh change in cultural as well as geographical, demographic and economic forms, through the ways in which the lough is evaluated by different people, by interchanges and interactions with political conceptualisations and by locational naming. To this we can also add the manner in which ideas and understanding of the lough have been transformed by differing human relations and changing exploitative practices. The various chapters represent only a brief introduction to the landscape significance of the lough, and it is hoped by the editors that these narratives will help stimulate the reader to investigate further the heritage diversity on their doorstep and function as a catalyst for people to reminisce, discuss and re-evaluate their sense of place and understanding of this valuable asset. As an outcome we hope that the readership will leave with an enhanced understanding of their heritage and are more aware of Lough Neagh's importance at both a local and global scale.

Finally, this book would not have been possible without the support, cooperation and dedication of a talented team of contributors. We trust that they will be happy with the end result that reveals a landscape rich in built, cultural and natural heritage diversity. We would especially like to thank the National Lottery Heritage Fund who have supported the work of the Lough Neagh Partnership, both in a financial and advisory capacity for the past five years and without whose backing this publication would not have happened. A special word of thanks goes to the Ulster Historical Foundation who have provided a level of expertise and support that was above and beyond our initial expectations.

WILLIAM BURKE
LIAM CAMPBELL
WILLIAM ROULSTON

Natural heritage
Geology
Ecology

The shoreline at Brookend.

1 The formation of Lough Neagh
a geological history

William Burke

Lough Neagh:
The Lake was that deep blue, which night
Wears in the zenith moon's full light;
With pebbles shining thro' like gems
Lighting Sultanas' diadems:
A little isle laid on its breast,
A fairy isle in its sweet rest

UNKNOWN, *c.* 1885

It is impossible for any observer to look at a map of Ireland and fail to notice the expanse of blue in the centre of Northern Ireland denoting what many have described as a freshwater inland sea. Standing on the shoreline, whether it be in Ballyronan, Washingbay, Oxford Island or Antrim, one could easily be transported to some coastal seascape but for the faint outline of the opposite shore often set in a haze by the winter drizzle or the summer heat. This is Lough Neagh. Lough Neagh (54.4°N 6.25°W) is the largest lake in Ireland and Britain, with a surface area of 383 km^2 and a catchment of 4,453 km^2, representing 43% of the land area of Northern Ireland. This extensive catchment is drained by seven major river systems (Upper Bann, Blackwater, Ballinderry, Moyola, Main, Six Mile Water and Crumlin) and numerous peripheral streams with the sole outlet to the Atlantic Ocean found at Toome, via the Lower River Bann. It would be easy to simply look at a geological map of Lough Neagh and from the key provide a rapid description of the rock underlying and surrounding the lough. However, the *terra firma* below our feet requires deeper thought. Geology defines who we are. It is the foundation of place, determines resource availability, impacts on our climate and weather, informs biological diversity, defines traditional livelihoods and underlies much of our cultural heritage.

FIG. 1.1

View from south east County Antrim looking west across lough with Selshan Harbour and Bartin's Bay in the foreground.

Since as early as the ninth century, many philosophers and researchers have attempted to explain the origins of this extensive body of water, trading local mythological creation stories with more academic treatise and, in combination, creating a place of uniqueness best described in the poetic eloquence of Nobel Laureate Seamus Heaney's *A Lough Neagh Sequence*. However, with the evolving trend during the 1800s towards authenticated observation reinforced by primary sourced data, the emphasis on folklore and stories diminished. Yet, while folklore and mythology will not provide a very complete picture of how Lough Neagh was formed, the cultural significance of these tales is seldom ignored by wider society. These stories can provide rich and interesting accounts of societal thinking prior to the introduction of scientific rigour and can often reflect the wider geophysical actions that have occurred over millennia.

There are many legends that attempt to explain the origin of Lough Neagh. A common theme in myths regarding the origin of many Irish lakes involves a magical well that, when left uncapped by an aloof townsman, overflowed and flooded an ancient city with all of the inhabitants either tragically drowned by the flood or still existing in a state of limbo along with the city in all of its glory, submerged in the depths. Thomas Moore, in 1922, based one of his famous melodies on the legend:

> On Lough Neagh's banks where the fisherman strays
> When the clear cold eve's declining
> He sees the Round Towers of other days
> In the waves beneath him shining.
>
> THOMAS MOORE, 1922

The best known story recounts how the famous Irish hunter and warrior Fionn Mac Cumhaill caused the creation of Lough Neagh. This legend proclaims that Fionn was chasing a Scottish giant across Ulster when he picked up a large piece of ground and hurled it at the giant. It overshot and fell into the Irish Sea forming the Isle of Man while the massive crater left behind became infilled with water and formed Lough Neagh. Today we can say with a very high degree of confidence that Lough Neagh was not formed by an overflowing magical well or an angry Irish warrior but created in response to an array of complex physical, chemical, biological and geological processes that occurred on a timescale ranging between millions of centuries, hundreds of metres, and thousands of kilometres.

The solid geology

It would not be an unfounded boast to say that despite its relatively small size, the island of Ireland hosts some of the most diverse geology in the world, covering all the major geological periods with the exception of those rocks

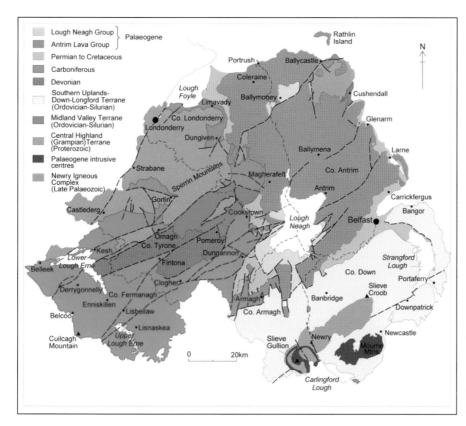

FIG. 1.2

Simplified geological map of Northern Ireland.

From W.I. Mitchell (ed.), *The Geology of Northern Ireland: Our Natural Foundation* GEOLOGICAL SURVEY OF NORTHERN IRELAND, BELFAST, 2004.

formed during the Cambrian (Fig. 1.2). Before embarking upon an exploration of the geological history of Lough Neagh, and in order to help view the rocks in their true context, it is worth very briefly considering the main events which have shaped the wider region and how they have contributed to the diversity of rocks, their composition, structure, the fossils and minerals they contain, and the processes which have shaped them. It is only with an understanding of this that geologists have been able to decipher the history and evolution of Northern Ireland.

Ireland's complex geological history has been evolving for over two billion years (Table 1). It spans several major orogeny's (mountain-building episodes), erosion of great mountain chains, the birth of oceans, and multiple ice ages. For much of the island's history, the north and south halves of the country (defined by a line between approximately Limerick in the south-west and Dundalk in the north) were located on separate continents up to ~5,000 km apart. Today, Ireland is a mosaic of sedimentary, igneous and metamorphic rocks, most of which are Precambrian and Palaeozoic in age (older than 250 Ma). Much of the bedrock of today is blanketed by glacial drift, i.e. unconsolidated sediments that were deposited during the most recent glaciation.

The oldest known rock on the island of Ireland is the granitic Inistrahull Gneiss, a type of metamorphic rock, dated at 1.7 billion years old, making it Paleoproterozoic in age, and found at Inishtrahull off the coast of Donegal. During this time and up to about 440 million years ago, the Irish landmass was divided in two, with both halves being located on opposite edges of the Iapetus Ocean. Formed from sediments laid down in basins on the American side of the Iapetus Ocean, the metamorphic schists found throughout the Sperrin mountains and north-east Antrim shows that not only did part of Ireland once form part of that continent, but also that massive collisions occurred, producing mountains out of materials formed on ocean floors. Other sediments which accumulated on this ancient ocean floor have been preserved as a series of sandstone and shale, forming the lowlands of Down and Armagh.

During a second phase of mountain building, granitic rocks were emplaced below the Earth's surface. Desert conditions prevailed during the Devonian period with Northern Ireland once again present as dry land. The erosion of a now vanished mountain chain and volcanoes produced sediments which in turn led to the formation of new rocks, for example, the conglomerates found at Cushendun. The Late Devonian, throughout the Carboniferous until the Early Permian saw the formation of the super continent Pangaea brought about by the collision of Gondwana and Euramerica. In this period, major faults were formed in Northern Ireland in the basement structures, following a NE-SW

TABLE 1
Geological succession of the rocks in Northern Ireland.

Era	Period		Epoch	Age (Myr)	Geological events in the Lough Neagh basin
CAINOZOIC	QUARTERNARY		Holocene	10,000	Present Lough Neagh formed
			Pleistocene	1.8	Glaciations, drainage disruption
	TERTIARY	NEOGENE	Piocene	5	
			Miocene		Normal landform development
		PALAEOGENE	Oligocene	22.5	Infilling by rivers and lake sediments
			Eocene	27.5 / 53.5	Crustal down warping of Lough Neagh basin; end of volcanic activity
			Palaeocene	65	Intense volcanic activity; basalt flows in north-east Ireland
MESOZOIC	CRETACEOUS			135	Ulster white limestone formation – chalk sea in north-east Ireland
	JURASSIC			195	Intense volcanic activity; basalt flows in north-east Ireland
	TRIASSIC			235	Subsidence and marine infilling of Lough Neagh basin

trendline. These faults were the first stages in the development of Lough Neagh. Between 400 and 300 million years ago north-west Europe was covered by a shallow tropical sea, that eventually created limestone which now makes up approximately two-thirds of the bedrock of Ireland. These marine conditions during the Carboniferous period resulted in the development of extensive limestone formations. Progressive shallowing of the ocean occurred later in the Carboniferous until river deltas dominated the area. Great thicknesses of sand and mud were preserved with organic remains forming the coalfields of Ballycastle and Coalisland. By the end of the Carboniferous all of Ireland was land.

In the Triassic (250–200 million years ago) a notable climatic change occurred with arid desert conditions prevailing. At this time, north-west Europe was located in equatorial latitudes within the Pangaean supercontinent. In the Early Permian, the North Atlantic rifting first affected Northern Ireland. Opening of the North Atlantic resulted in tensional stresses, causing crustal subsidence which was responsible for the development of fault-bounded sedimentary basins (including the Lough Neagh basin) due to reactivation of existing structures and faults, following the same NE-SW trend. The Lough Neagh basin developed due to a gradual down-throw by a series of faults, instead of one single major controlling fault, producing half-grabens. The development of the basin caused rapid burial with occasional flooding events depositing sand in shallow lakes producing sandstones. A gradual return to shallow marine basins resulted in the formation of great thicknesses of red mudstone sandwiching massive beds of salt, evidence of which can be found in the Carrickfergus area. The supercontinent of Pangaea continued to exist until its breakup in the Late Triassic. This brought an end to a long period of predominantly continental conditions that had influenced the climate of Ireland since the end of the Carboniferous and was the start of a period of marine conditions in Northern Ireland.

During the Jurassic period (205–104 million years ago) the seas deepened leading to the formation of grey mudstone and limestone now found mainly around the Antrim coast. Marine conditions were maintained through much of the succeeding Cretaceous period. Initially sandstones formed and were later overlain by white limestones. By the end of the Cretaceous a land mass broadly recognisable as Ireland had continued its northward movement to a position similar to southern France today. During the Jurassic-Early Cretaceous an ESE-WNW compressive regime affected Northern Ireland and caused a period of minor subsidence and subsequently a period of prolonged uplift and corresponding non-deposition, resulting in an erosional unconformity in the stratigraphic sequences of Lough Neagh basin.

The opening up of the north Atlantic, a process continuing today, was accompanied by widespread volcanic activity producing a basalt plateau, the eroded remains of which dominate Antrim and parts of Derry-Londonderry. Another period of uplift occurred in the early Tertiary (Paleocene), followed by NE-SW extension and rifting due to the spreading between Greenland and Eurasia. This rifting resulted in a period of magmatism in Northern Ireland during which the basalt flows of the Antrim Lava Group were deposited. After the period of magmatism in the Late Paleocene and Eocene, north-east Ireland and the lava plateau were affected by a post-magmatic extensional stress system. In the Oligocene (*c.* 20 million years ago), subsidence along NNW-SSE trending faults resulted in the deposition of the clays and lignite's of the Lough Neagh Group in the Lough Neagh basin.

This Lough Neagh clay formation marks the existence of a proto-Lough Neagh, forming under geological conditions not unlike those of today. This early lough covered at least 550 km^2 spreading across the southern end of the present lake, westwards into County Tyrone and eastwards in south-east County Antrim. The maximum thickness of the formation is 550 m near Washingbay, in County Tyrone. The deposits contain abundant plant fossils, derived from lake marginal swamps and woodlands. The sequence also contains lignite beds, up to 22 m thick near Crumlin and the presence of alluvial flood plain deposits. Westward the lignite beds split into numerous thin horizons as they become mixed with lacustrine deposits. Lignite or brown coal was first noted in the Oligocene Lough Neagh Group around Lough Neagh in 1757. However, neither the regional distribution of the Oligocene basins nor the quantity of lignite present was appreciated until the 1980s when large deposits were discovered. Since then, detailed exploration at Crumlin and Ballymoney has revealed a lignite resource of about one billion tonnes, with the largest deposit located at Ballymoney. The deposits are potentially mineable, although the only currently known use is for power generation. Near Crumlin, County Antrim, two thick seam groups sub-outcrop beneath superficial deposits close to the east shore of Lough Neagh and extend south-west beneath the lough. Another group of lignite seams are known between Coagh and the west shore of Lough Neagh in County Tyrone, and also between Stewartstown and the south-west shore of the lough.

Drift Geology – The Quaternary

The Pleistocene (180,000–10,000 years ago) brought a major change in climate to Northern Ireland. Ice masses moved over the land eroding and re-depositing vast amounts of material. Ice action in many lowland areas formed drumlin belts, while many upland areas were generally smoothed. As ice melted a range of landforms developed including moraines, eskers and deltas.

The surface of the Lough Neagh basin is largely mantled by thick glaciogenic formations of Pleistocene age. The somewhat chaotic, present day drainage network has developed on this Pleistocene cover. Both soils and land use are, to a considerable extent, determined by the distribution and character of the glacial deposits. Over the last 200,000 years Northern Ireland has been subjected to a number of glacial episodes. Only the most recent of these, the Midlandian which lasted from 35,000 to 13,000 and obliterated most of the evidence for earlier glacial events, is extensively represented in terms of sediments and landforms. Throughout the Pleistocene, there was a continual periodic development of a Lough Neagh ice sheet. Under gravitational stresses within the ice the mass would have spread out in centrifugal fashion with the directions of ice movement being determined, initially at least, by the pre-existing topography. However, as the ice mass thickened topographic control would have diminished resulting in Lough Neagh ice being fully capable of crossing the western basalt plateau and the Sperrin watershed and moving into the Foyle valley to the north-west. From field evidence we can estimate the ice thickness to have been at least 600–800m during the maximum glaciation. To the north, south-east and south-west the Lough Neagh ice also came into contact with other ice sheets. These movements and associations are shown in Fig. 1.3.

Beneath the main ice, mass erosional scouring accentuated the central Lough Neagh depression, while at the margins, deposition would have dominated. In the Bann valley and all the associated lowlands to the south and west of the

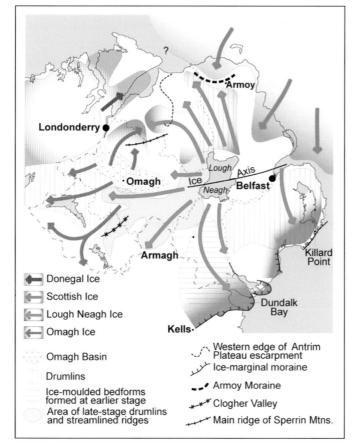

FIG 1.3

Ice-flow directions and glacial features of the late Midlandian.

From W.I. Mitchell (ed.), *The Geology of Northern Ireland: Our Natural Foundation* GEOLOGICAL SURVEY OF NORTHERN IRELAND, BELFAST, 2004.

present lough, depositional glacial landforms abound, including moraines, eskers, kame terraces and drumlins. In many places the Midlandian ice sheet simply reworked existing material; for example, many of the drumlins which are so characteristic of the Ulster landscape, were formed through the deformation of pre-Midlandian lodgement till.

The eventual decay and dissolution of the ice sheets around 18,000 years ago was probably unspectacular, with gradual melting in *situ* rather than measurable retreat. This is evidenced in the Lower Bann valley, and the Moyola valley, to the west of Magherafelt, which both contain numerous 'dead-ice' structures such as kettle holes. Withdrawal of the Lough Neagh ice from the Upper Bann valley allowed a final ice incursion from Scotland around 14,500 years ago, into Ulster. This is known as the Armoy Stage and is marked by an extensive push moraine around Ballymoney and Coleraine. The presence of ice in the northern Bann valley impeded drainage from the Lough Neagh basin and is likely to have caused extensive flooding. Evidence of late-Midlandian glacio-fluvial and glacio-lacustrine deposition abounds throughout west County Antrim, east County Tyrone and south County Derry. Around Tobermore and Cookstown thick deposits of sand and gravel are commercially important and small delta complexes around Moneymore, Cookstown and Antrim may all be associated with a single lake with a level about +60 m OD.

Temperatures throughout Northern Ireland in the late-Midlandian would have remained low evidenced by intense periglacial activity in and around the Sperrin mountains dating from this period. Open tundra vegetation would have prevailed (mosses, grasses, sedges, dwarf willow) until 13,000 years ago after which juniper became dominant. Between 12,000 and 10,500 years ago climate deteriorated rapidly, and open tundra returned. Giant deer, reindeer, bears, wolves and Arctic foxes are likely to have lived in central Ulster through the late Midlandian, evidenced by the numerous fossil remains of Quaternary age which have been found in and around the lough.

2 Lough Neagh and the Holocene

William Burke

All the world's landscapes and ecosystems are products of the natural and cultural processes that have shaped them over time. But what are those processes and how have they interacted to create the landscape we live in today? Geographically, it was 20 million years ago that Ireland ended up in the location it is now. Almost 300 million years before that, the super continent Gondwanaland began to separate in a north-south movement. Then 100 million years ago this shifted to an east-west separation, and by 40 million years ago the Atlantic Ocean was formed – and the continents, as they are now, were more or less in place 20 million years ago. The geology of Ireland and Britain reflects the various states of formation – everything from ice ages to tropical climates, and volcanic activities to changes in sea level.

FIG 2.1
The shoreline at Maghery looking towards the church at Milltown.

We have observed how structural and geophysical forces derived from tectonic movement, volcanism and sea level change had set the framework for the evolution of Lough Neagh as a sedimentary basin. However, the major determinant in defining the wider landscape over the past one million years has been climatic change with the climate oscillating between the Pleistocene glacials and interglacials. Ireland's landscape is studded with innumerable lakes, bogs and rivers whose location or configuration clearly owe much to glacial processes, either through erosive scouring of valleys and hollows, or by the damming and diversion of drainage networks by glacial deposits. However, among the many and diverse elements of Ireland's drainage network it might be anticipated that at least some of the larger lakes and rivers might, in part, be inherited from a pre-glacial landscape. This seems especially likely in those instances where geological structure has exerted a significant influence on the drainage configuration. Largest among Ireland's lakes, Lough Neagh is demonstrably pre-glacial in origin and occupies a structural and topographic basin that has been a focus for inland drainage since at least the Oligocene epoch.

It was only the after the end of the last glaciation *c.* 11,000 years ago that the world's climates and environments took on a recognisably modern form. However, the end of the Ice Age was not the final dramatic geological act for the lough. Since then, there have been intermittent, smaller magnitude and shorter duration climatic variations experienced across the northern hemisphere which have periodically affected physical geography and ecology of the lough. Yet, it has been the progressive impact of human activity over time that has created the most significant, measurable transformation of our landscape and the biodiversity it hosts. The period over which most of these cultural and environmental changes have taken place is known as the Holocene and it is this time that we see adjustments to plant and animal distribution, sea levels and soil forming processes as well as the emergence and evolution of agricultural practices.

The Holocene (also known as the Littletonian in Ireland and the Flandrian in Britain) began around 11,700 years ago (Table 1) and is an important period in the development of the present Lough Neagh. During the Holocene, the drainage pattern of the wider Lough Neagh catchment matured, the lough level stabilised and the sediment budget became established. Prior to this, towards the end of the Midlandian glaciation, Lough Neagh had become swollen when down wasting ice filled the Lower Bann valley and blocked the northwards outlet. Behind this barrier, the lough levels rose flooding the Lower Bann until a new temporary outlet was found to the south via Poyntzpass and Newry to Carlingford Lough. The eventual melting of the ice allowed the Lower Bann to establish its present route to the sea. The low-lying grounds at the margins of the existing lough are a relic of this late deglacial phase.

Period	Epoch	Age (Years BP)	Description	
QUARTERNARY	Holocene	2750–present	Sub-Atlantic	
		5950–2750	Sub-Boreal	
		8200–5950	Atlantic	Flandrian Marine Transgression
		10,500–8200	Boreal	
		11,700–10,500	Pre-Boreal	
	Pleistocene	1.8m–11,700	Glaciations	

Holocene dates are usually given in the form of years 'Before Present' (BP), where 'present' means the calendar year 1950. In most cases the dates are obtained from radiocarbon analysis of organic materials found within particular layers of sediment. The first stage of the Holocene, known as the 'Pre-Boreal' Age, from 11,700 to 10,500 BP, was initially very cold, with low shrubs and only sparse stands of birch and pine trees, but the period was then characterised by very rapid warming after 11,500 BP. It was during this interval when modern soil profiles would have finally begun to develop. These would have built on the remains of earlier, immature soils which had developed on freshly exposed glaciogenic parent materials. The process of soil formation has inevitably been extremely slow, continuing throughout the Holocene sub-period. It has also gone hand-in-hand with changes in climate, natural vegetation and human intervention. A significant outcome from the climatic changes experienced across Ireland at this time was the impact it had on local extinctions of large fauna including the giant deer also known as the 'Giant Irish elk' (*Megaloceros giganteus*), woolly mammoth (*Mammuthus primigenius*), brown bear (*Ursus arctos*) and reindeer (*Rangifer tarandus*) amongst others. Evidence for this can be found all around Lough Neagh. In 1953, a complete skull and antlers of a giant deer was found in glacial sand deposits at the Creagh outside Toome. Other similar discoveries have been made by fishermen on the lough with a skull netted off Rams Island in 1949 and a more recent find in the area known as 'The Thorns' in 2018.

The Boreal Age of the Holocene began some 10,500 years ago and coincided with the beginnings of a rapid, progressive rise in sea levels known as the 'Flandrian Transgression'. Interestingly, evidence from north-east Ireland has suggested that 18,000 years ago the sea-level stood at around plus 20 m above

TABLE 1

Holocene stratigraphy.

today's ordnance datum (OD) but then fell to about minus 30 m OD by 11,000 BP The early Littletonian climatic improvement saw a rapid rise in sea level to slightly above the present level around 6500 and 5000 BP. At present the Lower Bann drops less than 15 m over the 40 miles between Toome and Coleraine so it is easy to visualise how the lough would have changed in size and appearance during this time. Both the Flandrian Transgression and the development of Holocene peat deposits continued into the succeeding 'Atlantic' Age, which extended from 8000 to 5950 BP. This time interval was warmer and moister than today's climate, reaching a 'climatic optimum' – the maximum extent of forest ecosystems across Europe – around 6000 BP.

The time interval following 5950 BP is known as the 'Sub-Boreal' Age. It corresponds in time to the introduction of human cultures to Ireland and Britain, bringing increased rates of forest clearance for agriculture which increased further as the Neolithic gave way to the Bronze Age, especially between 4300 and 2900 BP. Historically, vegetation changes were characterised as adjustments to varying climate, but since c. 4000 BP man's activities have played an increasingly important role. A fluctuating, but steadily increasing, agricultural influence around Lough Neagh gradually altered the natural ecosystems, which today survive only by accident or in inaccessible, inhospitable spots. Spread of grasses, cereals and weeds paralleled the decline of the native trees; birch and hazel scrub replaced oak, elm and ash woodlands and raised bogs expanded in the wetter hollows.

The warm temperatures of the Holocene thermal optimum persisted until the start of the Bronze Age, but the climate then began to cool, marking the start of a generally downward trend, linked primarily to declining levels of incoming solar energy over this period. This continued into the succeeding 'Sub-Atlantic' Age, and through to the start of the 'industrial' era in Post-Medieval times, punctuated by relatively short-lived warming episodes during the Early Bronze Age and in the Early Medieval period. The early part of the Sub-Atlantic was characterised not only by climate change but also by the steadily increasing influence of humans on the landscape. Forest clearance continued to gather momentum during the Iron Age, particularly between about 2400 and 1800 BP, and again during the Early Medieval period. It is not specifically known whether these trends were mirrored in the Lough Neagh region, but Iron Age communities are likely to have been present in the area. Active soil erosion, especially after the introduction of iron coulters and mouldboards on ploughs around 2000 BP, provided minerals and nutrients perhaps increasing rates of both bog productivity and accumulation. Lowland raised bogs dominated by sphagnum mosses are common throughout the Lough Neagh basin, especially around Portadown and along the Lower Bann, Main and Moyola valleys. Increasing intensity of peat cutting, especially in the nineteenth century removed a number of bogs altogether, leaving either birch, willow or alder scrub on the marginal cut-over (as in The Birches Peatland Park), or rush pasture on the underlying gley soils, or, as in the Brackagh Moss Nature Reserve, south of Portadown, has caused the bog vegetation to revert to fen and fen carr.

Recent decades have been marked by unprecedented environmental changes which threaten the integrity of freshwater systems and their ecological value. Although most of these changes can be attributed to human activities, disentangling natural and anthropogenic drivers remains a challenge. Anthropogenic activities such as changes in land-use have induced major transformations within the lough system via increased catchment erosion and its effect on sedimentation rates and nutrient loads leading to eutrophication and ecological shifts affecting lake biota. The Holocene has witnessed all of humanity's recorded history and the rise and fall of all its civilisations. Humanity has greatly influenced the Holocene environment both around Lough Neagh and globally; while all organisms influence their environments to some degree, few have ever changed the globe as much, or as fast, as our species is doing. The vast majority of scientists agree that human activity is responsible for global warming, an observed increase in mean global temperatures that is still going on. Habitat destruction, pollution, and other factors are causing an ongoing mass extinction of plant and animal species; according to some projections, 20% of all plant and animal species on Earth will be extinct within the next 25 years.

Yet the Holocene has also seen the great development of human knowledge and technology, which can be used – and are being used – to understand the changes that we see, to predict their effects, and to stop or ameliorate the damage they may do to the Earth and to us. Tracing such environmental dynamics over short timescales and assessing the type and timing of the main drivers of change are needed for a better understanding of the complex cause-effect relationship between environmental responses, anthropogenic activities and natural climate variability, and therefore to improve management strategies. This is especially important for wetland landscapes like Lough Neagh where we must take affirmative action to protect not only the regions natural heritage assets but those intangible cultural attributes that mean so much to those people living on the loughshore.

3 What is diatomite?

David Jewson

Bann Clay is the local name for deposits of diatomite that are found along the Lower Bann valley from Toome to Agivey (Fig. 3.2). This chapter describes how and when they were formed, as well as the microscopic algae of which they are composed. The diatomites are important historically because they, and associated deposits, hold a 5,000-year record of the first settlers in Ireland after the end of the Ice Age. Also, in more recent times, the diatomites were an important industrial resource used in many products for over one hundred years.

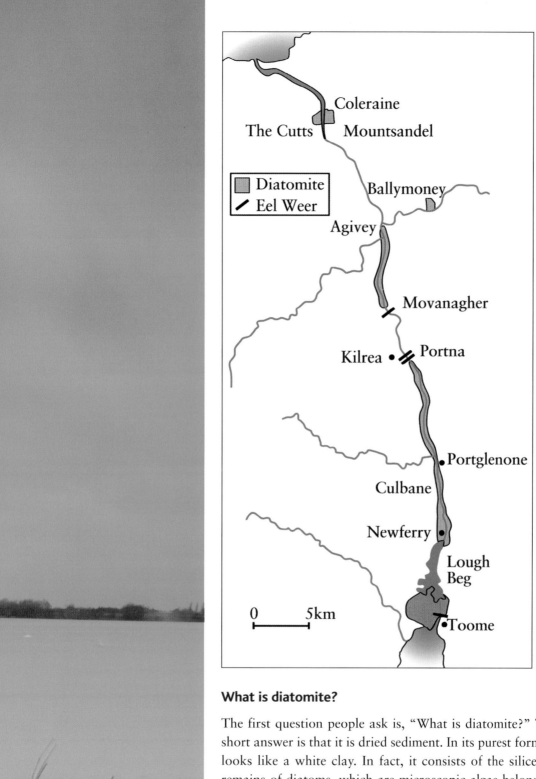

FIG. 3.2

Map of the distribution of diatomites and eel weirs along the Lower River Bann.

What is diatomite?

The first question people ask is, "What is diatomite?" The short answer is that it is dried sediment. In its purest form, it looks like a white clay. In fact, it consists of the siliceous remains of diatoms, which are microscopic algae belonging to one of the most important plant groups on the planet. Diatoms occur all around the world, growing in lakes, rivers and oceans. It is estimated that as a result of their photosynthesis, they turn over nearly 20% of the world's oxygen, which means that every fifth breath you take is due to diatoms!

FIG. 3.1

The south Lough Neagh shoreline.

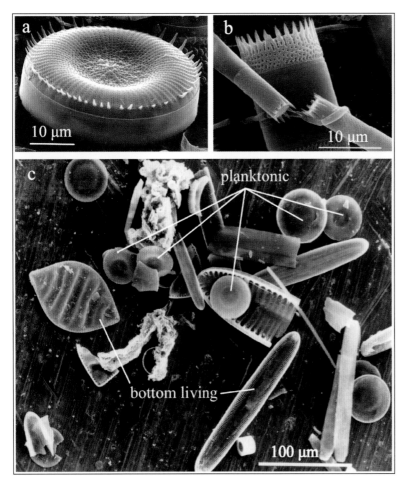

FIG. 3.3

Scanning Electron Microscope (SEM) pictures of planktonic diatoms a) *Stephanodiscus neoastrea* and b) *Aulacoseira subarctica* from Lough Neagh, while c) shows a range of species from the diatomite. The symmetrical shaped forms are eroded frustules of *S. neoastrea*, while the asymmetrical forms are benthic (bottom living) species, such as *Cymatopleura* on the left. The preparation for scanning makes the silica cell wall look opaque, but in life it is actually as clear as glass.

Diatoms are unusual plants in having cell walls impregnated with silica (Fig. 3.3). Put simply, it means that they are cells that live in a glass box. Silica is one of the commonest elements on earth and it actually takes less energy to make a glass cell wall than an organic one. Diatoms are too small to be seen by the naked eye, but when looked at through a microscope, then their beautiful shapes and ornate structures are revealed (Fig. 3.3). They can either occur as single cells, from two to over 300 m in size, or they can form into colonies and filaments up to several millimetres long. In life, they photosynthesise like all plants, but when they die and settle onto the bottom of a lake or ocean, then the organic parts rot away, leaving their silica cell wall. In the right conditions, this can then compact and form into diatomite.

Diatoms have been around since at least the Early Cretaceous, 110 million years ago, when we know of only 50 species. Now there are over 100,000 species. In their most basic form, their siliceous cell wall is made of two parts (called valves), which resemble a petri dish (see Fig. 3.3a), where one half is slightly larger than the other. One species that has this petri disc shape and lives in Lough Neagh is *Stephanodiscus neoastrea* (Fig. 3.3a). It is also found in the Toome diatomites. Other diatom species can attach to each other to form filaments. In Fig. 3.3b you can see such a species, which is called *Aulacoseira subarctica*. It is actually the most common species in the diatomites at Toome. It looks a bit like a Christmas cracker and has a range of diameters, from broad to narrow. This is an adaptation, seen in most diatoms, involving a cycle of diameter decline and size regeneration that is used like a clock to time the length of the life cycle. *Aulacoseira subarctica* is also a species that still lives in Lough Neagh, where it mainly grows during winter and spring, taking up the silica from the water to build its cell walls. Once the silica is exhausted, cells sink to the bottom, where they form a major part of the food source for the midge larvae. Many of the silica cell walls dissolve, but some remain preserved in the

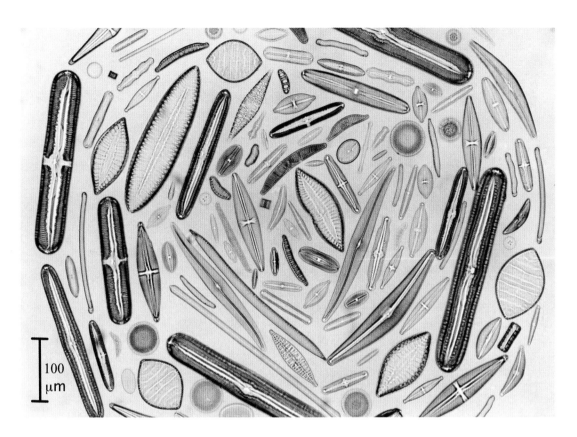

100
μm

FIG. 3.4

Light microscope picture of the main diatom species from Toome diatomite. Prepared and arranged by Klaus Kemp.

sediment. The result is that each new annual layer of sediment then becomes a time capsule of what conditions were like in the lake when they were buried. So, by taking sediment cores it is possible to unlock this information.

Professors Battarbee and Oldfield at the University of Ulster developed this technique using diatoms in the 1970s to investigate the past history of pollution in Lough Neagh. Since then the method has been widely used to quantify changes in pollution, acid rain and climate in lakes all around the world. Individual species of diatoms can be identified from their characteristic cell wall structures. A good example of the different sizes and shapes is shown in the picture of 'Toome diatoms' arranged on a slide by Klaus Kemp (Fig. 3.4). Klaus was one of many keen amateur diatomists given free samples of Toome diatomite by William Kenyon & Sons from the main factory in Cheshire. He made the slide to commemorate the setting up of the diatomite Areas of Special Scientific Interest in 1991. Most of the species shown are bottom living, with the more numerous and smaller planktonic species having been removed by filtering. Some bottom species secrete mucilage stalks or pads, which helps them form microscopic forests covering rocks. Other species are able to glide, so long as they are in contact with a surface, such as mud or rocks. So, they are plants that can move!

Diatomites and flooding

The diatomite deposits along the Bann valley were mainly formed during winter flooding between 4,500 and 7,500 years ago. At the height of this annual flooding, Lough Neagh and Lough Beg would have combined to form one large body of water, extending up as far as Portglenone, where a rocky outcrop acted as a partial dam (Fig. 3.2). The widest extent of the flooding was at Toome and reached westwards for nearly a mile. The flood waters contained large numbers of diatoms, which had been growing in Lough Neagh during winter and spring. Many of these settled onto the bottom and were left as a residue after the floods receded. Gradually the deposits then built up over many years. Similarly, further down the Lower Bann valley in basins between Portglenone and Portna, and Movanagher and Agivey (Fig. 3.2), other deposits were also being laid down, but their composition differed. For example, at Toome, the diatomites contained mainly planktonic or 'floating' species such as *A. subarctica* and *S. neoastrea* (Fig. 3.3c). These had grown in Lough Neagh and, therefore, were typical of deeper water. Whereas, further down the valley towards Movanagher and Agivey, the composition shifts to a greater abundance of bottom living (benthic) species (Fig. 3.3c and 4), which had grown *in situ* and are typical of shallower waters where sufficient light reaches the bottom. These species tend to be asymmetrical in shape (Fig. 3.4). Also, the more northerly deposits tend to have more inorganic material (clay and sand), which affects their chemical properties and reduces their commercial uses (see below). No diatomite deposits occur north of Agivey, as this was where the river descended to sea level and joined the estuary at the Cutts near Coleraine. As well as the spatial differences, there were also changes over time, with a shift from shallow to deep-water species in the later deposits at places such as Newferry.

Flooding and water level

The degree of annual flooding and long-term changes in level affected both the formation and later exploitation of the diatomites. The reason for the flooding was, and still is, because nearly half of Ulster drains into Lough Neagh, but the Lower River Bann is the only outlet. The result was that the annual water level rises could be as much as 2.7 m (9 feet). Such large changes inevitably affected the lives of people living around the lough and River Bann, from the first settlers right up to the modern day. Although some early attempts to lower the lough were made by trying to remove natural rock barriers, it was really the mid-nineteenth century that engineers began trying to manage lake levels across Europe. In Lough Neagh, there have been three major schemes aimed at lowering the lough level, controlling flooding and improving navigation on the Lower Bann. The first was the McMahon Scheme from 1847 to 1858, when the sluice gates were built at Toome as well as weirs and locks along the river. It resulted in a drop in 'normal' summer lough levels of about 1 m and a reduction in the extreme annual variations from 2.7 to 2.1 m. In a second attempt, 80 years later, the Shepherd Scheme (1930–42), lowered the lough level by a further 0.7 m and reduced annual fluctuations to 1.6 m (*c.* 5 feet). Finally, during the 1950s, a third attempt resulted in a further 0.6 m lowering of the summer level and control of annual fluctuations to within a regulated range between 12.46 and 12.61 m OD Belfast. However, in very wet winters, rises of over 1 m can still occur. The important consequence of these three schemes was that the diatomite sites became accessible for both archaeological study and economic extraction.

Diatomites and early man

The Ice Age ended about 10,000 years ago. It was followed by the first evidence of human settlement in Ireland at Mount Sandel at the mouth of the River Bann at Coleraine about 9,700 years ago (Woodman 1985). Subsequently, the settlers moved up the river to Culbane, Newferry and Toome. They were attracted to these river sites because of their potential for fishing, which could last for possibly six months of the year, as mature eels migrated out to sea and salmon returned to breed. It was also an advantage that shore-based techniques could be used, such as catching fish in the narrow channels when water levels were low, but also by using traps that were similar in principle to those still in use on the river today. The activities of these early settlers were closely linked to the seasonal changes in water level, which meant that they made their summer camps on the banks of the river to cook and dry their fish, but then retreated to winter camps on higher ground when levels rose. We know this from some of the excellent archaeological studies whose excavations coincided with the accessibility of sites after the lake lowerings. A particular stimulus was the tens of thousands of axes and flints being found as part of the commercial digging of diatomite (see below). The abundance of the artefacts gives an idea of what the size of the population must have been.

One of the first archaeological investigations was by Jackson (1909), but interest really took off in the 1930s by both local and international archaeologists at Newferry and Culbane. These included Prof. C. Blake Whelan from Queen's University and Prof. Hallam L. Movius from Harvard. At this stage, their investigations largely relied on artefacts found by the commercial diggers. Movius was reputed to have driven up to Newferry in a Bentley from his base at the hotel in Toome. One of the pioneering studies on diatomite deposits along the River Bann in the 1930s came as a result of an invite in 1934 from the Royal Irish Academy to a Danish professor, Knud Jessen, to come to Ireland to test out his innovative studies of using pollen preserved in the layers of peat bogs to study past changes in plant communities. His methods have been since been developed further and become a standard for investigating past conditions worldwide. One of Jessen's classic sites was Ballymacombs More at Newferry, where the peat formed over the diatomite. Unfortunately, this bog is now largely destroyed by removal of peat for horticulture. Interestingly, the student assigned to drive Prof. Jessen around Ireland was Frank Mitchell, who went on to to become a professor at Trinity College Dublin and was famous for his own research on interpreting past change to the Irish landscape. One of his classic study sites was on the diatomites at Toome (Mitchell 1955). At the time, it was thought to be the earliest evidence of humans in Ireland, at about 7,700 years ago. It was only the later excavations at Mount Sandel in Coleraine by Prof. Peter Woodman (Woodman 1985; Woodman and Mitchel 1993) that showed settlers had arrived there about 9,700 years ago. There is an excellent account of probable daily life for these early settlers at Mount Sandel by Thomas McErlean (2019) seen through the eyes of children.

Peter Woodman went on to make intensive studies of the diatomites at Newferry, building on earlier work by Smith and Collins (1971). They revealed the scale of operations along the Bann at Newferry and Culbane, including how the earliest occupation was on a sand bar where the Bann left Lough Beg (Fig. 3.4). It became dry when water levels fell in summer and so provided a temporary camp for fishing. However, over time the climate gradually became wetter and so winter water levels increased, which meant that each year deeper and deeper deposits of diatomite overlay the sand bar. With the rising water levels each autumn, the black charcoal layers from the fishermen's summer fires were spread out over the white diatomite. It is in the black charcoal layers that many flints and stone axes have been found, including some found by farmer Michael O'Neill in a channel beside the sand bar on the east side of the River Bann at Newferry (Fig. 3.5). In particular, Peter Woodman was able to establish that the diatomites were probably laid down between 7,500 and 4,500 years

FIG. 3.5
Newferry aerial view looking southwards to where the River Bann exits Lough Beg. Inset is a photograph of flints and axes from the east bank of the river, with baked mudstones, carbonated cherts and a picture of Prof. Peter Woodman at Newferry in 1990.

ago and he also showed how the design of their tools evolved with time. The earliest artefacts were actually found in the reed swamp layers underlying the diatomites, so together they span the Middle Stone Age (Mesolithic). The upper layers of diatomite and overlying peat contain evidence that probably extends into the Late Stone Age (Neolithic) and heralds the introduction of farming that replaced the hunter-gatherers. Peter Woodman always said that he had wished he had done more work at Newferry, because there are no other comparable sites in Ireland with evidence of continuous human occupation at one site for nearly 5,000 years.

Industrial use

Diatomites are also called diatomaceous earth or Kieselguhr (the original German name). They are found all around the world, with the majority of deposits marine in origin and hundreds of feet thick. Some date back as far as the Cretaceous, 80 million years ago. However, deposits formed in freshwaters, such as along the Bann valley, are not so extensive. One of the first diatomite deposits to be discovered was in 1836 in northern Germany by a man digging a well! However, it was the discovery in 1867 by Albert Nobel that diatomite could be used as an absorbent and stabiliser for nitroglycerin in artillery shells (both as dynamite and later gelignite) that was a major stimulus to look for other deposits. Diatomite became a strategic resource here too, because the Bann deposits were easily the largest in the UK and Ireland.

However, the first uses of diatomite in Northern Ireland can be traced back to around 1855 in the townland of Ballynease near Portglenone beside the River Bann. It was then known as Bann Clay and used to make Culbann bricks for house building in the local area around Portglenone. According to anecdotal reports, these bricks were not particularly appreciated, as they took up water in rainy weather. We now know that this occurs because the holes and open structures of diatoms gives diatomite a high porosity, such that it can absorb up to three and a half times its own weight. While this may not be good for house bricks, this and other properties of diatomite made it a useful material in many industrial applications, such as abrasive products and insulation bricks for kilns and furnaces. In 1898, the Grant brothers (Frank, Neill and John) built a factory to dry the diatomite and turn it into a light powdery form, which could be bagged for easy transportation across the sea to England. Their factory was just behind where the old RUC station stood at the eastern end of the bridge at Toome (marked on early twentieth-century Ordnance Survey maps as 'Kieselguhr Works').

At this time the market for diatomite was increasing all around the world. So, another company (United Kingdom Peat, Moss, and Litter Company Ltd), which had come to Ireland to extract peat, became interested in the potential of diatomite too. The demand was such that their own deposits were soon

exhausted, so they bought the Diatomite Company, which had a factory based in Glenone (close to Portglenone). When these deposits were exhausted too, they bought a business owned by the Grant family, which had the great advantage that it held the mineral rights of the O'Neill Estate. This was important, because you might own the land, but not the mineral rights below it. One other key local family throughout the whole period of diatomite extraction were the Quinns. They were originally involved with manufacture of Culbann brick, but Patrick, Frank and Dan, and later Dan's son Frank junior, all played a part. They had joined the United Kingdom Peat, Moss, and Litter Company, with Frank going on to become a director and general manager.

However, during this time, the business was sold in 1947 to an English company, William Kenyon & Sons, which specialised in insulation products. They built a new factory on the western side of the bridge at Toome. To supply this factory, deposits were still dug by spade and stacked to dry (Fig. 3.6), making it a highly labour intensive process, with up to 140 people employed at the peak. Seamus Heaney in his poem 'Bann Clay' from *Door into the Dark* (1969) pays tribute to the labourers who, 'pedalling at ease past the end of the lane, were white with it'. The depth of the diatomite varied between 0.5 and 1.5 m below the topsoil. The sods were cut in a similar way to peat digging, being first laid out to dry in rows, and then stacked to dry further. After this, the sods were moved to drying sheds, where they were broken up and laid out on the floor, before being milled. The resulting powder was then bagged for transport to England. Demand peaked in the 1940s at 6,000 tonnes per year during the Second World War (Fig. 3.7), but by the 1950s it had fallen dramatically. The decline coincided with the increase in extraction of diatomite in places such as California, Spain and Kenya. These deposits were marine in origin and hundreds of metres thick. They were both purer and cheaper to mine. So, the lower quality of the Bann valley diatomites became less in demand. By this time, the diatomite at Toome was used mainly

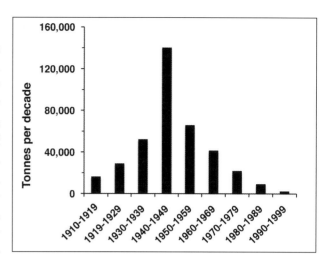

FIG. 3.7

Extraction of Toome diatomite per decade, including data from Smith (1983).

for making insulation bricks. By 1968, there were periods when the price fell so low that digging at Toome stopped altogether. It meant that Kenyon's had times when they had up to 600–700 tonnes of diatomite stacked and dried at Toome waiting to be sold. To try and reduce costs, a drying machine was brought in as well as a mechanical digger. This meant that only three or four people were needed, including the then manager, Frank Quinn Jnr. At this time, Kenyon's were also putting a lot of effort into testing for a whole range of potential products. Their manual is a fascinating compilation of the numerous experiments that were carried out. These included the traditional uses, such as abrasives (e.g. car polish, toothpaste, face creams, etc.), inert filters (e.g., cider, beer, sugar production), catalysts, absorbents, as well as the kiln insulation products, but they were still unable to compete in price. Once production fell to below 600 tonnes per year, Kenyon's finally decided to close their factory at Toome in 1995, after nearly 50 years of diatomite production. The site has now been turned into a series of small industrial units, with the main red brick processing building preserved, which is now used as a showroom and café by a bathroom company.

An important part of the local history of diatomite extraction is the different processing methods used in the other factory at Newferry (Fig. 3.8). The diatomite had a different composition, with more impurities than at Toome, which meant that it took a lot more effort (and cost) to bring it up to commercial quality. A good account of these methods and the families involved is given by Mary Breslin and John McCallion (2004). A brief summary is given here. For example, the diatomite under the peat of Ballymacombs More was 'greyish' and processing started with an initial period of drying, followed by heating in a sealed kiln for a week. This is called calcining and we now know that this is associated with health problems due to the formation of free crystalline silica. The kiln was heated using peat from the bog. A second process was where the diatomite was dried, milled and then ground after water was added. The resulting liquid suspension was piped off into large tanks (see Fig. 3.8), where it was left for four

FIG. 3.8
Disused diatomite factory
at Newferry (photo 1990),
showing the tanks used in
the processing of diatomite.

to six weeks to settle, before the water and impurities were drained off. After this, it was left for yet another week, before being dug out and dried on racks. Finally, it was heated in a kiln, as above. This lengthy process produced the purest and most valuable diatomite. As well as using the diatomite extracted from around the factory, other material was collected from the riverbanks to the north and especially from the deposits on the Antrim side at Newferry. There were two boats to do this, the smaller one, the *Fly*, could carry 40 tonnes and the larger, the *Kathleen*, carried 60 tonnes.

The lower levels of the fields on either side of roads around Newferry and Toome are a testament to the extent of the commercial extraction of nearly 400,000 tonnes over 100 years. This compares with a global extraction of diatomite worldwide of about two million tonnes per year in 2001. Most of the purest 'white' diatomite around Toome is in a layer about 0.6 to 0.9 m thick. However, in a field behind the eel factory there are areas where the diatomite deposits go down to 20 feet (6 m), but they become increasingly brown in colour as the organic matter content increases. Below this are well-preserved reed swamp layers, so this was probably a river channel that gradually filled in. It is now conserved as an Areas of Special Scientific Interest (ASSI). Frank Quinn (the last manager at Toome) said from his experience that the depth of diatomite varied between Lough Neagh and Lough Beg, probably due to channels going across the flood plain area.

Conservation

Unfortunately, the importance of the diatomite deposits has been largely overlooked in development plans for Lough Neagh and River Bann areas for many years. Important sites are still being lost for a variety of reasons, even though commercial extraction ceased 25 years ago. A good example is the loss of the archaeological site of Prof. Mitchell (1955) at Toome, which was once believed to be the earliest site of man in Ireland. During a visit in 1990, Prof. Mitchell confirmed that his site was now completely destroyed. This was partly due to the engineering works associated with the lowering of the lough in the 1950s, but also because the area has since been developed for processing and storing sand extracted from Lough Neagh. The lesson to learn from this is that destruction of the site may not be deliberate, but due to a lack of awareness of its importance, both locally and in government.

Unfortunately, the worst losses of archaeological sites occurred during the commercial extraction of diatomite for over 100 years at Culbane and Newferry. The sites of Whelan (1930), Movius (1936) and Jessen (1949) are all now largely dug-out or damaged. Part of Woodman's key site on the Antrim shore at Newferry containing charcoal layers was still there in the 1990s, but the fencing has not been maintained, although it is only a small area. To the north of his site is the largest undisturbed depth sequence of diatomite remaining. Overall, it was estimated that in 1983 that less than 20,000 tonnes of diatomite was left at Toome out of an original deposit of 337,500 tonnes (Smith 1983). In the final decade of extraction, there was probably a further 10,000 tonnes removed (Fig. 3.7). Unfortunately, even by the late 1980s, it was difficult to find undisturbed deposits and so the Conservation Branch of DOENI in 1990 agreed to support a six-month study by the University of Ulster and University College London (UCL) to try and identify possible sites for conservation (Jewson et al. 1991, 1999). As a result, in 1991 four ASSIs were established along the River Bann.

However, 30 years on, there are still no long-term plans in place for monitoring and management of these ASSIs. Also, other important sites not designated as ASSIs are increasingly under threat from road building to riverside developments. A typical example came from a farmer, Michael O'Neill (now deceased), who was the owner of the field at Newferry beside Woodman's site. He told me how, in attempting to improve the land beside the river, his brother thought it would be good idea to take soil from the top of the adjacent drumlin and move it down to improve the shore area, but, as he said, it ruined both. Similar examples of lack of awareness at other local sites are common. On a larger scale, the recent upgrading of the Belfast to Derry road, which included a new bridge and dual carriageway, has cut across the most extensive diatomite deposits both east and west of Toome. So, there are ongoing threats to this unique and important resource and it is becoming more and more important to increase local knowledge/interest as well as government involvement to protect a novel and historic area.

Bibliography

T.M. Baxter, 'An investigation of Holocene environmental change in the Lough Neagh basin using diatoms', DPhil. thesis, University of Ulster (1999).

M. Breslin and J. McCallion, 'The diatomite industry', *Life in the Past: Bellaghy Historical Society* (2004), pp 21–31.

J.W. Jackson, 'On the diatomaceous deposits of the Lower Bann valley, counties Antrim and Derry, and the prehistoric implements found therein', *Memoirs and Proceedings of the Manchester Literary and Philosophical Society*, 53 (1909), pp 3–18.

K. Jessen, 'Studies in the late Quaternary deposits and flora history of Ireland', *PRIA*, 52B (1949), pp 85–290.

D.H. Jewson, N.G. Cameron, R.W. Battarbee and N.C. Rhodes, 'Conservation of diatomite deposits', Department of the Environment Northern Ireland report (1991), 25pp.

D.H. Jewson, T. Baxter, R.W. Battarbee and N.G. Cameron, 'Lough Neagh and Bann valley diatomite deposits' in J. Knight (ed.), *Lower Bann and Adjacent Areas: Irish Association for Quaternary Studies Field Guide 23* (1999), pp 28–34.

T. McErlean, *The Salmon People* (Causeway Coast and Glens Borough Council Museum Services, 2019).

G.F. Mitchell, 'The Mesolithic site at Toome Bay, Co. Londonderry', *UJA*, 3rd series, 18 (1955), pp 1–16.

H.L. Movius, 'A Neolithic site on the River Bann', *PRIA*, 43C (1936), pp 17–40.

A.G. Smith, 'Palynology of a Mesolithic-Neolithic site in County Antrim, N. Ireland', *Proceedings of the 4th International Palynology Conference, Lucknow (1976–77)*, 3 (1981), pp 248–57.

A.G. Smith, 'Review of the diatomite resources of the R. Bann-Toomebridge area of Northern Ireland', Geological Survey of Northern Ireland, Open File Report 64 (1983), 8pp.

A.G. Smith, 'Newferry and the Boreal-Atlantic transition', *New Phytologist*, 98 (1984), pp 35–55.

A.G. Smith and A.E.P. Collins, 'The stratigraphy, palynology and archaeology of diatomite deposits at Newferry, Co. Antrim, Northern Ireland', *UJA*, 3rd series, 34 (1971), pp 3–35.

C.B. Whelan, 'The tanged flake industry of the River Bann', *Antiquaries Journal*, 10 (1930), pp 134–8.

P.C. Woodman, 'Recent excavations at Newferry, Co. Antrim', *Proceedings of the Prehistoric Society*, 43 (1977), pp 155–200.

P.C. Woodman, *The Mesolithic in Ireland*, BAR British Series 58 (Oxford, 1978).

P.C. Woodman, *Excavations at Mount Sandel, 1973–77*, Northern Ireland Archaeological Monographs 2 (Belfast, 1985).

P.C. Woodman and N.C. Mitchel, 'Human settlement and economy of the Lough Neagh basin' in R.B. Wood and R.V. Smith (eds), *Lough Neagh: the Ecology of a Multipurpose Water Resource* (Dordrecht, 1993), pp 91–111.

4 Dendrochronology lessons from the loughshore

Mike Baillie

One of the joys of research is that it can lead you to some very unexpected places. As someone closely involved with archaeology and dendrochronology, I had the opportunity to do quite a lot of pottering around Lough Neagh. In the late 1960s I assisted Peter Woodman, then assistant keeper in the Ulster Museum, in searching for evidence of the Mesolithic along the north-west loughshore, close to Toomebridge.

In the course of collecting quite a lot of Mesolithic stone axes we also located numerous bog-oak trunks. These were sampled, and the majority were subsequently dated by dendrochronology. In round figures they all dated to the period between AD 1 and AD 1600. It was never clear why they were there. Had they grown in that lough-side location, or had they floated from various locations around the lough, ending up stranded near the only exit? Here we encounter a typical Lough Neagh puzzle; oak is dense and does not float easily, so do we have to assume these oaks actually grew where they were found? The simple answer is that as with so much about Lough Neagh, we don't know.

However, it was interesting that we didn't find any oaks dating after 1600, because 1600 marks a point in time, the Plantation, when it is pretty certain that people started interfering with the level of Lough Neagh. So, if the drainage was altered, maybe that was why no further oaks ended up at the north-west corner. Or, maybe, people started clearing the oaks from around the lough? We will probably never know.

FIG. 4.1
The shoreline to the south of Ballyronan.

However, that takes me to another issue. Back in the 1970s an unfinished dug-out boat was found during the construction of a marina at Oxford Island on Lough Neagh. Attention was originally drawn to the boat by Richard Warner from the Ulster Museum, specifically because it was unfinished. What was an unfinished dug-out boat doing about 13 m from the shore? The boat was being made from an oak trunk, but, oak, as already mentioned, is really too dense to float. So, it is pretty certain that this boat (tree-ring sample Q3911) had been under construction when the lough was smaller than present; presumably it had been sitting on the old shoreline and was preserved by being left underwater. That was interesting in itself, but the interest really took off when it was dated. The last growth ring dated to AD 492 and, allowing for missing sapwood (normally the outermost 32+/-18 growth rings in oak in Ireland) it is pretty certain that it was felled sometime in the earlier sixth century (AD 514–550). We now know that there was a global environmental downturn in the time-window AD 536–550, when multiple volcanic eruptions (some in Alaska and others possibly from South America or Indonesia) caused massive cooling and triggered a major plague.

Here we see the joy of research. This AD 536–550 environmental event shows up dramatically in our oak trees from around Lough Neagh, including trees Q3108 from the Toome Bay collection and Q1948 from the River Blackwater The signs of the event are also there in oaks from the Upper Bann and from south of Portmore Lough to the east of Lough Neagh. In fact, it looks as if oaks in the vicinity of Lough Neagh were particularly badly affected; one of the Portmore oaks had actually been pushed over in AD 539! We can reasonably ask the question, were these oaks all affected by the rise in the Lough Neagh level around AD 540?

Let's consider a rise in lough level. Lough Neagh sits in a huge basin with numerous rivers flowing into it; but it has only one exit, i.e. the Lower Bann that drains the lough to the sea. What possible mechanisms could account for a significant rise in the lough level? Moreover a rise that appears to have lasted for decades if the duration of the reduced growth in the oaks is taken into consideration? The possible explanations for raised water level seem to be:

a) There was more water in the system; maybe the amount of rainfall increased;

b) Blocking of the exit perhaps due to sand bars forming at the north-west exit;

c) Blocking of the exit by tectonic movement, either at the same corner or further down the Lower Bann.

Just listing the possibilities allows ideas to flow. Which of these possibilities is more likely? For example, if you had a sudden deluge all sorts of debris, including tree trunks, might be washed towards the exit; it is then easy to imagine the exit blocking with sand bars forming and a general backing up of the waters of the lough. This change in water level could last until something changed the system once again. Frankly, blocking the exit sounds more plausible than simply adding more rainfall. However, it might be unwise to ignore the tectonic movement idea. It is known that an active geological fault runs down the Lower Bann. A sudden earth movement is all that might be needed to change the configuration of the Lough Neagh exit. Hopefully the reader can see the difficulty in pinning down a definitive cause for the unfinished dug-out location and the oak growth reduction.

Here is an observation. Notice how none of the story so far depends on anything other than dating some pieces of wood from a particular geographical location. We haven't used literature of any sort, no history or archaeology or local lore. All the questions about potential happenings involving Lough Neagh, around AD 540, were deduced from the finding and dating of an unfinished dug-out boat and some assorted bog-oaks. Was anything else going on around AD 540? As it turns out, quite a lot.

Take the issue of those bog oaks from the River Blackwater at the south-east corner of Lough Neagh. These oaks are a very recent population compared with most bog-oaks. This raises the question whether the River Blackwater had changed course; because, obviously, oaks can't have grown in a riverbed! As always with anything associated with Lough Neagh the questions outnumber the answers. However, there is one aspect of Lough Neagh that I have never seen discussed and that related to the recovery of north-east Ireland after the last Ice Age.

Everyone should know that during the last Ice Age enormous amounts of ice sat on top of Northern Ireland pushing the entire landmass down into the Earth's mantle. When the Ice Age ended and the ice melted the land rose in what is called isostatic rebound. The clearest evidence for this is the Antrim Coast Road which is built on an 8 m raised beach. That beach was formed by wave action when the sea level had risen to present day level after the Ice Age (eustatic recovery), but the land hadn't fully recovered. So, the sea level stabilised but the land kept rising; the raised beach we see today marks a period when the situation was stable enough for a defined beach level to form before the land rose again to the present level. Conventional wisdom has it that the raising of this raised beach (and the whole of north-east Ireland) was slow and gradual over the last 6,000 to 8,000 years. But what if it wasn't gradual? What if it rose suddenly, or in a series of jerks?

I ask this because nobody driving along the Antrim Coast Road ever asks themselves: "Hold on, if this beach suddenly rose by about 8 metres; what would have happened to the contents of Lough Neagh?" I pose the question to encourage people to think about what would happen to the water in Lough Neagh if at any stage the north-east corner of Ireland was raised by about 8 m. I also pose it because of two observations by palaeoecologists from Queen's University Belfast. Diatomite is a white clay formed from the silicon-rich remains of single-celled aquatic algae called diatoms; it is laid down in open water conditions. Deposits of diatomite are found around Lough Neagh and in locations up the Lower Bann valley. What the two researchers found has interesting implications. Richard Lamb was studying a thick peat deposit that sits on top of a substantial diatomite layer at Ballymacombs More, on the west side of the Lower Bann. In order to provide dating for the diatomite and peat he looked for known layers of volcanic glass shards (tephra) from Icelandic volcanoes. He found that just around the transition from diatomite to peat (think: diatomite laid down in water, i.e. wet; and peat growing on top of the diatomite, i.e. relatively dry) there was a layer of Hekla 4 tephra that is relatively well dated to around 2300 BC. Gillian Plunkett, by contrast, looked at a layer of diatomite that occurred above peat just to the south-west of Portmore Lough, the small near-circular lake to the east of Lough Neagh. Her findings indicated the same Hekla 4 tephra located at the Portmore peat-to-diatomite transition (suggesting relatively dry changing to wet conditions).

Now it does not require a rocket scientist to realise that, if you have a wet-to-dry transition to the north of Lough Neagh and a dry-to-wet transition half way down the east of Lough Neagh, something might have tilted; indeed, water might just have sloughed southwards. Simply raising these issues opens up a whole world of potential speculation. Most people in Ireland assume that Lough Neagh has 'always been there'; but has it? Why, for example, do we have a River Bann flowing into the south-east of Lough Neagh and another River Bann flowing out of the north-west corner? Why is the lough so shallow, relatively speaking, with only one deep trench up towards Toomebridge? Are we allowed to imagine a time when there was either no Lough Neagh or a very small lough? Can we imagine a River Bann flowing across a plain, to the sea, being joined by the Blackwater and the Moyola and a few others, with just a small deeper section involving the trench?

While this may seem fanciful, it transpires that across Celtic Europe there are stories of towns and villages below lakes, implying a persistent idea that the lakes once weren't there. Indeed Lough Neagh has just such a myth, presented in 1934 by John Marshall in his publication *Lough Neagh in Legend and in History*. In the story Lough Neagh was formed by the bursting forth of a magic well. If we add the persistent myths that make lakes 'home to fairies' it is clear that lakes were regarded with something approaching unease. Obviously a memory of a lake 'sloughing' could lie behind such unease, but it is also worth mentioning seiches. A seiche is when the waters of a lake are affected by the long wavelength effects of distant earthquakes. Take the known case of what happened on 1 November 1755, the day of the Lisbon earthquake. On that day it was recorded that a fisherman standing in a German lake had the water suddenly rise to chest level. In Scotland it was observed that both Loch Lomond and Loch Ness 'broke out'. In essence, the contents of these large lochs slopped about, the waters rising and falling repeatedly by a metre or more.

To get the right impression, imagine someone standing on the shore of Lough Neagh as he or she had done a hundred times before. Suddenly, one day, without any warning, the lough level rises to chest height and sweeps them off their feet. The water then retreats tsunami-like exposing more of the bed than they have ever seen; it then repeats this several times without a sound. What would the observer make of it? Imagine the thoughts; there must be something (a monster? fairies?) in the lake; what will it do next? Is it to be trusted? We can be pretty sure Lough Neagh would have seiched on 1 November 1755, there is just no record of it having done so (maybe the witnesses were drowned?). However, it is interesting that the prehistoric section of the Irish annals record several cases of 'lakes breaking out', two specifically in 1629 'BC' and in 2341 'BC'; comments that may indeed be records of ancient seiches. (The dates are presented as 'BC' to indicate that these are not true historic dates but dates incorporated in a quasi-mythological Irish narrative. However they bear a striking similarity to the known tree-ring dates of two seemingly catastrophic environmental events that took place in 2354–2345 BC and 1628–1623 BC, in what we might call the real world.)

In this vein, a very curious oak sample from a peat bog close to the southern shore of Lough Neagh preserves a remarkable, anomalous band of tiny growth rings (technically a phenomenon termed 'small early vessel' or SEV rings) starting in 2354 BC. When first noticed this led to the suggestion that the oak had been left standing in water from 2354 to 2345 BC; something that implied an unusual water level change. Later an oak from Ballymacombs, on the west bank of the Lower Bann (mentioned above), provided an oak sample with a very definite damage scar in the exact year 2354 BC. These two oaks, from opposite ends of Lough Neagh, could both be interpreted as symptoms of some sort of catastrophic flood event spanning 2354 to 2345 BC. Subsequently, it was very interesting to find in the Annals of the Four Masters that under the date AM 2820 (i.e. Year of the World 2820 = 5200–2820 = 2380 BC) it is said:

> 2380 BC Nine thousand of Parthalon's people died in one week ... Ireland was 30 years waste till Neimhidh's arrival.

FIG. 4.2
Peatland at Derrytresk.

While under the date AM 2850 (i.e. Year of the World 2850 = 2350 BC):

2350 BC Neimhidh came to Ireland ... with his people.

So, on the basis of the tree-ring evidence I am talking, quite realistically, about a possible inundation of an area surrounding Lough Neagh in 2354–2345 BC, while ancient Irish literature refers to the island being 'waste' for 30 years before the arrival of a new people in 2350 BC. To this can be added the surprising fact that the annals, under 2341 BC, go on to list:

These were the forts that were erected, the plains that were cleared, and the lakes that sprang forth, in the time of Nehmhidh ... [including] ... Magh-Lughadh, in Ui-tuirtre ...

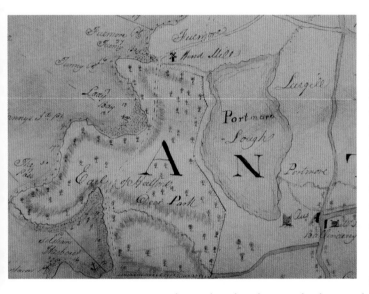

FIG. 4.3
Detail showing Portmore Lough from a map of Lough Neagh, 1785 (PRONI, D604/1).
PUBLIC RECORD OFFICE OF NORTHERN IRELAND

O'Donovan, in editing the Annals of the Four Masters in the nineteenth century, then proceeded to interpret this place name as follows 'Magh-Lughadh: i.e. Lughadh's Plain, a district near Lough Neagh'. How do we explain, in the context of what we now know from the trees about 2354–2345 BC, a pre-existing reference to lakes springing forth in 2341 BC which includes a mention of the plain of Lough Neagh? It seems that there is some real similarity between the events that affected Lough Neagh around 2350 BC and around AD 540.

It should by now be obvious to the reader that Lough Neagh may not always have been the placid water body we observe today. Its history deserves a lot more study. But it would be churlish to leave this discussion without reference to another Lough Neagh myth. Most children in Ireland learn that Lough Neagh was formed when the giant Finn McCool lifted a gigantic clod of earth to throw after a fleeing Scottish giant. He missed and the clod fell in the Irish Sea where it is now known as the Isle of Man. A nice little fairy story most would say; but is it? Remember I mentioned Portmore Lough, the little near-circular lake to the east of Lough Neagh. Well, Portmore Lough is as much a puzzle as Lough Neagh itself. It is a 1.6 km across but water-wise it is only one metre deep. Portmore Lough should long ago have filled in and become a peat bog; but it isn't a peat bog! So what might the story be?

Imagine a fragment of a comet, maybe as little as 30 m in diameter, streaking across the sky at about 11 km per second. It would be exceedingly bright as its outer layers peel away, hair-like. It might look remarkably like Finn McCool to a distant observer. As it gets deeper into the Earth's atmosphere the resistance is such that suddenly, a few kilometres above the ground, the vast amount of energy it carries, due to its mass and velocity, is released as it is vaporised in an explosion equivalent to about one megaton of TNT. By chance it has exploded directly over a peat bog on the eastern shore of Lough Neagh. The peat bog, like a giant sponge saturated with water, is blown away by the air-burst explosion leaving a shallow crater only some 3 m deep. The crater fills with water and over many centuries it starts to fill up with sediment so that now water only occupies one third of its initial depth.

Now I can imagine a lot of readers rolling their eyes on first exposure to this idea. However, there is more. Remember Finn when he removed the 'clod of earth' threw it eastwards where it fell in the Irish Sea forming the Isle of Man. Obviously that is not true, the Isle of Man is a real island. But remember that Man is associated with the Celtic god Manannan and the island's symbol is the triskelion, a three-legged swastika; something interpreted by Carl Sagan, among others, as the symbol of a spinning comet. So, buried in the Finn McCool fairy story is a lightly concealed allusion to a comet symbol. However, there is another Irish story wherein 'Manannan is buried, standing upright, in a lake that was formerly a red peat bog'. Where on Earth did anyone ever get the idea of a lake that was formerly a red peat bog? Unless, of course, they knew of a case where a peat bog had indeed been blown away and replaced with a lake.

There is no need to labour this story. But as an explanation for an anomalously shallow, near-circular lake beside Lough Neagh, it will have to do till a better explanation becomes available. It is worth remembering that oak found just one kilometre away from Portmore Lough that was pushed over in AD 539...

Hopefully the reader gets the general idea. Simply collecting ancient oak samples from around Lough Neagh, and dating them, introduces us to an intriguing set of questions about what the lough looked like in the past, its size and its depth, and when changes took place. The final true story is still a long way off.

FIG. 4.4
Cutover bog at Derrytresk.

Dunmore Rock +

Coledagh Head
Portrush I.
Gyants Caufvay
Fair Head

Portrush
Ban R.
Red Bay

Colerain
Bemoney
GlanarmBay

gh
N.T. Limnevaddy
Ban R. abounds with Salmon

Rawlwater
Skirry

Garvagh
DONDERRY
Killrea
Ballymenagh
Maggel

Maghera
A N T R I M
Connor

Randalls T. Carrickfergus
Carrickfergus T.

Magherafelt
Antrim

T E
R
Belfast
Bangor

Munimore
Lough
Glanevy
Newtown

N E
Ballynderry
R.
Neagh
C. Reaagh
Cumber

Stewarts T.
Rams I.
Lisburne

Mc Joy
This Lough turns Wood especially Holly into Stone

Altmore
Moyra

Dungannon
Hillsborrow
Killeagh

Charliamont
Blackwater
Legacory
Dromore
DOWN
Down
Patrick

Augnacloy
Ban R.
Tanrage

Kinard or Calledon
Ardmagh
Loughbrickland

Glaslough
Market Hill
Killogh

pooksburow
ARDMAGH
New C.

Monaghan
Newry

Maherowcely
Ballaghanery

Clounish
Garetevelin

MONAGHAN
Green C.

oot Hill
C. Blany
Carlingford
Carlingford Bay

n Stradone
Carrickmaacross
Dundalk

5 Turning wood to stone
Lough Neagh's second most famous legend

David Jewson

There have been many references to the legend of Lough Neagh turning wood into stone. One of the earliest was by Boethius (477–524), a Roman senator, which makes it possible that Lough Neagh was discussed in the forum over 1,500 years ago! Other references to the legend occur across Medieval Europe. One is by Nennius, an Englishman writing somewhere between the seventh and ninth centuries, while another is in a Scandinavian book called 'Kongs Skuggio'. This book includes a section on Ireland and describes how a local told a Norseman that petrification only works with the wood of holly. By the fourteenth century, the accounts had become more detailed, with Higden, another English writer, describing how if a stake of holly was driven into the bottom of the lough and left for seven years, then the part in the mud would have become iron, the part in the water would have turned to stone, and the part that was above the water would still be holly.

Such reports of how wood and petrified stone could be found together is a key component of why the legend appeared plausible and then endured over such a long time. But before investigating that further, it is important to mention that the petrified stone was a revered local asset, because it was good for sharpening knives and razors. Such stones, often called whetstones or hones, were favoured by itinerant tinkers, who travelled around Ireland sharpening utensils. The tinkers were an early form of the internet, because they passed on gossip and news as they travelled. It is easy to imagine a tinker telling the legends of Lough Neagh to an audience that had gathered to watch him sharpening knives. At the same time, maybe he recited the old jingle:

> Lough Neagh hones,
> Lough Neagh hones,
> you put in sticks
> and take out stones.

OPPOSITE
FIG. 5.1
Detail from 'A New Map of Ireland' by John Senex, 1720; the script within Lough Neagh reads, 'This Lough turns Wood especially Holly into Stone'.

LIBRARY OF THE OIREACHTAS, DUBLIN

FIG. 5.2
A piece of silicified wood.

The high esteem of the Lough Neagh 'hones' is demonstrated by Patrick Joyce in his book, *The Wonders of Ireland* (1911), where he relates an anecdote of how 'a very intelligent Limerick man' told him that Lough Neagh hones were the best in the world, because they could be made so sharp that you could even shave a sleeping mouse without waking it!

By the seventeenth century, questions over the validity of the legend were increasingly being asked. The debate was often intense. For example, in 1652 Dr Boate (one of the earliest writers on the natural history of Ireland) expressed skepticism about the petrifying properties of the lough. However, in 1684, Dr Molyneux thought it necessary to send a communication to the Royal Society in London supporting the petrification properties. This then led a Rev. Smith to challenge this on the basis that he had observed fossilised wood in areas away from the lough. To him, this suggested that burial in the ground, rather than immersion in lake water, might be important. As we shall see, his was a perceptive observation. Such exchanges were typical of the time, but often only carried out in correspondence with each other.

However, in 1751, a wider interest was generated by the publication of a book in Dublin by Rev. Richard Barton that contained six lectures on the natural history of Lough Neagh. Although, the book was described at the time as including 'much useless matter', Barton did make the important link between the lignite deposits around the lough and the petrification process. His evidence included descriptions from a number of sites, such as diggings in the lignite at Ardmore and Glenavy on the east shore of the lough. In the diggings were found different degrees of petrification from soft wood to hard stone. One person who is listed as a subscriber to Barton's book was the famous Irish-born physician and president of the Royal Society, Sir Hans Sloane. Unfortunately, although Barton's observations were fine, his reasoning was less so. He proposed that the petrification was the result of evaporation because he noted that the lough had eight rivers flowing into it, but only one leaving! However, a fuller understanding began to emerge with the improving scientific and geological methods in the nineteenth century. This can be seen in a series of interesting articles by Scouler (1837), Eagen (1881), Gardner (1885), Swanston (1893), amongst others. They show a gradual shift from purely observational to more investigative techniques. This was aided by the founding of the Geological Survey of Ireland in 1845, under the directorship of Sir Henry James, which began a period of systematic cataloging, mapping and research into the geology of the whole of Ireland. It continues today in the Geological Survey of Northern Ireland and Geological Survey Ireland (Suirbhéireacht Gheolaíochta Éireann).

In fact, the actual explanation behind the legend is an interesting story in itself. It begins with plants that grew in a mid-Tertiary basin (about 28 to 23 million years ago) that was a precursor to the present Lough Neagh basin, and probably of the order of 550 km² in size. The climate was warm temperate (Wilkinson et al. 1980) and the basin was a mix of open water offshore and extensive areas of coastal deltas and marginal swamps, where a luxuriant vegetation grew that included ferns, conifers, palms and swamp cypress. Over time, the plants in these swamps became buried by sediment, which protected them from decay by excluding oxygen and decomposer organisms. However, the groundwater percolating through the plant remains gradually replaced the original plant structures with silica in a process called silicification. In some circumstances, where the burial gives rise to reducing conditions, then iron can replace the wood to form pyrite (iron sulphide). However, in these sediments, the water during burial was fresh and low in sulphur, which favoured the formation of a different mineral called siderite, which is actually iron carbonate (Parnell et al. 1989). The overall result was the sediments gradually developed into what we now know as lignite or 'brown coal'. During their formation, the degree of silicification of plant material varied, so some parts remained as soft wood, while others parts became stone.

The thickness of the lignite deposits around and under Lough Neagh can vary from very thin layers up to tens of metres thick. There are actually two main types. One is the woody type described above while the other is non-woody lignite. This latter type was formed when the swampy inshore material in the original mid-Tertiary basin was eroded and carried offshore before sedimenting. The present day locations of lignite around Lough Neagh are in four main areas (Parnell et al. 1989). One is near Crumlin, close to the east shore and extends south-west beneath the lough. A second lies between Coagh and the west shore of Lough Neagh. A third is between Stewartstown and the south-west shore of the lough. The fourth and largest deposit is close to Ballymoney, County Antrim, about 40 km north of Lough Neagh. Together the Ballymoney and Crumlin deposits contain about one billion tonnes of lignite. This was sufficiently large that in the 1980s the possible use of lignite to fuel a power station was considered, though this was subsequently shelved, on both environmental and economic grounds. However, the evaluation process did stimulate detailed investigations into the distribution, formation and properties of the deposits (Parnell et al. 1989; Parnell and Meighan 1989).

One enduring question is what was it about the legend that gave it such longevity and notoriety? Part of the answer is the location of

FIG. 5.3
A cross-section of a silicified tree trunk.

some lignite deposits close to the lough shore, which meant that when fossilised wood was eroded, it gave the impression that silicification had occurred in the water rather than as the result of burial. A second reason was the variation in silicification. This gave the appearance that the transition from wood to stone was an ongoing process in the lough today, rather than something that had happened over millions of years. Also, a very powerful marketing tool was the story about how after seven years a holly stick would turn to iron in the mud, stone in water, but remain wood above the surface. Such descriptions would have been circulating orally around Ireland long before spreading to the Roman Empire. It tells us a lot about how quickly ideas can spread, especially when they seem to challenge accepted understanding. However, although the legend may have now become a myth, the story of how the true explanation emerged is an amazing tale in its own right.

Bibliography

R. Barton, *Lectures in Natural Philosophy, designed to be a foundation, for reasoning pertinently upon the petrifications, gems, crystals and sanative quality of Lough Neagh in Ireland; and intended to be an introduction to the natural history of several counties contiguous to that lake, particularly the County of Ardmagh* (Dublin, 1751).

F.W. Egan, *Memoirs of the Geological Survey: Explanatory Memoir to Accompany Sheet 27 of the Maps of the Geological Survey of Ireland, including Magherafelt, Moneymore, Castledawson, Desertmartin, Curran, and Ballyronan, in Londonderry; Cookstown and Coagh, in Tyrone; and Toome, in Antrim* (Dublin and London, 1881).

A. Fowler and J.A. Robbie, *Memoir of the Geological Survey of Northern Ireland: Geology of the Country around Dungannon* (Belfast, 1961).

J.S. Gardner, 'On the Lower Eocene plant-beds of the basaltic formation of Ulster', *Quarterly Journal of the Geological Society*, 41 (1885), pp 82–92.

Geological Survey of Northern Ireland, *Mineral Exploration Programme*, vols 2, 3, 5, 6, 8 (1984).

P.W. Joyce, *The Wonders of Ireland* (Dublin, 1911).

J. Parnell, B. Shukla and I.G. Meighan, 'The lignite and associated sediments of the Tertiary Lough Neagh basin', *Irish Journal of Earth Sciences*, 10 (1989), pp 67–88.

J. Parnell, and I.G. Meighan, 'Lignite and associated deposits of the Tertiary Lough Neagh basin, Northern Ireland', *Journal of the Geological Society, London*, 146 (1989), pp 351–2.

J. Scouler, 'Observations on lignites and silicified woods of Lough Neagh', *Journal of the Geological Society of Dublin*, 1 (1837), pp 231–41.

W. Swanston, 'The silicified wood of Lough Neagh', *The Irish Naturalist*, 2 (1893), pp 102–06.

G.C. Wilkinson, R.A.B. Bazley and M.C. Boulter, 'The geology and palynology of the Oligocene Lough Neagh clays, Northern Ireland', *Journal of the Geological Society of London*, 137 (1980), pp 65–75.

6 Natural heritage designations

Peter Harper

Lough Neagh has been designated a Ramsar site, a Special Protection Area (SPA) and an Area of Special Scientific Interest (ASSI). There are also nine Special Areas of Conservation (SACs) around the lough shoreline and several National Nature Reserves. Take all those designations into account and you start to get the picture. Lough Neagh is clearly a very important place for wildlife. So as the TV ad might say, "This is not just Lough Neagh, this is an internationally important wetland, an Area of Special Scientific Interest and a Special Protection Area." But what do the designations mean? Answering that question is easy for anyone working within the environment sector, but less so for the general public. So, what *do* the designations mean and why is Lough Neagh so important for wildlife and biodiversity?

Ramsar sites

These are globally recognised wetland sites of international importance. Ramsar sites are found all over the world and are named after Ramsar in Iran where a Convention on Wetlands of International Importance was held in 1971. The UK Government signed the convention in 1973 and ratified it in 1976. Lough Neagh

FIG. 6.1
The shoreline at Brookend.

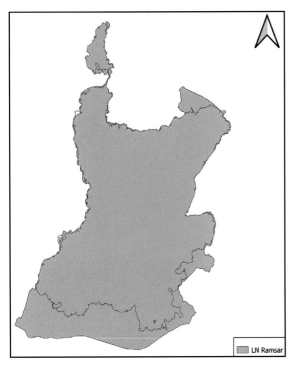

LN Ramsar

FIG. 6.2
Lough Neagh Ramsar site.

and Lough Beg Ramsar site has been designated primarily because of its importance to breeding and overwintering waterfowl. It covers an area of 39,500 ha.

Special Protection Areas (SPAs)

These sites are designated under the European Commission Directive on the Conservation of Wild Birds. They are sites identified by the UK Government as being of international importance for breeding, overwintering and migrating birds. There are 16 SPAs in Northern Ireland. Lough Neagh and Lough Beg SPA, covering an area of 41,188 ha, is one of the largest. This accounts for 36% of the total area designated as an SPA in Northern Ireland. It has been designated primarily because of its importance to overwintering waterfowl and as a breeding site for Common Terns.

Some birds overwinter in significant numbers. For example, it has been estimated that Lough Neagh supports 80% of the Irish population of Pochard and 9% of the north-west European population. It has also been estimated it supports 100% of the Irish, or just over 4% of the north-west European, population of Goldeneye. The lough supports over 80% of the overwintering Irish population of Scaup. Other feature species include Whooper Swan (6.5% of the Irish population), Common Tern (7.4% of Irish population), Great Crested Grebe (25% of the Irish population), Little Grebe (26% of the Irish population), Mute Swan (23% of the Irish population) and many more.

It is the sheer number and wide variety of birds that come to Lough Neagh every winter; otherwise known as 'the assemblage', which makes it so important. Having said that, bird numbers on the lough have shown a steep decline and many of the above species, for example, Pochard, Goldeneye, Whooper Swan and Gadwall, are categorised as 'Amber Listed' in the UK. That means that either the breeding numbers or range of these birds within the UK has contracted by between 25% and 50% over the last 25 years, that breeding takes place in less than ten sites or that the UK population represents at least 20% of the European population of breeding and non-breeding birds. Special Protection areas are exactly that, incredibly important sites for wildlife and biodiversity and, as bird numbers continue to decline, it has never been more important to undertake measures to protect them.

Special Areas of Conservation (SAC)

These are sites designated under the European Commission Habitats Directive. They are chosen by the UK Government to represent the most seriously threatened habitats and species in Europe. There are 57 SACs in Northern Ireland. SACs are designated as Category A, B or C. Category A represents an outstanding example of a particular habitat type within the European context. Category B sites hold excellent stands of a particular habitat type above the threshold for ASSI/SSSI designation. Category C sites are of national importance. Three of these are situated close to, or along the Lough Neagh shoreline.

Rea's Wood and Farr's Bay SAC (Grade B), 41.81 ha.

Rea's Wood and Farr's Bay have been designated because of their importance as a wet woodland or alluvial forest site with common alder, grey alder, white willow and ash. This site supports a wide variety of plants known as the 'higher plant assemblage' and this in turn supports many rare invertebrates including snails, butterflies, beetles, millipedes and various two-winged flies. Rea's Wood and Farr's Bay SAC is one of only 16 Category A wet woodland sites in the UK and as such another very special place. Management issues arise from the underlying hydrology of the site. The regulation of the water level on Lough Neagh has meant that there is less flooding along the loughshore. Ground water infiltration is also a factor but this needs to be considered further. Arising from this are management issues in relation to the control of invasive species such as Himalayan balsam, salmonberry or Japanese knotweed, all of which are present at the site.

Montiaghs Moss SAC, 151.28 ha.

This site has been designated because of the flora and fauna associated with the wetland, adjacent grassland and semi-natural woodland. Montiaghs Moss is a lowland raised bog from which much of the peat has been removed by cutting. It is now an intricate maze of ramparts, trenches, pools and drains interspersed with small hay fields, alder and willow carr and tall hedgerows. This supports a wide range of plant and animal communities. Its invertebrate population is of national importance. Typical woodland species include alder, downy birch, grey willow. Ground flora includes purple moor grass, bramble and nettle. There are rare species in the acid grassland including bog asphodel, cotton grass, bog myrtle, wild angelica, birds-foot trefoil, lesser butterfly-orchid and Irish lady's tresses.

FIG. 6.3
Special Protection Area (SPA).

FIG. 6.4
Fungi in Farr's Bay.

Montiaghs Moss is particularly important for wetland invertebrates such as dragonflies, damsel flies, beetles, butterflies and moths. For several species this is the only site where they have been recorded in the UK. Montiaghs Moss has international and national significance. It is currently being managed by the RSPB.

Peatlands Park SAC, 207.5 ha.

This is one of the largest blocks of semi-natural woodland in Northern Ireland dominated by downy birch but also willow, oak, holly, rowan, hawthorn and hazel. It also includes the open water of Derryadd Lake. This was a former peat cut which has left behind a mosaic of former cuttings and still intact bog some of which is still regenerating. This supports a wide range of sedge, grass and moss and other species such as bog myrtle, purple moor grass, bog asphodel and cranberry are present at the site. There are good examples of swamp and fen around the lake. Notable invertebrates include the marsh fritillary and green hairstreak butterflies. This site is open to the public and is being managed by DAERA.

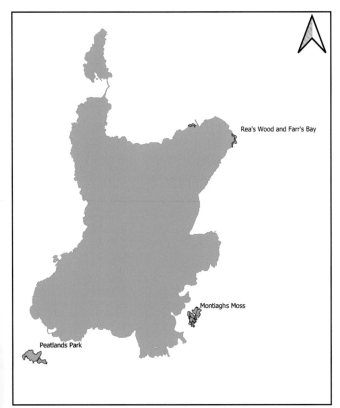

Together, our Special Protection Areas and Special Areas of Conservation form part of a European network of sites known as Natura 2000.

Areas of Special Scientific Interest (ASSIs)

These are areas which have been identified as being of high scientific interest for either their flora, fauna, geological, physiographical or other features. They have been designated by DAERA under the Nature and Conservation and Amenity Lands Order 1985. Most Areas of Special Scientific Interest are found on private land and subject to management agreements between DAERA and the landowners. There are 394 ASSIs designated in Northern Ireland. Lough Neagh and Lough Beg account for 36% of all land or water designated.

Lough Neagh ASSI

The Lough Neagh designation includes the entire water body and a marginal fringe of land along

FIG. 6.5
Special Areas of
Conservation (SAC).

the shoreline. The geology of the lough, the character of the shoreline, its submerged, floating and/or swamp and fen vegetation together with the wet woodland stands at several sites around the shoreline are all of interest.

Collectively these habitats support an exceptional variety of rare plants such as Irish lady's tresses and invertebrates including rare water snails, freshwater shrimps, beetles and hoverflies. For several species this is the only recorded site in Ireland. There are 15 species of fish including the European eel, river lamprey and Lough Neagh pollan. These features are all in addition to the internationally important numbers of overwintering birds that visit the lough every winter and the very large number of breeding birds discussed earlier in relation to the SPA designation.

Lough Beg ASSI

This is a very shallow lough and particularly important for submerged, acquatic plants. The western shoreline contains some of the most extensive area of unimproved wet meadow in Northern Ireland. Notable species include penny royal, water-wort, slender-leaved pondweed and again Irish lady's tresses. In terms of birdlife Lough Beg also supports internationally important populations of overwintering wildfowl. It is particularly important for Whooper Swan, Shoveler, Pochard and Teal. Lough Beg is also a passage site for Black-tailed Godwit and Ruff whilst the western shoreline supports breeding populations of Curlew, Redshank and Snipe. This is another precious site of national importance. Whilst most of these birds are under pressure and several amber listed, RSPB has been working hard with a range of stakeholders to improve the site for breeding waders.

Lough Beg
Lough Neagh

FIG. 6.6
Areas of Special Scientific Interest (ASSIs).

FIG. 6.7
Whooper Swans.

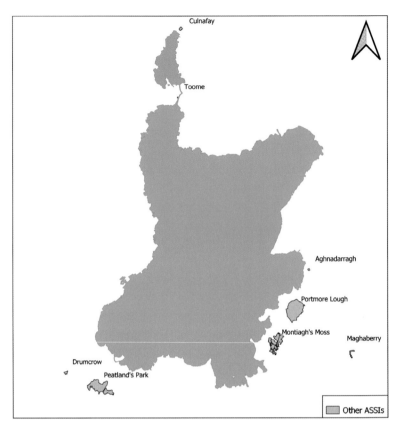

FIG. 6.8
Other Areas of Special
Scientific Interest (ASSIs).

There are a further seven ASSIs around the lough as follows:

Portmore Lough ASSI, 286 ha.

This has been designated as a good example of a transition between open water through swamp and fen to fen and carr woodland. It is also very important for overwintering wildfowl such as Tufted Duck, Pochard and Coot. This site is managed by RSPB and is also becoming an important site for breeding waders.

Montiaghs Moss ASSI, 207.3 ha.

This is an internationally important site (also designated as an SAC) because of the quality of its wet woodland and acid grassland habitat. There are also good examples of swamp and fen and supports a wide range of flora, fauna and invertebrates as discussed under the SAC designation.

Maghaberry ASSI, 9.95 ha.

Maghaberry supports a nationally important population of Lapwing. It is one of the most important sites for breeding waders in Northern Ireland.

Drumcrow (Earth Science) ASSI, 7.6 ha.

This site has been designated because of the importance of its wetland flora. It contains good examples of fen, fen meadow, wet grassland and vegetation associated with drains. There is a wide range of flora on site including marsh pennywort, lesser spearwort and several rare sedges.

Culnafay (Earth Science) ASSI, 8.41 ha.

This site has been designated because of the deposits of diatomite (Bann Clay) at the site. These deposits were formed between 7,500 and 5,000 years ago and are evidence that Lough Neagh extended beyond its current boundary.

Toome (Earth Science) ASSI, 0.89 ha.

This site has also been designated because of the importance of its diatomite deposits. This is one of the best geological sequences there is and the site has international importance for biological, climatological, geological and hydrological reasons.

Aghnadarragh (Earth Science) ASSI, 3.51 ha.

This site has been designated primarily for its geological interest. Extraction of lignite revealed the best example of the stratigraphy of the 'Midlandian Cold Stage' (c. 120,000–10,000 years ago). The site has also revealed remains of mammoth and musk ox.

National Nature Reserves (NNRs)

National Nature Reserves are designated in areas where there are nationally important populations of plants, animals, birds or where the area is of outstanding geological interest. DAERA is responsible for declaring nature reserves under the Nature and Amenity Lands (Northern Ireland) Order 1985. There are currently 48 NNRs in Northern Ireland. Nine of these are in, or around, the lough as follows:

Annagarriff NNR

Woodland with birch and oak, six species of Warbler and a rich flora including several rare and interesting carnivorous bog species.

Brackagh NNR

Raised bog with alder and willow carr, woodland, fens and shallow ponds supporting a wide range of butterflies and insect life.

Brookend NNR

Scrub woodland supporting a wide range of birds such as Sedge Warblers, Cuckoo and Curlew. It is also good for damsel flies and dragonflies and a range of wetland plants such as bird's-foot trefoil.

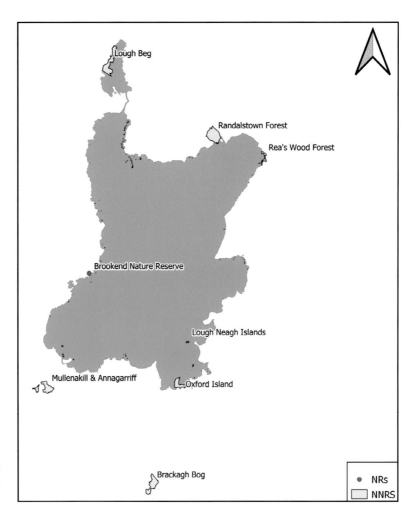

FIG. 6.9

National Nature
Reserves (NNRs) and
Nature Reserves (NRs).

Lough Beg NNR

A very important site for breeding waders such as Lapwing, Curlew and Redshank. This site has many rare plants including Irish lady's tresses. It is also a very important site for passage birds and overwintering wildfowl.

Lough Neagh Islands NNR

There are over 80 islands in Lough Neagh. Many of these are important breeding bird sites for species such as Black-headed Gull, Common Tern, Lesser Black-backed Gull, Tufted Duck, Mallard, Great Crested Grebe and many others. Fourteen of these islands are monitored on a regular basis by Lough Neagh Partnership staff.

Meenadoan NNR

This is a raised bog supporting a wide range of sphagnum moss, sedges, moss and lichen.

Mullenakill NNR

This raised bog is 8,000 years old and supports a rare flora such as sundew and sphagnum moss. The site supports Snipe and Woodcock and a wide range of invertebrates.

Randalstown NNR

This part dry woodland supports ash, hawthorn and blackthorn and part wet woodland with willow and alder, and has a wide variety of birdlife.

Rea's Wood NNR

Wet woodland site as previously discussed under the SAC and ASSI sections.

Conclusion

One lough, many designations. Lough Neagh means different things to different people but if you take one thing from this article, it's this: Lough Neagh *is* an internationally important site for wildlife, that's something we need to appreciate and value before it is too late.

FIG. 6.10 Lesser Black-backed Gull eggs.

7 The vegetation of Lough Neagh's wetlands

Bob Davidson

The shorelines of Lough Neagh and the surrounding lowlands support extensive areas of wetland vegetation. In recent times these wetlands have been greatly modified by the impact of man. Drainage schemes that lowered the lake level have had the most dramatic impact, forcing entire plant communities to shift their ground while others have been altered significantly by the new water regimes. This has led to the reduction or extinction of some species and the increase and spread of others. For example, Harron and Rushton (1986), in reviewing the effects of successive lough lowerings on the wetland flora, use the term 'devastating' and report severe reductions of willow, reeds, bulrush, reedmace, sedges and yellow loosestrife.

More extremely, they found that *Thelypteris thelypteroides* (*T. palustris*), *Teesdalia nudicaulis, Sium latifolium, Cladium mariscus, Carex lasiocarpa* and *Carex buxbaumii*, previously found in but one or two stations in the Lough Neagh area, had disappeared. *Lathyrus palustris* and *Carex acuta* were in particular thought to have suffered from the effects of drainage, while the macrophyte covered Lough Beg has lost some 30% of its pre-drainage area. Other less dramatic and sudden, but nonetheless influential, impacts include woodland clearance, peat cutting, grazing, eutrophication and agricultural reclamation. More generally, Harron and Rushton briefly outline the characteristics of the Lough Neagh wetland flora (some 700 species) in terms of its significance for rare Irish species and for the general distribution of the Irish flora.

FIG. 7.1
View of the southern shoreline of Lough Neagh.

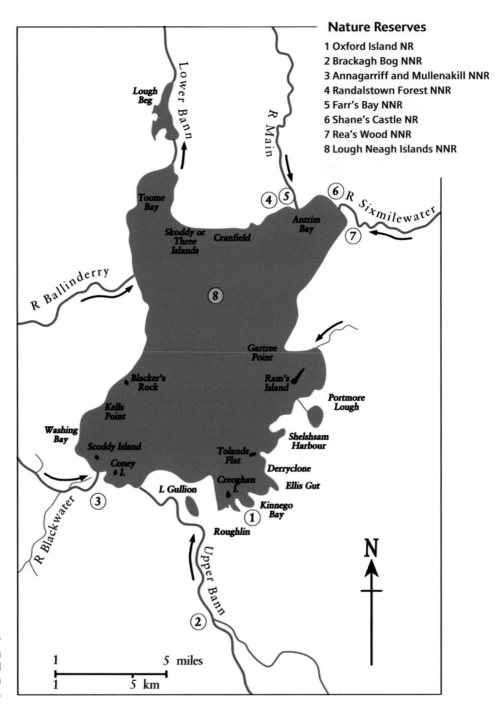

Nature Reserves

1 Oxford Island NR
2 Brackagh Bog NNR
3 Annagarriff and Mullenakill NNR
4 Randalstown Forest NNR
5 Farr's Bay NNR
6 Shane's Castle NR
7 Rea's Wood NNR
8 Lough Neagh Islands NNR

FIG. 7.2
Map of Lough Neagh showing nature reserves and other places mentioned in the text.

It is the aim in this essay to discuss the vegetation not only of the open waters of the lough itself but also the vegetation that is found today on ground that has had at least an historical association with its floodwaters. The lough level today is fairly stable, but it used to be both higher and more variable before the various drainage schemes of the last 100 years or so. The influence of these floodwaters can still be seen on low-lying ground around the lough margin but is particularly evident on the extensive flat land to the south of the lough. The vegetation will be discussed in terms of plant communities of open water, peatlands, woodlands and grasslands. No recent work has concentrated effort to examine the vegetation in terms of plant communities alone, but considerable effort has gone into the examination of the occurrence and distribution of individual species. Particular sites referred to in the text can be located in Fig. 7.2.

Physical and historical background

Most of the lough shoreline is composed of drift deposits which include boulder clays, sands and gravels with the underlying basalt only outcropping along some sections of the north shore. Landward the shore is gently shelving but is in most cases marked by low cliff sections cut in slightly elevated boulder clay drift. These steep cliff sections are all now a short distance from the present lake margin as they mark the pre-drainage shoreline established before the first lake lowering of the mid-nineteenth century. On the lake bed, offshore sand bars occur in many places to produce local sheltered conditions suitable for aquatic plant life. To the south and south-west of the lough the drift is overlain by extensive areas and in places considerable depths of peat. These extensive flat lands bordering most of the shore and rivers in the area were regularly flooded before drainage and are thus composed of fen peat deposits while areas further inland are more often raised bog peatlands. The peatlands are frequently broken by slightly elevated boulder clay drumlins. Three major drainage schemes have reduced the level of the lough and restricted flooding. The first scheme was carried out between 1847 and 1858 with further schemes in 1942 and 1959. The combined result of the drainage schemes has been the lowering of the level of the lough by an estimated 2.3 m and the reduction of fluctuations from an estimated 3.5 m to notionally <0.5 m today.

Other changes have taken place which were not directly influenced by the drainage schemes. Forest clearance from the better soils was more or less complete by the seventeenth century. Over many centuries peat extraction, with controlled drainage, has reduced the extent and level of most of the raised bogs. Drainage of the raised bogs means that their surfaces are no longer actively growing. The water of the lough is only slightly alkaline (~ pH 8.2) but a recent development affecting the aquatic plant communities has been the rapid increase in the eutrophic status of the lough which may have led to the extinction of some species and the spread of others.

Plant communities

The association between the plant communities of open water, reedswamp, fen, raised bog, grasslands, alder and willow carr, birch woodlands and mature woodlands are outlined diagrammatically in Fig. 7.3. Shallow waters not subject to violent wave action support submerged plant communities. If the water is

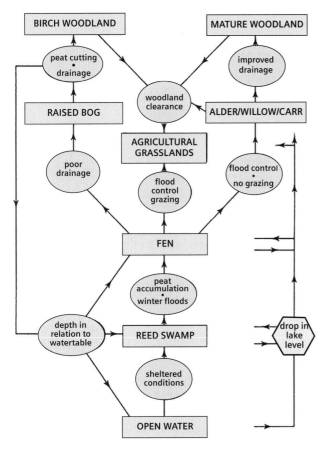

FIG. 7.3

Diagram of the relationships between plant communities of Lough Neagh.

sheltered enough an emergent reedswamp community can establish itself. The tendency then is for the sheltered water within the reedswamp to trap silt and organic debris to build up an organically-rich sediment layer. As the accumulation proceeds, the landward side of the reedswamp tends to progress to a more terrestrial plant community. The resultant species-rich fen community, influenced by floodwaters but not permanently submerged, can, in suitable local hydrological conditions of poor drainage, pass to a more oligotrophic plant community dominated by sphagnum mosses. The water-logged acid conditions greatly inhibit plant decomposition so the accumulation of peat within raised bogs tends to be relatively rapid. Deep peat cutting on raised bogs down to the level of eutrophic groundwater can re-establish the succession of the open water stage. 'Improved' drainage within raised bogs causes them to lose their formative plant communities which are altered by an increase in species better adapted to drier conditions and a decrease in hydrophilous species such as sphagnum mosses.

A common consequence of improved drainage on raised bogs is the development of birch (*Betula pubescens, Betula pendula*) woodland. Fen communities not overtaken by raised bogs may pass to alder (*Alnus glutinosa*) and willow (*Salix* spp.) carr in the absence of grazing or to wet grassland with heavy grazing. Agricultural development has, in many areas, completely ousted fen plant communities and replaced them with commercial grassland mixtures. Alder and willow carr will eventually pass to more mature woodland but commonly reverts to grassland due to clearance. The birch woodlands of the raised bogs are similarly often cleared to be replaced by grassland or open moorland.

The natural progression of plant communities from submerged aquatics to mature woodland is a very slow process but has been violently disrupted each time the lough level has been lowered and the flood levels reduced. New plant communities have developed very quickly on freshly exposed lake shore while other communities have shifted their ground or altered their composition.

Several 'typical' cross-sections of the lake shore and a river have been drawn to outline the physical relationship between the water margin and some of the major plant communities already discussed. Fig. 7.4 shows a section at Rea's

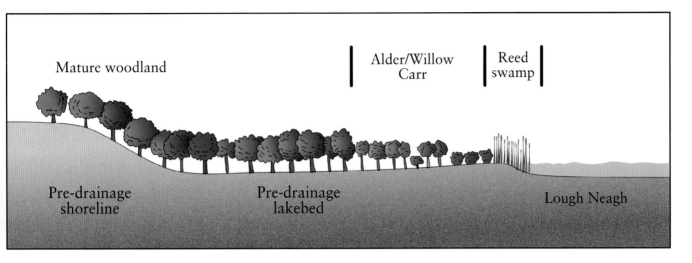

Wood Forest NNR, County Antrim, on an ungrazed site. Reedswamp, alder/willow and mature woodland have all developed on ground that was formerly lake bed. The trees, by fairly sharply distinct successive stages of growth, still show quite clearly the position of the pre-drainage shorelines. A series of low sand ridges running parallel with the shore within the wood confuse this picture slightly by creating wet and dry sections, with their associated plant communities. In contrast, a similar section through grazed ground lacks the alder/willow carr. The example given in Fig. 7.5 is taken from Derryclone, County Antrim, where the alder/willow carr is replaced by wet grassland. On grazed shores such as these, a narrow band of alder occasionally occurs close to the water's edge while the steep face of the old shoreline fairly consistently supports mixed scrub.

A shore with a very different character is found at Blacker's Rock, County Tyrone (Fig. 7.6). Here the water was very shallow and broken by several islands before the first drainage scheme. The drop in water level has left the landward side of extensive reedbeds dry, broken by stands of more mature trees on the old island sites. The raised bog comes quite close to the shore in this area and is

FIG. 7.4

Cross-section of shoreline at Rea's Wood.

FIG. 7.5

Cross-section of shoreline at Derryclone.

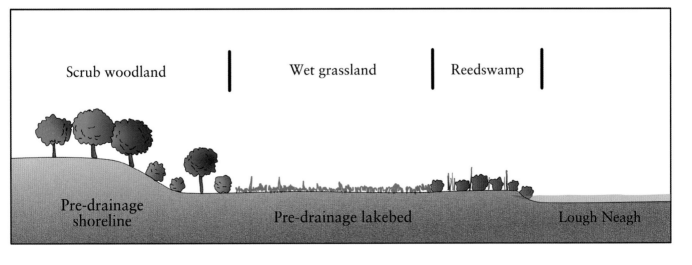

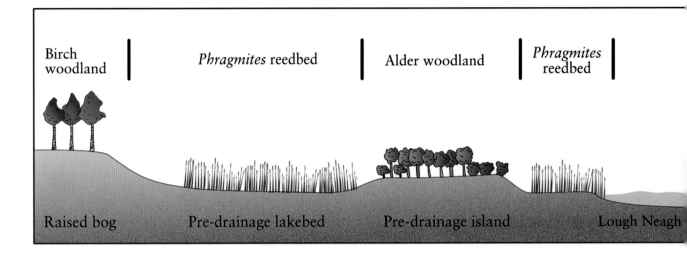

Birch
woodland

Phragmites reedbed

Alder woodland

Phragmites
reedbed

Raised bog

Pre-drainage lakebed

Pre-drainage island

Lough Neagh

FIG. 7.6
Cross-section of shoreline
at Blacker's Rock.

clothed in birch woodland. Along sections of the north shore the shoreline is rocky (Fig. 7.7). Peatlands are absent here and reedswamp is rare but an unusual 'rock garden' type flora grows in the rock crevices and in places the shore is well wooded. Offshore, submerged aquatics are found where the water is shallow.

Fig. 7.8 is a typical section through a river and its margins to the south of the lough, the floodplain of which once supported fen vegetation. The fen communities have been replaced by large fields of re-seeded grassland. The margins of these rivers generally support submerged, floating and emergent aquatic plants.

Plant communities of open water

Plants growing in open water are either completely submerged, floating attached, freely floating or emergent. These communities have been strongly influenced by man in recent times through lowered water levels, increasing eutrophication and the introduction and spread of new species. Two formerly abundant species were awlwort (*Subularia aquatica*) and quillwort (*Isoetes lacustris*). These are now very rare. This may have arisen because of the eutrophic state of the lough as they are essentially plants of mesotrophic waters.

FIG. 7.7
Cross-section of
shoreline at Cranfield.

Rock garden flora
&
scrub woodland

Submerged aquatics

Basalt outcrop

Lough Neagh

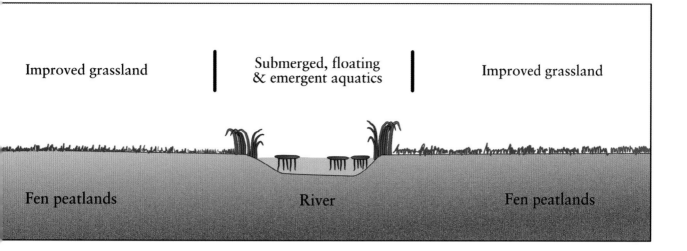

| Improved grassland | Submerged, floating & emergent aquatics | Improved grassland |

| Fen peatlands | River | Fen peatlands |

Submerged plants

Completely submerged plants can photosynthesise only where sufficient light penetrates and as the euphotic zone rarely exceeds 3 m in summer these plants survive only in the shallower waters of the lough. They are also excluded from open, exposed shores by turbulent wave action and unstable substrate. As a result, they occur only where they are protected from strong wave action by the configuration of the shoreline or by the presence of off-shore sand bars or islands, or in inlets, pools and drains around the shores of the lough. Lough Beg is shallower than Lough Neagh and is particularly rich in submerged aquatics. The group includes many pondweeds (*Potamogeton* spp.). The commonest are *Potamogeton pectinatus* and *P. filiformis*, the latter growing in shallower water (10–70 cm) and quite often in more exposed conditions. Other fairly frequent pondweeds include *P. lucens*, *P. gramineus*, *P. perfoliatus*, *P. berchtoldii* and *P. crispus*. Of these *P. lucens* occurs in the deepest waters (2 m in Kinnego Bay). Less common pondweeds include *P. zizii*, *P. alpinus*, *P. praelongus*, *P. pusillus* and *P. obtusifolius. Zannichellia palustris* is frequent in the lough and two fairly abundant species in suitable sheltered waters are spiked water milfoil (*Myriophyllum spicatum*) and Canadian pondweed (*Elodea canadensis*), the latter having been introduced *c*. 1836.

A rare water milfoil from North America (*Myriophyllum alternifiorum* var. *americanum*) occurs on Lough Neagh and Lough Beg. It occurs in other lakes in Ireland but in Britain it is only found in the west of Scotland. *Ranunculus fiuitans* has its only Irish station on the lower reaches of the Six Mile Water in County Antrim. Several species of starwort (*Callitriche* spp.) belong to this group, the most widespread being *Callitriche stagnalis* although it is found in pools and drains, rather than in more open situations where *C. hermaphroditica* is more frequently found. An interesting plant which has a scattered and local distribution elsewhere in the British Isles but which has become locally common

FIG. 7.8

Cross-section through River Bann.

in Lough Neagh is *Elatine hyropiper*. It was first noted last century in the Newry Canal and is a low creeping plant which grows on muddy substrate in shallow water (0.5 m) where the bottom is not shaded by mats of filamentous algae or larger aquatics.

Floating attached plants

This group is less tolerant of exposed conditions than the submerged group and is therefore even more confined to sheltered waters. Many plants of the group grow in inlets and drains and find the margins of slow flowing rivers particularly suitable (Upper River Bann and River Blackwater). The species are cosmopolitan and include the yellow water lily (*Nuphar lutea*) amphibious bistort (*Polygonum amphibium*), unbranched bur-reed (*Sparganium emersum*), broad-leaved pondweed (*Potamogeton natans*) and flote-grass (*Glyceria fluitans*).

Free floating plants

Free floating plants are often found growing in association with floating attached plants; they tend to shade out submerged aquatics. Four species of duckweed (*Lemna*) occur on Lough Neagh. Common duckweed (*Lemna minor*) and greater duckweed (*L. polyrrhiza*) are the most widely distributed and frequently occur together, usually scattered throughout emergent plant communities. *L. polyrrhiza* is worthy of note as it is a rapidly increasing species first recorded on the Lagan Canal in 1880 and now very common on Lough Neagh. The other duckweeds are ivy leaved duckweed (*L. trisulca*) which is fairly frequent although it can be easily overlooked as it has a submerged growth habit; and fat duckweed (*L. gibba*) which is described as rare and local. The frogbit (*Hydrocharis morsus-ranae*) is rare, occurring only in drains at Lough Gullion, and it shares a feature with *Lemna polyrrhiza*, that it reflects the northern extension of the flora of the Central Plain of Ireland. In Britain there are many plants associated with wetlands that are confined to lowland lakes in southern regions; many of these plants recur on the Central Plain of Ireland where they find similar conditions in the numerous, shallow, limestone lakes. In turn many of these plants have extended their northwards along a narrow tongue of limestone that extends up the corridor of the Blackwater valley to south-east Lough Neagh. *Hydrocharis morsus-ranae* and *Lemna polyrrhiza* are two examples from this group of species with a southern distribution in Britain; others will be referred to later.

Emergent plants

This is the reedswamp group composed of plants that are permanently rooted underwater but send up emergent shoots. The water between the plant stems is often sheltered enough to trap not only silt but also dead plant material; this leads to the accumulation of organic matter and the gradual elevation of the rooted surface. It is therefore a transitional community between open water and various terrestrial communities. Reedswamp communities were much reduced immediately after the 1959 lowering when considerable sections were left dry; most of the shoreline is grazed by cattle so most of these species were quickly lost on the landward side to better adapted marsh and grassland species, while the reedswamp plants re-established themselves at the new shoreline. Where grazing was excluded the freshly exposed areas were invaded by willows (*Salix* spp.) and alder (*Alnus glutinosa*) giving rise to swamp and fen carr; this scrub development is well represented at Farr's Bay, Antrim Bay, Rams Island, Raughlin Peninsula and Coney Island. Most of the shoreline is very exposed so contrary to expectations for such a shallow body of water reedswamp communities on Lough Neagh are by no means extensive. Abandoned gravel pits and the peatlands where turf cutting has reached down to the level of nutrient rich groundwater provide additional sites.

A very common plant on the shores of Lough Neagh is the reed canary grass (*Phalaris arundinacea*). This is considered a reedswamp species as it tolerates flooding but in fact it often establishes itself just above the mean water level where it is very efficient at binding the soil and withstanding strong wave action. Where the water is shallow, common spike rush (*Eleocharis palustris*) establishes itself in even the most exposed conditions, given a suitable substrate. More sheltered shores support other reedswamp plants, often in pure stands; characteristic are common reed (*Phragmites australis*), reed-mace (*Typha latifolia*), bulrush (*Scirpus lacustris*), branched burred (*Sparganium erectum*) and bottle sedge (*Carex rostrata*). Lesser reed-mace (*Typha angustifolia*) is local and rare in Ireland but occurs in significant stands on the outer margins of the *Phragmites* beds of Portmore Lough and Lough Gullion.

Common emergent plants of shallow water, though not usually in pure stands, include watercress (*Nasturtium officinale*), fool's watercress (*Apium nodifiorum*), water speedwell (*Veronica anagallis-aquatica*), yellow flag (*Iris pseudacorus*), water plantain (*Alisma plantago-aquabca*) and lesser water plantain (*Baldellia ranunculoides*). Plants of particular interest in this group are the flowering rush (*Butomus umbellatus*) and arrowhead (*Sagittaria sagittifolia*), both of which are frequent in the area but are of definite southern distribution in Britain and have their principal Irish distribution in the Central Plain. *Butomus* is common in drains and inlets while *Sagittaria* is more frequent along the sides of slow moving rivers. Emergent plants are found in a narrow fringe around the entire lough except where the shore is too exposed. In such cases plant communities are replaced by shifting accumulations of sand and gravel often intermixed with flotsam of tree branches and leaves. Where the shore is rocky, many plants of the emergent group establish themselves in the relative shelter between boulders. The most significant stands of *Phragmites*, with their associated emergent plants, are found at Shane's Castle, Selshan Harbour, Ellis

Gut, Kinnego Bay, Raughlin Peninsula, Croghan Island and Scaddy Island. The smaller lakes are all fringed with *Phragmites* but the most extensive reedbed in the area stretches from Blacker's Rock to Kells Point on the west shore and is in places several hundred metres wide.

Plant communities of peatlands

The tendency of reedswamp communities to accumulate partially decayed organic deposits has already been referred to above. In such waterlogged anaerobic conditions, the organic layer (peat) can build up above mean water level. The reedswamp plant community then progresses to one of fen; a plant community of peatlands subject to more or less continuous waterlogged conditions but not constantly under standing water. In these situations, the ground-water is similar in chemistry to that of the lough and the local rivers, i.e. neutral or slightly alkaline in reaction but rich in nutrients. This suits a wide range of plants and the fen community is an extremely rich one.

Raised bog communities supersede fen communities where local conditions of poor drainage cause the fen peat to accumulate to such a level that the surface vegetation is influenced more by rainwater than by more nutrient-rich groundwater. The leaching of the surface by rainwater leads to the replacement of fen vegetation by more acidophilous vegetation dominated by *Sphagnum* mosses, which quickly accumulate as acid peat and spread to form low, domed, raised bogs. In Ireland, the initiation of these raised bogs took place in Atlantic times, about 7,000 years ago. They have developed extensively on low-lying ground in some places to a depth of 10 m, especially to the south of the lough in the north of County Armagh, but also along the west shore as far as Toome Bay.

Before the drainage scheme of 1847–58, large tracts of land were seasonally flooded along the shores of the lough and along the lower courses of many rivers. These areas must have supported well developed fen communities, but the extent of the fen has been reduced to almost nothing by various drainage schemes which have progressively eliminated the winter floods. With improved drainage the lowland fens make excellent agricultural land, so the natural plant communities were quickly replaced by artificial ones. Where agricultural development has not taken place the restriction of flooding has allowed the ecological succession of herbaceous fen communities to progress to woodland. As late as 1930, before the final lowering, Duff (1930) recorded well developed fen communities still surviving over large areas.

At this time, the mean water level was about 1 m higher than today and fluctuated considerably from summer to winter. The extent of the fen was described by Small (1931) and included the Three Islands area, Shane's Castle, Selshan Harbour to Portmore Lough, from Oxford Island shore to Maghery, all along the Upper Bann and Blackwater rivers, around Annagarriff and Derryadd lakes, numerous small patches to the south-west and south-east, along the entire margins of the lough and at the mouth of all rivers. Today, with improved drainage and greater control of water levels, these areas are no longer subject to winter flooding and fen communities are restricted to narrow margins adjacent to open water and deeply cut over sections within the raised bog areas. An especially interesting mosaic of fen communities in cut over sections within remnants of raised bog is well illustrated at Brackagh Moss. This site has been slightly damaged by improved drainage from the surrounding agricultural land but is now protected as a National Nature Reserve and efforts are being made to maintain the water table at the highest practical level.

Fens

The fen community is species-rich and includes many plants which are also found in the reedswamp community. Other plants include marsh marigold (*Caltha palustris*), meadowsweet (*Filipendula ulmaria*), purple loosestrife (*Lythrum salicaria*), great willowherb (*Epilobium hirsutum*), cowbane (*Cicuta virosa*), nodding bur-marigold (*Bidens cernua*), tripartite bur-marigold (*B. tripartita*), marsh ragwort (*Senecio aquaticus*), yellow loosestrife (*Lysimachia vulgaris*), marsh forget-me-not (*Myosotis scorpioides*), bittersweet (*Solanum dulcamara*), water mint (*Mentha aquatica*), gypsy-wort (*Lycopus europaeus*), marsh woundwort (*Stachys palustris*), common spotted orchid (*Dactylorhiza fuchsii*) and northern fen orchid (*D. majalis*). Common sedges include *Carex disticha, C. paniculata, C. nigra, C. flacca, C. rostrata and C. vesicaria*.

Not all the fen plants have survived the new water regime. Some were especially dependent on seasonal flooding and have now disappeared from the area. Notable amongst these are the marsh fern (*Thelypteris palustris*) and saw sedge (*Cladium mariscus*). There have been more recent single records for marsh pea (*Lathyrus palustris*) and northern bedstraw (*Galium boreale*), but these too may now have disappeared completely. Fen plants that are very rare or have recently become extinct in the Lough Neagh area but are much more frequent in the more base-rich East Anglian fens and wetlands of central Ireland are the marsh fern (*Thelypteris palustris*), buckthorn (*Rhamnus catharticus*), alder buckthorn (*Frangula alnus*), marsh pea (*Lathyrus palustris*), saw sedge (*Cladium mariscus*) and the tufted sedge (*Carex elata*).

An orchid worthy of note associated with the fragments of fen that remain is *Spiranthes romanzoffiana*. It is an American plant known to occur in the Lough Neagh basin and in a few other sites in the British Isles, but not elsewhere in Europe. It was first discovered at Brackagh Bog by Praeger (1892). Unfortunately, it is near extinction at this site, but it is still thriving at several other sites around Lough Neagh and at Lough Beg. Its occurrence here is difficult to explain but Praeger (1934) points out that there are several North American plants in north-west Europe and similarly several European plants on the north-east American coast. He suggests a possible early migration via Iceland and Greenland when the two continents were closer together.

Two extremely rare grasses of fen communities in the British Isles have been found in the Lough Neagh area; holy grass (*Hierochloe odorata*) occurs at Selshan Harbour and northern small reed (*Calamagrostis stricta*) which has not been found recently at a large number of its former sites but has been recorded from nearby Lough Beg and from some areas in Lough Neagh.

Raised bogs

All of the raised bogs have been altered by various degrees of cutting, draining and burning. As a result, there is very little active growth of peat; the *Sphagnum* moss communities that developed most of the peat have been much reduced or eliminated locally. Typical plants of the raised bog surfaces today include sundew (*Drosera rotundiflora*), cross-leaved heath (*Erica tetralix*), heather (*Calluna vulgaris*), cotton grass (*Eriophorum angustifolium*), bog asphodel (*Narthecium ossifragum*) and royal fern (*Osmunda regalis*). Cranberry (*Vaccinium oxycoccus*) and bog rosemary (*Andromeda polifolia*) are found only locally in the area within the Peatlands Park, County Armagh, but are interesting in that they are typical constituents of lowland raised bogs in the British Isles. Andromeda occurs here as an extension of its range from the Central Plain of Ireland where it is very common. All three species of Drosera – *D. rotundifolia*, *D. anglica* and *D. intermedia* – occur within Peatlands Park.

It has already been pointed out that the drained peat surfaces support fewer *Sphagnum* species than a raised bog in its natural condition. Instead, they often have a more or less continuous cover of *Calluna* with a ground cover of *non-Sphagnum* mosses. Burning encourages purple moor grass (*Molinia caerulea*), bracken (*Pteridium aquilinum*) or rosebay willowherb (*Epilobium angustifolium*), and, where burning is less effective, vigorous stands of hairy birch (*Betula pubescens*) develop. Areas that are cut over to a fairly low level and regularly burnt develop a poor fen community dominated by *Molinia* associated with devil's bit scabious (*Succisa pratensis*), marsh pennywort (*Hydrocotyle vulgaris*) and sweet vernal grass (*Anthoxanthum odoratum*). This poor fen community is well represented over a large area at Derrymore south of Portmore Lough. The drains in this area support bogbean (*Menyanthes trifoliata*), greater bladderwort (*Utricularia vulgaris*), bog pondweed (*Potamogeton polygonifolius*) and bottle sedge (*Carex rostrata*).

Plant communities of woodlands

According to McCracken (1971), oak woodlands were extensive around the shores of the lough during the early seventeenth century; the only areas devoid of woodland cover at this time were a small section in the south-west at Washingbay and a larger section on the east shore between Portmore Lough and

Antrim. To the south of the lough, in north Armagh, alder and willow grew on the low-lying fens and oak was restricted to the protruding pockets of glacial drift. By the beginning of the eighteenth century these oak woodlands had all been cleared except for a few remnants on the north shore which were finally cleared at the end of that century.

The land that once supported these oakwoods is now almost entirely converted to agricultural use. Many of the townland names on the southern shores of the lake contain the word 'derry' which strongly indicates earlier extensive occurrence of oak woods. Oak woodlands have been lost but other semi-natural woodlands have been established. The scarp of the old lake shore supports a band of seminatural woodland dominated by blackthorn (*Prunus spinosa*) and ash (*Fraxinus excelsior*) with occasional spindle (*Euonymus europaeus*), crab apple (*Malus sylvestris*), guelder rose (*Viburnum opulus*) and hazel (*Carylus avellana*). Buckthorn (*Rhamnus catharticus*) was never common but may now have disappeared, Harron and Rushton (1986) describing it as rare, sparse and decreasing.

The scarp is generally cut in boulder clay, and wooded sections support a fragmented woodland ground flora. The Cranfield shore in the north of the lough is something of an exception as here the basalt outcrops reach the lake shore and the scarp is marked by large boulders and bare rock. The ash woodland on this site is interesting in that it supports native oak (*Quercus petraea*) and wych-elm (*Ulmus glabra*). The long history of woodland cover on the site is reflected in the richness of the ground flora which includes many woodland grasses, namely *Festuca gigantea*, *Melica unifiora*, *Bromus ramosus*, *Brachypodium sylvaticum*, *Elymus caninus* and *Milium effusum*. A curious occurrence is the fern, the giant large-leaved polypody (*Polypodium australe*) which is otherwise rare in Northern Ireland and not normally found away from chalk or limestone.

There are several large estates on the shores of the lough. The owners of these lands set aside sections for woodland management that today support mature beech (*Fagus sylvatica*) and sycamore (*Acer pseudoplatanus*) with a mixture of native trees. Woodland of this type is best represented along the Antrim Bay shore, but other examples occur at Gartree Point, Rams Island, Raughlin Peninsula and on Coney Island. As a result of the various lough lowerings freshly exposed margins of the lake bed have been colonised by vegetation. The areas best protected from grazing have generally been those adjacent to existing woodland and it is these areas that have developed the best alder and willow carr. There is typically a marked break in the character of the canopy between the planted hardwoods and the naturally regenerated alder and willow carr which in itself reflects, by stage of growth, successive lake lowerings.

Additional carr woodland has also developed on numerous small, scattered sites along the shore of Lough Neagh and in association with the other small lakes notably on the north-east shore of Portmore Lough. Alder, perhaps aided by its ability to fix nitrogen, quickly colonises freshly exposed sands and gravels; the peatier and wetter sites support a wide range of willow species, the most frequent of which are *Salix fragilis, S. alba, S. atrocinerea, S. caprea* and *S. viminalis*. Blackcurrant (*Ribes nigrum*) and guelder rose (*Viburnum opulus*) are frequent but alder buckthorn (*Frangula alnus*), a common constituent of East Anglian carr, is very rare. On drier ground, as on old sand and gravel bars, ash (*Fraxinus excelsior*) and hairy birch (*Betula pubescens*) are common and planted sycamore (*Acer pseudoplatanus*) spreads easily.

The herbaceous vegetation of drier sections is locally dominated by bluebell (*Hyacinthoides non-scriptus*), but the wetter areas support a rich and luxuriant flora with several rarities. Tall plants typical of fen are found here such as meadowsweet (*Filipendula ulmaria*), hemlock water drop-wort (*Oenanthe crocata*) and iris (*Iris pseudacorus*). Growing in great sheets in damp sites in the Antrim Bay area is the greater bittercress (*Cardamine amara*), which is otherwise rare in Ireland. Characteristic sedges are *Carex remota, C. vesicaria, C. paniculata* and *Scirpus sylvaticus*. A sedge thought to be extinct in Ireland, *C. elongata*, was re-found at several damp woodland sites by Harron. The Himalayan balsam (*Impatiens glandulifera*) first recorded in 1937 has established itself in several localities and as a very successful introduced plant that is having detrimental effects on the native vegetation locally. Birch (*Betula pubescens*) forms vigorous pure stands throughout much of the cut-over bog in the area. It is especially characteristic of overgrown ramparts that were once used as paths to traverse the bog but now retained only as land boundaries. Its distribution is, therefore, closely associated with that of the raised bog.

Plant communities of grasslands

All the grasslands in the immediate vicinity of the lough are man-made and are mostly used for summer grazing of domestic livestock. In the absence of management, the natural transition from open water to dry land passes through reedswamp to willow and alder carr to oak woodland. Where seasonal flooding is more persistent the tree species do not colonise, and a tall fen vegetation develops. The reclamation of the fen areas has already been mentioned; they have, for the most part, been re-seeded with agricultural grassland mixtures to produce a sward which is, incidently, much favoured by flocks of wintering swans. The narrow strip of exposed lake bed that fringes the lough is grazed throughout its length apart from the reedswamp and woodland sections already mentioned and other small and inaccessible sites. The type of grassland that develops is controlled by the soil (which is neutral but varies from sands and gravels to boulder clay and peat), the water regime of the site and the management. All these factors vary on a very local scale and as no systematic work on the grassland communities has been carried out it is possible to make only very general comments about their species composition and their distribution.

On the lake shore, poorly drained ground that is not continuously saturated supports a wet meadow flora which includes meadow buttercup (*Ranunculus acris*), creeping buttercup (*R. repens*), ladies' smock (*Cardamine pratensis*), moneywort (*Lysimachia nummularia*), common rush (*Juncus effusus*) and the grasses *Deschampsia cespitosa, Holeus lanatus, Agrostis canina, A. stolonifera,* and *Poa trivialis*. Heavy clay soils often support hard rush (*Juncus inflexus*) while peat soils yield the sedge *Carex disticha*. Very wet grasslands on mineral soils are termed marshes and typical species of this group include many that are found in both reedswamp and fen. Examples are the marsh marigold (*Caltha palustris*), ragged robin (*Lychnis flos-cuculi*), marsh cinquefoil (*Potentilla palustris*), marsh pennywort (*Hydrocotyle vulgaris*), marsh bedstraw (*Galium palustre*), the rush *Juncus acutiflorus* and the grass *Agrostis stolonifera*.

The distribution of the re-seeded grasslands corresponds with that of former fen and to a lesser extent to reclaimed raised bog. Other local sections of former lake bed have also been re-seeded; the reclamation is often done by bulldozing higher ground onto lower ground occupied by reedswamp or marsh communities on the margin of the lough to produce a uniform, efficiently drained surface.

Conservation

With each fall in water level the plant communities of Lough Neagh have been subjected to severe and rapid changes. All have been altered in character by the loss of some species and the addition of others. Some plant communities have almost disappeared completely, as was the fate of the once extensive fen communities. Further lowerings are unlikely, but other pressures are mounting which will threaten the continued survival of the natural and semi-natural areas that remain. Agricultural development is the main threat, and many sites have been destroyed in recent years. The Northern Ireland Environment Agency through the statutory powers vested in it by the Amenity Lands Act NI (1965) and the Nature Conservation and Amenity Lands (NI) Order 1985, have taken certain measures to control damaging development. This has been done in two ways, firstly, by declaring the entire shoreline and much of the low-lying ground to the south of the lough an Area of Special Scientific Interest. Secondly, a more effective but a very local measure is the establishment of National Nature Reserves. These have been set up on several prime sites of scientific value by acquiring the land or drawing up agreements with the landowners for the reserves to be managed primarily for the protection of the flora and fauna. Nine nature reserves have been established in the Lough Neagh area and although they are small in extent, they encompass a wide range of vegetation types.

Bibliography

M. Duff, 'The ecology of the Moss Lane region, Lough Neagh', *PRIA*, 39B (1930), pp 477–96.

J.E. Harron, 'A preliminary study of areas of special ecological interest occurring in the Lough Neagh basin' (Report to Conservation Branch, DoE(NI), 1977).

J. Harron and B.S. Rushton, *Flora of Lough Neagh* (Irish Naturalists' Journal Committee, Belfast and University of Ulster, Coleraine, 1986).

E. McCracken, *The Irish Woods Since Tudor Times* (Newton Abbot, 1971).

R.L. Praeger, 'Botanical rambles in County Armagh', *Report and Proceedings of the Belfast Natural History and Philosophical Society, Session 1893–4* (1894), pp 34–6.

R.L. Praeger, *The Botanist in Ireland* (Dublin, 1934; reprinted Wakefield, 1974).

J. Small, 'The fenlands of Lough Neagh', *Journal of Ecology*, 19 (1931), pp 383–8.

S.A. Stewart and T. Corry, *A Flora of the North-East of Ireland* (Belfast, 1938).

J.M. White, 'Recolonisation after peat cutting', *PRIA*, 39B (1930), pp 453–76.

FIG. 8.1
Bluebells on Coney Island.

8 The ancient and modern flora of the Lough Neagh region

Jonathan Pilcher

A geological view

During the mid-Tertiary (around 20 million years ago) a lake basin sat in approximately the position of the present day Lough Neagh. In the warm temperate conditions at this time, peat formed in the low-lying swamp and this preserved the remains of trees that fell into the swamp. These tree remains exist today as lignite which is an organic deposit intermediate between peat and the much older coal.

Lignite beds are present at several points around the lake basin with the best-known at Aghnadarragh townland, near Crumlin. The deposit here extends westwards under the present day lough and was the subject of much academic, economic and political excitement in the 1980s when a commercial test pit was dug and proposals were put forward for a major extraction project linked to a lignite-burning power station. The claim was made for 250 million tonnes of fuel, enough to fire a power station for 30 years. Fortunately for the environment this project never came to fruition. However, the test pit did give a glimpse into this much earlier, Tertiary, 'Lough Neagh' and its temperate vegetation and forests (McCabe et al. 1987). A typical Tertiary forest composition reads like the plant list of a modern arboretum – *Sequoia* (coastal redwood), *Taxodium* (swamp cypress), *Nyssa* (tupelo), *Liquidambar* (sweetgum), *Castanea* (sweet chestnut), *Ostrya* (hop-hornbeam), *Juglans* (walnut), *Sciadopitys* (umbrella pine), *Carya* (hickory) and *Pterocarya* (wingnut). The sediments above the lignite provide a uniquely detailed record of the subsequent glacial and interglacial events. A well preserved mammoth tooth was the first find that indicated the importance of this site.

Glaciation and early post-glacial development of the lough

While glacial ice advanced and retreated several times during the Pleistocene period, there is little hard evidence of what the Lough Neagh basin would have looked like during the warm periods. The lack of deposits dating from these periods suggests that they were wiped away by the succeeding ice advances. A peat deposit preserved under glacial clays at Benburb (Boulter and Mitchell 1977) has provided the most detailed interglacial record from Northern Ireland. Pollen analysis from Benburb peat (Gennard 1984) shows a sequence from pine woodland with birch, alder, willow, juniper and grass, followed by pine and yew woodland and then deciduous woodland with oak, beech, ash, elm and alder with spruce (*Picea*), arriving towards the end of the deciduous woodland stage. The final phase has fir (*Abies*) and yew forming coniferous woodland with rhododendron. Thus a number of plants common in Europe today and not considered as native to Ireland – beech, spruce, fir and rhododendron – arrived in Ireland during this interglacial but were then lost in the following cold period.

With current interest in conservation, climate change and re-wilding schemes, the question of what is considered a native plant has practical implications. The long timescale view of the Irish flora confirms that this is not a simple question, particularly in the light of future climate change.

In the final cold stage of the last glacial period an ice sheet developed with its centre over Lough Neagh. This was deep enough to spill over the Sperrins, so it must have been some 600–800 m thick. Ice from other centres of ice-sheet formation fused with the Lough Neagh sheet to give a continuous cap over most of Ireland. When this ice sheet began to thaw, huge volumes of melt water were trapped by the ice to the north leading to delta deposits at altitudes that seem to make no sense in the modern Lough Neagh context. As the Lough Neagh ice melted, the Lower Bann continued to be blocked by ice leading to the lough water level being 60 m above present levels and thus the lake was far larger than at the present time.

Size of the lough in the past

The Holocene history of Lough Neagh lake levels is complex. Lough Neagh is at present about 12.5 m above mean sea level (OD Belfast). A clear indication of the complication of the lake level story is provided by presence of diatomite at Toome on the Lower Bann (and at various other locations) at +12 to +13 m OD and wood-rich peat deposits well below present lake level around the south and west shore of the lough dating to between 4000 and 1000 BCE.

Diatomite is formed of the remains of lake-water algae and its presence implies a high lake level, at least periodically; submerged wood-rich peat with identifiable woodland species clearly indicates that there had been a low lake level for long enough for woodland to develop. The present day water level is due to drainage operations on the Lower Bann in 1847–58, 1942 and 1959. These interventions lowered the water level by about 1 m and reduced the variability in water level so reducing flooding. One metre may not seem to be very significant, but due to the drainage a large area of flat land to the south of the lough became amenable to agriculture.

There is no sharp boundary to what may be called the lough basin. Wood and Smith (1993) include the whole water catchment which would allow us to include the Lower Bann valley and even part of the Sperrin mountains in this account. This brings in many sites from which much of the vegetational history of Northern Ireland is derived. To understand the present vegetation of the area we need to delve into the past. As we have seen, the Lough Neagh area was totally covered by an ice sheet at about 22,000 years ago. This simplifies the post-glacial vegetational history as the slate was wiped clean and all present vegetation post-dates the melting of this ice.

Late glacial vegetation

The following sequence is a composite built from the records of sediments in many present day lakes (e.g. Cannon's Lough: Smith 1964) and in pre-peat deposits under present day bogs for example Fallahogy (Smith 1958) and Sluggan Bog (Smith and Goddard 1991).

15,000 to 13,000 years ago (BP)

Although the Northern Hemisphere ice sheets had begun to melt, global sea levels were still low and Ireland, England and the continent were still joined by land. The land bridges provided a passage for the return of plants to Ireland. Ice-free land to the south of present day Ireland may have provided a source of the first plants to colonise the newly ice-free mainland – a sparse alpine vegetation including juniper, crowberry (*Empetrum nigrum*), dwarf willow (*Salix herbacea*) and dwarf birch (*Betula nana*) developed without any tall trees.

12,000 BP

Temperatures were relatively warm. Much of Ireland was covered by grasslands with few trees. Giant Irish Deer grazed the rich grasslands, and indeed several sets of Giant Irish Deer antlers have been found in the Lough Neagh area. Organic silt was laid down in lakes.

11,800 BP

Later, a sudden and catastrophic climate deterioration occurred, the Giant Irish Deer disappeared, and organic lake sediments were capped by a clay layer. Plants such as mugwort (*Artemesia vulgaris*) and sedges (*Carex* species) replaced the grassland leading to an alpine vegetation similar to that before this cold snap.

11,000 BP

At 11,000 years ago the temperature was rising rapidly and sea levels continued to rise as the Northern Hemisphere ice sheets melted. Temperate plants began to return from refuges much further south in France and Spain, but as the rising sea level cut the connection between Ireland and England before the land bridge between England and the continent was submerged, fewer plants came naturally to Ireland. Thus Ireland has a depauperate flora with some 820 flowering plants recorded in Ireland as opposed to about 1,150 in England and over 2,000 in northern France.

Post-glacial vegetation

The summary vegetational history below is based on a large number of studies on Northern Ireland bogs and lakes (see for example: Smith 1958; Smith and Goddard 1991; Pilcher and Smith 1976).

10,000 BP

The first plant to increase in abundance as the temperature rose was juniper (*Juniperus communis*). It is presumed to have survived the cold snap and was able to expand rapidly. It was quickly followed by birch (*Betula pubescens*). This, the tree birch rather than dwarf birch (*Betula nana*), is a classic pioneer tree producing huge amounts of wind-blown seed.

9500–8000 BP

The birch woodland was reduced as hazel (*Corylus avellana*) increased. Hazel, because of its larger seeds was slower to migrate into the north of Ireland than the wind-dispersed birch but able to replace it because its seeds can germinate under the shade of birch. Very quickly the hazel was reduced to understory status by the arrival of the major forest trees, oak and elm. Once this mixed deciduous woodland was established, forest dominated almost the whole of Ireland and extended well into the mountain ranges of the Mournes and Sperrins. Almost the whole of the Lough Neagh catchment would have been densely forested. There is no present day woodland that gives an adequate picture of the continuous dense forest cover indicated by pollen diagrams of this period.

7000 BP

Alder (*Alnus glutinosa*), present in small amounts earlier, expanded at this time. This may have been due to a lowering of lake levels providing a suitable wet but fertile habitat for alder. Meanwhile the dense mixed deciduous woodland continued to dominate the landscape.

5900 BP

The first people to arrive in Ireland were hunter-gatherers (the Mesolithic culture). There is evidence of their presence at a number of coastal sites and they entered the Lough Neagh basin via the Lower Bann. Settlements are known at Mount Sandel (Collins 1983) and at Newferry (Smith and Collins 1971; Woodman 1977) both on the Lower Bann. At Newferry there seems to have been a seasonal camp, probably connected to salmon fishing. Charcoal from their fires and salmon bones were found in the diatomite, the assumption being that it was a seasonal camp at times when the area was not flooded. Botanical remains at the Mount Sandel site show that hazelnuts formed part of their diet. So far there is no evidence that this population moved far from the shores and rivers into the dense forest and there is little sign of their presence in the pollen diagrams. However, from this time the vegetation story becomes dominated by human influences

5500 BP

Everything changed with the arrival of the Neolithic farmers. They moved into the forests and began to clear trees for farming. One of the early settlements at

Ballynagilly in County Tyrone (Pilcher and Smith, 1976) had a rectangular house built of oak planks and the pollen evidence showed that they were growing cereal crops. Initially the farmers may have kept to the higher ground, staying away from the wet, heavy soils of the Lough Neagh basin.

5500 BP to the present

Successive waves of people continued to come into the area, with new technology – bronze tools then iron axes and ploughs – each reducing the forest and increasing the land under agriculture. Pollen diagrams from sites all over Northern Ireland paint a similar picture, with the wettest areas being developed more slowly.

The present flora of the Lough Neagh basin

Leaving aside the effect of human populations, there is a natural progression of lake and lake-margin vegetation. Plant populations are not static, but undergo a succession, often leading to a stable climax vegetation. Here is a very brief outline of a typical lake-to-bog succession such as must have occurred in many of the marginal parts of the Lough Neagh basin.

Transition from water to bog

1 Open water and floating vegetation

The open water of Lough Neagh has a rich algal flora including a wide range of diatoms. Floating vegetation develops in bays and lakes that become cut off from the main lake. Both native water lilies are present, *Nuphar lutea*, yellow water lily is more common in the south, particularly in the rivers entering the lough. *Nymphaea alba*, white waterlily, has been recorded from the area but is rare (Harron 1986).

2 Marginal vegetation in shallow water

Common reed (*Phragmites communis*) is found throughout the lake margins. Reeds form a dense monoculture, producing annual growth up to 2 m tall. With abundant nutrients from the lake water, they produce a prodigious biomass each year. Much of this builds up, eventually turning into reedswamp peat and providing the solid substrate for the development of fen. Also seen on the lake margins is bullrush, *Schoenoplectus lacustris*, long harvested as a valuable thatching material superior to both reeds and cheaper barley straw.

3 Fen

This is still subject to seasonal flooding but not usually with standing water throughout the year. The fen has a very diverse flora and is often visually very attractive, including meadowsweet (*Filipendula ulmaria*), yellow flag iris (*Iris pseudacorus*), pink-flowered lady's smock (*Cardamine pratensis*), common spotted orchid (*Dactylorhiza fuchsii*) and marsh cinquefoil (*Potentilla palustris*).

4 Fen carr

As the level of fen vegetation builds up, the surface becomes suitable for the germination of tree seedlings. Willow and alder are most tolerant of waterlogging, but often birch will be the first to arrive as it produces such large quantities of wind-blown seed.

5 Woodland

At the present day there are few areas of true woodland around Lough Neagh. The oak woodland in Shane's Castle estate dates back to at least the seventeenth century as demonstrated by dendrochronology, but it is unlikely to be a natural woodland. Present day oak woodland is different, in both extent and composition, to the ancient woodland represented by the preserved bog oaks from the bogland margins of the lough. The main peak of oak growth in the Lough Neagh basin was 4000 to 1000 BCE. These native oak forest trees were tall and straight-stemmed and unlike the oaks seen in modern oak woodland in Ireland (e.g. Breen wood, Kilbroney oak wood (Pilcher 1976)). The degeneration of the native oak stock can be traced to centuries of exploitative felling that removed the best trees leaving the runts to set seed for the next generation. Ireland's woodlands lacked the protection afforded to royal forests such as Sherwood forest in England and Fontainebleau forest in France where the finest trees were kept to set seed for the next generation.

A picture of the composition of ancient forests of this area can be gained from pollen analysis. The most informative pollen records for the Lough Neagh area come from the large bogs bordering the Lower Bann valley (at Fallahogy, Ballyscullion and Newferry for example). Pollen preservation in the sediments of Lough Neagh itself is generally poor – superior records are obtained from work on nearby bogs. All of these studies paint a picture of a dense mixed woodland up to the early centuries AD, dominated by oak, but with a range of other species, particularly alder, hazel, ash and birch. Pollen analysis does not tell us exactly where individual species were growing within the catchment of the pollen diagram, so we must use a combination of knowledge of the ecology of the plants and botanical intuition. It is clear from what is known of past Lough Neagh water levels that any areas of woodland close to the lough must have been subject to seasonal flooding. Alder and willow are particularly tolerant of occasional flooding and would have grown close to the lough shore as they still do today. The little patches of wet woodland that exist today have survived mostly because they were either too wet or too inaccessible for farming. More obvious patches of woodland such as Coney Island – nine acres of woodland about 1 km from the present day shore – have been occupied, managed and modified since Neolithic times and can hardly be considered as natural.

Drainage of bogland and the recent reduction in peat cutting is allowing the development of new woodland in some areas. Often this woodland includes non-native species such as rhododendron, hemlock (*Tsuga heterophylla*) and various pines. Conservation of bogland, as in Peatlands Park, involves the labour-intensive work of removing these invasive 'non-native' species. In other areas it is native birch that invades drying peatland and this is seen as part of a 'natural' succession that could eventually lead to the establishment of a mixed deciduous woodland. Deciduous woodland always has a rich understory of vegetation, particularly of species that can make use of the brief window of opportunity in the spring before the leaf cover becomes dense. Bluebells, primrose and celandine all flower and set seed early.

6 Bog

Bogs are characterised by a specific plant composition that develops when the vegetation is cut off from the source of ground water and is fed entirely by rain water. They are usually the end point of a succession from open lake water, to water with floating vegetation, then to fen or reedswamp. Sometimes there may be a fen woodland stage, but eventually the build-up of dead vegetation raises the surface out of contact with ground water. Without the mineral supply from ground water the incipient bog becomes more acidic which limits the range of plants that can survive. Typically at this point sphagnum mosses become the dominant plant. Any remaining trees are killed as the roots are starved of oxygen by the blanket of sphagnum. The ancient stumps of bog oaks and bog pines are

FIG. 8.2
Bogland at Derrytresk.

testament to this process. The area of bogland in the Lough Neagh basin originally extended over a large area to the south of Lough Neagh and also along the Lower Bann valley. Much of this bogland has been drained for agriculture and additionally drained for peat to fuel the demands of the linen industry. The extent of the ancient bogs and associated wet woodland became clear during the construction in the 1970s of the M1 motorway which passed through low-lying land near the River Bann and River Blackwater. Many thousands of bog oaks were dragged out of the construction trench of the motorway. At this time, grants for agricultural 'improvement' encouraged the drainage of further areas of bogland extending south and east of Lough Neagh (Baillie 1995). Under the bog oaks there was usually a layer of reedswamp peat and often lake clays or sometimes diatomite indicating the area had once been part of the lough.

The development of bog from any of the above stages depends on local conditions. We can follow the sequence from open water to bog by studying a vertical section through a bog (either by digging or by taking a core). In many cases the transition seems to be directly from reedswamp to bog, in others through a fen or fen carr stage and in others through an oak woodland. In each case the fossilised remains such as reeds or wood or sphagnum moss bear witness to the different stages leading to the bog. It is also clear that variations in climate play a role in this sequence. Many of the bogs show signs of periodic drying leaving to colonisation by pine followed by a surge in sphagnum growth that killed the pine, preserving their stumps in the peat. Clearly, present day rapid climate change is going to have a significant impact on the few intact bogs that are left in Ireland.

7 Invasion by alien species

Rhododendron (*R. ponticum*) is invading bogland in a number of areas in Northern Ireland; in the Lough Neagh area at Toomebridge and in County Armagh (Harron 1986). Non-native conifers can also invade bogland. There is an argument that rhododendron, fir and spruce should be classed as native vegetation as they were here in the interglacials under similar climatic conditions and should be allowed to develop where they have self-seeded. Open lake water is under threat from alien water plants brought in for aquaria, while fens are being invaded by balsam (*Impatiens glandulifera*) brought in to Ireland as a garden plant and first recorded in the wild by Praeger in 1937. It is now found around almost all of the loughshore. Another garden escape is the skunk lily (*Lysichiton americanus*). There are only a few records of the skunk lily in 1986 but its rapid rise to dominance in a bog in County Down demonstrates its ability to colonise. A more surprising invader is the pitcher plant (*Sarracenia purpurea*) which was introduced deliberately in Peatlands Park for education purposes, but has got a strong hold and is seeding across the bog.

The future of vegetation in the Lough Neagh basin

The rather optimistic prediction of a mere 2°C rise in global temperature in the next century will nevertheless have some dramatic effects; it is, after all, about half of the global temperature change from the middle of the last Ice Age to the present. The two main effects of man-induced climate change are likely to be sea level rise and temperature rise. Both will have an impact on Lough Neagh and its surroundings.

Sea level rise will affect the drainage through the Lower Bann and eventually, in the distant future, lead to a marine sea-lough Lough Neagh. Temperature rise will change the composition of the flora, lead to drying of the bogs and their colonisation by trees and will enable many more alien species to thrive, probably at the expense of the native vegetation. Much of the vegetation further south in Europe may be spread to Ireland deliberately or accidentally and increase naturally. Woodland species that are common in France are likely to form a component of our woodlands. The sweet chestnut, *Castanea dentata*, which normally is not able to set viable seed here, is likely to be able to set seed and spread into the oak woodlands. On top of these changes, more exotic introduced species such as sycamore, Norway maple, eucalyptus and the Australian cabbage palm (*Cordyline australis)* all of which are already setting abundant seed in sheltered areas, are likely to spread dramatically.

Set in the context of the huge vegetational changes during geological timescales outlined above, these future changes may not be as extreme as they appear from our very limited viewpoint.

Bibliography

M.G.L. Baillie, *A Slice Through Time: Dendrochronology and Precision Dating* (London, 1995).

M. Boulter and W.I. Mitchell, 'Middle Pleistocene (Gortian) deposits from Benburb, Northern Ireland', *Irish Naturalists' Journal*, 19 (1977), pp 2–3.

A.E.P. Collins, 'Excavations at Mount Sandel, Lower Site, Coleraine, County Londonderry', *UJA*, 3rd series, 46 (1983), pp 1–22.

D.E. Gennard, 'A palaeoecological study of the interglacial deposit at Benburb, Co. Tyrone', *PRIA*, 84B (1984), pp 43–56.

J. Harron, *Flora of Lough Neagh* (Irish Naturalists' Journal Committee, Belfast and University of Ulster, Coleraine, 1986).

A.M. McCabe, G. Coope, D. Gennard and P. Doughty, 'Freshwater organic deposits and stratified sediments between early and late Midlandian (Devensian) till sheets, at Aghnadarragh, County Antrim, Northern Ireland', *Journal of Quaternary Science*, 2 (1987), pp 11–33.

J.R. Pilcher, 'A statistical oak chronology from the north of Ireland', *Tree-Ring Bulletin*, 36 (1976), pp 21–7.

J.R. Pilcher and A.G. Smith, 'Palaeoecological investigations at Ballynagilly, a Neolithic and Bronze age settlement in County Tyrone, Northern Ireland', *Philosophical Transactions of the Royal Society of London, Series B*, 286 (1979), pp 345–69.

J.R. Pilcher, 'History of the vegetation of north east Ireland' in *Stewart & Corry's Flora of the North-east of Ireland*, ed. P. Hackney (Belfast, 1992), pp 59–70.

J.R. Pilcher and S. Mac an tSaoir (eds), *Wood, Trees and Forests in Ireland* (Royal Irish Academy, Dublin, 1995).

J.R. Pilcher and V.A. Hall, *Flora Hibernica* (Cork, 2001).

A.G. Smith, 'Pollen analytical investigations of the mire at Fallahogy Td, Co. Derry', *PRIA*, 59B (1958), pp 329–43.

A.G. Smith, 'Cannons Lough, Kilrea, Co. Derry: stratigraphy and pollen analysis', *PRIA*, 61B (1961), pp 369–83.

A.G. Smith and A.E.P. Collins, 'The stratigraphy, palynology and archaeology of diatomite deposits at Newferry, Co. Antrim, Northern Ireland', *UJA*, 3rd series 34 (1971), pp 3–25.

A.G. Smith and I.C. Goddard, 'A 12,500 year record of the vegetational history of Sluggan Bog, Co. Antrim, N. Ireland (incorporating a pollen zone scheme for the non-specialist)', *New Phytologist*, 118 (1991), pp 167–87.

A.G. Smith and J.R. Pilcher, 'Radiocarbon dates and vegetational history of the British Isles', *New Phytologist*, 72 (1973), pp 903–14.

R.B. Wood and R.V. Smith (eds), *Lough Neagh: the Ecology of a Multipurpose Water Resource* (Dordrecht, 1993).

P. Woodman, 'Recent Excavations at Newferry, Co. Antrim', *Proceedings of the Prehistoric Society*, 43 (1977), pp 155–99.

9 The birdlife of the lough

Ciara Laverty

FIG. 9.1
Mallard eggs.

Lough Neagh is the largest lake in the British Isles covering an area of approximately 383 km². It is a wetland of international importance or Ramsar site, a Special Protection Area (SPA), and an Area of Special Scientific Interest (ASSI) because of the wealth of wildlife it supports. In fact it is paradise for birdwatchers! As well as large numbers of resident species that can be seen throughout the year, we are treated to an influx of summer and winter migrants.

Mallard (Anas platryhynchos)

For many of us, the humble Mallard is the first connection with nature we experience as children. It is one of our most widespread species of duck. They are found on most types of water body and are just as at home on urban ponds as they are on Lough Neagh. This familiar species is the ancestor of many of our farmyard duck breeds. Mallards are dabbling ducks, which means they typically feed in shallow water, often upending. They have a varied diet consisting of plant matter like seeds and aquatic vegetation, as well as insects and crustaceans. Males sport a vibrant green head, yellow bill, chestnut breast and a white neck ring. They have pale grey flanks, a vivid blue wing bar (speculum) and a black rump. Females are much more drab in appearance, with brown streaked plumage for camouflage.

In spring the female Mallard will choose a secluded spot, hidden in vegetation not far from water, in which to build her nest. She uses grass and leaves to construct the nest, and lines it with soft down feathers which she plucks from her breast. She can lay 12–14 eggs and is the sole incubator, only leaving the nest for short intervals to feed or stretch her legs. After about 28 days the ducklings hatch. There are many potential predators for young ducklings like Herons, foxes, rats and crows so there is a significant chance that not all of the youngsters will reach maturity. This is why

FIG. 9.2
Mallard.

FIG. 9.3
Mallard duckling.

Mallards lay so many eggs, in the hope that at least one or two ducklings will survive to adulthood. It takes around 60 days for the young Mallards to become independent.

Great Crested Grebe (Podiceps cristatus)

The Great Crested Grebe is a resident species and can be seen all year round on the lough. They are truly adapted for life on the water. Legs set far back on the body makes them strong, elegant swimmers but very ungainly walkers on land. During the spring and summer months, mature birds are adorned with striking chestnut and black crests. Adults form pair bonds by performing an elaborate courtship dance in which they rise from the water shaking their heads from side to side, a remarkable wildlife spectacle which signals the beginning of spring on the lough shore. The Great Crested Grebe is a conservation success story. The species was almost hunted to extinction in Britain in the late nineteenth century. Their beautiful feathers were used decorate ladies' hats and accessories. Thankfully, a group of passionate women known as the 'Fur, Fin and Feather Folk' campaigned for the protection of these birds; this was the precursor to the Royal Society for the Protection of Birds (RSPB). Today Lough Neagh holds the largest breeding population of Great Crested Grebe in Ireland.

FIG 9.4
Great Crested Grebe.

Grey Heron (Ardea cinerea)

Another familiar sight is the resident Grey Heron. Patient, stealthy hunters; they are often seen standing statue-still on the shoreline waiting to spear an unsuspecting fish with their dagger-like beak. They are opportunists and feed on a range of species – fish, eels, frogs, small mammals and reptiles – and are equipped with a 'pectinate' claw, which are small comb-like teeth on the side of the claw on their middle toe. This is a fascinating adaption which allows them to preen feathers that they are unable to reach with their bill. They also have 'powder downs', a gland that produces a fine powder which is spread over their wet plumage with their special claw helping the feathers to dry. Although the Grey Heron is a solitary hunter, they tend to nest in colonial groups or heronries. Large stick nests are made in tall trees and tend to be used year after year, some of which can be in use for over 100 years. They are one of the earliest nesters with some birds laying their first eggs in February.

Wander along the lough shore during the months of April and May you will witness a magnificent wildlife spectacle – the chironomid fly swarm. These non-biting flies have an extremely short life span of just two to three days. They emerge from the lough in order to find a mate and lay eggs. Insect-eating summer migrants like Swifts, Swallows and House Martins rely on these flies to successfully rear young.

Sand Martin (Riparia riparia)

The Sand Martin is the smallest member of Hirundine family (Martins and Swallows) that nests on our shores. They lack the white rump seen on House Martins and have sandy brown upperparts, a white belly with a brown breast bar. The first Sand Martins arrive in late March. True to their name, they excavate tunnels in sand banks ending in a nesting chamber. Both the male and female carry out the excavation work, with some tunnels measuring almost a metre in length. The nest chamber is lined with feathers, leaves or grass into which the female lays an average of five eggs. Both parents take it in turns to incubate the eggs and chicks hatch after 14 days. The parent birds feed the chicks a diet of insects, until the young birds fledge around 22 days old. Sand Martin fledglings are still reliant on their parents for a further week after leaving the nest. It is common for Sand Martins to raise two broods of chicks in a summer before migrating back to the Sahel region in Africa, south of the Sahara desert. An extremely busy summer for birds weighing just 14 grams!

FIG. 9.5
Grey Heron.

Sedge Warbler (Acrocephalus schoenobaenus)

The Sedge Warbler is a small attractive warbler, with brown streaked plumage and a prominent cream coloured eye stripe. They tend to be quite difficult to spot as they are perfectly camouflaged in their preferred habitat of reedbed or scrub. The male's scratchy, chattering calls give their presence away. Sedge Warblers do not sing the same song twice; their ability to mimic other bird species is woven with their own chattering and creates a unique song. The greater a male's song repertoire the greater his breeding success. A small cup-shaped nest made from grass, animal hair and spider webs is weaved around the reed stalks about 30 cm above the ground. An average of five eggs are laid with chicks hatching after 14 days of incubation the chicks then fledge after a further two weeks. The abundance of insect life that Lough Neagh provides makes up the diet of insectivorous birds like the Sedge Warbler. This species first appears in April and by October will have left to migrate back to sub-Saharan Africa to overwinter. Before they depart from our shores they double their body weight in preparation for the long journey south.

FIG. 9.6
Sedge Warbler.

Common Tern (Sterna hirundo)

Every summer Common Terns make the gruelling migration journey from west Africa to our shores. They have a black cap, long red-orange bill with a black tip. In flight they look like a small, elegant gull with slender wings and buoyant movement. Their long tail streamers have earned them the nickname 'sea swallows'. Common Terns readily breed in coastal habitats as well as inland waterways. The small islands on Lough Neagh are important breeding sites for this Amber List bird species. A thin scrape in sand, gravel or short vegetation is created into which they lay two to three eggs. After about 22 days of incubation, the eggs hatch and the young terns fledge after a further 28 days. Common Terns sometimes nest among other species like Black-headed Gulls because of the aerial protection they provide from predators. By the end of September our Common Terns will have left our shores, and continue their migration back to the southern hemisphere to overwinter.

FIG. 9.7
Common Tern.

FIG. 9.8
Pochard.

Although the departure of our summer breeders like the Sand Martin, Sedge
Warbler and Common Tern signals the end of long summer evenings and warm
temperatures, autumn and winter bring their own seasonal joys. Thousands of
wildfowl flock to Lough Neagh from much colder climes to spend the winter in
milder temperatures.

Pochard (Aythya farina)

Pochards are a resident diving duck species and can be seen all year round on
the lough. Their population grows during the winter months as thousands of
Pochard migrate from north-eastern Europe along with other wildfowl species.
As with most duck species, males and females look very different. Male Pochards
sport a stunning chestnut-red head, black breast and tail with silver flanks and
back while females have brown plumage with a pale face and sides. Pochards
are omnivorous, diving to feed on invertebrate and plant material. One of their
favourite prey items is the larvae of the Lough Neagh fly – the 'bloodworm'
which lives in the mud on the floor of the Lough. The Pochard is a Red List
species, which means its population has declined drastically. Pochard numbers
on Lough Neagh declined from 40,000 birds to less than 8,000 between the early
1990s and 2004.

Whooper Swan (Cygnus cygnus)

The loud trumpeting call of the Whooper Swan reverberating across the lough on a frosty morning is a profound winter experience. These graceful birds migrate all the way from Iceland, travelling in family groups to spend their winter on Lough Neagh and Lough Beg. Northern Ireland is extremely important for this species, with 20% of the UK population overwintering here. At first glance they appear similar to our resident Mute Swan, but there are a few ways to tell the two species apart. Whoopers have a yellow bill tipped with black and lack the 'knob' seen above the orange bill on Mute Swans. Whoopers are a sleeker bird than the familiar Mute Swan and do not hold their wings arched over their backs. They first arrive in mid-October. Whoopers are herbivorous and can be seen feeding on arable fields and wet grassland of the Lough Neagh Shoreline during the winter months. By April most of our Whoopers will have departed our shores to return to Iceland to breed. However, some pairs have been noted spending the summer on Lough Neagh.

No matter the season, Lough Neagh has a wealth of wildlife wonders to explore and this article has just scratched the surface. Get out and explore the different habitats, see what species you can spot and notice how the landscape and species differ from season to season. I promise you will not be disappointed.

FIG. 9.9
Whooper Swans.

10 Two decades of AFBI eel research on Lough Neagh

turning fishery folklore into fishery fact

Derek Evans

The eel fishery on Lough Neagh first crossed my academic radar as a marine biology student in Edinburgh in the early 1990s. Any university of repute teaching Fisheries Biology 1.0.1 would contain within this module a lecture on the '*Commercial eel fishery on Lough Neagh*', an example of how an organised fishing community can manage sustainably and harvest a natural resource.

We learned that this fishery, worth millions of pounds, was organised as a co-operative, developed and lead by a local priest, yet incredibly almost the entire catch was exported to Continental Europe. As a harvested fish species the European eel was a bit of a curiosity. Following a life history the polar opposite to that of a salmon, the oceanic half of its life cycle was an unknown. Described as *Catadromous*, we were taught that European eels are hatched at sea, believed to be somewhere in the Sargasso region of the North Atlantic and wild spawning had yet to be seen. Artificial breeding had proved impossible and so the juvenile glass eel and elvers were the only source of seed stock to populate natural recruitment, fisheries and eel farms. These juveniles swam across the ocean, entered European estuaries, and travelled upstream into rivers and lakes without showing any sign of 'homing'. Adults lived upwards of 18–35 years before migrating downstream to swim back across the ocean to the Sargasso, breed once and die. This dual migration of European eels across the North Atlantic remains one of the greatest unseen movements of animals on planet Earth.

Fast forward ten years and, I'm employed as a Senior Fisheries Scientist within the Fisheries and Aquatic Ecosystems Branch of the Agri Food and Biosciences Institute NI (AFBI), tasked as the Project Leader into all things eel. May 2003 and I'm sitting in a large office in the HQ of the Lough Neagh Fishermen's Co-operative Society in front of Fr Oliver Plunket Kennedy, about to embark on what has (so far) turned out to be two decades of research into every aspect of the eel population in Lough Neagh. But why the need for research? What's the interest?

FIG. 10.1
Lough Neagh eel.

Across Europe, where there is a long tradition of consuming eel, particularly northern Europe, Lough Neagh is synonymous with the eel, often referred to simply as Irish eel. Many buyers in the main markets in Holland would frequently call them *Kennedy eels*. This had a wonderful symmetry by association, when one considers that in 432 St Patrick invented eels, after he banished Satan in the form of the serpent from the lands of Ireland, culminating in them wriggling into the rivers becoming eels. To this day few people in Ireland eat eel (and we don't have snakes...), and one of Patrick's ecclesiastical descendants has helped create Europe's largest inland fishery for eel on our very own doorstep. At 16% of the entire annual EU catch, Lough Neagh is home to the largest wild European eel fishery in the world, with average outputs (~250t) equivalent to that of entire European countries. The individual qualities of Lough Neagh eel make it such a unique product that in 2011 the European Commission awarded it special status, giving 'Lough Neagh Eel' a protected label as a regional speciality food known as Protected Geographical Indication (PGI).

Since the creation of the current co-operative in the late 1960s, numerous households and families have earned a living through the decades from one of our most primal, yet most arduous activities – fishing. Eel fishing is a very hard way of life, the working conditions are often grim, the hours are long and when you go to bed at 8pm to rise for a storm at 3am, the work life balance necessitates a 'certain kind of folk'. Every fisherman will also tell you that 'the difference between fishing and catching is like night and day ...'.

In 1983 it was European fishing communities such as that around Lough Neagh which noticed that the annual bounty from the sea of the influx of millions of elvers into European estuaries had not happened. Elvers had almost vanished compared to previous years – in Lough Neagh terms the arrival of elvers into the River Bann at the Cutts in Coleraine fell from 12 million to three-quarters of a million, a drop of 94%. The hope amongst fishing communities was that it was a blip, a bad year, something that they had seen previously in other species, and that it would 'right itself next year', no panic. But it didn't, in fact, the drop in elvers continued to get worse. Across the European eel's natural range spanning Europe and North Africa the annual immigration now fluctuates around the lowest numbers ever recorded at about 7–10% of that seen pre-1983. These dramatic changes in the numbers of a fish species once considered to be in every 'shuck and stream' around the country culminated in the listing of eel as 'critically endangered' by the International Union for the Conservation of Nature (IUCN), and as a 'species of conservation concern' under the Convention of International Trade in Endangered Species (CITES). The factors thought responsible for the decline of eel are being studied widely and include overfishing, habitat loss, pollution, the impacts of hydro-electric dams, climate change and the introduction of alien parasites (from Japan, not Jupiter...). While there are those with pet theories who persist in seeking a single dominant cause, it is most likely an accumulation of these factors that has resulted in significantly fewer silver eels making it to the Sargasso Sea to spawn, fewer elvers produced and the present low state of the stock.

This continuing collapse in recruitment, and the knock on effect this would have, not only on commercial harvests, but the production of adults eels to spawn at sea was the impetus for pan-European action. And so began the Department of Agriculture, Environment and Rural Affairs-funded AFBI programme of research and monitoring in response to requests for answers. High level intervention followed when the European Parliament and Commission became involved in devising a recovery plan for EU eel stocks. Based around the creation of Eel Management Plans (EMP), the thrust is increased escapement of at least 40% of silver eels to sea. In 2007 scientists across the EU were asked to present to the EC what an EMP should look like, and I essentially gave an updated version of the Fisheries Biology 1.0.1 lecture on Lough Neagh; when you've a winning formula, you've a winning formula. For the insomniacs amongst you the 116 EMPs are available on the EC website, and in many of these you can see an echo of the management of the Lough Neagh fishery which proved to be a blueprint for how it should be done.

Given the common biological characteristics of eels and the fact it was one genetically indistinct pan-European stock (all European eels have the same DNA profile), the driver behind many of the research themes on Lough Neagh was that the findings could be applied to other river systems across the eel's range.

If you are a fisheries scientist, curious about all those things which affect or influence the lives of aquatic organisms, then Lough Neagh is a fish nerd's paradise. Combine this with the opportunity to work with a unique co-operative and fishery management team, backed by a community and fishing fleet with a willingness and desire to be fully engaged with scientific research – it would only be a matter of time before we started to get meaningful, applicable results. Unlike many of our collaborators across Europe (which focus on one eel life cycle stage), Lough Neagh provided AFBI with access to live specimens from *all* of the life cycle, ranging from the juveniles (glass eel and elver), through the yellow eels (of the main commercial fishery) to the seaward migrating silver eels (caught at

FIG. 10.2
Fishermen on the
lough.

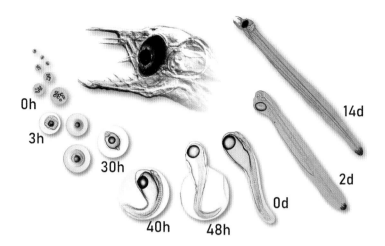

FIG. 10.3

European eel development from egg via embryonic stages to hatch in hours and yolk sac larvae derived from Lough Neagh female silver eels in days after hatch at 20°C.

Photo courtesy of Dr Jonna Tomkewitz, Danish Technical University.

the famous weir at Toome). In addition the Lough Neagh Fishermen's Co-operative Society provided access to a dataset, the envy of the eel world, spanning 108 years from the turn of the twentieth century, with continual catch records right up to the current day.

To give a flavour of some of the key areas of research which AFBI developed in attempting to understand the biology and ecology of Lough Neagh eels the following are some highlights from each of the eel life phases.

Glass eel and elvers

After a year of oceanic drifting as a willow leaf shaped stage called a Leptocephali, juvenile eel destined for the Bann transform into glass eel as they cross the European continental shelf 500 km to the south-west of Ireland. As each of these respective stages from Lepto to glass eel to elver age, they get shorter, and after six weeks in the estuary with the onset of rising water temperatures they're stimulated to feed and to grow. Years of surveying have established the arrival timing of the glass eel, and we have found changes with a wide variation from the traditional pattern of spring arrivals and summer elver runs. Glass eels have been caught at the Cutts in Coleraine as early as January, and more recently sporadic elver runs have continued into the autumn with collections from traps in September. The year 2011 was the lowest recorded catch for Bann elvers, falling to 16 kg (approximately 48,000 individuals), but has risen since then to an average over the last ten years of around 470 kg (1.4 million). Glass eels are 'lazy', though it is probably more biologically correct if I say they are clever. They surf their way into an estuary and upstream using a rising tide, swimming as little as they can in the surface water layers, and heaven forbid they should ever climb up a ramp into an elver box. The correct biological terminology for eel surfing is selective tidal transport and it is quite a sight to see the little strands of silver spaghetti riding the head of the tide, ducking out of the spotlight when beamed with a torch.

AFBI's first research focus was on determining if there were any locally derived impacts which may be negatively influencing the migration of elvers into the Bann estuary and onward up the Lower River Bann. This is a heavily flow mediated system with a series of sluice gates controlling the movement of water out of Lough Neagh since their construction in the 1930s. Changes in rain patterns linked to climate change have been recorded across Northern Ireland and at times these now coincide with juvenile eel migrations which are interrupted by the heavy outward river flows following sluice gate openings. We found no other significant barriers to migration, and so, as with so many other countries, the drop in recruitment was confirmed as a stock-wide phenomenon. Given the absence of local impacts affecting elver numbers, the research changed direction with efforts now moving to optimise the trap and transport of juvenile eel from the barriers at the Cutts into Lough Neagh. A range of netting methods have been trialled and deployed linked to various environmental parameters such as river flow, water temperature and lunar/tidal phases. The upshot of these trials was that drag netting is ideal for catching glass eel, as they're on the surface, but once conditions in the Bann pass the magic temperature threshold of 8°C, things change, 'elvering' begins and juvenile eel activity becomes a bottom dwelling behaviour, which no net could conquer. As the biology shifts from surfers to crawlers so too did the applied nature of the research switching to the sequence of elver traps and passes at the sluice gates and weirs along the Bann. Over the years AFBI have trialled a collection of new elver boxes, ramps, collection devices and crawling substrates to varying degrees of success. Two clear winners quickly became apparent, neither of which were rocket science and have remained part of the measures used to aid the assisted migration of elvers into Lough Neagh.

The first is affectionately referred to as the 'grass skirt', in which strands of old rope are embedded into a resin block and placed at the upper most pinch point of the rising tide in the Bann. Unable to get past this point due to water flow, the mat acts as an artificial substrate into which juvenile eels bury themselves as the tide falls. Developed by Dr Cedric Briand, a French glass eel expert, AFBI brought it to the Cutts in 2005, and over the last 15 years it alone has caught 2.2t of elvers, worth the equivalent of £0.5 million and proof positive that there can indeed be money for old rope. The second was the introduction of bristle mat as a climbing substrate to help elver movement up the ramps into elver boxes or over elver passes at the side of the sluice gates at Portna. Resembling an upturned yard brush, the bristle mat accommodates the movement of eels (and lamprey) from a range of sizes and their sturdy nature forgoes the need for the replacement and removal of straw ropes which did the job admirably for the previous 70 years.

Yellow eels

The main commercial fishery on Lough Neagh has a fleet of around 80–90 boats, crewed by two and each boat a standard size and effort. This is the beating heart of the co-operative and provided an opportunity to study eel fishing up close and personal in a way that does not exist anywhere else across the European eel range. Many hours on boats with fishermen were the stimulus for undertaking specific research topics and have helped fuel the academic progress of 17 university students through various undergraduate degrees, masters and doctorates. With forearms like Popeye, but the dexterity of a weaver, watching their two-handed motion as they run a long line, baiting hooks, steering the boat, whilst quizzing the nerd, teaches you that despite 'public' perception to the contrary, there are men out there who can multi-task. AFBI have measured 60,000 yellow eels and sampled 5,000 of them. We know their gender (mostly females), where they tend to live, the best way to catch them, their preferred food, how much fat they have, any viruses and parasites, their (thankfully very low) accumulated chemicals, and crucially what age they are.

At an average age of 12–16 years old, this finding proved to be of great interest across the fleet as most felt their eels were much younger, five years maximum. But this is a standard age for eel of this size, they are a long lived fish species which has direct implications in terms of fixing the 'eel problem'. AFBI trialled alternative eel baits, making use of marine trawler discards and frozen Lough Neagh fry to see if catch compositions changed – in a nutshell, none of these worked, as the release of their respective odour trails in the water was disrupted by the freezing process. Surveys into hook sizes found that by increasing the size of hooks it reduced the capture of smaller eels – known as gape limited, if it's too big for their mouth, the eel won't touch it. We have tattooed 1,000 small eels that ended up in catches sent to the HQ at Toome to investigate if such eels released on site into the Bann made their way back upstream into the lough; a year later three of them reappeared in catches.

Silver eels

The series of weirs at the exit of Lough Neagh and downstream at Kilrea, provided immediate access to thousands of silver eels. AFBI have been able to analyse much of the same parameters as those for yellow eel, with additional focus on assessing and quantifying the number of silver eels escaping to sea. Unlike the yellow eels, the silver eels are pretty much an even split between males and females. Males are smaller, younger, 12 years old (vs 18 for females), and dominate the early weeks of the silver eel run in the autumn as they need a head start over the females for their swim across the Atlantic. Silver eels do not eat, their swim fuelled by the fat they have accrued during their time feeding as a yellow eel in the lough. This fat it turns out is crucial in the transformation of a yellow eel into a silver eel and we now know that there is a critical threshold of

16–18% fat. This triggers changes, causing physical adaptations in the eels becoming more suited to an oceanic environment, producing a black back and silver belly, more rounded fins, larger eyes and the recycling of their redundant digestive system.

Old fishermen often told me tales of how 'silvers liked the sun' and how they would use the sand on the bottom of the lough to 'rub off their backside'. Amusing observations until years later in our research we found a link between warm summers and silver eels, and sure enough silver eels have no backside as they have stopped feeding. Over the two decades there have been many similar experiences where AFBI science has confirmed a fisherman's suspicions and I like to think that this synergy has somehow helped turn fishery folklore into fishery fact. Studies of the migration of silver eels from Lough Neagh has produced the largest eel tagging programme in Europe with 12,100 eels tagged and their escapement out of the lough assessed. You may be familiar with the silver eel weir at Toome, an iconic landmark for that stretch of the Bann, which since its installation in 1947, and a total catch of 6,900 tonnes, is recognised across the eel world as a 'serious piece of kit'. Yet our research has shown that it is not as effective as it may seem, and that this, combined with the 10% free gap known as the Queen's gap, currently enables the required quantities of silver eels to escape from the Neagh-Bann system.

Amongst these migrants AFBI developed methods for acoustically tracking the eels on their journey, listening to them as they passed various receivers swimming down the Lower Bann. Colleagues in the Loughs Agency in 2015 reported two rogue signals from their listening station along the Donegal coast which turned out to be two of our Lough Neagh migrants that had transited the Bann, turned left at Castlerock, heading in the right direction for the Sargasso Sea. Finally, in 2017, silver eels from Lough Neagh were transported to Denmark where a team at the Danish Technical University had been attempting to breed eels in captivity, with limited success. It became apparent that they had been working with farmed eels, which when hormonally induced to mature them, lacked an essential nutrient in their feed meaning their eggs would not fertilise. The wild Lough Neagh eels had no such impediment and six months later the first larval eels from a known Lough Neagh origin were hatched in Denmark.

Over these two decades wider eel science has progressed. We now understand the link between fat and spawning, we've used satellite tags to track them to the Azores halfway to the Sargasso Sea and we have located an inbuilt compass in their eye to help steer this course – but as I watch NASA flying a drone on the surface of Mars through my phone, we still know nothing of where or how this fish breeds here on planet Earth.

Many people have been involved in assisting so much of this research; their knowledge, ideas and good nature are what made it the success it has been thus far. However, it would be remiss not to single out this particular character

without whom many facets of AFBI's work would not have happened. Criticised often (if he caught you), a cornerstone of the co-operative and crucial to so many of our studies, former Head Bailiff Bill McElroy is due our appreciation for his can-do attitude and encyclopaedic knowledge of fishing. Thanks Bill.

FIG. 10.3

The author Derek Evans (left) with Bill McElroy.

11 What the Curlew and bogs do for us …

Siobhan Thompson

I work as the Natural Heritage Project Officer for Lough Neagh Landscape Partnership, and I first heard Curlew around Lough Neagh one May afternoon in 2017. I was walking through an area known as the Old School Lands. This is an area of low-lying raised bog that is part of a network of fragmented bogs that lie along the southern shores of Lough Neagh.

The Curlew flew over my head, calling that beautiful bubbling crescendo. Its long, graceful beak was silhouetted against the sky, and it flew low over the heather and cotton grass, skimming past the trees and coming to land on a patch of bog. I could see it for a minute and then that dappled brown bird disappeared, blending with the muted colours of the landscape around it. I watched the area for a long while, but I had no hope of seeing that bird again, and had I not seen it coming in to land, I would have had no idea that she was there.

FIG. 11.1
Curlew on agricultural land adjacent to the southern Lough Neagh shoreline.

It is possible that this could have been a migrating Curlew passing through the Lough Neagh basin. The Lough Neagh and Beg Special Protected Area was designated in April 1999 under European Natura legislation. This was in recognition of the natural resources and the support that internationally important communities of breeding waders, terns, and wildfowl find along its shores and islands. The lough offers shelter and natural haven, with its mild climates and key position on the Atlantic flyway ensuring we see large populations of different birds returning to our shorelines every year.

Now four years on, I have spent many hours out on the bog watching these Curlew. As a ground nesting bird, they will land a good distance away from their nest and work their way across the land. The backdrop of cotton grass, and heather combined with the natural dips and hollows of the bog make it a wonderful place for them to nest. Even with my scope I have lost sight of them as they weave their way cautiously across land, stopping to listen or watch something that catches their eye every so often. Curlew are an iconic bird of our peatlands, meadows and wetlands, they are the largest of the breeding waders found in the Irish landscape and along our coasts. In recent decades, their decline has been monitored by conservation bodies and government agencies throughout the island of Ireland and the United Kingdom.

When we look at this decline, we can see that several pressures are acting to accelerate it. Farming practices have intensified, leaving less available habitat for the birds to nest on. The available land that there is for the birds to nest on, is also increasingly separated and fragmented. In combination with this is the increase in predators such as foxes and crows. As the Curlew is a ground nesting bird it is much more vulnerable to attack than birds that nest in trees. Without doubt for the Curlew to survive throughout Ireland the UK, there is a need for conservation bodies and government agencies to set up funding programmes that will deliver the restoration and conservation of habitat that the Curlew nest and feed on. As well as steps to increase the number of eggs and chicks that survive to fledging age. For the survival of the Curlew and to sustain and grow population numbers for the future there needs to be young chicks surviving every year.

The low-lying bogs are remnants of the working connect that local people had with this landscape, up until the turn of the century these bogs were cut by locals for domestic peat to heat their homes. A turbary payment was made to the landlord, and it accounts for the many ditches and the symmetrical patterns you see from the air when looking down at this site. With the event of new easier to access fuels, most people turned away from the cutting of peat, and these lands have laid undisturbed for the past few decades. Now carpets of colourful sphagnum mosses, heathers and cotton grass, dotted with bog asphodel, sundews, and bog rosemary spread out in front of you as far as the eye can see.

At first glance our bogs may seem like barren and empty landscapes, but spend some time walking through, sitting or indeed lying in one and you soon come to realise that there is a whole community of bog dwellers who depend on this specialist habitat. When you walk through them, feet squelching across the waterlogged surfaces, you see the abundance of insects that live on them, four spot orb spiders, large heath butterfly, emperor moths, daddy longlegs, various dragon and damsel flies. These insects form the base of the specialised ecosystem that live in and around our bogs.

Bogs are formed when rainwater congregates for many decades, creating a waterlogged acidic environment that is often nutrient poor. Specialised species like sphagnum moss cover the surface of the bog, forming dense undulating mats. These top layers can in some instances be several metres deep. Sphagnum moss is an amazing species in that it can hold up to 20 times its weight in water. It is a key component in storing water in these habitats. In a healthy peat forming bog, the water levels are close to the bog surface. As new layers of sphagnum moss form, the older layers are submerged, and sink to the bottom of the system. Because conditions within the bog are very acidic, the sphagnum moss through anaerobic decomposition forms peat. Scientifically the profile and importance of bogs and peat has become well known. We hear them referred to as the Amazonian rain forests of the UK. Their role in removing carbon from the atmosphere and helping us to combat climate change is well researched. We know that healthy bogs are vitally important to the life systems of this planet that supports us. These areas that were once exploited for the removal of peat, are now recognised as one of the most important habitats to combat climate change.

I have worked in conservation since 2002, and the work gives me access to many pockets of nature throughout our countryside, and along Lough Neagh's shores. These areas are often fragmented and are not very large in size. They are interwoven with farmland, and housing for local people. Increasingly our countryside and the nature that lives in it, are under pressure. Some from man-made activities, such as development and agricultural intensification, and others from the impact of climate change. Evidence of this can be seen in the increase in flooding that has occurred around the Lough in the last ten years, with the lough's levels rising and causing extreme flooding around the southern shores.

The message we now hear is that our bogs and peatlands when restored and in a healthy condition can play a vital role in mitigating impacts from a warming planet. They are one of the largest natural carbon stores. They can absorb flood waters, help reduce greenhouses gases, and can make the air we breathe cleaner. Our Lough Neagh and Irish bog are critical habitats, playing an important part in helping to combat climate change. Essentially science shows that these bogs and peatlands are worth so much more to us as restored habitats in the long term, providing benefit for the masses.

FIG. 11.2
Tagged Curlew at Derryloughan.

However, it is not the science that makes us love nature. Many of us love getting out into the countryside, the natural world is our playground, in these wilder landscapes, away from people, and the fast pace of life we can find space to reconnect with who we are as individuals. Studies show that living in nature or near to nature, or even listening to a soundtrack of nature, or looking at pictures can have a positive impact on our brains. It calms our nervous system, lowers blood pressure, helps us maintain physical fitness and creates a positive cascade of soothing emotions within our nervous system. When were calmer and feeling less anxious we have more resilience to deal with stressful events in our daily lives and can cultivate more empathy and connect to the people around us.

We seek out nature, not only for our physical wellbeing but for our social and emotional development. Walking through the ramparts of south-west lough Neagh and listening to the call of the Curlew, Cuckoo, Lapwing and Meadow Pipits is a beautiful restful experience. It soothes the soul, much like listening to waves breaking on the shore. Problems and worries that you were in the grip of seem to be a distant memory, and some much-needed perspective can be gained. There is also a sense of connect, that feeling that I can be part of their secret world.

The natural world of Lough Neagh is inspirational. It is a haven for us as people, in an ever increasingly fast paced world. Our bogs, wetlands, rivers and Loughs provide us with the food we eat, the water we drink and the clean air that we breathe. It sits at the core of everything that we do, providing for us on so many different levels, and is truly woven into the fabric of our existence.

FIG. 11.3
Curlew at Derryloughan.

Built heritage
Archaeology
History

FROM TOP:
Tullyhogue.
Cranfield.
Rams Island.

12 The prehistoric archaeology of Lough Neagh

William Burke

Introduction

Prehistory in Ireland spans the periods known as the Mesolithic (8000–4000 BC), the Neolithic (4000–2500 BC), the Bronze Age (2500–700 BC) and the Iron Age (700 BC–AD 400). How we investigate human societies from those times is through the medium of archaeology, especially through the study of material remains that resulted from ancient human behaviour and activity. The study of prehistory allows us to understand a great deal about how communities functioned and how they learned from each other.

Before farming, inherited knowledge of the natural world allowed communities to thrive. Later, agricultural know-how facilitated the settling of the land and the development of many new crafts and skills. Contact with the rest of Europe brought new ideas, while technological innovations ushered in whole new ways of life. This is especially true of Lough Neagh and its immediate shorelands which, together with Lough Beg and the Lower River Bann, is recognised as an area of outstanding archaeological importance, reflecting a settlement history and societal evolutionary narrative of international significance. The lough has a long and fascinating history of human occupation with people making it their home and leaving their mark on the landscape and environment for over 10,000 years. There is hardly a place along the shoreline of the lough that does not bare the imprint of human use and habitation, and much of the landscape and environment which we see today has been influenced, if not determined, by our forebears.

FIG. 12.1

Flint recovered from excavation at Mountjoy Fort, Brocagh.

The Mesolithic

The earliest phase of Irish prehistory is the Mesolithic and is defined by the first human inhabitants arriving in Ireland. As the ice sheets retreated north, the Mesolithic hunter-gatherer societies of Europe followed, populating these newly forested regions. Evidence indicates that the first humans crossed the Irish Sea around 8000 BC, travelling to the east coast of Ireland from western Britain. This was a time when sea levels were significantly lower, indeed much of the Irish Sea basin was dry land, so crossing the sea in a small boat, perhaps one similar to the canoe formed from a hollowed-out log (dating to 5490–5246 BC) uncovered on the western shore of Lough Neagh at Brookend, would have been less perilous during the Mesolithic than today. As well as dug-out logs, it is likely that wooden-framed boats covered in bark or skin would have been constructed. These would have appeared similar in form to modern-day curraghs or coracles and would only have held two or three people at most.

These first colonists were hunters, trappers, fishers, and foragers who initially settled on the coast and then accessed the interior of the island along the rivers. Ireland was heavily forested at this time and access to resources and communications was easiest via the rivers and loughs. The resources within and along the edges of waterways like the Lower Bann and around the Lough Neagh shoreline provided both food and shelter to a people who were highly mobile hunters and gatherers and who exploited not just wild animals, fish and shellfish but also developed a characteristic chipped stone tool technology. It is these stone tools that have allowed archaeologists to subdivide the Mesolithic into Early and Later Mesolithic. In general, the material culture from the earlier Mesolithic is characterised by small flint blades known as microliths. These were too small to have been used on their own and probably formed part of composite tools, for example, a number of microliths may have been inserted along the length of a wooden handle to form a cutting blade or at the end of a wooden pole to make a harpoon or spear. In contrast the Later Mesolithic was characterised by large flint blades, often referred to as Bann flakes or butt-trimmed flakes, which could have been used on their own as spear points or cutting knives. The reason for this change in flint technology remains unclear and it is not paralleled in Britain or the continent.

Evidence for Mesolithic settlement around Lough Neagh can be found at two major occupation sites, one at Mount Sandel near Coleraine, and a second at Newferry just north of Lough Beg, both of which have produced a wealth of archaeological material that has helped inform an understanding of Irish Mesolithic society more so than any other sites on the Island.

At Newferry, the remarkable number of finds is largely due to major drainage operations including the Bann Drainage Scheme and the Lough Neagh Drainage programmes with artefacts providing a picture of how Mesolithic communities functioned. At Mount Sandel, the excavations carried out between 1973 and

1978 have provided important information on the way of life in the Irish Mesolithic. Mesolithic activity is strong around the shores of Lough Neagh with numerous flint and stone artefacts from both the Early and Later Mesolithic recovered from along the shores at Toome, the mouth of the River Main, Shane's Castle, Gartree and Ballyvanen townlands, near Selshan Harbour, from areas between Lough Neagh and the towns of Glenavy and Crumlin, from Clanrolla and Kinnego, Coney Island near the southern shore, the Creagh, Traad Point, and most recently during the construction of the new A6 road at Toome. Artefacts include Bann flakes, stone axes, blades, tanged points and flint cores.

This hunter-gatherer lifestyle seems to have been replaced by a farming economy during the fourth millennium BC. The mechanism for change is open to debate – invasion or transferral of ideas – but the new way of life brought with it a distinctive range of equipment which gives its name to another period – the Neolithic.

The Neolithic

The Irish Neolithic spanned some 1,500 years from approximately 4000 to 2500 BC. At the beginning of this period, Ireland was still a frontier land at the

FIG. 12.2

Stone implements from Lough Neagh.

John Evans, 'On some discoveries of stone implements in Lough Neagh, Ireland', *Archaeologia* (1867), vol. 41, pp 397–408

remote edge of Europe. The first farmers arriving from Britain and Europe found a heavily forested land rich in wildlife, which was already home to scattered groups of hunter-gatherers who had coexisted with this world for centuries. The Neolithic marks both a technological and economical change throughout Ireland. New settlers arrived bringing with them the first domesticated plants (wheat and barley) and animals (sheep, goats and cows) to these shores. This period stands in stark contrast to the preceding Mesolithic which was a largely mobile hunter gatherer lifestyle to a more sedentary agricultural one.

As these farmers set about clearing the woodland to lay out their farms and construct the first robust houses, they would give rise to a society which in time would build a range of megalithic tombs, various earthen monuments such as henges and mounds, and great ritual complexes spread over many acres. Today the megalithic monuments of these early farmers are the most visible surviving remains; court tombs, passage tombs and portal tombs (dolmens), representing the funerary and ritual monuments of these Neolithic peoples. Other sites do exist, mainly as earthwork remains such as henge monuments which were large earthen enclosures used for ritual and tribal gatherings. The majority of Neolithic settlement sites, however, have only been discovered through excavation. Single or groups of rectangular houses of timber construction have been found in areas of well-drained soils, including areas that were later covered in bog. The quality of the land is a most important factor in settlement location and one of the most diagnostic tools of this period are stone artefacts, especially the polished stone axe, used no doubt to clear stands of trees to open the landscape for farming and to use the subsequent felled wood in building houses, settlements and dug-out boats.

It might be expected that traces of the activities of these farming communities would be recorded in Lough Neagh but, while the Lower Bann and to a lesser extent Lough Neagh were of crucial importance to hunter-gatherer communities, with the change from hunting and gathering to farming, the lough assumed lesser importance during the later part of prehistory. The Neolithic period experienced a series of climatic oscillations towards a wetter, colder weather which resulted in a rise in wetland water levels and the development of massive peat bogs, in particular along the southern and north western edges of the lough. These low-lying, water-logged areas would have been of little attraction to the initial Neolithic colonists. As an outcome of climate change, we tend to find Early Neolithic settlements located on the lighter glacial gravels which lie round the edge of the Lough Neagh basin with the best and earliest known Neolithic farming settlements in the north of Ireland being found along the eastern foothills of the Sperrins.

The arrival of agriculture had marked a shift away from the lough and the river systems as the major source of food however there are occasional traces of shoreline settlement in later periods, in particular in the Later Neolithic suggesting that the lough and drainage system may have had temporary importance. Significant scatters of Later Neolithic material have been found at Toome, including flint javelin heads and two decorated, intact Neolithic bowls. These bowls were found during the lowering of Lough Neagh in the mid-1950s. They were embedded in shoreline peat deposits and may represent occupation on a shoreline which was at least as low as that of today. They are not an isolated occurrence as another such bowl was found at Newferry near the levels of the River Bann. The presence of a partially drowned dolmen on the west shore of the lough also suggests that the water level may have been lower during a part of the Neolithic. Other artefacts including polished stone axes have been recovered from Creagh and Toome, River Main, Shane's Castle, Dungonnell townland, Rams Island, Deer Park and Lady Bay, Selshan Harbour and Coney Island. Occupation sites have been identified through excavation at both Shane's Castle (1972) and at Langford Lodge (1960) where investigation of early Christian raths revealed earlier Neolithic activity. Excavations on Coney Island in 1962–4 revealed Neolithic features including a short ditch, occupation layers and a series of pits and hollows all of which contained burnt flints and flint knapping debris.

The Bronze Age

The Bronze Age is, as the name suggests, characterised by the extensive use of metals, particularly copper, tin (bronze), lead and gold. The period is normally divided into two broad sub-periods based on development of artefact types, the Early Bronze Age (2500–1550 BC) and Later Bronze Age (1550–700 BC) and activity relating to both periods have been uncovered around Lough Neagh. During the Bronze Age, the landscape seems to have been managed or controlled to a much greater degree than in the Neolithic. Extensive areas were deforested for farming, and hamlets and field systems appear in the archaeological record. The importance of the individual was accentuated, and society became much more stratified and less egalitarian. It is during the Bronze Age that conspicuous displays of wealth appear, and bronze tools and weapons, as well as gold and other exotic jewellery such as amber and jet are found in the archaeological record. It is uncertain whether the introduction of metal working to Ireland came about through the arrival of a new people, but it is certain that the skills including the mining and production of tools, weapons and ornaments was not one suddenly learnt and may have grown and developed in Ireland through contact with other peoples who had experience of this technology from Britain or Atlantic Europe.

The Irish Bronze Age was an agricultural economy and the mainly round houses of its domestic settlements have frequently been discovered through excavation. These can turn up singularly or in small groups or clusters, but the main visible remains of this period are however the funerary and ritual monuments including its standing stones, stone circles, wedge tombs and round burial cairns. Alongside metal tools and weapons, hand-made pottery was still important. A variety of pottery styles and techniques were in use throughout the period, including Food Vessels, Encrusted Urns, Irish Bowls, Collared Urns, and Cordoned Urns. These eventually were superseded by a variety of undecorated vases or barrel-shaped flat-bottomed undecorated pottery in the Late Bronze Age. These pots were used for cooking, storage and also for burial, both as containers for food and offerings for the afterlife, and also as the containers for the burnt remains of the deceased. Flint continued to be used in tool construction, alongside copper and then bronze. Bronze tools included socketed spearheads, axes and sickles, woodworking tools, and a plethora of sword designs; ranging from long, thin rapiers with riveted handles to locally produced copies of European style swords. Evidence of Early Bronze Age settlement has been found at Coney Island on the southern shore of Lough Neagh, and it can be argued that the resources of the lough, notably its fish, must have played an important role in maintaining this settlement on such a tiny island. Another type of lake shore settlement was found on Lough Eskragh close to the Blackwater. Here the footings of numerous dwellings were uncovered when the lough level was lowered.

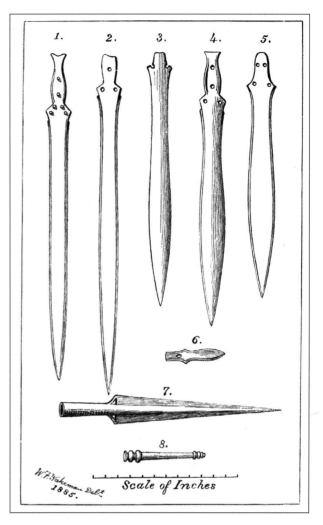

FIG. 12.3

Bronze weapons recovered from crannog sites on Toome Bar.

W.G. Wood-Martin, *The Lake Dwellings of Ireland* (Dublin and London, 1886), plate XXXVII

Artefacts of Late Bronze Age date recovered from Lough Neagh include a riveted spearhead from Derrymacash townland, a bronze dagger from Duckingstool Point, a bronze socketed axe head from the River Blackwater, a sword from Maghery and a palstave axe from the Creagh near Toome.

The Iron Age

From around 700 BC to AD 400 there was a transition from the Bronze Age to the Iron Age with the gradual introduction of new technologies – bronze was superseded by iron, stone implements fell out of use, and ceramic pottery appears to have been mostly replaced with vessels made from leather or wood. Decorative metal artefacts, glass and amber jewellery, as well as new weapon types were created. These artefacts all fall within what is termed the 'Celtic' tradition which is found across much of Europe at this time. The continuation and proliferation of heavily fortified settlements and defensive earthworks, combined with the increase in weapon types, indicates that this was a turbulent time in Ireland. This is reflected in the mythology surrounding the Irish Iron Age, as depicted in the Ulster Cycle of tales involving Cú Chulainn, 'The Hound of Ulster', the Red Branch Knights, and the infamous Cattle Raid of Cooley. Despite this, the Irish Iron Age is generally perceived as somewhat of an enigma, particularly following on from the richness displayed in the settlements, ritual and material culture of the preceding Bronze Age. There are no known Iron Age sites around Lough Neagh, but Iron Age artefacts have been recovered from Toome and in dredging material from the River Blackwater in 1968–72 and 1984–91. These included a bronze decorated scabbard, an iron axe head, a spear-head from Moy, a cylindrical spear-ferrule from Derrytresk townland (near Maghery townland), and two spear-butts from Maghery and Derrytresk.

FIG. 12.4
Experimental archaeology demonstration at Antrim Castle Gardens led by Brian Sloan from the Centre for Community Archaeology, QUB.

This cursory examination of the prehistoric record suggests that the Lower Bann valley and a significant extent of the Lough Neagh shorelands with its vital fords, ample resources and secure living space maintained settlements for much, if not all of, the span of Irish prehistory, from 8000 BC until the fifth century AD.

13 Archaeological investigations at Aghagallon

Cormac McSparron

In 2017 the Centre for Archaeological Fieldwork at Queen's University Belfast conducted a community archaeological excavation on behalf of the Lough Neagh Landscape Partnership at a large and enigmatic enclosure at Aghagallon, County Antrim.

In the townland of Derrynaseer, in the village of Aghagallon, there is a very large, sub-circular enclosure, located just behind St Patrick's Church, about which, before this project, almost nothing was known. The monument measures approximately 151 m east to west and 156 m south-west to north-east, *c.* 470 m in circumference, enclosing an area of 1.76 hectares (4.3 acres). It is defined by an earthen bank, best preserved along the north-east, where it stands to a

FIG. 13.1
The excavation at Aghagallon with St Patrick's Church in the background.

height of 1 m, surmounted by hedgerow along the east and south-east, but now absent from the south and south-west of the enclosure. Apart from the north-west quadrant, which has been entirely built over, there is a drop of up to about 1 m to the land surrounding the enclosure, the site being a platform raised slightly above the surrounding terrain. The northern half of the enclosure is largely taken up by St Patrick's Church, graveyard, car park, and St Patrick's Primary School.

The first edition Ordnance Survey map of 1833 marked the site, labelling it a 'fort', and represented the feature as an almost perfectly circular enclosure to the rear of the church, defined on the map by a dotted line measuring 154 m north-south by 157 m east-west. Later editions variously depict it as a slightly raised platform or an enclosure with a substantial bank (larger than today), but always with dimensions comparable with the modern monument.

In addition to mapmaking, in the 1830s the surveyors and officials of the Ordnance Survey compiled 'Memoirs' on the people, customs and antiquities in the districts they mapped in Ulster. In the parish of Aghagallon the 'Chapel Fort' was described as 'remarkable' (*OSM*, vol. 21, 2), and 'one of the largest forts known in the north, but has been destroyed many years back' (ibid., 8). Its size was estimated at '5 English acres' and to have had 'stood 1 mile in circumference'. The account noted dilapidation over the previous decades and that 'a large portion of the parapet, which was composed of earth and stones, still remains and averages 4 feet high and from 4 to 8 feet thick' (ibid., 12), clearly a much larger bank than survives today. The Ordnance Survey Memoirs also recorded that race meetings called the 'Aghagallon Races' had formerly been held in late autumn around the exterior of the enclosure, with traders of all kinds present and that these had been abolished around the time of the 1798 Rebellion.

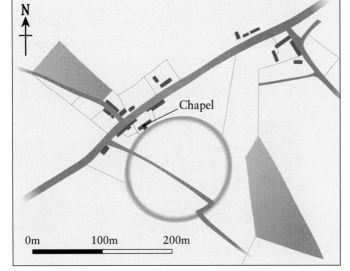

FIG. 13.2

The enclosure at Aghagallon, redrawn from the first edition Ordnance Survey map of 1833.

The place-name Derrynaseer, contains two elements, *doire*, which is conventionally translated as an oak wood, and *saor*, literally freeman but which usually referred to the craftsman class (MacNeill 1929). A conventional translation of Derrynaseer would therefore be 'the oak wood of the craftsmen'. However, it is possible, or even likely, that the element *doire* in Derrynaseer may mean not a wood as such, but a dry area within a marshy area, which was suitable for trees (Muhr 2002, 47), suggesting that *Doire na Saor*, may mean a dry area within a marshy landscape used by craftsmen.

Aghagallon and the townlands surrounding it are close to the southern boundaries of the Early Medieval lordship of *Dál Buinne* (MacCotter 2008, 234). This was created by the expansion into south Antrim, around 800, of the *Dál Fiatach*, who controlled most of north and east Down. *Dál Buinne* had its capital at *Dun Echdach* or Duneight and inaugurated their kings at *Cráeb Tulcha*, or Crewe Hill.

There are only a few references to the *Dál Buinne* in Early Medieval texts. One fascinating reference to the *Dál Buinne* is found in *Lebor na Cert*, the Book of Rights, a twelfth-century collection of poetic descriptions of the tribute paid by local kings to over-kings and the redistributed gifts paid back to the local kings, from the over-kings. Verse 12 outlines the gifts given to the *Dál Buinne*:

> The king of bright Dál mBuinde is entitled
> to eight horns, eight cups, eight slaves,
> eight valuable women,
> and eight horses for racing (Dillon 1962, 87).

In the late twelfth century part of east Ulster came under Anglo-Norman rule. Dál Buinne became an Anglo-Norman cantred, called *Dalboing* or *Dalbingu*. The de Courcy and de Lacy deeds show that it was granted to the church by the thirteenth century and it is described as the Deanery of Dalboyn in the papal taxation of 1306 (MacCotter 2008, 234).

In the later Medieval period the western part of the Deanery of Dalboyn, the parishes of Ballinderry, Aghalee, Aghagallon, Magheramesk, Magheragall, began to be referred to as *Coill-Ulltach*, the wood of Ulster, anglicised to Killultagh (Reeves 1847, 234). Perhaps the earliest reference to the use of this name is from the Annals of Ulster for 1515, which indicates that by this stage the territory was in the hands of the Clandeboy O'Neills (MacAirt and MacNiocaill 1983). Killultagh suffered heavily during the Nine Years' War, partly because of its strategic location and the presence of an important Irish fortification there at Inisloughlin (Macdonald 2012). Killultagh had been granted to Sir Foulke Conway by 1608 (*CSPI, 1608–10*, 89).

In advance of excavation a number possibilities presented themselves as to the nature of the Derrynaseer enclosure:

A henge monument

Because the Derrynaseer monument was a large sub-circular enclosure, it was considered possible that it might be a henge. The term henge is widely used, and encompasses a somewhat disparate group of earthen banked enclosures, which vary in scale and exact form, and which are found across Britain and Ireland from about 3000 BC onwards. In many cases henge enclosures seem to be constructed with their bank defining the outside of their enclosure with a ditch

FIG. 13.3
Grace McAlister of the Centre for Community Archaeology analyses finds from the excavation.

on the inside, the opposite way round from a defensive fortification where the ditch would be external. Based on this fact, Warner (2000) has speculated that a henge's function might be to protect those outside the henge from what is on the inside of the henge, possibly dangerous spiritual entities which are contained by the henge in some manner. Brophy and Noble (2012) have very usefully suggested that henge should not be seen as a noun, but rather as a verb and that *henging* something may be a solution, through the construction of an inward facing bank and ditch, to one of a set of spiritual problems.

An *óenach*

The *óenach* was a form of assembly noted in early Irish literature, from about the seventh century AD, where the community gathered to hear the promulgation of laws, the creation of alliances and where feasting, games and in particular horse racing, took place. It is probably similar to the *moot* or *thing* of Germanic and Scandinavian society in the Early Medieval period (Gleeson

2014). Each *tuath*, the basic unit of political organisation of Early Medieval Ireland, had an *óenach*. The *óenach* is not a simply described object, however, its exact physical nature varied from one lordship and kingdom to the other. In some cases the *óenach* was located at the same site as the administrative capital and the inauguration site of the *tuath* (Gleeson 2015, 33). In other cases these sites of community rituals were located at several sites within a discrete landscape, or even at several distinct locations within the wider tuath. There are few clear descriptions of *oenaige* in early Irish documents, but two glosses in the Book of Armagh and the Book of Leinster give some hints. Both gloss the term *óenach* with the Latin words *theatrum*, *circus* and *spectaculum,* or theatre, oval racecourse and the seating area of a *circus* respectively (Hicks 2009, 36). Hicks further suggested that henges may have been reused at some *óenaige* as the *circus* component of the *óenach*. He cites *Óenach Carman* and its association with a *circus,* now unlocated, in the Curragh, County Kildare, as a possible example of the reuse of a henge, as well as possible henge monuments close to Rathcrogan, County Roscommon, and Lough Gur, County Limerick, all noted as *oenaige* in Early Medieval Irish texts (Hicks 2009, 38–42).

A settlement-cemetery

These are a recently discovered monument class, consisting of a settlement with an associated communal burial ground (O'Sullivan et al. 2014, 306). They are quite large enclosures, their diameters are larger than raths, typically 40–70 m in size, the largest, Knowth Site M, being approximately 100 m in diameter (ibid., 308). The burial areas are usually partitioned off from the rest of the site with evidence for dozens of burials, the largest yet found at Balriggan, County Louth, revealed evidence for 57 burials (Delaney 2010). In addition to their settlement and burial functions, many show evidence for industrial activity, especially metalworking, and/or large scale food production (ibid.). A good example is the settlement-cemetery at Raystown, County Louth, where, in addition to a settlement area consisting of Early Medieval buildings, souterrains, and a cemetery, evidence for five cereal drying kilns, and eight watermills were uncovered (Seaver 2010). Settlement-cemetery sites appear not to predate the fifth century AD, with some possibly being established in the seventh or eighth century, and most only used for a relatively short period of time before falling into disuse (O'Sullivan et al. 2014, 311).

A monastery

Early Medieval Irish monasteries were enclosed sites. The eighth-century Collectio Canonum Hiberninsis (O'Sullivan et al. 2014, 145), notes how a monastery had three enclosures of increasing sacredness; clergy were admitted to the central enclosure, the observant populace to the middle enclosure, and murderers, adulterers and prostitutes only to the outer enclosure of the monastery. Other texts, such as the Book of Mulling (ibid.), imply that there were sometimes only two enclosures. Archaeological excavation seems to suggest that industrial activity was commonly carried out within the outer enclosure (McErlean and Crothers 2007, 370), with tillage perhaps conducted in the outer enclosures also (O'Sullivan et al. 2014, 147).

The geophysical survey

A geophysical survey was carried out at Aghagallon in advance of the excavation (McDermott 2015, 2017) and identified a number of anomalies, including two possible inner enclosures within the monument.

Trench 1

This trench measured 14 m by 2 m and was located to test the curving anomaly identified by McDermott (2017). The excavation identified a ditch, in the same position as the geophysical anomaly, with a bank faced with a stone revetment. A single fragment of coarse Medieval pottery was found with the bank reveting material. The ditch had two fills, an upper loam fill which contained flecks of charcoal and lumps of slag from metalworking, and a lower layer of clay rich, waterlogged soil in which was found more metalworking slag as well as some preserved plant matter, including a deposit of hundreds of raspberry seeds. A sample of these raspberry seeds was radiocarbon dated to between AD 704 and

FIG. 13.4
Trench 1.

972, most likely within the year range 777–886. The location of the excavated ditch, coupled with the evidence from the geophysical survey, indicates that it was part of a second inner enclosure, within the outer bank. The form of the geophysical anomaly suggests that this ditch enclosed an area with a diameter of about 30–40 m. This is similar in diameter to a rath ditch, but at only 1.5 m deep it is less substantial than a typical rath ditch.

Trench 2

This trench was L-shaped. The northern leg of the 'L' measured 7 m north-south by 2 m east-west, the western leg, 6 m by 2 m. It was located to test a series of geophysical anomalies identified by McDermott (2017). Several truncated pits and small postholes were found cut into an old ground surface situated just above the subsoil. Two fragments of glass slag were found in the topsoil above these features along with a single fragment of possibly Medieval wheel thrown pottery and a seventeenth-century clay pipe bowl. Within the features cutting the relic topsoil were two flint flakes and a hammer stone. The glass-working waste certainly indicates glass-working at the site. One of the pieces, a large transparent globule of dark green glass, had part of a mandrel, the iron rod around which glass beads are wound, embedded within it, the mandrel possibly having snapped during the production of a bead and the globule of glass falling into a pail of water. Glass worked in this way in Ireland is certainly not earlier than the later Iron Age (early centuries AD) and most probably dates to the Early Medieval period (Guido 1978). The hammer stone found in pit cut into the old ground surface is a type of artefact which has a very wide date range. Artefacts like this are often found on Neolithic and Bronze Age sites, but they could also be of use for grinding up pigments and pounding silicates, like sand, in the processing of the raw materials of Medieval glass production.

The shallow pits and postholes may indicate some kind of light wooden building and with pieces of waste from glass-working in this trench it is tempting to see these features as the remains of structural elements of a glass-makers workshop. Early Medieval glass-making was typically carried out in small furnaces with bellows used to raise the temperature, up to about 1100°C. Excavation and experimental archaeological evidence from Denmark has identified small open glass furnaces for the production of beads (Frankiewicz and Kryzyzanowska 2015) in the Early Medieval period. There were, however, no indications of a furnace or similar for the heating of silica and additives to make glass, at Aghagallon. The truncation which seems to have occurred in this area of the enclosure may have removed any direct evidence of Medieval glass-working, with only the small amount of glass-making waste found in the topsoil left to show that glass objects had ever been manufactured there.

FIG. 13.5
Trench 3.

Trench 3

This trench measured 4 m by 2 m. Only the southern half of the trench was actually excavated to subsoil. Excavation in the northern half was not continued beyond exposing a modern field drain. Excavation in the southern half revealed a wide shallow ditch approximately 0.7 m deep and 2.6 m wide. The stratigraphic sequence in this feature was complex, it having been cut and then recut on at least two occasions. There were only a few definite artefacts including two pieces of coarse pot of uncertain age, but with a fabric which is reminiscent of some types of Neolithic pottery, and a flint end scraper likely to date to the Neolithic or Early Bronze Age. The location of a shallow ditch, just inside the bank of the enclosure is reminiscent of the internal ditches sometimes found at Neolithic and Bronze Age henges. A radiocarbon date, however, of AD 703–957, probably within the range 778–884, obtained from a fragment of charcoal from the earliest layer in the ditch seems to suggest that this must be an Early Medieval feature.

Trench 4

This trench measured 8 m north-south by 1 m east-west. It was positioned to test a curving geophysical anomaly identified by McDermott (2017). Trench 4 revealed a bowl furnace, iron slag, and associated features, which, apart from the furnace, were largely left unexcavated because of the small size of the trench and the apparent complexity of the features. There was a single small piece of, probably Medieval, coarse pottery found in the furnace derived material. A Neolithic or Early Bronze Age retouched flint blade, which was itself waste from the manufacture of an arrow head, was also found in these furnace derived materials (pers. comm. Brian Sloan).

Discussion

The two radiocarbon dates, along with the evidence of Medieval glass-working and copper and iron production, have established that this is a site where craft-working took place during the Early Medieval period. The excavations were small compared to the large size of the site, however, and earlier activity at Derrynaseer cannot be ruled out, especially considering that the excavation found some Neolithic or Early Bronze flint work, and a few small fragments of pottery which have a fabric similar to some types of Neolithic pottery. As noted above, in advance of excavation a number possibilities had presented themselves as to the nature of the Derrynaseer enclosure. Its morphology and location were potentially compatible with it being; a henge; part of an *óenach*; a settlement-cemetery; or perhaps an Early Medieval monastery. It is now possible to winnow this list.

The craft-working evidence, and the Early Medieval dates from the two radiocarbon samples, is consistent with interpreting the site as a settlement-cemetery, an *óenach* or a monastery. The main enclosure at Derrynaseer, with a diameter, of approximately 150 m is much larger than the largest known settlement-cemetery, however, and there is not the density of settlement and industrial activity that might be expected in a settlement-cemetery site.

Considered on their own, the archaeological remains uncovered at Derrynaseer are more compatible with its interpretation as a monastery. The evidence for an internal enclosure, within a large outer enclosure, is what typically would be expected at a monastery, as is the presence of craft-working in the outer monastic precincts. There is not the level of general occupation waste which you might expect to find in a monastic enclosure, however, although it could be argued that perhaps the monastery was an unsuccessful, short-lived foundation, or that there is more concentrated occupation and ecclesiastical architecture in the parts of the enclosure under the modern car park, church, school and graveyard. This still begs the question, however, why there are no Early Medieval literary sources referring to a monastery at this site?

Early Medieval Ireland was a literate society. The lack of any historical reference to a church or monastery here makes this site's interpretation in a monastic context very problematic. It is difficult to see how a large monastic enclosure like this could have escaped any passing reference to a founding saint, the death of an abbot, or a sacking in war. Also place-name evidence suggests craft-working, for which we have evidence, but if this was an early church site it would be expected that it would be the site's ecclesiastical associations which would be remembered rather than its industry. Folklore is similarly silent regarding any church or saintly associations with the site, in contrast to ecclesiastical sites in the immediate vicinity. On balance, although the archaeological evidence is compatible with a monastic interpretation, the weight of historical, place-name and folklore information seems to rule out this explanation for the monument.

The form, dating, evidence for craft-working, but absence of settlement evidence within the enclosure, does seem to support, however, the interpretation of Derrynaseer as part of an *óenach* landscape. The problem with studying *óenaige* is the fact that they are not a single, unitary monument type. They are rather a set of principles and social practices, which become superimposed with myth and practice on the landscape, and reusing earlier antiquities such as henges or megalithic tombs. The evidence for craft-working fits the market function of the assemblies which were frequently an integral part of the *óenach*, and traders may have set up camp a few days before the commencement of the fair to make their wares. The historical, place-name, and folklore evidence of the site at Derrynaseer, can also be viewed as giving *some* support to the suggestion that the site was the *circus* component of an *óenach*. The tradition of horse racing around the enclosure at Derrynaseer, in the autumn, and the associated collection of traders, noted in the Ordnance Survey Memoirs, is consistent with the types of activities which continued in Early Modern times at the sites of former

FIG. 13.6
Broadcaster Joe Mahon visits the excavation for the UTV series *Lough Neagh*.

óenaige, such as *Óenach Tailtu,* at Telltown in County Meath where the Irish antiquarian, linguist and historian John O'Donovan noted the continuation of games at Lughnasa until the end of the eighteenth century (MacNeill 2008, 336), the same period when they ceased at Aghagallon. It is probable that when the site became part of the Anglo-Norman cantred of *Dalboing,* the ritualistic aspects of the *óenach,* its lordly and legal functions, ceased, but the market and games functions may have continued.

In addition to the large enclosure at Derrynaseer, other antiquities in the landscape may also have been components of a landscape where the rituals of lordship were enacted. In particular, the other church sites, holy wells, raths and the, now destroyed, prehistoric cairn are reminiscent of the collection of monuments at *Óenach Tailtu* (Gwynn 1941, 149–57; MacNeill 2008, 313–36). Despite the absence of firm evidence that it is prehistoric it would still be unwise to rule out the possibility that Derrynaseer was originally a henge which was reused in the Early Medieval period. Although several excavation trenches were dug, they collectively made less than 0.5% of the area of the monument, and excavations in the interior of henges typically find few archaeological features. Without actually excavating more of the interior of the monument, and possibly placing a trench over the bank, it is impossible to entirely rule out the site having a previous incarnation as a henge, repurposed by later lordships, to emphasise the legitimacy, and timelessness of their rule.

Acknowledgements

I would like to take this opportunity thank the Lough Neagh Landscape Partnership for supporting the excavation, and in particular Liam Campbell and Chris McCarney for all their help, and the Heritage Lottery Fund for funding the excavation. I also would like to thank St Patrick's Parish for hosting the excavation, in particular Fr Declan Mulligan, as well as the parish secretaries for all their help and enthusiasm. The children and staff from St Patrick's Primary School deserve special thanks both for their enthusiasm, visiting the excavation regularly to see what we were discovering, and their dedicated recording of our findings. We would especially like to thank the principal, Kevin O'Hara, and Emma Jayne Morgan, whose P3 class visited us regularly through the project, keeping us on our toes with the most excellent questions. I am indebted to Gail Russell, Inspector of the Historic Monuments Division of the Department for Communities, for her help with the Scheduled Monument Consent. Finally, I would particularly like to help all the volunteers, and students of the Centre for Community Archaeology, QUB.

Bibliography

K. Brophy and G. Noble, 'Henging, mounding and blocking: the Forteviot henge group' in A.M. Gibson (ed.), *Enclosing the Neolithic* (Oxford, 2012).

S. Delaney, 'An Early Medieval landscape at Balriggan, Co. Louth' in C. Corlett and M. Potterton (eds), *Death and Burial in Medieval Ireland in the Light of Recent Excavations* (Dublin, 2010), pp 91–102.

M. Dillon, *Lebor na Cert: the Book of Rights* (Dublin, 1962).

M. Frankiewicz and M. Krzyzanowska, 'An archaeological experiment with Early Medieval glass bead production in an open hearth – the results', *Slavia Antiqua*, 7 (2015), pp 109–28.

P. Gleeson, 'Assembly and élite culture in Iron Age and late Antique Europe: a case-study of Óenach Clocair, Co. Limerick', *Journal of Irish Archaeology*, 23 (2014), pp 171–87.

P. Gleeson, 'Kingdoms, communities, and óenaig: Irish assembly practices in their northwest European context', *Debating the Thing in the North: the Assembly Project II*, *Journal of the North Atlantic*, Special Volume 8 (2015), pp 33–51.

M. Guido, *The Glass Beads of Prehistoric and Roman Periods in Britain and Ireland* (London, 1978).

R. Hicks, 'Some correlations between henge enclosures and óenach sites', *JRSAI*, 139 (2009), pp 35–44.

P. Macdonald, 'Excavations at Inisloughin Fort', unpublished Data Structure Report, Centre for Archaeological Fieldwork, Queen's University Belfast (2012).

S. Mac Airt and G. Mac Niocaill, *The Annals of Ulster (to AD 1131)* (Dublin, 1983).

P. MacCotter, *Medieval Ireland: Territorial, Political and Economic Divisions* (Dublin, 2008).

E. MacNeill, 'Early Irish laws and institutions', *New York University Law Quarterly Review*, 7:4 (1929), pp 849–65.

M. MacNeill, *The Festival of Lughnasa* (Dublin, 2008).

S. McDermott, 'Aghagallon enclosure interior, Co. Antrim', unpublished Geophysical Survey Report No. 34, Centre for Archaeological Fieldwork, Queen's University Belfast (2017).

FIG. 13.7
Brockish Island.

T. McErlean and N. Crothers, *Harnessing the Tides: the Early Medieval Tide Mills at Nendrum Monastery, Strangford Lough* (Belfast, 2007).

K. Muhr, 'Manx Placenames: an Ulster view' in P. Davey and D.F. Davey (eds), *Mannin Revisited: Twelve Essays on Manx Culture and Environment* (Edinburgh and Douglas, 2002), pp 37–52.

Ordnance Survey Memoirs of Ireland, Vol. 21: Parishes of County Antrim VII, 1832–8, South Antrim, ed. A. Day and P. McWilliams (Belfast, 1993).

A. O'Sullivan, F. McCormick, T. Kerr and L. Harney, *Early Medieval Ireland: the Evidence from Archaeological Excavations* (Dublin, 2014).

E. Gwynn, *The Metrical Dindshenchas* (Dublin, 1941).

W. Reeves, *Ecclesiastical Antiquities of Down, Connor and Dromore* (Dublin, 1847).

M. Seaver, 'Against the grain: Early Medieval settlement and burial on the Blackhill: excavations at Raytown, Co. Meath' in C. Corlett and M. Potterton (eds), *Death and Burial in Medieval Ireland in the Light of Recent Excavations* (Dublin, 2010), pp 261–79.

R.B. Warner, 'Keeping out the otherworld: the internal ditch at Navan and other 'Iron Age' hengiform enclosures', *Emania*, 18 (2000), pp 39–44.

FIG. 14.1
Iron railings were erected around the cross in 1911 to prevent people taking chippings from it for souvenirs or charms.

14 Lough Neagh and Ardboe Cross

Pat Grimes

Colman's monastery

Few people who visit Ardboe for the first time can fail to be impressed by its magnificent stone cross which stands on the banks of Lough Neagh, adjacent to the monastic ruins. An anonymous poet, writing about Ardboe at the beginning of the nineteenth century, conveyed something of its effect on people

> *I've travelled France and I've travelled Flanders*
> *And all the countries beyond the Rhine,*
> *But in all my rakings and undertakings*
> *Ardboe your equal I ne'er could find.*

For the poet, as for the local people, the true Ardboe was the site of the sixth-century monastery on the loughshore, not the extensive parish of later centuries. Little is known about this monastic settlement; the facts concerning it are few and brief. Everything else must necessarily be conjecture, based on what took place in other religious sites in Ireland and Britain at that time. It is known, however, that the abbey was founded in 590 by Colman, son of Aed, who was a chieftain of the ruling clan in Mid-Ulster. That clan was the Úi Tuirtre, which controlled the lands between Slieve Gallion and Lough Neagh in the time of St Patrick, and retained control of this district for more than 700 years until the Cineal Eoghain swarmed down from Inishowen in present-day Donegal and eventually drove the Úi Tuirtre across the Bann. These details have come down to us today because they were recorded in the Annals of Ulster, a history of Medieval Ireland written in Irish and Latin. It is by means of the annals and other written sources such as *Codex Ardmachanus* (The Book of Armagh) that the names Ardboe, Lough Neagh, and Colman have passed down to us through the course of more than 1,400 years:

FIG. 14.2
Ardboe abbey and cross as seen from Lough Neagh, looking east. The cross can be seen in the middle of the stand of beech trees to the left of the photograph.

Colmán, ó Ard-bó for brú Locha eachach in Ultoibh
(Colman of Ardboe on the shore of Lough Neagh in Ulster)

When a few Ardboe people got together in 1970 to produce a parish magazine, they asked Rev. Fr Eamon Devlin, a native of The Loup, South Derry, and at that time parish priest of Ravensdale, County Louth, if he would contribute a short article on the history of Ardboe. Father Devlin, recognised as a specialist in early Irish history, readily complied with the request. The first part of his article dealt with the Early Christian period, and it is worth quoting it verbatim, rather than paraphrasing the words of the scholar.

Some aspects of Ardboe history

We are told – in *The Tripartite Life of St Patrick* (1890) – that the territory between Slieve Gallion and Lough Neagh was brought to the faith by the National Apostle himself. For the ancient people of this territory – the Úi Tuirtre – he founded seven churches, the names of two of which survive to the present day. None of these seven churches, however, can be identified with the church of Ardboe. It was not a Patrician foundation but it has a link with St Patrick. The king of the territory to whom St Patrick came was Cairthein Beag, and the line that descends from this man has been preserved in the genealogies. It runs as follows – Mac Cairthein; Mac Muiredoich; Mac Amalgada; Mac Aeda Guaire; Colman Maccaid. Colman Maccaid, who appears in this line, was the man who founded the monastic church of Ardboe in the year 590. This information is given in the *Annals of Ulster*.

The impact of Christianity on this ancient territory is seen from the number of people who are acclaimed as saints. Seventeen saints are listed as having descended from the Cairthein Beag who succoured Patrick on his missionary activities, and perhaps the most important of these was Colman, who founded the monastery of Ardboe in 590. The memory of St Colman of Ardboe had a profound significance for more than one thousand years. In the late 17th century we find the founder's name still venerated in the district. The great native reaction to the conquest and plantation of Ulster had broken down. A new plantation was under way, and scions of the Old Irish stock were being transplanted to Connaught. Feardorcha O'Meallain, a local poet, sensing the sadness and tragedy of it all, wrote his poem *In ainm an Athar le buaidh* and in it he called on Colman Maccaid to assist them in the days of their affliction. This is clearly a reference to founder of Ardboe, and probably the last reference to him in the sources. If he is unknown and unhonoured in Ardboe today, that is only a further symptom of the national degradation.

In the 9th and 10th centuries a new element appears in Ardboe's history. The vigorous Cineal Eoghain had pushed southwards from Inis Eoghain to the shores of Lough Neagh. There were many branches of this people, but the branch that settled on the shores of Lough Neagh was the Úi Echach Droma Lighin. From this sub-sept of the Cineal Eoghain two surnames evolved about the year 1000 – O Doibhlin (Devlin) and O Donnghaile (Donnelly). The territory of the former became the parish of Ardboe when parishes were established in the 12th century and the owners – perhaps it would be better to say the occupiers – of the territory had an important official role in the internal arrangements of the O'Neill kingdom, from that time till the break-up of the clan system with the Flight of the Earls in 1607. These people actually gave their name to the territory. On the maps that were drawn for the purposes of the Plantation of Ulster (1609) two pieces of letterpress appear as Munterevlin iochtar and Muntirevlin vachtar i.e. upper and lower O'Devlin territory. The significance of this is that these two territories lay on the southern and western borders of the ancient monastic lands, twelve townlands in all that surrounded the old monastic church and the Old Cross of Ardboe. At the time of the Plantation these churchlands were passed to the Protestant Archbishop of Armagh and the secular lands came into the possession of one of the Stewarts, Lord Ochiltree. What exactly the churchlands of Ardboe were, is made explicit by the grant of these lands in 1620 to Christopher, Archbishop of Armagh – Kilnecanavan, Kilneskally, Killogonlan, Tirevalvallon, Ballymurchy, Mullowtra, Dirrichrin, Anaghmore, Mellon, Aumagherta, Clonto, Dromany, Kenrose.

The last named townlands – a tolerable rendition by an English scribe unused to the Irish language – are known today as Killycanavan, Kilmascally, Killygonland, Trickvallen, Ballymurphy, Mullaghwhitra, Derrychrin, Annaghmore, Mullan, Aneeter, Drumaney, Kinrush.

The high cross of Ardboe

The high cross at Ardboe always impresses the viewer. Almost 20 feet in height and standing on a slight eminence with the vast stretch of Lough Neagh for a back-drop, its grandeur and serenity are both awesome and enigmatic. The cross is sculpted from several massive blocks of local sandstone, and its shaft and arms are decorated with scenes from the Old and New Testaments. It was not erected in the time of Colman: there is no written record of its creation but in all probability it dates from the ninth or tenth century. The provenance of Ardboe cross has been a matter of guesswork on the part of most scholars who have studied or tried to interpret the scriptural panels; invariably the verdict was, "We just don't know." However, it became possible to make an educated guess following the dating of crosses at Monasterboice and Clonmacnoise by Peter Harbison, Homan Potterton, and Jeanne Sheehy in their 1978 book, *Irish Art and Architecture: from Prehistory to the Present*. They concluded, from their studies of inscriptions and artwork, that those crosses were probably created around 840. Given that the Ardboe panels share many of the same biblical scenes, and that the sculptural art of all three crosses is so similar, it is entirely feasible that the Ardboe cross dates from the same period, and was probably decorated by the same sculptors. It is also very likely that the Ardboe cross became a focus for pilgrims from this time forward. The anonymous poet of the early nineteenth century declared:

> From the twenty-fourth of June to the second of August
> They do assemble from every part
> For to petition the Queen of Heaven
> To pardon sinners with contrite heart.

It is known that the capstone – the topmost stone of the cross, shaped like a miniature house – fell off in a storm in the winter of 1817. In 1845 the top half of the cross fell and was subsequently restored in 1850 by Colonel William Stewart of Killymoon. This latter fact was not reported in any newspaper, but it was attested to by Rev. Thomas Twigg, vicar of Swords, County Dublin, when he gave a lecture in Ardboe schoolhouse on 23 January 1872. Twigg had been curate in Ardboe in the years 1845–7 and he would have been personally acquainted with the colonel, not least because the colonel's brother, Rev. Richard Stewart, was the rector of Kildress. In the course of his lecture, Twigg stated:

> I remember having them [*the engravings*] explained to me many years ago by Christopher Trainor, a kind and friendly gentleman who lived in the neighbourhood, and they all plainly represented scenes from scripture. At the foot of the shaft were represented Adam and Eve in Paradise; above that Abraham's sacrifice; then I think Daniel in the lion's den; then the three children in the fiery furnace; and in the centre Christ coming in glory to judge the world. This interesting monument of antiquity, shortly before I came to Ardboe parish, fell and was set up again at the expense of the late Colonel Stewart of Killymoon; but from comparing what I recollect of it and the description given in *O'Neill's Irish Crosses*, I am inclined to think that the workmen in replacing it have turned that side to the east that was formerly to the west.

Colonel Stewart deserves a special word of praise for his good deed: what would have been the fate of the cross if he had not intervened? Very possibly broken up and lost for all time. The colonel, to whom is owed a considerable debt of gratitude, was in fact that very rare person in Ireland – a landlord who was beloved by his tenants and workers. Born in 1780, he succeeded his father, Colonel James Stewart, in 1821, living in Killymoon Castle near Cookstown. He was for many years the Member of Parliament for Tyrone, and was Lieutenant Colonel of the Tyrone Militia. He owned 30 townlands around Cookstown and Dungannon. When the potato crop failed in 1845 he immediately reduced the rents of his tenants, and published the details in the press so that other landlords could take the hint. During the Famine years he was chairman of the relief committee for the Cookstown district. He encouraged his gardener to plant different varieties of potato, even as early in the year as January, in an attempt to find one which was not prone to blight. He died on 2 October 1850, and this notice in the *Dublin Evening Post* of 8 October 1850 gives some indication of his character:

> Death of Colonel Stewart, of Killymoon – We have heard of the death of this amiable and highly respected gentleman, proprietor of the splendid seat and magnificent demesne of Killymoon, county Tyrone, for which proposals of purchase were lately made by Lord Gough. The deceased was for many years representative for the county Tyrone, and was reputed to be "one of the most polite men of his age."

At a meeting of Cookstown Board of Guardians and Rural District Council on Saturday, 26 November 1910, a discussion took place regarding damage to the Ardboe Cross, as the *Mid-Ulster Mail* reported:

> A letter was read from Mr Treanor, asking paling to be put up in the Old Cross graveyard. This was referred to Messrs John Devlin JP and James McGuckin. Mr MacGregor Greer said he noticed on a recent visit to Arboe that pieces had been chipped off the Old Cross.
>
> The Clerk said that sort of thing was blamed on tourists. It was said they took away bits of the Cross as souvenirs. In reply to a enquiry as to whether the Old Cross had been scheduled as an ancient monument with the County Council, Mr Devlin said he understood that Mr Treanor, on whose land the Cross was situate, had not given the necessary permission. The Clerk – If it had been scheduled the County Council would have looked after it. Mr Devlin said the chippings had been taken off the Cross in the harvest time. Mr MacGregor Greer said the other old monuments were protected by railings. The Clerk said that was suggested at one time but the local people objected.

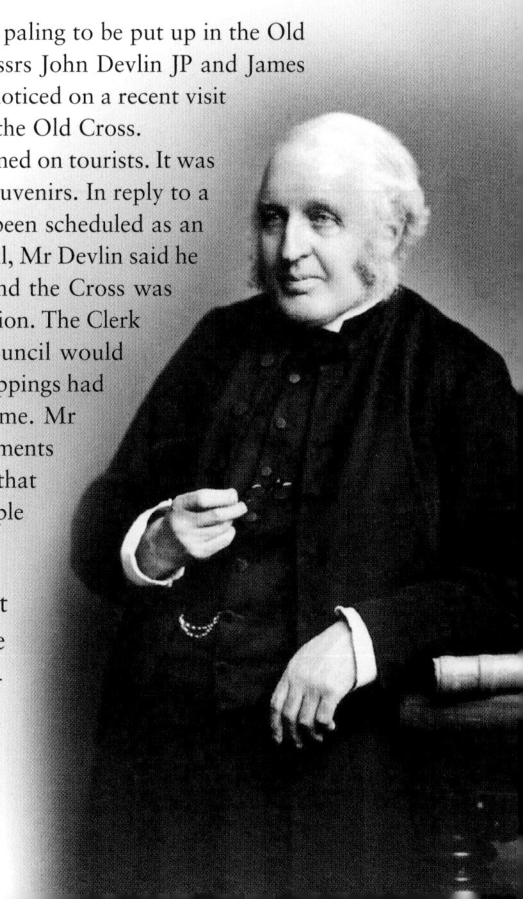

FIG. 14.3
Rev. Thomas Twigg, vicar of Swords, who had been Church of Ireland curate in Ardboe during the Famine in 1845–7, and who was the first person to write a comprehensive history of Ardboe's abbey and cross.

At this time Cookstown Rural District Council decided to build a wall around the graveyard adjacent to the cross, as the *Mid-Ulster Mail* of 25 February 1911 reported:

'James Booth secured the contract for building the wall at Arboe Churchyard (for which £100 was passed) at £74 12s. 6d.' Iron railings were erected around the cross in the same year. Six feet in height, the railings enclosed a space around the cross, 12 feet by 12 feet, thus preventing anyone from damaging the fabric of the cross. The original railings safeguard the cross to the present day, unchanged save for the occasional coat of paint.

FIG. 14.4

An early photograph of the cross, taken by R.J. Welch on 22 July 1897. The girl is Ellen Coyle, whose family lived beside the cross and fished the waters of Lough Neagh.

15 Cranfield church and holy well

William Roulston

The townland of Cranfield on the northern shore of Lough Neagh extends to just over 850 acres. The name in Irish is *Creamhchoill*, 'wild-garlic place'. Uniquely in Northern Ireland, this single townland is co-extensive with a civil parish of the same name. In earlier times Cranfield was subdivided into four smaller townlands.

The Down Survey map of *c.* 1657 names 'The Foure Townes of Cranfeild [sic]' as Urinstowne, Tanvilla, Kellstowne and Farranstowne (or Ferranstowne). Towards the middle of the nineteenth century a 'respectable inhabitant' informed the noted antiquarian William Reeves that the four townlands were Ballykeel, Ballyharvine, Ballyarny and Tamnaderry. The earliest apparent reference to Cranfield dates from *c.* 830 and can be found in the 'Martyrology of Tallaght'. In the papal taxation of the beginning of the fourteenth century the parish is listed under the name Crewill. In a further document of *c.* 1540 the church of Crannchyll is mentioned. The church was in ruins in 1622 and thereafter it ceased to have any significance as an ecclesiastical parish.

The remains of the parish church, measuring 13 m east-west by 6.5 m north-south, stand on a slight rise close to the shoreline with extensive views over the

FIG 15.1

This memorial sits just beyond the headstone in the foreground of the photograph of the church.

Fig. 15.2
Detail showing Cranfield from a map of Lough Neagh, 1785 (PRONI, D604/1).
PUBLIC RECORD OFFICE OF NORTHERN IRELAND

FIG. 15.3
The ruins of Cranfield church.

FIG. 15.4
The holy well.

lough. Prior to the lowering of the lough in the mid-nineteenth century, the church and adjoining graveyard were on the water's edge. The ruins are devoid of architectural detail, but have been dated tentatively to the thirteenth century. The graveyard contains headstones dating back to the 1700s, but has been a place of burial for much longer. The saint most associated with Cranfield is St Olcan, who is said to have been baptised by St Patrick, and is supposed to have been buried here in soil brought from Rome.

A short distance from the church is the famed holy well, a popular site of pilgrimage for centuries. Pebbles drawn from the well were believed to have miraculous powers and were used to protect women in childbirth as well as being carried by emigrants on the long voyage to the New World. Visits to the well continue with numerous rags and other cloth items attached to overhanging branches. In more recent times the vicinity of the church has been developed with a slipway and jetty, large car-parking area, public toilets and picnic tables. Just over a mile north of the church, close to Kickhams GAC at Creggan, stands a stone cross in the style of an Irish high cross. This replaced an earlier oak cross which is believed to have been positioned here as a termon cross to mark the boundary of the church lands of the Medieval parish. A replica of the wooden cross can be found within the ruined church at Cranfield.

Bibliography

Siobhán McDermott with Ruth Logue and Grace McAlister, 'Cranfield Church, Co. Antrim', Geophysical Survey Report No. 37, Centre for Archaeological Fieldwork, QUB (2017).

Pat McKay and Kay Muhr, *Lough Neagh Places: Their Names and Origins* (Belfast, 2007).

William Reeves, *Ecclesiastical Antiquities of Down, Connor and Dromore* (Dublin, 1847).

16 The Gaelic landscape surrounding Lough Neagh

Thomas McErlean

This paper attempts to take you on a journey anticlockwise around the lough in Gaelic times. Its purpose is to map out how the loughside communities were organised into territories and parishes during the fifteenth and sixteenth centuries. The journey starts at the Bannside at Portglenone and travels southwards past Lough Beg and down the west side of Lough Neagh and then proceeds across the southern, eastern and northern sides to complete the circuit back at the bridge over the Bann at Portglenone.

FIG. 16.1
Excerpt from an early seventeenth-century map of Ulster attributed to Willem Blaeu, showing the area around Lough Neagh.
PUBLIC RECORD OFFICE OF NORTHERN IRELAND

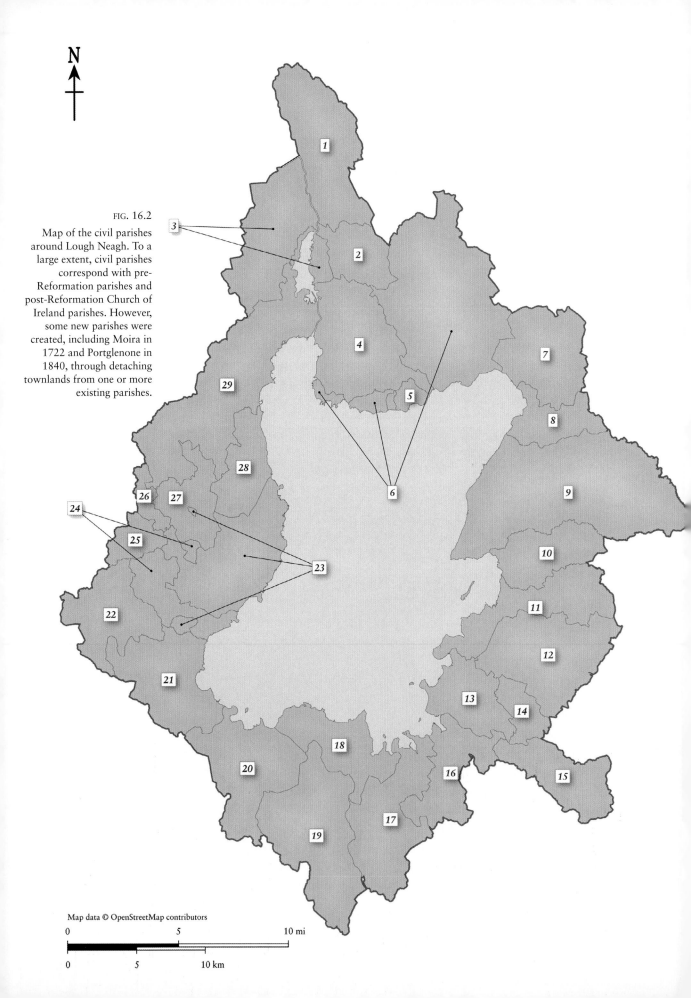

N

FIG. 16.2
Map of the civil parishes around Lough Neagh. To a large extent, civil parishes correspond with pre-Reformation parishes and post-Reformation Church of Ireland parishes. However, some new parishes were created, including Moira in 1722 and Portglenone in 1840, through detaching townlands from one or more existing parishes.

Map data © OpenStreetMap contributors

0   5   10 mi

0   5   10 km

Lough Neagh civil parishes

Map no.	Parish name	Map no.	Parish name
1	Portglenone	16	Shankill
2	Grange of Ballyscullion	17	Seagoe
3	Ballyscullion	18	Montiaghs
4	Duneane	19	Drumcree
5	Cranfield	20	Tartaraghan
6	Drummaul	21	Clonoe
7	Antrim	22	Donaghenry
8	Grange of Muckamore	23	Arboe
9	Killead	24	Ballyclog
10	Camlin	25	Artrea (Tyrone portion)
11	Glenavy	26	Arboe (Derry portion)
12	Ballinderry	27	Tamlaght
13	Aghagallon	28	Ballinderry
14	Aghalee	29	Artrea
15	Moira		

A short note on the Gaelic landscape and its organisation into various lordships and parishes is necessary as an introduction. By the fifteenth century Lough Neagh was an O'Neill lake. The western and southern sides of the lough were in the lordship of the O'Neills of Tyrone while the north-west and eastern sides, apart from a tiny portion on the south-east controlled by the Magennises, were in the lordship of the O'Neills of Clandeboy. Gaelic lordships were organised into estates called ballybetaghs composed of townlands and owned by the principal territorial families and their freeholders. These elite families resided in crannogs or less frequently in this area, tower-houses. On the ecclesiastical side the landscape was divided into dioceses, deaneries, and parishes. The central focus of the local religious landscape was the parish church and each was provided with several church townlands which were held by erenagh families. There were also extensive estates owned by religious houses, especially in this area by the Augustinians. Those that were located at a distance from the monastery were called granges. Overlying the parochial structure was a devotional and pilgrimage (turas) geography. Pilgrimage to places of revered sanctity where stations were performed, and cures obtained added a spiritual dimension to the landscape. Above all, the land was farmed and the lough fished by local families who have left us with a detailed surname landscape best appreciated by a visiting the graveyards around its shore.

The sources of information on the Gaelic territorial geography around the lough are meagre. However, for the western and southern shores the baronial maps of South Derry, East Tyrone and North Armagh compiled in the summer of 1609 are of outstanding importance. These are commonly known as the Bodley maps, but officially as the 'Maps of the Escheated Counties of Ulster' (Bodley 1609). Those of the baronies of Loughinsholin, Dungannon and Oneilland cover part of the lough shore. Another useful primary source is the Patent Rolls of James I (CPR Jas I). Space prevents full academic referencing here, but an extremely valuable and fascinating secondary source is the volume *Lough Neagh Places* (McKay and Muhr 2007) to which the reader is directed for the meaning of the local townland names and for the comprehensive list of references contained therein. Online further information can be explored in the Northern Ireland Place-name Project website (www.placenamesni.org).

For the wider context of Gaelic territorial organisation, albeit at a slightly earlier horizon, *Medieval Ireland* by Paul MacCotter (2008) is of great interest, while a general summary of the significance of the Irish townland system of landscape organisation is provided by McErlean (1983). In contrast to the sources for territorial geography, the sources for reconstruction of the Medieval parish layout are relatively plentiful, especially from seventeenth-century documentation. To a great degree the ancient parishes have been fossilised in the Post-Medieval civil parishes layout. A useful source in map form for these on an all-Ireland basis is provided by Mitchell (2002).

The western shore, Lough Beg and Bannside

Starting on the west side of the Bann at Portglenone, the journey begins in the parish of Tamlaght O'Crilly, named from its erenagh family, the O'Crillys, who held the extensive church lands of the parish. We are on the boundary between the territory called 'Brian Carragh's Country' and that of Killetra. Brian Carragh was the head of the Clandonnell O'Neills, a branch of the Clandeboy O'Neills, who in the late sixteenth century ruled an extensive territory on both sides of the Bann. His principal crannog lay north-west at Inishrush and was garrisoned by the McErleans, his gallowglass (Gaelic mercenary soldiers from the Scottish Isles). Heading south, we pass into the parish of Ballyscullion also named from their erenagh family, the O'Scullins, who are still prolific in numbers in the parish. The spiritual centre of the parish is the iconic Church Island in Lough Beg where the feast of St Teague/Teady (latinised Thaddeus) is still venerated every September by hundreds of pilgrims. The surrounding townlands formed the estate of the O'Mulholland family whose great claim to historical fame is the joint guardianship, along with the O'Mellans, of the national relic of St Patrick's Bell.

Leaving O'Mulholland's Country and crossing over the Moyola river, we pass from the diocese of Derry into that Armagh and from the parish of Ballyscullion

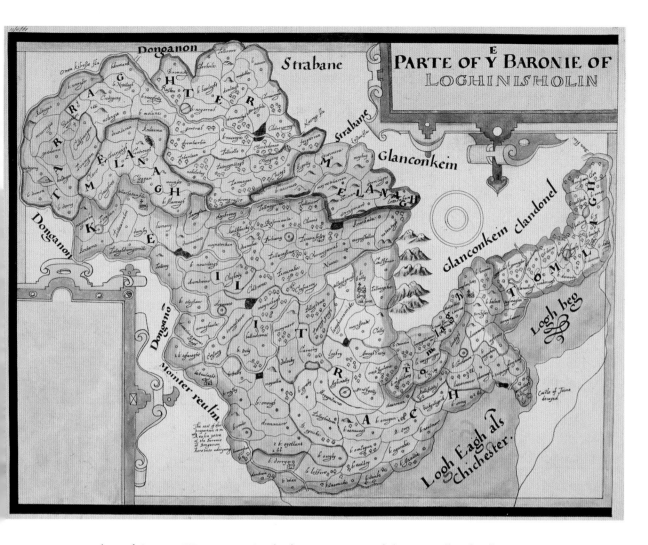

FIG. 16.3

Bodley map of the barony of Loughinsholin, which at this time (1609) was still part of County Tyrone (PRONI, T1652/13).

PUBLIC RECORD OFFICE OF NORTHERN IRELAND

to that of Artrea. We are now in the large territory of the O'Neills of Killetra, another branch of the Clandeboy family. Killetra extended from the western shore of the lough to Slieve Gallion and contained large oak woodlands. It was controlled from several crannogs including one situated near the lough shore on the west bank of the Bann opposite Toome. Their principal one appears to be that at Lough Lug near Moneymore. Killetra was subdivided into many estates occupied by landholding families under their O'Neill lord. Leading families along the lough shore were the McVeys/MacVeighs and the McGuigans. Most of the Killetra lands bordering the lough were in the large parish of Artrea whose parish church was in a detached portion far to the south across the Ballinderry river in the modern County Tyrone. The part in Killetra was served by local chapels of ease at Eglish near The Loup and other sites.

Travelling into the southern part of the territory, we pass into Ballinderry parish. The site of the old Medieval parish church is beautifully sited on a hilltop with a panoramic view just south of Ballylifford. The erenagh family of its four church townlands were the McGuckians. Crossing the Ballinderry river, we leave Killetra but not Ballinderry parish, which extends for a short distance into Tyrone, after which we enter the parish of Ardboe and the large territory of Tullaghogue. The latter was the domestic (mensal) territory of the Great O'Neill, based at Dungannon. The parish of Ardboe along with extensive church lands contained the sub-territory belonging to the O'Devlins. They along with the O'Hagans, the O'Quinns and the O'Donnellys were the chief support or service families of the Tyrone O'Neills, the O'Devlins supplying their chief force of kerns (foot soldiers). Their lands were known as Mounterevlin and were divided into two parts, 'Revelinowtra and Revelinyetra' (Revelin Upper and Lower). Their main crannog with an associated tower-house was at Lough Crew at Stewartstown. Ardboe parish was formed in the twelfth century out of the lands and pastoral sphere of the ancient abbey of the name situated on the very shore of the lough. The early monastery is beautifully represented by its surviving impressive high cross which is regarded as the iconic ecclesiastical monument of Lough Neagh.

FIG. 16.4
Excerpt from Richard Bartlett's map of south-east Ulster, *c.* 1602, showing Gaelic territories adjoining the southern half of Lough Neagh.

CARDINAL TOMÁS Ó FIAICH MEMORIAL LIBRARY AND ARCHIVE

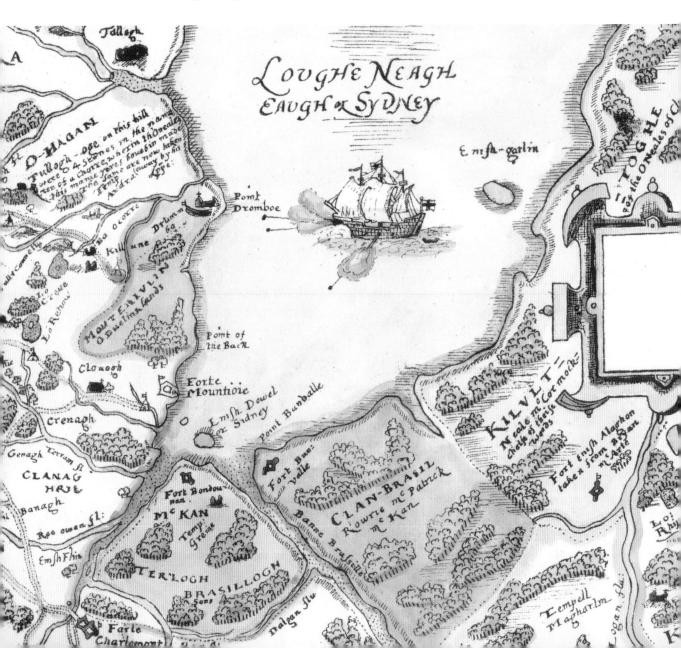

Leaving Ardboe, we pass briefly through a very narrow corridor of Ballyclog parish and enter the sub-territory of Clonagherie and the parish of Clonoe. Clonagherie extends from Mounterevlin to the Blackwater river and was held by a branch of the Tyrone O'Neills. It contains *c.* 29 townlands and had large area of bog in the south-east around Washingbay but is shown in the Bodley map in 1609 as having little tree-cover. The ancient parish church is in Killary Glebe townland, the site now occupied by the Church of Ireland's St Michael's. Flowing into the lough at Washingbay is the Holy river which issues out of a former lake now a marsh called Doon Lough in which was a probable crannog. This little stream was believed to have been blessed by St Bridget as she crossed it travelling from her convent in Kildare to Ardboe thus bestowing miraculous properties to its waters. In Gaelic times it was a place of pilgrimage and stations were performed in its waters at a little pool near where it enters the lough.

The southern shore of the lough

As we cross the Blackwater just beyond the Tamnamore roundabout and travel along the M1 as far east as Lurgan we are in the sub-lordship of the McCanns. This family originated in South Tyrone and obtained land in North Armagh in the mid-twelfth century as part of the expansionist strategy of their overlords the O'Neills Their lands were divided into two territories, Clancan between the Blackwater and the Upper Bann, and Clanbrasil to the east of the latter river. Though extensive, their landscape was largely composed of forest and bog. This is reflected in the makeup of their contribution to military hostings where they supplied only foot soldiers and no horsemen. Clancan is approximately coterminus with parish of Tartaraghan. In this parish the Augustinian monastery of St Peter and Paul in the city of Armagh had a small grange with a chapel at Maghery on the lough shore.

This was a place of pilgrimage in honour of St Patrick commemorated in the name of an ancient, possibly prehistoric, timber togher or trackway through local bogs called 'St Patrick's Road' which led to it. It was also believed that the road continued as causeway in the shallow waters leading to Coney Island. This island, once called Inis Dabhaill ('Island of the Blackwater'), occupied a strategic position at the mouth of the latter river and was fortified at various times, including by Shane O'Neill in the mid-sixteenth century who renamed it Fuath na nGall ('Hatred of the Foreigners') in reference to his English enemies. Crossing the Upper Bann into the second McCann territory, Clanbrasil, we enter the diocese of Dromore and ancient parish of Seagoe but in the Late Medieval period the portion adjacent to the lough shore was encompassed by a separate little parish called Annaloist whose church was situated on Oxford Island. To a certain degree this lost parish was recreated in the late eighteenth century when Montiaghs parish was delineated. On the southern boundary of Clanbrasil just south-east of Portadown the McCanns had a tower-house near the edge of the

Upper Bann called 'Knockballybrianbuy' (now Knock townland) called after one of their lords, Brian Boy McCann. One of the last lords of Clanbrasil was Rory Mac Patrick McCann whose name is recorded on Bartlett's map of south-east Ulster.

The eastern shore

Leaving Clanbrasil and passing through Shankill parish, we enter briefly into County Down travelling through the large townland of Kilmore. The latter was part of the Magennis lordship of Iveagh providing it with a very narrow land bridge to Lough Neagh. Turning to the north we leave Dromore diocese and enter the diocese of Down and the large territory of Killultagh. The latter stretched from Lisburn in the east to the lough shore on the west and from the Crumlin river on the north to the Lagan on the south. Along the lough shore and in its interior were large oak woods interspersed with open country. On its southern boundary near the Lagan was the crannog site of Inisloughlin which guarded the entrance into the territory through a pass in dense woods from

FIG. 16.5
The ancient ecclesiastical site of Laloo, Portmore, Ballinderry parish.

Iveagh and Kilwarlin the Magennis territories to the south. By the fifteenth century this ancient territory had passed to a branch of the Clandeboy O'Neills, referred to as the O'Neills of Killultagh, who by tradition resided at Portmore.

The first loughside parish we meet is Aghagallon. On its western part adjacent to the shore is the townland of Derrymore which contains the ancient church and pilgrimage site of Magheranagaw one of the lough's holy places. Here both St Patrick and St Culin (probably a form of St Coleman or possibly St Comgal) were venerated. The chapel and two surrounding townlands belonged to Movilla abbey at Newtownards and presumably supplied that abbey with fish from the lough. We now pass north into Glenavy parish with another Ballinderry parish to its east. Lying about a mile offshore is the monastic site of Inis Dairgreann (Rams Island). Before the lowering of the lough level in the mid-nineteenth century the island was a mere six acres. Along with Ardboe, Rams Island is one of the major church sites of the lough but sadly, apart from a Viking raid in the ninth century, little is known about its history. Its splendid round tower testifies to its former importance and wealth. It may have started as an island hermitage of one of the major local monasteries, but which one is presently unknown. Possible candidates are Ardboe, Muckamore, Antrim or Glenavy.

Next to the north is the parish of Camlin of which the four townlands of Ballygortgarve, Ballyshanaghill, Aghnadarragh and Ballvollen along the shore were collectively known as 'O'Hamill's Country' and were the estate of this prominent South Antrim Gaelic family. Crossing over the Crumlin river, we leave Killultagh and enter the estate of Kilmackevet and the large parish of Killead. We have now left the ancient diocese of Down and are now in that of Connor. These two dioceses were officially united in 1441. Kilmackevet was a long narrow estate which extended from the lough shore up to the western side of the Belfast hills. After the Plantation it remained in native hands being granted to Aodh Méirgeach O'Neill of the Clandeboy family. The ancient church of Kilmackevet which gave the estate its name was in the townland of Gartree which extends peninsula-like into the lough. This church and its former lands were associated with Bangor abbey.

The northern part of the Killead parish consisted of the territory of Killelagh. Like Kilmackevet it remained in native hands after the Plantation being granted to Sir Niall Óg O'Neill, brother of Aodh Méirgeach. A large part of the western side of Killelagh along the lough shore was held by the O'Mulholland family, a branch of whom presumably moved from west of the Bann along with the Clandeboy O'Neills in the fourteenth century. In the townland of Ballyginniff and about a mile from the lough shore was the church of Kilmaneeve ('the church of the holy woman'). By tradition the holy woman of the dedication was Lí Ban (see Chapter 33 of this book), the mermaid baptised by St Comgall of Bangor. The nearby Ballymacilhoyle townland is called after the land of the McIlhoyle/McConnell family whose surname translates as 'son of the servant of

Comgal' (St Comgal of Bangor) who were probably erenaghs of the local church lands.

Leaving Killelagh, we enter the parish of the Grange of Muckamore. The parish was formed from the extensive estate of the Augustinian abbey of Muckamore situated a short distance to the east of Antrim town. Muckamore monastery was important in the Early Medieval period and was re-founded under Augustinian rule in the mid-twelfth century and was heavily patronised by the Anglo-Normans and became rich being endowed with the tithes of many churches in the diocese of Connor. The last recorded prior at the dissolution was Bryan Boy O'Mulholland. In the townland of Balloo on the south side of the Six Mile Water river in the area east of the Antrim Forum was the small tertiary Franciscan friary of Massereene, presumably founded sometime in the late fifteenth century by the Clandeboy O'Neills. Beside the friary was a small castle or tower-house called *Clogh na mbrather* ('the Friars Castle'), a name rendered as 'the castle of Mowbray' in early seventeenth-century documentation.

FIG. 16.6

The old graveyard at Muckamore adjoins the site of the Augustinian abbey.

Crossing over the Six Mile Water, we enter the parish of Antrim and the large territory or tuath of Moylinny (*Maighe Line*) extending eastwards from the lough shore to near Ballyclare. The town of Antrim takes its names from the

important early monastery of the name whose surviving round tower, 'the Steeple', stands impressively to the east of the town. In the late twelfth century, the monastery became a parish church and its lands, 'the 16 towns of Antrim', became an Anglo-Norman manor. Around the royal motte which survives in Antrim Castle Gardens a small town developed. In the late fourteenth century the whole territory of Moylinny passed into the control of the O'Neills of Clandeboy.

The northern shore, Lough Beg and the east Bannside

A short distance north of Antrim town we enter the parish of Drummaul and tuath of Munterividy. Interestingly, in most of County Antrim the early Irish term 'tuath' meaning territory is retained. Munterividy was occupied by the main branch of the Clandeboy O'Neills and controlled from their castle of Edenduffcarrick (Éadan Dúcharraige), now called Shane's Castle,

FIG. 16.7

The Anglo-Norman motte in Antrim Castle Gardens.

situated on the shore of the lough. Another control point was the crannog in Kilknock townland on its north-west boundary. Heading west, we arrive in Duneane parish and the tuath of Feevagh. This territory was also occupied by an influential branch of the Clandeboy family. Their principal places were the castle or tower-house at the ford across the Bann at Toome on its western boundary and a crannog in Derryhollagh townland on its eastern one. Within Feevagh was the miniscule parish of Cranfield whose church, like Ardboe, was located on the very shoreline of the lough. Cranfield was a major place of pilgrimage with St Olcan's well one of the most venerated in the north of Ireland (see Chapter 15 of this book).

From Feevagh we pass north into the parish of the Grange of Ballyscullion overlooking Lough Beg. This parish was formed out of large estate or grange of the Augustinian abbey of St Peter and Paul in Armagh. In turn the origin of this grange lies in some of the lands which formerly belonged to the ancient monastery on Church Island in Lough Beg which appears to have passed to the ownership of the Augustinians in the twelfth century. Going north along the Bann we pass into the tuath of Muntercallie and the parish of Ahoghill. This tuath formed the eastern portion of the large territory previously mentioned known as 'Brian Carragh's Country', which extended from near Ballymena in the east across the Bann to Maghera on the west. On the northern boundary of

Muntercallie bordering the McQuillan lordship of the Route in north Antrim was a crannog in Lisnahunshin townland. Located in Muntercallie was the important Gaelic assembly site on Knock Mullagh (Tully Hill). In August 1557, the viceroy of Ireland, the earl of Sussex, camped with large army camped here during a military campaign against the MacDonnells of North Antrim.

Crossing over the important ford over the Bann at Portglenone we have arrived back at where we started and our journey though the Gaelic landscape of the Lough Neagh has been completed.

Bibliography

Bodley 1609: *Facsimiles of Maps of the Escheated Counties and Baronies in Ulster, from the Originals Executed about 1609* (Ordnance Survey Office, Southampton, 1860).

CPR Jas I: *Irish Patent Rolls of James I: Facsimile of the Irish Record Commissioner's Calendar prepared prior to 1830*, with a foreword by M.C. Griffith (Irish Manuscripts Commission, Dublin, 1966).

Paul MacCotter, *Medieval Ireland: Territorial, Political, and Economic Divisions* (Dublin, 2008).

Thomas McErlean, 'The Irish townland system of landscape organization' in Terence Reeves-Smyth and Fred Hamond (eds), *Landscape Archaeology in Ireland*, BAR British Series 116 (Oxford, 1983), pp 315–40.

Pat McKay and Kay Muhr, *Lough Neagh Places: Their Names and Origins* (Belfast, 2007).

Brian Mitchell, *A New Genealogical Atlas of Ireland* (2nd ed., Baltimore, 2002).

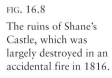

FIG. 16.8
The ruins of Shane's Castle, which was largely destroyed in an accidental fire in 1816.

17

Lough Neagh in Medieval times
its political and social context

Katharine Simms

The sheer size of Lough Neagh meant that it would inevitably have an influence on the settlements and societies around it, but over the centuries this impact was not always the same. Sometimes it acted as a boundary, sometimes as a centre, economic or political.

From the dawn of history we can see a tendency to a threefold division across the north of Ireland dictated by the Mourne-Foyle rivers in the west, behind which the two branches of the Northern Uí Néill, the Cenél Conaill and Cenél nEógain, first rallied their forces, and to the east Lough Neagh itself with the Upper and Lower Bann rivers, beyond which lay the various kingdoms collectively known as the Ulaid, or 'true Ulstermen'. In between these two frontier areas, lay a string of subordinate kingdoms known as the Airgialla, their rulers claiming descent from three brothers, Colla Úais, reputed ancestor of the Uí Macc Úais, located across modern Derry and Tyrone, Colla Menn, claimed by the Mugdorna, who gave their name to the barony of Cremorne, County Monaghan, and Colla fo Chrí, the ancestor-figure for kingdoms in the Monaghan-Fermanagh-Armagh area.[1]

However, a map of 'Land Use Capability' in the Royal Irish Academy's *Atlas of Ireland*[2] shows the largest expanse of prime soil in Ulster stretching southwards from the peninsula of Inishowen, and the Uí Néill fortress of Ailech, or Grianán Ailig (Greenan fort, Inishowen), along the river basins of the Mourne and the Foyle, and

FIG. 17.1
Tullyhogue.

another exceptionally fertile area along both banks of the Lower Bann. This naturally meant that both these border areas, between the modern Donegal and Tyrone on the one hand, and the modern Derry and Antrim on the other, would repeatedly become subject to competing claims from either side.

The earliest historical records show an Ulaid people known as the Cruithin, or Irish Picts, in control of both the Antrim and Derry sides of the Lower Bann. In AD 563 a succession struggle among their leaders led to the battle of Móin Doire Lothair, identified with Moneymore, parish of Derryloran, County Derry.[3] The winning side had recruited the Northern Uí Néill as allies, and rewarded the Cenél nEógain with a grant of the north coast of Derry from Magilligan Point to the mouth of the Bann. The significance of this episode for the subsequent history of the Northern Uí Néill is underlined by a tradition in the seventh-century Life of St Columba by Adomnán, which depicts their patron saint, already on his mission to Scotland, seeing the outcome of the battle in a vision.[4]

Once across the barrier posed by Lough Foyle, the Cenél nEógain rapidly expanded their control across the lands of the Uí Macc Úais, annexing territories or subduing their original rulers. An important acquisition was the western shore of Lough Neagh, which is shown on the Royal Irish Academy's 'Land Use Capability' map as largely comprised of Grade 3 soil, valuable, but somewhat limited by its coarse texture, whereas the eastern shore is Grade 8, considerably less useful due to its poor drainage. The outline of this comparatively profitable soil to the west of the lake approximately coincides with the boundaries of what an early thirteenth-century Anglo-Norman record called 'the cantred of Talachot', that is, a territory named after the hill-fort of Telach Óc or Tullyhogue near Cookstown, though in sixteenth-century maps it was to be labelled the 'Lotie' (*lucht tige*) or 'household' lands of the Great O'Neill, the ruler of Cenél nEógain.[5]

Telach Óc had been a political centre for the Uí Thuirtre, a sub-kingship of the Uí Macc Úais, whose territory stretched between the modern Cookstown and Toomebridge. Pressure from the expanding forces of the Cenél nEógain induced the Uí Thuirtre to compensate for losses in the west by advancing north and eastwards along the banks of the Bann and eventually across Toomebridge, beginning as early as the late eighth century.[6]

After a great victory won by the Cenél nEógain king, Niall *Caille*, at the battle of Leth Cam (AD 827), all Airgialla became tribute-paying subjects of the Cenél nEógain. The lands once ruled by the Uí Mac Úais gradually became known as Tír Eógain, a name continued into modern times as Tyrone, though the earlier kingdom comprehended Derry also. With this doubling or trebling of their territory, the Cenél nEógain kings now outshone their kinsmen the Cenél Conaill, still confined to the Donegal area, and monopolised the title 'kings of Ailech', although by the late tenth or eleventh century they had moved their centre of power to Telach Óc. Professor Hogan has speculated that Telach Óc had been a site with significance for all Airgialla, and not just the Uí Thuirtre, since it attracted the Cenél nEógain kings away from their imposing fort of Ailech, but it was in any case more geographically suitable as a power-base for their expanded territory, and references in the annals to Ua hÓcáin (O'Hagan) as the 'rechtaire' or 'major-domo' of Telach Óc suggests that it became the site of a royal palace.[7]

Already in the late eleventh-century Book of Rights, we are told that the cantred of Telach Óc was tax-free, that is, its inhabitants paid no tribute to the overking of Ailech, because: 'kingship of the men of Ireland may come from their strong country'.[8] This is the first explicit reference to the function of Telach Óc fort as an inauguration site for the head of the northern Uí Néill dynasty, who might not only rule most of Ulster as king of Ailech, but could claim on occasion to rule all Ireland as 'king of Tara' or 'high-king'.

By the late eleventh century the displaced Uí Thuirtre rulers were led by the O'Flynn or O'Lynn (Ó Floinn) dynasty and were colonising the south Antrim area, changing the function of Lough Neagh and the Lower Bann once more from a barrier between the Ulaid and Tír Eógain, to the centre of a new lordship. They were hotly opposed by the original inhabitants, and so conducted their attacks from island strongholds. In 1121 the annals say that the chieftain Cú Muige son of *An Deorad* ('the Exile') O'Flynn committed suicide in the lake after his stronghold on Rams Island in Lough Neagh had been captured by the Uí Echach,[9] and 44 of his followers slain.[10] In 1129 a second entry recorded the plundering of Church Island in Lough Beg by the Ulaid. The list of those slain indicates that the Mac Laughlin (Mac Lochlainn) rulers of Cenél nEógain were allied to the O'Flynn dynasty on this occasion, but it also seems that another O'Flynn fought on the opposing side.[11]

In 1176, just one year before the Anglo-Norman baron, John de Courcy, invaded Downpatrick and commenced his conquest of Ulster, the chief Cú Muige O'Flynn was assassinated by his own brother, Cú Mide. His obituary in the annals describes him as ruler of Uí Thuirtre, Fir Lí, Dál Riada and Dál nAraide, territories approximating to the baronies of Coleraine and Loughinsholin in east County Derry, and the northern two-thirds of County Antrim, thus the most fertile lands in that neighbourhood. Cú Muige was a loyal subject of the kings of Cenél nEógain. In 1156–7 he is recorded as witnessing the charter of the high-king Muirchertach Mac Laughlin, endowing the new Cistercian monastery at Newry.[12] His dynasty's success in colonising east Ulster made him not only the most powerful king in that area, rather more so than the Mac Donlevy (Mac Duinnshléibe) titular kings of Ulaid, whose rule was centred on modern County Down, but he was an instrument by which Mac Laughlin overlordship extended past the Lower Bann and Lough Neagh and into eastern Ulster.

When de Courcy invaded Downpatrick in 1177, his armoured knights inflicted a series of resounding defeats on Ruaidri Mac Donlevy, king of Ulster, and on his overlord, the Mac Laughlin king of Cenél nEógain, but he was less able to deal with the fratricidal Cú Mide O'Flynn, who burned Armoy, his chief seat in Dál Riata, to prevent de Courcy occupying it, and next year defeated the Norman baron so soundly at 'Sgrig Arcaidh' (parish of Skerry, near Slemish mountain), that de Courcy barely escaped, as the chronicler, Gerald of Wales, tells it:

> scarcely eleven knights remained by his side, while some of the remainder were killed and others scattered about the woods. But since John was a man of invincible valour, he and this tiny number of followers fought their way through to his castle, despite the fact that they had to cover a distance of thirty miles over which they continually had to defend themselves against a large force of the enemy, without their horses, which had all been lost, wearing their armour, on foot, and having had nothing to eat for two days and nights.[13]

However, de Courcy's setback was temporary, his conquest of Ulaid east of the Bann and Lough Neagh continued. In 1193/4 Cú Mide O'Flynn, 'king of Uí Thuirtre and Fir Lí', was treacherously killed at Antrim town by de Courcy's followers. In 1201/02 Ruaidri Mac Donlevy, king of Ulaid, and Niall O'Flynn met a similar fate.[14] After de Courcy was superseded by Hugh de Lacy the Younger, first earl of Ulster in 1205, and the latter in turn was banished from Ulster by King John and his army in 1210, the 'Irish pipe roll of 14 John' contains sheriffs' accounts for the Antrim area which mention a 'war of Tuirtre' lasting nine weeks, the capture of booty from the Irish, and the successful collection of two years' arrears of the 'fixed rent of Tuirtre', implying that O'Flynn and his subjects had already been paying regular tribute or 'rent' to Earl Hugh de Lacy.[15]

The same 'pipe roll' records the justiciar's war against the O'Neill king of Tír Eógain (Áed *Méith*, d. 1230). Although this king had defied King John's demand for hostages and submission in 1210, and subsequently destroyed three castles built by the justiciar at Belleek, Clones and a site near Newry, he ended by rendering 321 cows in payment of the 'rent of Tír Eógain', and a further herd of 293 cows as a fine for his rebellion.[16]

For the first three-quarters of the thirteenth century most of Ulster east of Lough Neagh and the Bann was controlled and colonised by the incoming Normans, with the less profitable eastern shores of the great lake largely occupied by rent-paying Irish chieftains, O'Flynn and MacGilmore (Mac Gilla Muire), and their subjects.[17] The land west of the lake was more independently governed by chieftains who might or might not acknowledge the authority of the king and the earl of Ulster, most spectacularly the famous Brian O'Neill, who took advantage of an interregnum in the earldom after Hugh de Lacy's death in

1242–3 to claim the highkingship of Ireland and invade Anglo-Norman settlements east of the Bann, only to be defeated and killed with heavy losses at the Battle of Down in 1260. This period saw the erection of bridges and castles along the line of the Upper and Lower Bann, at once to increase accessibility to the west for punitive government expeditions and to close the doors into eastern Ulster against raids from that direction.[18]

The Battle of Down made clear the need for a strong resident authority in Ulster and the earldom was revived in 1263 for Walter de Burgh, lord of Connacht. In the time of his son, Richard, the 'Red Earl' of Ulster (d. 1326), colonisation crossed the Bann and settlements were commenced along the River Roe, in the port of Derry and on Inishowen, around the castle of Northburgh (now Greencastle). The strong resident authority, however, was represented not by the absentee earl, but by a succession of seneschals of Ulster drawn from the de Mandeville family, closely allied with the line of the grandson of Áed *Méith* O'Neill, known as Áed *Buide* (d. 1283), king of Cenél nEógain, ancestor of the Clann Áeda Buide or 'Clandeboy' O'Neills.[19]

This expansion westward was severely threatened by the invasion of Edward Bruce and his army of Scots in 1315–18, but ultimately came to an end when the de Mandevilles assassinated William de Burgh, the 'Brown Earl' of Ulster, in 1333, and mounted a full-scale rebellion against the English government in alliance with Henry, chief of the 'Clandeboy' O'Neills (d. 1347). After five years of war, the peace talks in 1338 included the condition that Henry O'Neill and his heirs should receive for an annual rent a swathe of war-wasted land to the east of the Bann, much of which had previously been occupied by the O'Flynn chiefs, who were now forced into a subordinate role.

Henry O'Neill had been vainly trying to maintain a dominant position as king of Tír Eógain against the claims of his kinsman Áed *Remor* ('the Fat') O'Neill (d. 1364), son of King Domnall O'Neill (d. 1325), the instigator of the Bruce invasion. Finally, in 1344 the justiciar of the day, mindful of Henry's complicity with the Anglo-Irish assassins of the Brown Earl, officially deposed him and appointed Áed *Remor* as sole ruler.[20] For most of the rest of the Middle Ages, Lough Neagh and the Upper and Lower River Bann returned to the role of a frontier between, on the one side the Great O'Neills of Tír Eógain, descendants of Brian of the Battle of Down and his son Domnall of the Bruce invasion, and on the other the Clandeboy O'Neills, sometimes submitting to the Great O'Neill, sometimes forming an independent buffer state between the Great O'Neill and the colonists. In 1515 a tract reviewing the state of Ireland remarked that the Anglo-Irish colonists remaining in Lecale and the Ards, County Down, rendered 'black-rent', an annual sum of protection-money: 'to the captayne of Clanhuboy payeth yerely £40, or elles to [the Great] Oneyll, whether of them be strongest'.[21]

Somewhat counter-intuitively, the regular payment of black-rent during the fifteenth century stabilised relations between the colonists and the Irish and allowed a growth in trade – as late as 1528 the duke of Norfolk, who had been consulting with one Thomas Bathe, a merchant of Drogheda, advised the king to send money to Piers Butler, earl of Ossory:

> aswell to yeve unto Irishemen, to take part with the Kynges Deputie, and hym, as at the lest to syt styll without doing hurt, nor to suffer none others to come thorow them, to do hurt to the Kinges obeysaunte subjectes.[22]

King Edward IV had sent Henry son of Eógan, the Great O'Neill, his livery of 48 yards of scarlet cloth and a gold chain in 1463, and described him in an official record as 'the King's friend'. Also in 1463 O'Neill authorised the archbishop of Armagh to grant safe-conducts in his name to a number of merchants from Drogheda 'to come and go with their goods through the seaports of the earldom'.[23]

The principal goods merchants brought into Gaelic Ulster were iron, salt, wine and English cloth, and the goods they brought away in exchange were mostly hides and fish. The Bann was celebrated for its salmon fishery, using weirs erected both along the river and in the estuary, and large quantities of salted salmon were exported to England mainly through Bristol. Already in the 1350s the widowed mother of the murdered Brown Earl, Elizabeth de Burgh, was receiving significant income from the lease of boats and fishing-rights on the Bann, the Bush and the Lynn rivers.[24] In 1473 a projected grant to Henry, Lord Grey, of Lecale and the Ards together with any other lands and manors of the earldom of Ulster he could reconquer, to hold for 40 years, included the fisheries of the Bann, 'all of which premises are parcel of the king's earldom of Ulster'.[25] While salmon formed a significant export item, the eel fisheries were a sought-after commodity for the home market in Dublin and Drogheda, as eels could be transported and stored alive for long periods in boxes of running water.[26]

The 'lasts' of hides that the merchants received were a product of the increasingly pastoral economy of Late Medieval Ulster. All Europe in the wake of the Black Death (1347–9) experienced a shift in emphasis towards pastoralism, in response to the higher wages demanded by a reduced labour force, but in Ulster this general trend was exacerbated by chronic wartime conditions.[27] The registers of the archbishops of Armagh abound in complaints of the chiefs' military following deliberately driving herds onto the lands of church tenants to destroy their crops, as a preliminary to annexing them.[28] From the last decade of the fourteenth century onwards, a new word occurs in the Irish annals, *cáeraigecht*, which became 'creaght' in Hiberno-English, signifying a massed herd of livestock, cows, sheep, goats etc with their owners and shepherds, like a whole village on the move, sometimes migrating into a next-door territory as refugees, sometimes aggressively accompanying an invading army. An important article by Prendergast in 1855[29] argued from extensive descriptions in the State Papers of the Cromwellian period for the existence of true nomadism in Ulster 'from early ages', involving most of the population

FIG. 17.2

Excerpt from Richard Bartlett's map of south-east Ulster, *c.* 1602, showing Tullyhogue. The text reads: 'On this hill were 4 stones in the manner of a chaire, wherin th' O'Neale this manie yeres have bin made. The same are now taken away by his Lpye [Lordship, i.e. the Lord Deputy, Lord Mountjoy]'.

CARDINAL TOMÁS Ó FIAICH MEMORIAL LIBRARY AND ARCHIVE

there. However, evidence from the Early and High Medieval periods points rather to a mixed farming economy, combined with the practice of booleying, or transhumance, driving the community's cattle on to coarse hill pastures in the summer, wherever geographical conditions favoured the practice. The Cromwellian papers, especially the 1641 depositions, rather suggest that the Plantation of Ulster resulted normally in planters taking possession of the more fertile lowlands, while they leased out the associated summer grazing to dispossessed original inhabitants, who were forced to live in the hills all year round with their wandering herds, forming a discontented community ripe for rebellion.[30]

Interestingly the cantred of Tullyhogue, the household lands of the Great O'Neill, were cultivated more intensively in the English style, by Shane O'Neill the Proud (d. 1567) and Hugh O'Neill, the Great Earl of Tyrone (d. 1616), both of whom encouraged an influx of Palesmen or even English tenants to boost productivity,[31] as indeed did Sir Phelim O'Neill, the instigator of the 1641 rebellion.[32] By that period, however, the whole of Ulster had been absorbed into the Stuart kingdoms, and Lough Neagh and the Upper and Lower Bann were never again to form a political boundary.

Notes

1 See Brian Lacey, 'County Derry in the early historic period' in *Derry & Londonderry: History and Society*, ed. Gerard O'Brien (Dublin, 1999), pp 115–48 at pp 120–04, 138–43; A.S. MacShamhráin, 'The making of Tír nEógain, Cenél nEógain and the Airgialla from the sixth to the eleventh centuries' in *Tyrone: History and Society*, ed. Charles Dillon and H.A. Jefferies (Dublin, 2000), pp 55–84, at pp 64–79.

2 *Atlas of Ireland: Prepared Under the Direction of the Irish National Committee for Geography* (Royal Irish Academy, Dublin, 1979), p. 28.

3 Edmund Hogan (ed.), *Onomasticon Goedelicum* (Dublin, 1910), p. 541.

4 F.J. Byrne, 'The Ireland of St Columba' in *Historical Studies* 5, ed. J.L. McCracken (London, 1965), pp 37–58 at p. 44.

5 Paul MacCotter, *Medieval Ireland: Territorial, Political and Economic Divisions* (Dublin, 2008), pp 224, 259; Éamon Ó Doibhlin, *Domhnach Mór (Donaghmore): an Outline of Parish History* (Omagh, 1969), pp 43–62, and maps facing pp 40, 41.

6 F.J. Byrne, *Irish Kings and High-Kings* (London, 1973), pp 125–6; T. Ó Fiaich (Fee), 'The kingdom of Airghialla and its sub-kingdoms', unpublished MA thesis, University College Dublin, September 1950 (UCD Library thesis no. 820), pp 175–8.

7 James Hogan, 'The Uí Briain kingship in Telach Óc' in *Féilsgríbhinn Eoin Mhic Néill*, ed. John Ryan (Dublin, 1940), pp 406–44 at pp 420–23; Anthony Candon, 'Telach Óc and Emain Macha c. 1100', *Emania*, 15 (1996), pp 39–46: 40–41; Katharine Simms, *From Kings to Warlords* (Woodbridge, 1987), pp 32, 81.

8 Myles Dillon (ed.), *Lebor na Cert* (Dublin, 1962), pp 64–5.

9 Presumably the Uí Echach Ulad, who occupied the barony of Iveagh, diocese of Dromore, County Down, and were led by Magennis and MacCartan chieftains.

10 Seán Mac Airt and Gearóid Mac Niocaill (eds), *The Annals of Ulster to 1131* (Dublin, 1983), pp 564–5; Seán Mac Airt (ed.), *The Annals of Inisfallen* (Dublin, 1951), pp 280–81; John O'Donovan (ed.), *Annals of the Kingdom of Ireland by the Four Masters* (7 vols, Dublin, 1856, reprinted Dublin, 1990), pp 1012–13 (AD 1121).

11 *The Annals of Inisfallen*, pp 292–3 (AD 1129).

12 Marie-Thérèse Flanagan, *Irish Royal Charters: Texts and Contexts* (Oxford, 2005), pp 292–3, 301–02 n.42.

13 B. Scott and F.X. Martin (eds), *Hibernia Expugnata: the Conquest of Ireland by Gerald of Wales* (Dublin, 1978), pp 178–9.

14 Séamus Ó hInnse (ed.), *Miscellaneous Irish Annals* (Dublin, 1947), pp 74–5, 80–81; W.M. Hennessy (ed.), *The Annals of Loch Cé* (2 vols, London, 1871, reprinted Dublin, 1939), vol. 1, pp 186–7, 214–15, 222–3 (AD 1193, 1201); Bartholomew MacCarthy, ed., *The Annals of Ulster* (4 vols, Dublin, 1887–1901), vol. 2, pp 220–21, 234–5, 236–7 (AD 1194, 1201, 1202).

15 'Irish Pipe roll of 14 John', ed. O. Davies and D.B. Quinn, *UJA*, 3rd series, 4 (1941) supp., pp 62–5.

16 Ibid.; Sean Duffy, 'King John's expedition to Ireland', *Irish Historical Studies*, 30 (1996), pp 1–24.

17 T.E. McNeill, *Anglo-Norman Ulster: the History and Archaeology of an Irish barony, 1177–1400* (Edinburgh, 1980), pp 4 (Map I), pp 22–31.

18 Ibid., pp 22, 29–30; Katharine Simms, 'Late Medieval Tír Eoghain: the kingdom of the Great Ó Néill' in *Tyrone: History and Society*, ed. Dillon and Jefferies, pp 127–162 at pp 136–40.

19 McNeill, *Anglo-Norman Ulster*, pp 32–4 (Map 9); Katharine Simms, 'Tír Eoghain "North of the Mountain"' in *Derry and Londonderry: History and Society*, ed. O'Brien, pp 149–173 at 160–61.

20 Katharine Simms, *Gaelic Ulster in the Middle Ages* (Dublin, 2020), pp 115–22.

21 *State Papers Published under the Authority of His Majesty's Commission, King Henry VIII*, pt III, section 1 (London, 1834), p. 9.

22 Ibid., p. 136.

23 *Annals of Ulster*, AD 1463; PRONI, Register of Primate John Prene, Lib. I, fo. 182r; see Simms, *Gaelic Ulster*, pp 187–9.

24 McNeill, *Anglo-Norman Ulster*, pp 137–40.

25 Simms, *Gaelic Ulster*, pp 188–9.

26 Timothy O'Neill, *Merchants and Mariners in Medieval Ireland* (Blackrock, Co. Dublin, 1987), pp 37–42.

27 Katharine Simms, 'The origins of the creaght: farming system or social unit?' in *Agriculture and Settlement in Ireland*, ed. Margaret Murphy and Matthew Stout (Dublin, 2015), pp 101–118.

28 *The Register of Primate John Swayne*, ed. D.A. Chart (Belfast, 1935), pp 18, 64, 72, 93, 198; *Registrum Iohannis Mey*, ed. W.G.H. Quigley and E.F.D. Roberts (Belfast, 1972), no. 178.

29 J.P. Prendergast, 'The Ulster creaghts', *JRSAI*, 3 (1855), pp 420–30.

30 Katharine Simms, 'Nomadry in Medieval Ireland: the origins of the creaght or caoraigheacht', *Peritia*, 5 (1986), pp 379–91.

31 Nicholas Canny, 'Hugh O'Neill, earl of Tyrone, and the changing face of Gaelic Ulster', *Studia Hibernica*, 10 (1970), pp 7–35 at pp 27–9; Simms, *Gaelic Ulster*, pp 495–8.

32 Hilary Simms, 'Violence in County Armagh, 1641' in *Ulster 1641: Aspects of the Rising*, ed. Brian Mac Cuarta (Belfast, 1993; reprinted Newtownards, 2020), pp 123–38 at p. 130.

FIG. 17.3
Views of Tullyhoge.

18 Mapping Lough Neagh
c. 1570–1625

Annaleigh Margey

The Early Modern period gave rise to an increased interest in the geography and landscape of Ulster amongst English officials.[1] Events, such as Shane O'Neill's rebellion and the Nine Years' War, exposed their poor geographical knowledge of the province, as they sought to outwit the Gaelic Irish in their military manoeuvres.

While written accounts of Ulster's wild and remote landscape had made their way to the officials, including successive lord deputies and Queen Elizabeth I herself, visual representations, such as maps, had been few and far between. The province did, of course, feature in some of the maps of Ireland, which had become more prevalent from the 1550s, but in terms of definitive geographical knowledge, they were lacking in particulars. By the late 1560s, Elizabeth I had recognised their deficiencies and requested 'plats of Ulster to be sent' to help in settling the province with English subjects.[2] Over the ensuing decades, maps of the province, and its regions, became much requested, as officials built their knowledge, and as England's relationship with Ulster changed from one of reconnaissance, to subjugation and then full-scale plantation.[3]

Maps that did issue from English cartographers in Ireland included some of Ulster's most prominent geographical features, such as Lough Neagh. Some of the earliest maps of Ireland merely located the lough in the landscape. However, as England's involvement with Ulster increased in the late sixteenth and early seventeenth centuries, the lough featured more heavily, as part of a growing military landscape, with lough-side fortifications becoming core parts of the mapping agenda. By the plantation period, the lough continued to feature, as the backdrop to land grants and new settlements in the Londonderry Plantation. This chapter seeks to introduce this wide spectrum of maps of, and including, Lough Neagh. Beginning with a look at the earliest representations of Lough Neagh in maps of Ireland and Ulster, it will move to explore the military maps that emerged during the Nine Years' War campaign, including both the landscape and fortification maps, before exploring the continued inclusion of the lough on plantation maps from the province.

In 1567/8 John Goghe's map gave one of the first clear representations of Lough Neagh. Although somewhat elongated, the depiction did show four islands within the lough, recognising features such as Coney Island, as well as the clear flow of the River Bann (Fig. 18.1).[4] The banks of the lough also

FIG. 18.1

'Hibernia Insula', John Goghe, c. 1567 (TNA, MPF1/68).

THE NATIONAL ARCHIVES, LONDON

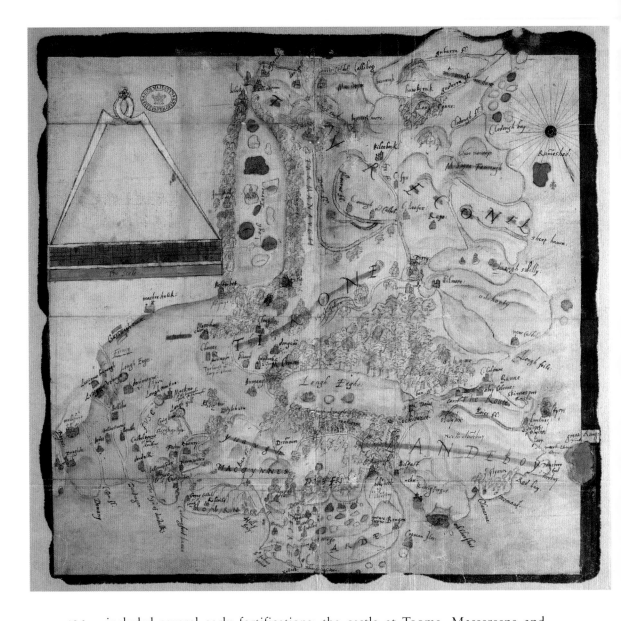

FIG. 18.2

Ulster, *c.* 1580
(TNA, MPF1/90).

THE NATIONAL ARCHIVES,
LONDON

included several early fortifications: the castle at Toome, Massereene and 'Corkrey'.[5] The map had several annotations from Sir William Cecil, Elizabeth I's Secretary of State, who obviously used it to assist in his administering of the province in the aftermath of Shane O'Neill's campaigns. Early provincial maps did little to improve on this rudimentary geography. A map of Ulster of *c.* 1580, now at The National Archives in London, for example, included 'Lough Eaghe', but again gave it an elongated shape (Fig. 18.2).[6] On this occasion, three islands were included in the lough, one of which had an unroofed building. This may be a representation of the Coney Island tower, which possibly marks Shane O'Neill's original stronghold.[7]

By the 1590s, new mapmakers had arrived in Ulster. Francis Jobson, for example, who had worked as part of the 1586 Commission in Munster, produced several maps of the province. He had originally been commissioned in 1591 'to take the plot of the countreys of Tyrone, both the Clandeboyes, the Route and other parts of the Province of Ulster'.[8] His 1598 map of the province incorporates this brief, showing the changing political geography of the province,

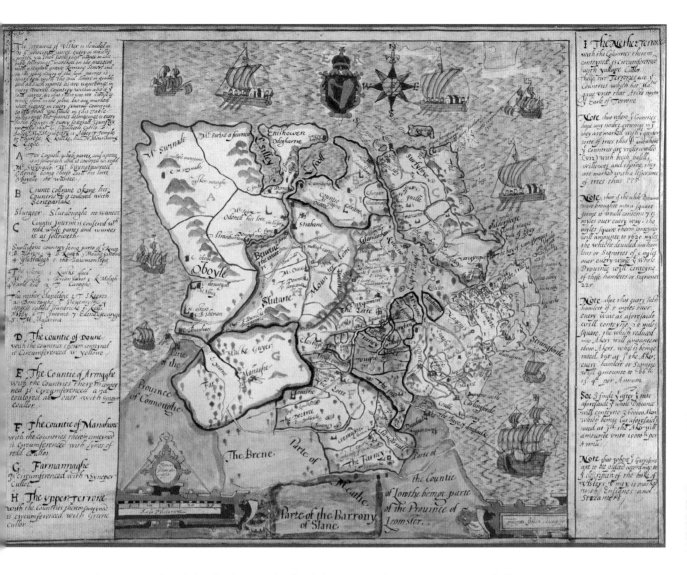

FIG. 18.3

Ulster, Francis Jobson,
c. 1598 (TCD, MS 1209/17).

TRINITY COLLEGE, THE UNIVERSITY
OF DUBLIN

as he encapsulated both the Gaelic lordships and the new counties of the province in the aftermath of shiring (Fig. 18.3).[9] This geography showed that Lough Neagh formed part of the boundary of several counties, including Tyrone, Antrim, Down and Armagh. The map also gave some of the earliest insights into the emergence of the lough, as a core part of Ulster's military landscape.[10] These included a fort at Toome, on the opposite bank of the Bann to the castle at Toome, as well as Blackwater Fort.[11] This fort, depicted in red on the map, would have been a 'rectangular palisade earthwork'.[12] Blackwater Fort's inclusion here merely marked out its importance, as part of the early military landscape of the province. It had been, as O'Neill notes, 'established to curb the growing power of Turlough Luineach O'Neill and provide support to the 'enterprise of Ulster' by Walter Devereux, first earl of Essex, and Sir Thomas Smith'.[13] Moreover, as a fortification, it became a core part of the action of the Nine Years' War, forming a centrepiece of a 1595 battle.[14]

Lough Neagh's strategic importance grew across the Nine Years' War. As the boundary of multiple new counties, and multiple lordships, the lough emerged as a zone of interest for both Tyrone's and the English armies. O'Neill

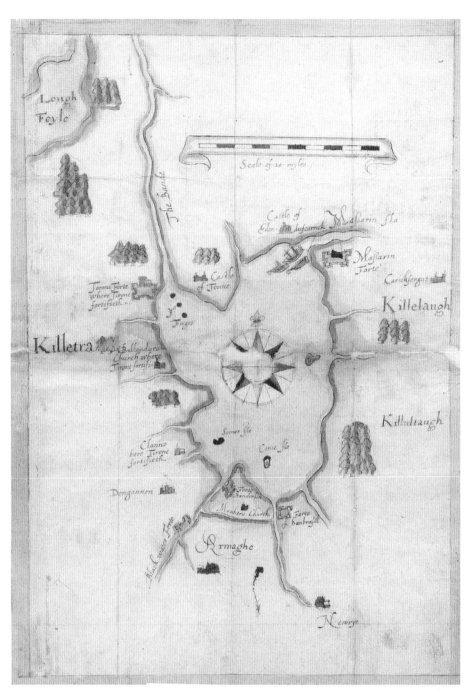

Fig. 18.4
Lough Neagh and its
surroundings, *c.* 1601
(NLI, MS 2656/xix).
THE NATIONAL LIBRARY OF IRELAND

constructed multiple fortifications along the western shore of Lough Neagh in 1601, 'barring riverine access into County Tyrone'.[15] These fortifications became more important, in the face of English attempts to pacify the province in the aftermath of the Nine Years' War. The English strategy gave rise to a three-pronged attack in the province, with Sir Henry Docwra leading forces from the north-west, at Lough Foyle and his fort at 'the Derry'; Sir Arthur Chichester's forces coming from the east at Carrickfergus; and Charles Blount, Lord Mountjoy, the new lord deputy, leading forces from the south-east.[16] Maps became a fundamental part of the reconnaissance process, with Lough Neagh and its fortifications featuring heavily. A 1601 map displayed some of this reconnaissance in action, as the map marks out what fortifications were built

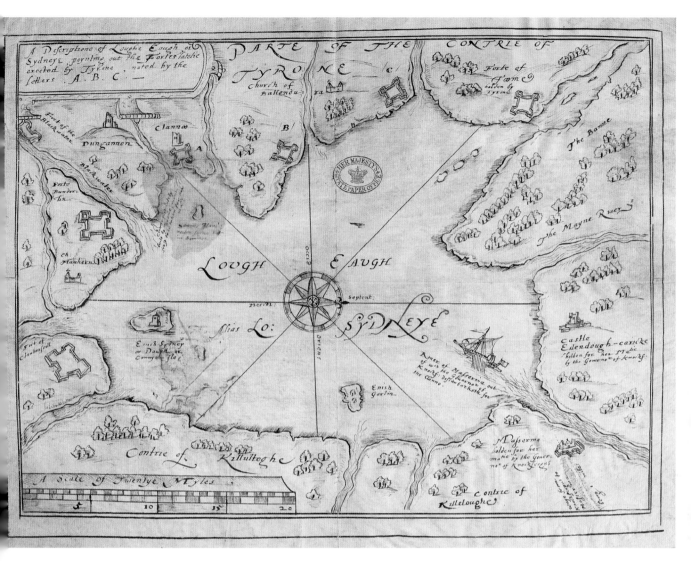

FIG.18.5

Lough Neagh, Richard
Bartlett, *c*. 1601–02
(TNA, MPF1/133).

THE NATIONAL ARCHIVES, LONDON

and not built (Fig. 18.4).[17] Although unsigned, the map gives a strong insight into Tyrone's fortification of the lough. This included inscriptions, such as 'Ballendura Church where Tirone fortifie' and 'Clanno here Tirone fortifieth'. Moreover, the map included small drawings of the forts surrounding the lough. For example, the map noted the complex riverine geography at Blackwater Fort, with the three sides of the forts and angular bastions included. Other forts, such as Toome Fort and 'Massarin Forte', also added to this military landscape.[18]

The landscape of Lough Neagh continued to be an important feature of the provincial military maps, which emerged from Mountjoy's campaigns. These maps were the work of Richard Bartlett, a cartographer, who joined Mountjoy's forces in Ulster and mapped his campaign. Amongst his earliest maps from the province was his 'A Description of Loughe Eaugh or Sydneye poynting out the Fortes latelie erected by Tyrone noted by the letters A. B. C.' (Fig. 18.5).[19] A pen and ink drawing, with north on right, the map included multiple forts, such as 'Clanoo', 'Toome', 'Blackwater' and 'Clanbrassill'.[20] Bartlett added multiple inscriptions to reflect the contested nature of the loughside military landscape. For example, at Clanno Fort, he added 'lately built by Tyrone, ment first to be taken for her Maiestie', while Massereene Fort was 'holden for her Maiestie by

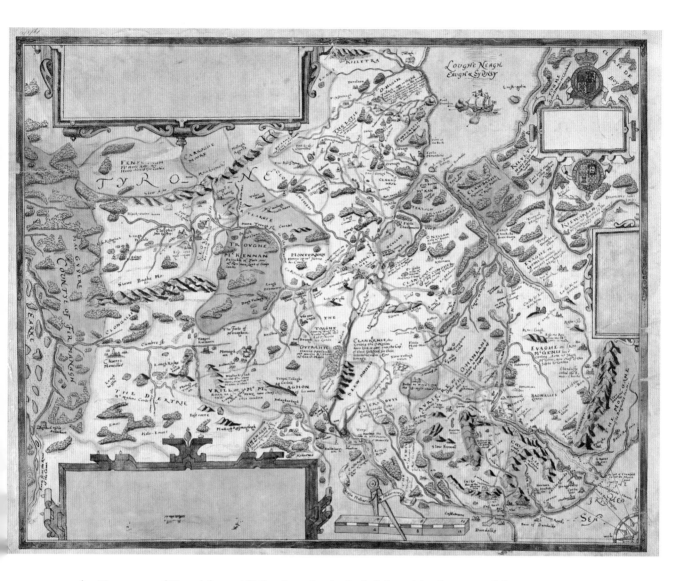

the Gouernor of Knockfergus'.[21] Bartlett also included the wider features of the natural, physical landscape, which formed part of the defences used by both sides. These included the multiple rivers, islands and forests within, and surrounding, the lake.

As Bartlett continued within Mountjoy's retinue, he produced multiple fortification and provincial military maps. His series of provincial maps provided the first look at the newly emerging landscape of English fortifications around Lough Neagh. His 'A Generalle Description of Vlster', for example, included both the existing forts and the new forts built by the English at the turn of the seventeenth century (Fig. 18.6).[22] He took a closer look at the landscape in his 'Campaign Map' for south-east Ulster, which included the newly-built Fort Mountjoy on the banks of Lough Neagh, the Moyry Pass in the south, and fortifications in the wider landscape, such as Charlemont Fort (Fig. 18.7).[23]

FIG.18.7

South-east Ulster, Richard Bartlett, *c.* 1602–03 (PRONI, T1652/2).

PUBLIC RECORD OFFICE OF NORTHERN IRELAND

FIG. 18.6

'A Generalle Description of Vlster', Richard Bartlett, *c.* 1602–03 (TNA, MPF1/35).

THE NATIONAL ARCHIVES, LONDON

FIG.18.8
Mountjoy Fort, 1960s; based on original from c. 1602 (NLI, MS 2656/vii).
NATIONAL LIBRARY OF IRELAND

Bartlett also produced a detailed plan of Mountjoy Fort (Fig. 18.8).[24] This plan offered the first insight into the English fortifications built along the banks of Lough Neagh. Bartlett's plan notes the fort as a star-shaped fortification, with angular bastions, cabins, cannons, wet and dry ditches, drawbridges, gates, houses, palisade, platforms, ramparts and connecting roads.[25] The fort then became operational in summer 1602.[26]

As English, and later British intervention in Ulster, moved from military subjugation to full-scale plantation, cartographers made fewer provincial maps of the province. Those provincial maps that did emerge aimed to identify the proportions granted to settlers in the landscape. Lough Neagh became a feature of maps from the Londonderry Plantation in 1622. Under the 1622 Commission, Sir Thomas Phillips engaged Thomas Raven, a surveyor and cartographer with extensive experience working in Ulster, to produce maps of the proportions and villages of the Twelve Great Livery Companies of London. The Salters' Company received a grant adjacent to Lough Neagh, building their new village, Salterstown on the banks of the lough. The proportion map shows the Salters' lands nestled on the bank of Lough 'Chichester' with a small representation of Salterstown included (Fig. 18.9).[27] The village map, 'The Salters Buildings at Salters Towne Six Miles from Maghary felt', shows multiple house plots along the banks of the river (Fig. 18.10).[28] Both houses, with an exoskeleton wood frame and cabins, are included. The settlers' names are inscribed beneath the houses, displaying a strong mix of both English and Scottish settlers on the site. (See Chapter 23 for more on Salterstown.)

There can be little doubt that Lough Neagh was a significant element of the mapping agenda of Early Modern Ireland. The lough formed a natural focal point in the province for both the Gaelic Irish and the English, and later, British, settlers. As the largest enclosed lough, it became a core element of the defensive, and later, settlement, landscape of counties including Armagh, Down, Antrim, and Derry/Londonderry. The use of the lough's islands, for example, by Shane O'Neill for his stronghold showed the central value of the natural landscape for his defences. As the decades progressed, these defensive uses increased, as both Gaelic and English fortifications adjoined the lough on every edge. Moreover,

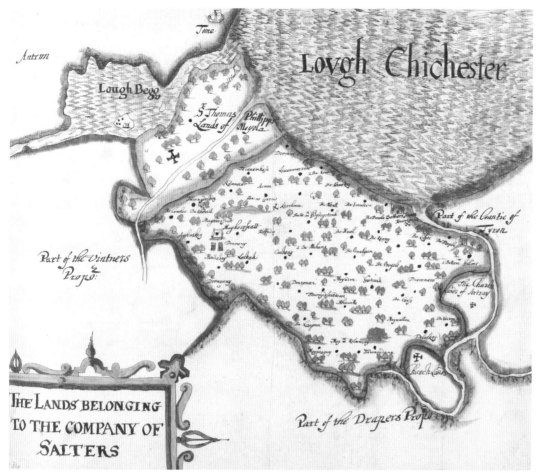

FIG.18.9

'The Lands belonging the Company of Salters', Thomas Raven, 1622 (PRONI, T510/1/34).

PUBLIC RECORD OFFICE OF NORTHERN IRELAND AND LAMBETH PALACE LIBRARY

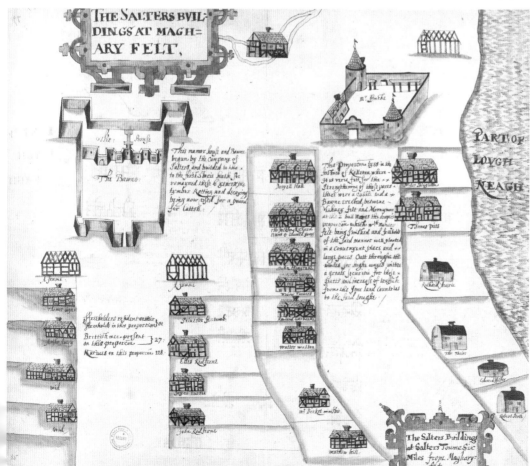

FIG. 18.10

'The Salters Buildinges at Salters Towne six miles from Maghary felt', Thomas Raven, 1622 (PRONI, T510/1/35).

PUBLIC RECORD OFFICE OF NORTHERN IRELAND AND LAMBETH PALACE LIBRARY

the lough also became a core part of the settlement plans for the province. As the natural hinterland of the Londonderry Plantation, its banks became home to settlements, such as Salterstown, providing an economic and security boast to the new plantation. As such, Lough Neagh continued to be not just a geographic feature in the landscape, but a source of security, power and economic development in the province during the Early Modern period.

Notes

1 A. Margey, 'Representing plantation landscapes: the mapping of Ulster, *c.* 1560–1640' in J. Lyttleton and C. Rynne (eds), *Plantation Ireland: Settlement and Material Culture, c. 1550–c. 1700* (Dublin, 2009), p. 140.

2 Ibid., p. 141; *CSPI, 1550–70*, p. 336.

3 For a wider exploration of these categories of Ulster maps, please see: Margey, 'Representing plantation landscapes', pp 140–64.

4 TNA, MPF1/67, 'Hibernia Insula', John Goghe, *c.* 1567; P.V. Addyman, 'Coney Island, Lough Neagh: prehistoric settlement, Anglo-Norman castle and Elizabethan native fortress', *UJA*, 3rd series 28 (1965), pp 78–101.

5 R. Ó Baoill, 'Excavations at the site of Toome Castle, Co. Antrim', *UJA*, 3rd series 58 (1999), p. 90.

6 TNA, MPF1/90, Ulster, *c.* 1580.

7 Addyman, 'Coney Island, Lough Neagh', pp 80–81.

8 Rawlinson Manuscript A. 317, *Analecta Hibernia*, 1 (1930), p. 99.

9 TCD, MS 1209/17, Ulster, Francis Jobson, *c.* 1598.

10 Ibid.

11 M. McGowen, 'Seventeenth-century artillery forts in Ulster', *Clogher Record*, 10 (1980), p. 246.

12 Ibid., p. 241.

13 J. O'Neill, *The Nine Years War, 1593–1603* (Dublin, 2018), p. 46.

14 Ibid., p. 47.

15 J. O'Neill, 'Half-moons and villainous works', *Archaeology Ireland*, 24:4 (2014), p. 13.

16 J.H. Andrews, *The Queen's Last Mapmaker: Richard Bartlett in Ireland, 1600–3* (Dublin, 2008), p. 21.

17 NLI, MS 2656/xix, Lough Neagh and its surroundings, *c.* 1601.

18 Ibid.; see also the recent discussion in A. Fee and F. Mayes, 'Mountjoy Fort and Mountjoy Castle, Co. Tyrone', *UJA*, 3rd series 71 (2012), p. 118.

19 TNA, MPF1/133, 'A Descriptione of Lough Eaugh or Sydneye poyning out the Fortes latelie erected by Tyrone noted by A. B. C.', Richard Bartlett, *c.* 1601–02.

20 Ibid.

21 Ibid.

22 TNA, MPF1/35, 'A Generalle Description of Vlster', R. Bartlett, *c.* 1602–03.

23 TNA, MPF1/36, South-east Ulster, *c.* 1602–03. See also: Andrews, *The Queen's Last Mapmaker*, p. 112. Andrews coined the term 'The Campaign Map' in this work.

24 NLI, MS 2656/vii, Mountjoy Fort, 1960s; based on original from *c.* 1602.

25 Ibid.

26 Fee and Mayes, 'Mountjoy Fort and Mountjoy Castle', p. 121.

27 PRONI, T510/1/34, 'The Lands belonging to the Company of Salters', Thomas Raven, 1622.

28 PRONI, T510/1/35, 'The Salters Buildings at Salters Towne six Miles from Maghary felt', Thomas Raven, 1622.

19 The Nine Years' War and Lough Neagh

James O'Neill

The Nine Years' War, fought from 1593 to 1603, was the last attempt by Irish lords to throw off English rule and preserve Gaelic systems of law and noble privileges. The confederation of Irish lords came closer than many imagine to extinguishing the authority of Queen Elizabeth I in Ireland. The conflict was fought along the length of Ireland, but is most often associated with the fighting in Ulster, more specifically Armagh, and the devastating defeat of the Irish at the Battle of Kinsale in December 1601.

Lough Neagh, also known by the Crown as Lough Sydney, is rarely mentioned. This was because for most of the war it sat in the settled security of the Ulster heartlands, well away from war zones further to the south. However, the region was witness to the events at the very outbreak of war and the devastating terror of scorched earth warfare and famine that brought the war to its close.

In a chance of fate, the first effects of the burgeoning conflict came to the shores of Lough Neagh, not as a clash between Irish and Crown forces, but between Irish lords as Hugh O'Neill, the earl of Tyrone, took action to neutralise any threat to his power in Ulster. As a shooting war raged in Fermanagh, the commitment of Crown military assets to engaging with Hugh Maguire (Tyrone's son-in-law) allowed the earl to move against politically suspect Irish lords in central and east Ulster. This was his plan all along: with no military forces available to shore up the position of the Crown's client Irish lords, Tyrone could act with impunity.

Though Tyrone had become the most powerful Irish lord in Ulster, he was still opposed by others who chose to ally with the English Crown. One of these was Phelim MacTurlough O'Neill, who held the lordship of Killetra. Situated where the River Bann flowed from Lough Neagh, it was strategically vital as it sat on the boundary between the lordship of Tyrone and north Clandeboy. Tyrone had moved against Phelim before, when the earl tried to supplant Phelim with an O'Hagan. However, Phelim killed Tyrone's man and went into open hostilities against the earl. Moreover, Sir Henry Bagenal arranged to have Phelim pardoned and returned to his lands. Worse for the earl, Tyrone was forced to swear before Lord Deputy Fitzwilliam to guarantee Phelim's safety. Though the matter appeared settled, an ally of Bagenal's on Tyrone's doorstep was irreconcilable with the earl's plans to dominate the province. In Fermanagh, Hugh Maguire had ejected the English sheriff during Easter 1593 with the aid of forces led by Tyrone's brother, Cormac MacBaron. A meeting of Tyrone's key allies and adherents gathered at Toome, likely to plan Maguire's expansion of the conflict into Connacht. It was at this gathering that Phelim met his fate.

Phelim and his small group arrived at Toome on Friday evening, 11 May. Ostensibly, Phelim was there to discuss Tyrone fostering one of his sons, but when he arrived he did not have immediate access to the earl, who was camped in the earthwork fort on the west bank of the River Bann (Toome Castle is on the east bank). Tyrone had secretive meetings with Maguire and the O'Hagans over the weekend, in plain view but beyond earshot of anyone who wished to listen in. On Sunday Phelim asked Tyrone to meet with him but the earl put him off until Monday morning. Despite the days, Phelim and his men were well-entertained, 'all that time did eat and drink with the earl himself, and were well used by him'.[1]

Phelim met privately with Tyrone early on Monday morning, after which Tyrone boarded a boat to set off down the Bann. Saluting the earl's departure, Phelim shouted, "God be with you, my lord." Tyrone responded, "*Slán dé fút go hoíche*" ("God's defiance to you till nightfall").[2] Phelim's companions were terrified but Phelim 'stood in good hope that he [Tyrone] used those words only in jest'.[3] As Tyrone left, an Owen O'Hagan 'flattered the said Phelim', walking back with him to the earl's camp, but as they reached the gate of the fort Owen 'clasped him [Phelim] about the neck drew his sword and struck off one of his arms'. Two more O'Hagans piled in, hewing Phelim into pieces. Phelim's companions made a break for it and two managed to escape, but Donal Og MacEvagh was caught and drowned in the river. A small distance downriver Tyrone received news of Phelim's murder. The news caused Countess Mabel to clasp her hands over her ears in shock at the brutal act, leading the earl to strongly admonish her. Three days later Phelim's lands were spoiled and his kinsmen banished from the territory under threat of similar treatment. This was one of Tyrone's more well-known assassinations, but others who attempted to defy Tyrone met similar ends.

Though shocking and brutal, Tyrone used assassination as a final recourse, preferring instead persuasion and conciliation and it was along the lough shore in 1594 that Tyrone engaged in some dynastic dealing and bridge building, as well as cementing his position as the pre-eminent lord in the region. Captain Charles Eggerton, the constable of Carrickfergus, noted the earl was camped near Edenduffcarrick (modern Shane's Castle), where he settled disputes over land ownership between local lords, making himself guarantor for the observance of said agreements. Though at this time Tyrone was still claiming loyalty to the Crown (while conducting the war by proxy) this was not about

Fig. 19.1

Map of Lough Neagh from 'State of the Fortes of Ireland as they weare in the yeare 1624' by Nicholas Pynnar, (BL, Add. 24,200, ff. 35v–36).

© BRITISH LIBRARY BOARD

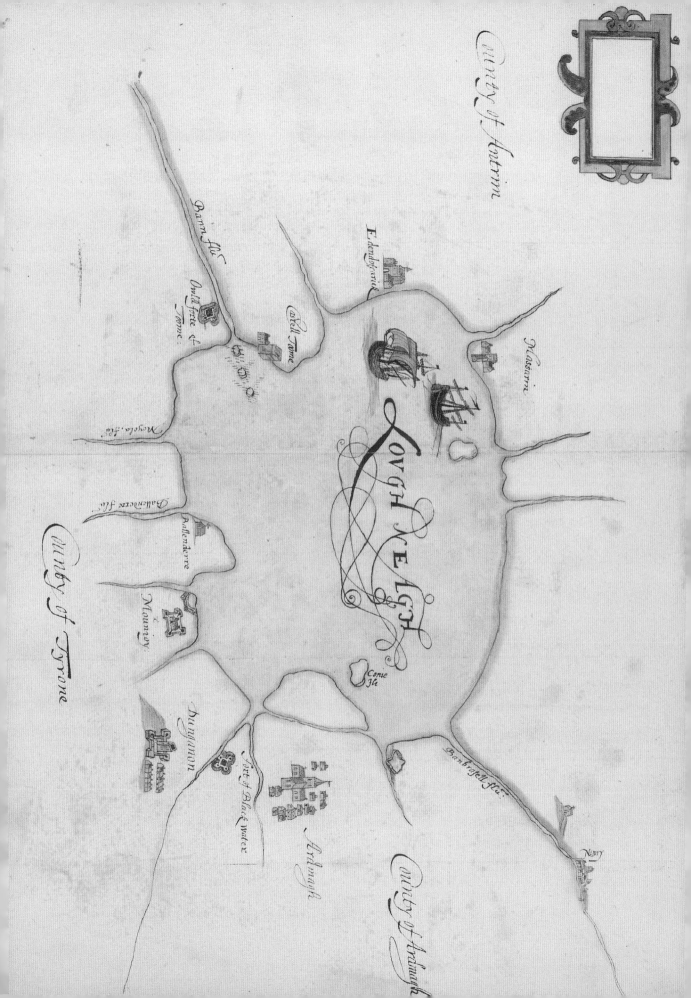

County of Antrim

County of Tyrone

County of Ardmagh

Lough Neagh

Barm flu
Owld forte of Tome
Catell Tome
Edendgrarie
Massarin
Moyola flu
Ballenderre flu
Ballenderre
Mountioy
Come Ilh
Dunganon
Fort of Black water
Ardmagh
Banbreffell flu
Newry

maintaining the queen's peace but underpinning his authority. Lord Burghley wryly noted in the margin of the document that Tyrone was 'a busy officer without warrant'.[4]

That Lough Neagh was a vital strategic asset was not lost on Queen Elizabeth's officers in Ireland. Its central position in the province and access to rivers north and south provided unmatched levels of access to Antrim, Derry, Armagh and Tyrone. Writing in 1594, Captain William Piers, a veteran with many years' service in Ireland, noted that establishing a naval force on the lough would be key to engaging Tyrone and his allies in the home territories. He recommended the construction of boats capable of transporting 200–300 troops out of Clandeboy to be landed anywhere of their choosing in surprise raids. This he hoped, would keep Clandeboy safe from invasion and disrupt 'rebellious or traitorous' plans.[5]

Almost two years later, Sir John Dowdall recommended that an amphibious force be established on the lough. He noted that 500 troops

> with good provisions of boats and victuals, they will annoy the traitors more than 3,000 men any other way employed, for they may do service in one place, and the next day be thirty or forty miles from it upon the sudden by night as the cause shall require.[6]

Dowdall knew what he was writing about, as he had commanded an effective amphibious campaign on Lough Erne during 1593–4. However, the tide of Irish military success made any attempt to exploit the lough pointless, as successive defeats pushed English military power out of Ulster. By 1597 just a few English garrisons remained: Carrickfergus, Newry and the fort on the River Blackwater. In the relative security Irish agriculture flourished, with plentiful harvests providing the resources for Tyrone to pay for the largest and best-equipped armies deployed by the native Irish.

The next action on the lough shore happened almost by mistake, as Sir John Chichester raided west out of Carrickfergus in July 1597. After a series of engagements with Brian MacArt O'Neill's men, Chichester moved against Edenduffcarrick, but he admitted that it fell much to his surprise. Chichester had planned to send his men to steal cattle and horses from around the castle, while using one-third of his small force to counter any attempt by the Irish garrison to intervene. However, 'some of them issuing out that end, we fell in presently pell-mell with them and entered their bawn, after two assaults given them, we gained so near the castle as to set it fire, wherein was said to be infinity store of provisions'.[7] Some hoped that the new position would be 'a great bridle to the earl [Tyrone]' but this hope proved false.[8] Indeed, the garrison may not have been aware of just how vulnerable the position was, as shown by their rash behaviour in January 1598.

The ward of the castle enjoyed well-stocked stores but still felt the need to spoil the surrounding countryside. They took 'eighteen mares and garrans from the poor inhabitants around and demanded beeves of them'.[9] In response the Irish attacked the position, breaking into the bawn and burning the door of the main keep, leading the ward to kill all the stolen horses in the castle cellar 'and by this wilful accident put the house in danger to be lost'.[10] Taking Edenduffcarrick was the high watermark of John Chichester's success against the Irish, as just over three months later he was killed in the Battle of Aldfreck near Carrickfergus. James MacDonnell sent his head to Tyrone in Dungannon, where it was allegedly kicked around like a football. It was his brother, Sir Arthur Chichester, who came to shape the nature of the war around the lough.

Sir Arthur Chichester arrived in Ireland in 1599 and was garrisoned in Carrickfergus. Chichester referred to the loss of Edenduffcarrick in October 1600. He noted how a number of boats had been stationed at the castle 'in the hands of a neutral, who betrayed the ward. I must recover that or pay dearly for it'.[11] The 'neutral' mentioned by Chichester was Niall MacHugh O'Neill. He had become disgruntled by Tyrone's arbitration of a land dispute and had submitted to the Crown.[12] During December 1600 Niall MacHugh contacted Chichester with promises to deliver the castle, and more importantly the boats, to the Crown. However, in the febrile landscape of conflicting loyalties and self-interest, Niall had set a trap for Chichester who noted:

> Had I given him [Niall MacHugh] more time, I had endangered all these Her Majesty's forces here, for he had sent the Scots, Brian Mac Art [O'Neill] and other, to come upon us, and when I came he defended the castle against me, declaring himself by killing a sergeant and discharging diverse shot upon us.[13]

Unable to breach the defences and in danger of being cut off from Carrickfergus, Chichester and his men withdrew. It was only in the spring of the following year that Chichester was able to retake the castle and the boats, but by then Chichester no longer needed it as a base for his operations on the lough. During the same expedition in April, Chichester took and fortified Massereene friary (in modern Antrim town), and it was from here that Chichester would make an indelible and distinctly brutal contribution to the war. Chichester despised the native Irish and advocated the most severe methods possible to defeat Tyrone and his allies. He regarded famine as the best tool for defeating the Irish as it would kill 'multitudes'.[14] Moreover, Chichester advocated daily raids, spoiling and killing all who could be found, man, woman child or beast 'until the nation be wholly destroyed or so subjected as to take a new impression of laws and religion, being now the most treacherous infidels in the world and we have too mild spirits and good consciences to be their masters'.[15]

Massereene was reputedly a Third Order Franciscan friary established by the O'Neills around 1500, but in eight days in April 1601, Chichester raised earthwork fortifications around it, transforming it into his base of operations on Lough Neagh. He had the small number of boats from Edenduffcarrick, but in May 1601 he requested supplies:

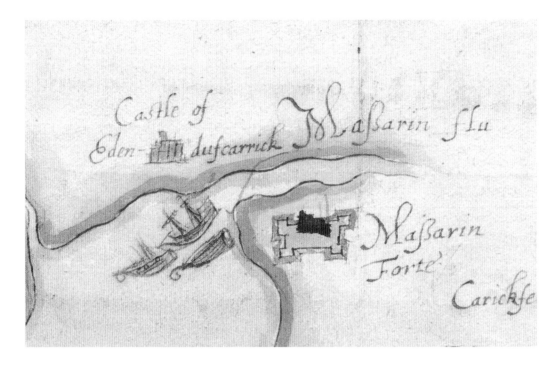

FIG. 19.2

Detail from map of Lough Neagh, *c.* 1601, providing a view of the fortifications in the vicinity of Antrim town (NLI, MS 2656/xix).

NATIONAL LIBRARY OF IRELAND

to have certain boats built upon the Lough Neagh, in addition to other boats already there, and for that purpose that there is sent pitch, tar, oakum, resin, ropes, nails, sails, masts, boards, and other necessaries.[16]

Chichester recognised that Tyrone and his allies were adept at neutralising the Crown's field armies by forcing them into dangerous overland journeys. Moreover, access into Ulster was limited by the drumlin belts and lakelands of the southern borderlands. Access for large Crown armies was limited to Ballyshannon in the west and the Moyry Pass in the east. Tyrone's strongest line of defence along the River Blackwater on the Tyrone/Armagh had stopped repeated English attacks dead in their tracks. The lough provided a highway for amphibious operations, enabling swift attacks into Tyrone's previously secure heartlands. This vulnerability was soon ruthlessly exposed.

Chichester's small flotilla could only carry around 60 troops, but in May they descended on the lough's western shore where Chichester reported 'we have burnt and destroyed along the lough, even within four miles of Dungannon, where we killed man, woman, child, horse, beast, and whatsoever we found'.[17] He added that during one of the raids they attacked Patrick O'Quinn's lands: 'we lighted upon him and killed him, his wife, sons, daughters, servants, and followers, being many, and burnt all to the ground'.[18] As this region was previously thought secure Tyrone had only a small force with which to respond and, therefore, Chichester and his men returned home unscathed. Chichester reported that the region had been unaffected by war so his sudden arrival had 'spread much terror in the people, who heard not a drum, nor saw not a fire there of long time'.[19] Lord Deputy Mountjoy was well-pleased with the raids and ordered Sir George Carey (the Crown's treasurer at wars in Ireland) 'to furnish him [Chichester] with money and such other things as he writes for, and dispatch them with all speed; for I doubt not but he will be able to do great matters'.[20]

The amphibious raids depended on speed and surprise to be effective, so Tyrone took measures to ensure Chichester's next raids would not find the country so defenceless. The month after Chichester's raids Tyrone ordered a series of earthwork fortifications built along the lough shore. Six were recorded on an English map drawn up in June 1601.[21] Furthermore, Tyrone ordered troops to guard the lough. Chichester later noted: 'they have such a good watch towards the lough, that without good strength I can do them no great annoyance'.[22] As the Irish strengthened their defences along the western lough shore, Chichester's plans to support Mountjoy's summer campaign to the River Blackwater were abandoned. However, Chichester was not going to be so easily put off, switching his attention to easier targets on the south-east shores of the lough.

During July Chichester attacked Clanbrassil, a territory around modern Lurgan, where he 'fetched such cows as were left on this side of the Bann, killed such people as we lighted upon and cut as much corn as possibly we might ... I found all that country as plentifully stored with corn as any part of England, and I will labour by all means to destroy it, which will cut their throats faster than our swords, from which flight keeps them'.[23] Clearly, many Irish civilians were managing to evade Chichester's troops, but anything they were forced to abandon was destroyed. English raids moved into Killultagh. Described as one of the strongest holds in Ireland, Chichester had made a start on wasting it and in August made another attempt to burn to the River Bann, but could not stay in the region due to Tyrone's garrison at Inishloughan. Lord Mountjoy planned to reinforce Chichester with 1,000 troops to enable a permanent garrison to be established on the western lough shore, four or five miles from Dungannon, but the arrival of a large Spanish landing force at Kinsale forced the English to abandon this plan for now.

The Spanish landed at Kinsale on 21 September 1601. Don Juan del Águila commanded the army, totalling 3,400 troops, which dramatically altered the balance of power in Ireland. Mountjoy was forced to confront the Spaniards, bottling them up within the Medieval walls of Kinsale, but in doing so he was obliged to draw every available man out of the north, leaving only a skeleton force to hold the ground gained during the 1601 campaign. As the weather turned, Chichester was thrown on the defensive:

> This lough water is, in a storm, very rough, our boats weak and of small burden, and the weather hath been so foul that I have been forced to turn, when half way over, and run the boats ashore, for safety of our men, upon the enemies' country near Toome. I am overmatched with numbers on every

side of the Scots revolt, and so pestered with disloyal Irish in our own companies that we cannot without great danger attempt much.[24]

Though attention was focused on Kinsale, Chichester could not rest easy as at the end of October he was forced to scuttle his boats to prevent their capture, though he planned to recover them later.[25] Nevertheless, as Chichester bided his time he constructed more boats 'with these I hope to make a sure plantation in Tyrone … from which the country will be wasted'.[26]

Kinsale ended in disastrous defeat for Tyrone, who returned north, reaching Dungannon on 10 January 1602 with the broken remains of his army. However, the Crown army had also taken a battering, with Mountjoy losing almost 6,000 men in the frozen trenches around Kinsale. Only at the start of March 1602 did Chichester send his boats with 140 men to raid Killetra where they killed and spoiled all who fell to them. By 31 May Chichester had placed Captain Hugh Clotworthy in charge of the flotilla, which consisted of: 'One barque close decked of 30 tons, one boat of 14 tons, and two at 10 tons, and three smaller boats to load and unload victuals and munitions and other matters of service.'[27]

While waiting for Mountjoy and his troops to march north, Chichester moved on Tyrone's fort at Toome. It had controlled the west bank of the River Bann since the start of the war and checked any advance by English land forces from the east, but it fell to Chichester on 20 June 1602. The following day Tyrone fired Dungannon and retreated to Glenconkeyne forest. With Mountjoy on the Blackwater and Chichester at Toome, the earl did not want to get trapped between the two. At the start of July, Mountjoy and Chichester met on the shore a few miles from Dungannon where they began construction of a large campaign fort made 'defensible to contain above one thousand foot, and one hundred horse, which was to be victualled from Carrickfergus by way of the lough'.[28] The fort was named Mountjoy Fort after the Lord Deputy. (See Chapter 20 for more on this fort.)

The polygonal fort was recorded in detail by the cartographer Richard Bartlett.[29] It was built to the most modern *trace italienne* design, with earthwork ramparts and three spear-shaped angle bastions. The ramparts were protected by a wet ditch and earthwork glacis and the bastions had platforms mounting three cannon which provided long-range firepower. Supplied by boats from across the lough, this position would have proved near-impossible to crack at the height of Tyrone's powers. At this stage of the war, with Tyrone's allies defecting to the Crown and the back of Irish military power broken, the fort was an impregnable base for Mountjoy to conduct his scorched earth campaign.

Mountjoy had started a programme of crop destruction the previous year. His goal was to instigate a famine in the region, describing these operations where 'we do continually hunt all their woods, spoil their corn, burn their houses and kill so many churls'.[30] Mountjoy had hoped the privations brought on by famine would force someone to betray Tyrone to the English, bringing a rapid conclusion to the war. Others, notably Chichester, were content that famine would bring mass mortality upon the Irish. He wrote 'no course … will cut the throat of the grand traitor … and bring the country into quiet but famine, which is well begun but will daily enlarge'.[31] Chichester had known how damaging famine could be when he wrote two years earlier that 'a million of swords will not do them so much harm as one winter's famine'.[32] He was now achieving this aim, but the English campaign coincided with a collapse of agriculture in the region under the strain of supporting years of war. What would have been a brutal campaign of suppression became a catastrophe for the Irish, as famine struck quicker and became more devastating than Mountjoy could have predicted.[33] Hunger ravaged the country and it was reported, 'with our eyes daily seen the lamentable estate of that country, wherein we found everywhere men dead of famine … between Tullagh Oge and Toome there lay unburied a thousand dead'.[34] Nevertheless, despite the death, hardship and misery brought on by famine, Mountjoy could not induce anyone to betray Tyrone. Chichester ranged from the fort at Toome, troops scoured the countryside from Mountjoy Fort and English forces pushed down from the north-west, but the Lord Deputy admitted at the start of 1603 that only by a stroke of luck would they capture Tyrone. However, Tyrone bowed to the inevitable, when from his refuge in Glenconkeyne forest he sought terms for submission, surrendering to Mountjoy at Mellifont, County Meath, on 30 March 1603.

For much of the Nine Years' War, the area around the lough was relatively peaceful. Most of the fighting took place in the south Ulster borderlands, on the hotly contested line of the River Blackwater or further still in the Wicklow and Curlew mountains. The region was relatively safe and in that security agriculture prospered. Yet, when the tides of war shifted the lough provided a fast and secure means for the Crown to by-pass Tyrone's defences in the region, and through that brought the horrors of war to Tyrone's heartlands, devastating the land and killing thousands who lived around the lough.

Notes

1 Declaration of Ever O'Neill, 1 June 1593 (TNA, SP 63/170, f. 3).
2 Hiram Morgan, '"Slán dé fút go hoíche": Hugh O'Neill's murders' in David Edwards, Pádraig Lenihan and Clodagh Tait (eds), *Age of Atrocity: Violence and Political Conflict in Early Modern Ireland* (Dublin, 2007), p. 95.
3 Declaration of Ever O'Neill, 1 June 1593 (TNA, SP 63/170, f. 3).
4 Charles Eggerton, constable of Carrickfergus to Lord Deputy William Fitzwilliam, 20 June 1594 (TNA, SP 63/175, f. 128).
5 Plat by Captain William Piers, 6 Nov. 1594 (TNA, SP 63/177, f. 3).
6 Sir John Dowdall to Lord Burghley, 9 March 1596 (*CSPI, 1592–6*), p. 484.
7 Sir John Chichester to Lord Burghley, 16 Sept. 1597 (TNA, SP 63/200 f. 317).
8 Sir Henry Wallop to Sir Robert Cecil, 27 July 1597 (*CSPI, 1596–7*), pp 356–8.
9 Captain Charles Eggerton to Lords Justice Loftus and Gardiner, 6 Jan. 1598 (TNA, SP 63/202 pt 1, f. 76).

10 Ibid.

11 Sir Arthur Chichester to Sir Robert Cecil, 21 Oct. 1600 (*CSPI, 1600*), pp 484–5.

12 Hiram Morgan, *Tyrone's Rebellion: the Outbreak of the Nine Years War in Tudor Ireland* (Dublin, 1993), p. 190.

13 Chichester to Cecil, 16 Dec. 1600 (*CSPI, 1600–01*), pp 83–5.

14 Chichester to Cecil, 2 May 1600 (TNA, SP 63/207 pt 3, f. 24).

15 Chichester to Cecil, 8 Oct. 1601 (*CSPI, 1601–03*), pp 110–12.

16 Anthony Dawtry to Sir Arthur Chichester, 15 May 1601 (TNA, SP 63/208 pt 2, f. 189).

17 Chichester to Cecil, 15 May 1600 (*CSPI, 1600–01*), pp 332–5.

18 Ibid.

19 Chichester to Lord Deputy Mountjoy, 14 May 1601 (*CSPI, 1600–01*), pp 355–8.

20 Lord Deputy Mountjoy to Sir George Carey, 23 May 1601 (*CSPI, 1600–01*), p. 355.

21 A description of Lough Eagh [Neagh] or Sydney, pointing out the forts lately erected by Tyrone, 1601 (TNA, MPF 1/133). One of these was at Ardboe church. Later occupied by Crown troops, its earthwork defences can still be seen today.

22 Chichester to Cecil, 21 July 1601 (*CSPI, 1600–01*), pp 447–8.

23 Ibid.

24 Chichester to Cecil, 20 Oct. 1601 (*CSPI, 1601–03*), pp 134–5.

25 Sir Arthur Chichester to the English Privy Council, 6 Nov. 1601 (*CSPI, 1601–03*), pp 152–3.

26 Ibid.

27 Note of the boats kept in Lough Sidney or Lough Eagh [Lough Neagh] for her majesty's service, and the charge thereof, 31 May 1602 (*CSPI, 1601–03*), pp 396–7.

28 Fynes Moryson, *An Itinerary*, vol. iii (Glasgow, 1908), p. 167.

29 Mountjoy Fort, 1602–03 (NLI, MS 2656, vii).

30 Lord Deputy Mountjoy to Sir George Carew, 2 July 1602 (*Calendar of the Carew Manuscripts, 1601–03*), pp 263–4.

31 Chichester to Cecil, 14 March 1602 (TNA, SP 63/210, f. 188).

32 Chichester to Cecil, 21 May 1600 (*CSPI, 1600*), pp 192–3.

33 For a discussion of the scorched earth policy and its effect, see James O'Neill, *The Nine Years War 1593–1603: O'Neill, Mountjoy and the Military Revolution* (Dublin, 2017), pp 175–8.

34 Moryson, *An Itinerary*, vol. iii, p. 208.

20 Excavations at Mountjoy Fort, Brocagh

Ruairí Ó Baoill

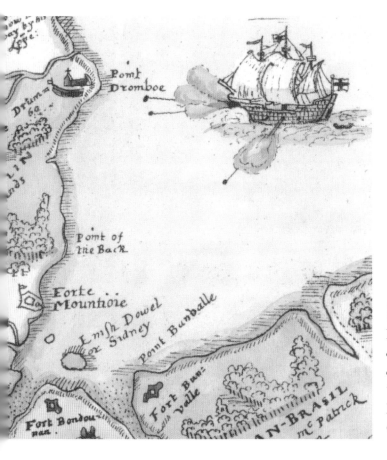

In June 2018 Archaeology and Palaeoecology, Queen's University Belfast, carried out its annual student training and community excavation at the site of the 'lost' late Elizabethan earthen fortification known as 'Mountjoy Fort' (NISMR TYR 047:020) at Brocagh, County Tyrone.

Historical background

The principal Gaelic lordship in western Ulster in the Late Medieval period was that of Tír nEóghain, controlled by the Ua Néill/O'Neills which encompassed what is now modern County Tyrone as well as parts of what are now counties Derry to the north and Armagh to the south (Loeber 2001; Simms 2000; 2020). In the fourteenth and fifteenth centuries, two branches of the O'Neill lords controlled the areas around Lough Neagh. The major branch of the family, based in Tyrone, controlled the western and south-eastern shores of the lough. A smaller branch, the Clan Áeda Buide (Clandeboy) O'Neills controlled the north-eastern and eastern shores from their castle at Edenduffcarrick (known later by the English as Castle

FIG. 20.1
Excerpt from Richard Bartlett's map of south-east Ulster, c. 1602, showing Mountjoy Fort.
CARDINAL TOMÁS Ó FIAICH MEMORIAL LIBRARY AND ARCHIVE

FIG. 20.2
Mountjoy Fort by Richard
Bartlett
(NLI, MS 2656/vii).

NATIONAL LIBRARY OF IRELAND

Mowbray and then Shane's Castle) near modern Randalstown in County Antrim (Greer 2019; Simms 2000, 2020).

With increasing Tudor interference in the affairs of Ulster, things came to a head in the 1590s. War broke out between the forces of Queen Elizabeth I and a confederacy of Irish lords led by Hugh O'Neill, second earl of Tyrone, in what historians call the Nine Years' War (1593–1603) (Morgan 1993; O'Neill 2017).

Although the Irish confederates won most of the engagements during the war, they lost the major battle that took place in late 1601 at Kinsale in County Cork, where the Irish and their Spanish allies were roundly defeated by the English, after which O'Neill was forced to retreat back to the safety of Tyrone. This left Elizabeth's Lord Deputy in Ireland, Charles Blount (Lord Mountjoy) able to move large numbers of English troops to different parts of the country safely again.

As part of his new strategy, Lord Mountjoy instructed Sir Arthur Chichester, the English governor of Carrickfergus, to launch amphibious attacks into O'Neill territory across Lough Neagh. The flotilla of ships for these attacks was to be based at Massereene (Antrim), on the north-eastern shore of the lough. Anticipating renewed attacks on O'Neill territory, O'Neill had a series of new earthen fortifications constructed, or old forts regarrisoned, around the north-western, western and south-eastern coast of Lough Neagh. The Irish forts included those at Toome, Ballinderry, Clonoe, Bundorlin, Bunvalle, Inishloughlin and possibly Coney Island. Useful work on locating these forts has been carried out by Kathy McCluney (McCluney 2005).

The construction of Mountjoy Fort

Despite planning for such an eventuality, O'Neill was not able to prevent the construction of English fortifications in Ulster. It was during this period that the English fort at Mountjoy, on the south-west shore of Lough Neagh, was built in the summer of 1602. The fortification must have been fairly substantial, as it was capable of holding at least 1,200 infantry and cavalry. Presumably these soldiers also helped construct the fort. Mountjoy Fort was used as a forward base for assembling troops for further operations into core O'Neill territory.

English cartographers drew up a series of campaign maps during the Nine Years' War. The maps produced are an invaluable aid to identifying archaeological monuments of the period, many of which no

FIG. 20.3
The ruins of Mountjoy Castle.

longer survive above ground. Important military maps include those produced by Richard Bartlett in 1601–02 (Andrews 2008). These maps illustrate both the series of Irish forts around Lough Neagh constructed in late 1601 and the also English ones erected in late 1601 and 1602, including Mountjoy Fort.

Richard Bartlett's map of Mountjoy Fort

The 1602 Bartlett map of Mountjoy Fort (Fig. 20.2) shows it to be a large, seven-sided earthwork fortification, consisting of four self-contained but inter-connected sections surrounded by ditches. These sections contain buildings for the garrison, including stables for the cavalry, and housing for 'loyal' Irish troops. The fort is built on a headland projecting into Lough Neagh and possibly over a small earlier O'Neill earthen fortification. Almost as soon as the fort was completed, the construction of a new high-status stone fortification (Mountjoy Castle) commenced adjacent to the earthen one. Smaller than the fort, the castle was completed by 1605 and was established on high ground looking downslope towards the fort and loughshore (Fig. 20.3).

Mountjoy Fort is portrayed on Nicholas Pynnar's map of Lough Neagh in 1624 and an estate map of 1682. After this period it disappears from history. Whether the fort was simply abandoned and allowed to erode or whether it was deliberately slighted to improve facilities at the shoreline for shipping connected with the slightly later Mountjoy Castle is unknown. Prior to the 2018 excavation taking place, there had been much interest in the site of the 'lost' fort at Mountjoy from local historians in County Tyrone (Fee and Mayes 2010, 2012; Walshe and Dilworth 2012). The 2018 excavation was the first opportunity to actually investigate what survived below the ground at Brocagh.

In April and May 2017, a substantial QUB geophysical survey under the leadership of Dr Siobhán McDermott was carried out in two fields that would appear to constitute much of the eastern portion of Mountjoy Fort (McDermott 2017). This survey suggested strongly that significant *in situ* remains of the fort survived below the surface of the field and it was within the southern of the two fields surveyed that the 2018 excavation took place.

The 2018 excavation

The 2018 excavation was a QUB archaeology student training and community excavation and was directed by Ruairí Ó Baoill of the Centre for Archaeological Fieldwork (now the Centre for Community Archaeology), QUB. It was hoped that the investigation would shed important new light on the types of fortifications being constructed by both Hugh O'Neill's Irish forces and the forces of Elizabeth I in what was the cockpit of the Nine Years' War, a monument type that before now has hardly been identified, let alone studied in depth by historians and archaeologists. It was also a community excavation and local volunteers and schoolchildren had an opportunity to do some excavation under

FIG. 20.4
Schoolchildren at the excavation at Mountjoy Fort.

the supervision of the QUB archaeologists. The investigation was carried out on behalf of the Lough Neagh Landscape Partnership, funded by the Heritage Lottery Fund. The excavation revealed four main phases of activity on site dating from the prehistoric to the Post-Medieval periods.

Evidence of prehistoric activity

Prehistoric finds included struck flint tools such as an incomplete Late Mesolithic Bann flake, a projectile head, and a planno-convex knife. These finds are a testament to the importance of the resources to be found in Lough Neagh to people living in this part of Tyrone from the time of the first colonists in Ireland onwards. The incomplete nature of many of the flint artefacts suggests that there may have been prehistoric settlements in the area during the Late Mesolithic and Neolithic periods.

Medieval finds

Finds relating to life in Late Medieval Tyrone included sherds of decorated Medieval Ulster Coarseware, a type of unglazed Irish pottery dating from the fourteenth-early seventeenth centuries. A fragment of German stoneware pottery was also recovered. This type of high-status pottery was being imported into the Gaelic Ulster during the Late Medieval period and sherds were found at Hugh O'Neill's castle at nearby Dungannon during the QUB/HED/*Time Team* excavation carried out there in 2007. It may date to the sixteenth or seventeenth centuries.

The early seventeenth-century Elizabethan fort

FIG. 20.5
The east-facing section of the seventeenth-century ditch.

The most important discovery of the 2018 excavation was one of the internal defensive ditches within the early seventeenth-century fort, along with its accompanying bank. Within the excavated trench the subsoil-cut ditch had a

recorded maximum width of 6 m wide and was 1.5 m deep. Many fragments of hand-made red brick from buildings that would have stood within the seventeenth-century fort were retrieved during the excavation. A small portion of the truncated wall of a red brick building within the fort was also uncovered during the excavation. It was roughly 0.5 m wide. Unfortunately, it was found right at the end of the excavation and it was not possible to excavate it after it had been recorded.

Military artefacts

A number of interesting military artefacts were found on the excavation, including lead pistol and caliver shot. Calivers were a type of light musket that were used by the English army from the early 1600s when Lord Mountjoy revamped the English army in Ireland at the end of the Nine Years' War. This is exactly the same date as Mountjoy Fort. A total of seven complete examples and several pieces of lead were recovered from the excavation. None of the complete examples had been fired.

Evidence of daily life

Two fragments of rotary quern for grinding corn to make bread were two found on the excavation, including one recovered from the fills of the early seventeenth-century ditch. Whether these were from a pre-existing settlement or brought by the English troops garrisoned at Mountjoy Fort is unknown. Finds associated with the Elizabethan fort included seventeenth-century pottery, animal bone, clay tobacco pipe stems, hand-made red brick and glass. Two particularly nice high-status finds were a fragment of an elaborate stem of a wine glass and a possible ceramic wig curler, both of which probably were the property of one of the officers in the fort.

The site in later centuries

Much Post-Medieval pottery, glass and metal work was recovered, dating from the eighteenth-twentieth centuries. These finds through light on the lives of the farming communities who worked the land at Brocagh after the fort went out of use. Pottery types included slipwares, refined earthenwares (pearlwares, creamwares, transfer-printed earthenware, tin-glazed earthenware and various whitewares), white salt-glazed stonewares and porcelain.

After the 2018 excavation was completed, all the excavated features were covered back over with soil and the field returned to pasture land to protect the sub-surface archaeological remains.

What does it all mean?

The large ditch that was uncovered during the excavation probably represents one of the ditches of the 'lost' Elizabethan fort at Mountjoy/Brocagh and the 2018 excavation proved successfully that there are significant *in situ* remains of

Mountjoy Fort surviving below the fields at Brocagh. It bears out the old archaeological maxim that just because you can't see it doesn't mean it isn't there! The discovery of the fort at Mountjoy is also another addition to the number of Ulster sites from the period of the Nine Years' War that have been archaeologically investigated, and the results published, by archaeologists from Queen's University Belfast. These include the O'Neill tower-house and Chichester's military fort at Castle Hill, Dungannon, excavated in 2007 with *Time Team*; Inisloughlin, County Antrim, excavated in 2008, and Ballycarry, County Antrim (possible site), excavated in 2008–09 (Donnelly et al. 2007, 2008; Macdonald 2012; Murray 2012). Another site at Dunnalong, County Tyrone, was excavated in 2012 and was published in 2013 by Derry City Council and the Foyle Civic Trust. There has also been work carried out by Dr James O'Neill and Dr Paul Logue at the site of the Battle of the Yellow Ford, County Armagh (O'Neill and Logue 2010, 2014).

Community involvement

There was great community interest in the excavation. Nearly 450 people visited the site while it was taking place, including members of the Ulster Archaeological Society. Pupils from the nearby St Brigid's School in Brocagh were able to participate in the excavation at the site under the direction of QUB archaeologists. The public open day, held on Saturday, 23 June 2018, was very successful and 350 people, including Belfast Young Archaeologists Club (YAC), visited the site and people got an opportunity to do a little excavation. The media coverage of the excavation included Joe Mahon (Westway Films); Stephen McAuley and Anne Marie McAleese (BBC Radio Ulster); Louise Cullen (BBC NI), and the *Dungannon Herald* newspaper.

Acknowledgements

Thanks are due to the Lough Neagh Landscape Partnership, especially Dr Liam Campbell and Chris McCarney; the Heritage Lottery Fund; Centre for Archaeological Fieldwork (now the Centre for Community Archaeology), Queen's University Belfast: Brian Sloan, Dr Cormac McSparron, Dr Colm Donnelly, Dr Siobhán McDermott, Marie-Therese Barrett, Georgia Vince, Naomi Carver, Megan Hughes, Charles Koubrek III and Adam Purvis; all of the QUB students who participated in the 2018 excavation; the pupils of St Brigid's School, Brocagh; all the volunteers who came on the open day to dig; Táilte and Cormac Óg McSparron; Adrian Fee, the landowner in whose field the excavation took place; Aidan Fee, Frank Mayes, James Walshe and William Dilworth, Stewartstown Historical Society; and Dr James O'Neill.

Bibliography

J.H. Andrews, *The Queen's Last Map-maker* (Dublin, 2008).

C.J. Donnelly, E. Murray and P. Logue, 'Excavating with the Time Team at Castle Hill, Dungannon, Co. Tyrone', *Archaeology Ireland*, 21:4 (Winter 2007), pp 16–19.

C.J. Donnelly, E. Murray and R. McHugh, 'Dungannon Castle: its history, architecture and archaeology', *Dúiche Néill*, 17 (2008), pp 11–24.

A. Fee and F. Mayes, 'Mountjoy Fort and Mountjoy Castle', *The Bell: Journal of the Stewartstown and District Local Historical Society*, 12 (2010), pp 18–32.

A. Fee and F. Mayes, 'Mountjoy Fort and Mountjoy Castle, County Tyrone', *UJA*, 3rd series, 71 (2012), pp 118–29.

R.H. Greer, *Con O'Neill: Last Gaelic Lord of Upper Clannaboy* (Belfast, 2019).

P. Macdonald, 'Archaeological excavation at Inisloughlin, County Antrim: identifying the Gaelic fort of "Enishlanghen"', *UJA*, 3rd series, 71 (2012), pp 88–117.

S. McDermott, 'Mountjoy Fort, Brockagh, Co. Tyrone', Centre for Archaeological Fieldwork Geophysical Survey Report No. 41 (2017): available online at http://www.qub.ac.uk/schools/CentreforArchaeologicalFieldworkCAF/PDFFileStore/Filetoupload,784960,en.pdf.

K. McCluney, 'The lost forts of Lough Neagh: an investigation into Gaelic artillery fortifications around Lough Neagh dating from the Nine Years' War, 1594–1603', unpublished MA thesis, Queen's University Belfast (2005).

H. Morgan, *Tyrone's Rebellion: the Outbreak of the Nine Years War in Ireland* (London, 1993).

E. Murray, 'Excavations within the scheduled enclosure at south-west Ballycarry, County Antrim, and the discovery of a Post-Medieval fort or fortified bawn', *UJA*, 3rd series, 17 (2012), pp 130–49.

J. O'Neill, *The Nine Years War, 1593–1603: O'Neill, Mountjoy and the Military Revolution* (Dublin, 2017).

J. O'Neill and P. Logue, 'The battle of the Ford of the Biscuits, 7 August 1594' in C. Foley and R. McHugh (eds), *An Archaeological Survey of County Fermanagh, Volume 1, Part 2: the Early Christian and Medieval Periods* (Belfast, (2014), pp 913–21.

J. O'Neill and P. Logue, 'Investigations at the site of the Battle of the Yellow Ford' in E. Murray and P. Logue (eds), *Battles, Boats and Bones: Archaeological Discoveries in Northern Ireland 1987–2008* (Belfast, 2010), pp 94–7.

K. Simms, 'Late Medieval Tír Eoghain: the kingdom of the 'Great O'Neill' in C. Dillon and H.A. Jefferies (eds), *Tyrone: History and Society* (Dublin, 2000), pp 127–62.

K. Simms, *Gaelic Ulster in the Middle Ages* (Dublin, 2020).

Various, *The Lost Settlement of Dunnalong* (Derry, 2013).

J. Walshe and W. Dilworth, *The Faire Field* (2012).

21 Tracing the past at Toome

Ruairí Ó Baoill

Historical background

Toome plays an important part in Ulster history. This is because of its strategic location on the eastern side of the junction of the Lower River Bann and Lough Neagh, at the north-west corner of the lough. For much of its history, it commanded the vital east-west crossing point between what are now modern counties Derry and Antrim. Settlement here was also well placed to exploit the abundant fish and other resources in the Bann and the lough, and this has attracted people to it from the time the first peoples colonised Ireland in the Mesolithic period onwards (Woodman 2015).

A number of crannogs are recorded as having been located on Toome Bar (NISMR ANT 042:011) and descriptions of impressive Bronze Age swords, spear heads, rapiers, spear butts and flint tools recovered from Toome Bar are detailed in Wood-Martin (1886, 169–71 and plate XXXVII). None of these crannogs are visible today. River crossings, especially one as important as the crossing at Toome, are traditionally the boundary markers of territories, places of battles and the location of prehistoric votive deposits. Whether the Bronze Age weapons recovered from Toome Bar belonged to the inhabitants of the

FIG. 21.1
Aerial view of Toome Bay.

crannogs or whether they were, in fact, votive offerings to a river god, perhaps to ensure a safe ferryboat journey across the Bann or on Lough Neagh is unknown.

In later periods, Toome was the route through which for centuries attack and counter-attack were carried out by various Gaelic lords and foreign adventurers in Ulster. It is mentioned in this regard in the entries for the years 1099, 1148, 1181, 1197, 1199 and 1200 in the Annals of the Four Masters. Whoever controlled the pass at Toome could also avail of the lucrative fishing and ferry rights there. The first substantial bridge construction spanning the Bann at Toome was only constructed in 1785.

In the thirteenth century, at the same time as the Anglo-Norman earldom of Ulster was being established, the land around Toome came in to the hands of the Ó Floinn kings of Uí Thuirtri in south-east Derry and south Antrim. To protect their kingdom, sometimes they allied themselves with other Gaelic lords, at other times with the Anglo-Normans (McNeill 1977, 81–2). They controlled this area until the mid-fourteenth century when they were supplanted by the new power in east Ulster, the Clandeboy (Clan Áeda Buide) O'Neills (McNeill 1980; Greer 2019; Simms 2020).

Medieval settlement at Toome

The story of the Medieval settlement at Toome is little understood, but tantalising evidence of this period was discovered during an excavation carried out in 1991 (Ó Baoill 1999). It took place when contractors working for the Department of Agriculture uncovered the remains of a substantial wall along the eastern side of the Toome Canal. It was suspected that the masonry might be the remains of the Elizabethan castle at Toome (NISMR ANT 042:012), built in the sixteenth century, and a rescue excavation took place at the site in autumn 1991. The work was carried out on behalf of the Environment Service: DOENI (now the Historic Environment Division, Department for Communities), under the direction of Ruairí Ó Baoill.

Evidence of Medieval occupation at the site that predated the Elizabethan castle was discovered in three locations across the excavation site. The first was a large pit (1.9 m long by 0.8 m wide and 0.7 m deep) cut into the subsoil and containing at least 17 irregularly spaced stones. It may have been a large hearth. The feature was discovered underneath the strata relating to the Elizabethan castle. Out of some of the fills of the hearth were recovered sherds of Anglo-Norman Saintonge Green Glazed pottery from a wine jug and found in association with sherds of Irish, locally produced, unglazed Cooking Ware (Everted Rim Ware) vessels, dating to the thirteenth/fourteenth century (Gahan 1999, 102–04).

Just beyond the north-east flanker, and so outside the limits of the sixteenth-century castle, a second and smaller hearth was uncovered. This was sub-circular in shape, roughly 0.8 m in diameter, and was composed of an arrangement of flat stones. From the rake-out of hearth material found close to the hearth, sherds of unglazed Cooking Ware (Everted Rim Ware) vessels, probably also dating to the thirteenth-fourteenth century, were also recovered along with animal bone. Finally, a sherd of unglazed Cooking Ware (Everted Rim Ware) and a sherd of glazed locally-produced Medieval pottery were discovered in and under a mortar surface revealed 6 m east of the Elizabethan castle and possibly related to an earlier building (a Medieval castle?).

So it would appear that there was substantial occupation on the site in the centuries before the Elizabethan castle was constructed. The Everted Rim Ware pottery, a native Irish ceramic type, suggests a Gaelic Irish settlement here. Although tempting to think that the remains of the Saintonge wine jug found in the very large hearth is evidence that there was an Anglo-Norman settlement here as well, they were found in association with sherds of Everted Rim Ware pottery. It may be that the jug was something bought or traded for in one of the centres of the Anglo-Norman earldom, such as Carrickfergus or Antrim, and brought back to Toome. Hence it might actually be evidence of trade and peaceful interaction between the Irish at Toome and the Anglo-Norman earldom, something that we rarely see mentioned in the historical sources of the time.

What size the Medieval settlement at Toome was, and how far back towards the modern village it stretched, is as yet unknown. However, the fact that significant Medieval remains would appear to still survive below the ground means that archaeologists might uncover more of the early history of Toome in the future.

The history of Toome Castle

Toome is mentioned as one of a string of forts to be erected by the English along the Bann in an entry, dated 6 July 1567, in the Calendar of the State Papers relating to Ireland (*CSPI, 1509–73*, 340). Interestingly, Toome is actually described in the entry as Castle Toome. By the end of the sixteenth century it appears to have fallen into disrepair and had to be refortified by Sir Arthur Chichester in July 1602 (*CSPI, 1601–03*, 334) towards the end of the Nine Years' War. The castle last saw action in the Williamite War and afterwards was allowed to fall again into disrepair. It was finally demolished in 1783 to help in the building of a bridge over the River Bann. Fragments of masonry from Toome Castle were still visible as late as 1835.

The building of the Toome Canal in the mid nineteenth century may have caused much damage to what remains were left, though no mention is made of the castle in contemporary journals or archive material relating to this work. By the twentieth century, no above ground remains of the castle were visible until their rediscovery by chance in 1991. There was another 'old fort of Toome' shown on the Derry side of the River Bann on a Thomas Raven map of 1622

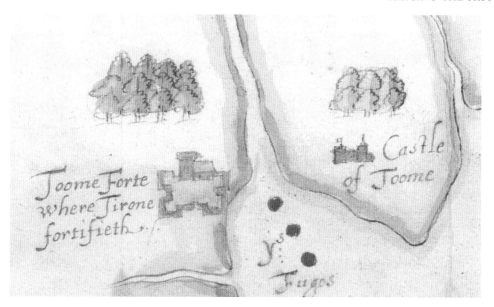

which also portrays 'The Castell of Toome', the one excavated in 1991 (Fig. 21.4). This may have been an O'Neill fortification constructed during the Nine Years' War. The monument is no longer visible.

FIG. 21.3

Detail from a map of Lough Neagh, *c.* 1601, showing the castle and fort at Toome (NLI, MS 2656/xix).

NATIONAL LIBRARY OF IRELAND

The excavated remains of Toome Castle

An 11 m stretch of wall from the Elizabethan castle was uncovered, surviving to a maximum height of nearly 4 m. Of this 11 m, a 6.2 m long section of masonry constituted the remains of a curtain wall (a wall connecting two towers which, when repeated around the sides of a castle, creates a strong defensive circuit), which was 2 m wide. A 4.8 m long section of masonry was the remains of a flanker (a small projecting tower at the corner of a castle wall that allows lines of fire along the outside faces of the castle walls to increase the defensive capabilities of the garrison). The external face of the wall was battered, the internal face was vertical and it sat on an offset plinth that projected out approximately 0.1 m, founded on subsoil. Excavation showed the masonry

FIG. 21.4

Detail (looking south) from Thomas Raven's map of the Vintners' Company estate showing the castle and fort at Toome, 1622 (PRONI, T510/1/31).

PUBLIC RECORD OFFICE OF NORTHERN IRELAND AND LAMBETH PALACE LIBRARY fragments to be the remains of the east curtain wall of the castle and its north-eastern flanker.

The wall was constructed of random coursed, uncut stones. It had a mortared rubble core, the mortar having been roughly poured amongst the stones rather than them being individually bonded together. This was perhaps evidence of the urgency with which the castle was built with the result that lumps of mortar were found adhering to the face of the wall at various points. The line of the curtain wall was robbed out to the south. The stratigraphy here was very disturbed, and close to where the wall ran out a later eighteenth- or nineteenth-century robber trench was visible.

A bank of earth approximately 5 m long, 2 m wide and 2.5 m deep was all that remained of archaeological deposits within the castle. Limited excavation was carried out around the base and top of this bank, and the north-facing section was drawn. But the bank of material was left unexcavated for future archaeologists to investigate. However, it was still possible to recover many details about the castle including the construction levels and internal floor surfaces of both cobbles and large mortared stones.

FIG. 21.5
Plan of the excavated area.

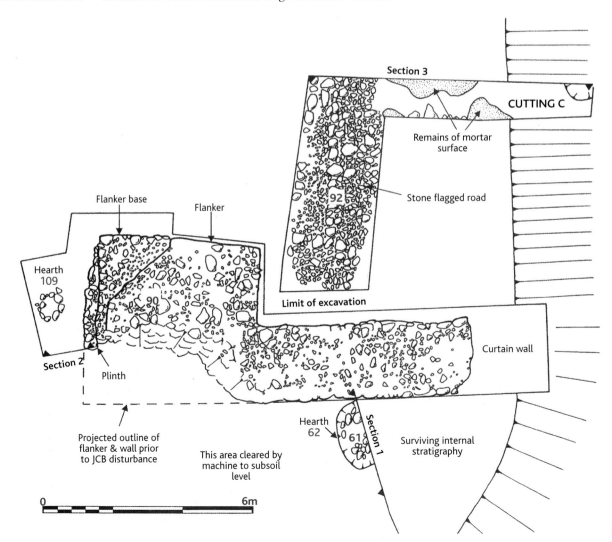

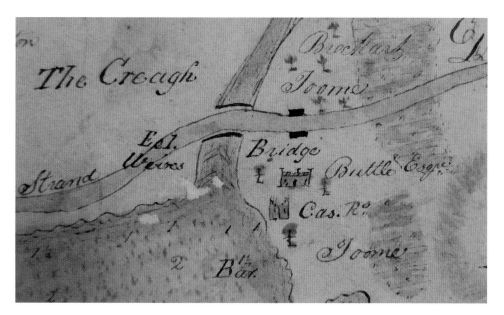

East of the surviving castle flanker and curtain wall, a surface of unmortared stones, 2.5 m wide was uncovered. The feature was located 0.3 m below modern topsoil and was excavated for a distance of 6 m east of the castle where it continued beyond the limit of excavation in the direction of Toome village. The surface is almost certainly a roadway leading up to the castle and is contemporary with it. Artefacts discovered amongst its stones dated the roadway to the seventeenth century. After the 1991 excavation was completed, all the archaeological features were covered over with soil to protect them for possible future investigation.

Although there is still much to discover about the history and development of Toome, future archaeological investigations will undoubtedly shed more light on the long story of the people who have lived in this most important and interesting of places on the shores of Lough Neagh.

Fig. 21.6

Detail showing the ruins of Toome Castle from a map of Lough Neagh, 1785 (PRONI, D604/1).

PUBLIC RECORD OFFICE OF NORTHERN IRELAND

For all the Corrs (past and present)
from Toome and the surrounding area.

Bibliography

A. Gahan, 'The pottery' in R. Ó Baoill, 'Excavations at the site of Toome Castle, Co. Antrim', *UJA*, 3rd series, 58 (1999), pp 102–04.

R.H. Greer, *Con O'Neill: Last Gaelic Lord of Upper Clannaboy* (Belfast, 2019).

T.E. McNeill, *Anglo-Norman Ulster* (Edinburgh, 1980).

T.E. McNeill, 'Excavations at Doonbought Fort, County Antrim', *UJA*, 3rd series, 40 (1977), pp 63–84.

R. Ó Baoill, 'Excavations at the site of Toome Castle, Co. Antrim', *UJA*, 3rd series, 58 (1999), pp 90–108.

J. O'Laverty, *An Historical Account of the Diocese of Down and Connor Ancient and Modern* (5 vols, Dublin, 1878–95).

K. Simms, *Gaelic Ulster in the Middle Ages* (Dublin, 2020).

W.G. Wood-Martin, *The Lake Dwellings of Ireland* (Dublin and London, 1886).

P.C. Woodman, *Ireland's First Settlers: Time and the Mesolithic* (Oxford, 2015).

22 Lough Beg and Church Island
a deep landscape

Liam Campbell

Church Island has been immortalised in Seamus Heaney's poem,
The Stand at Lough Beg

> ... *The lowland clays and waters of lough Beg,*
> *Church Island's spire, its soft treeline of yew ...*

OPPOSITE
FIG. 22.1
View of Church Island with marsh
marigold (*Caltha palustris*) in the
foreground.

FIG. 22.2
Detail (looking south) from
Thomas Raven's map of the
Vintners' Company estate
showing Lough Beg, 1622
(PRONI, T510/1/31).
PUBLIC RECORD OFFICE OF NORTHERN
IRELAND AND LAMBETH PALACE LIBRARY

This natural, built and cultural heritage library of riches exudes deep calm and contemplation that possibly only the poet can capture. Formerly known as *Inish Toide*, it is most likely the site of a pre-Viking monastery (Toner 1996, 65, 76–77). Church Island is positioned in Lough Beg, in what is essentially a widening of the Lower River Bann, one mile north of Toome. Called the 'little lake' by way of contrast with its much greater neighbour, Lough Neagh, its famous Church Island has an eighteenth-century spire, a ruined Medieval church of the parish of Ballyscullion and an old graveyard.

In a sense, though, when we now use the term island, it is more of a seasonal island due to the historical lowerings of Lough Neagh and dredging of the Bann over the last 200 years or so. It consists of seven acres of land much of which is wooded. The dredging of the River Bann in the 1930s and 1940s created a marshy wetland between the island and the west or County Derry side of Lough Beg. This low-lying wetland can be crossed by foot except when a swollen River Bann floods the marsh and water completely surrounds the island. Though, like Heaney implies, it is best viewed from the land.

It has been said that the ruins of the church date back to the time of St Patrick who used the River Bann to navigate to the island to meet with Taoide and found a Christian settlement. On the island is a stone known as the Bullaun Stone featuring a hole that holds water. A 'rag tree' is nearby. These are normally found near wells of other sources of water like this. Usually, the rags are placed there by people who believe that if a piece of clothing from someone who is ill, or has a problem of any kind, is hung from the tree the problem or illness will disappear as the rag rots away. Sometimes the rag represents a wish or aspiration which will come to pass as the rag rots.

The nearby Cranfield church site also has an impressive rag tree. The Bullaun Stone on Church Island is most likely associated with the first monastic settlement, though local tradition has it that the hole in the stone was made by St Patrick as he knelt to pray. It has been a focal point of pilgrimage and burial ever since and some continued to bury their dead there until the middle of the last century. The name of the parish of Ballyscullion is first recorded in 1397, when *Bally Oskullyn* was valued at 13 shillings and four pence in Archbishop Colton's Visitation (Reeves 1850, 76). The (O')Scullions were the Medieval erenaghs, or lay custodians of the church lands of the parish, and indeed the local community carry on this tradition in the care of this site. Interestingly, of the 22 townlands which make up the parish, 21 (including the townland of Ballyscullion West) lie west of Lough Beg in County Derry, while one townland (Ballyscullion East) lies east of Lough Beg in County Antrim.

What is reasonably certain, is that a man called Thaddeus came to the island where he founded a church and monastic settlement; the traditional name for both the island and the church is *Inish Taoide*, *Toide* being Irish for Thaddeus (Thaddeus is said to be buried against the inner wall of the church). Since the Vikings sailed up the Bann on their raids of Irish settlements, it is unlikely that *Inish Taoide* escaped their predations. However, it survived and is mentioned in the Annals of Inisfallen in 1112 and in the Annals of Ulster in 1129. In later years the monks were of the Dominican religious order. Traces of herbs and rare mints grown by the monks for cures are still found there today. The church on the island acted as the parish church until the early seventeenth century. In 1622 it was noted that 'the old church of Inistode or Ballineskullen, standing on an island invironed on every side with water, is ruinous.'

In the year 1642 the church was taken over by the military and a regiment of soldiers was billeted there. A contemporary poem highlights the state of the church and the turbulence of the period and attitudes of the military to the native inhabitants. The author was Payne Fisher and the poem, from which the following extracts are taken, is called 'Newes from Lough-Bagge, alias the Church Island, upon ye first discovery and fortifying of it' (Pinkerton 1860, 164–7).

> At last about Bellahy, a mile
> Or more, wee spye'd a little Ile:
> More by chance sure 'twas, then by
> Our cunning in Cosmography.
> This little Ile well view'd and scand
> To vs appeard some new-found-land
> And glad wee were since twas our happ
> To finde what was not in the Mappe.
> Arriueing heere wee could not lesse

Then think wee weare in a Wildernesse:
Soe dismall 'twas, wee durst engage
Our liues t'had beene some Hermitage,
And much it did perplexe or witts
To thinke wee should turne Anchorits.
 In this sad Desart all alone
Stands an old Church quite ouergrowne
With age, and Iuie; of little vse,
Vnlesse it were for some Recluse.
 To this sad Church my men I led
And lodge'd the liueing mong ye Dead
…
Wee haue put the Kirke in good Repayre.
 Without we keepe a Guard; within
The Chancell's made or Magazine,
Soe that our Church thus arm'd may vaunt
Shee's truly now made Militant.
With workes wee haue inuiron'd round
And turn'd or Churchyard to a Pound:
Forts gaurd vs on all sides; soe that
Thoe wee donte supererogat
Or stand precisely on Popish quirks
Yet heere wee are saned by our works
…
Yet 'tis secure'd by a counter scarfe.
As for the Rebells they keepe off
And seldome come within ye loughe;
Yet now and then wee at distance see
A Reasne stalking Cap-a-Pe.
About Bellahy lurke a crew
Of Canniballs that lie perdue:
These seldome range but closely keepe
Themselues like woolues yt watch for sheepe

FIG. 22.3
View of Church Island with ragged robin (*Silene flos-cuculi*) in the foreground.

Despite its ruined state, the church continued to play a role in the religious life of the local community. Mass is often celebrated within the roofless walls of the ancient church and burials continued there until the 1930s. During the 1798 Rebellion, many women and children were forced to take shelter on the island. The feast day of St Thaddeus falls on 7 September and an annual pilgrimage to the island in honour of the saint still takes place on the first Sunday in September. Under that date the Martyrology of Donegal (compiled in 1603 from earlier sources) includes a reference to *Toit, Insi Toite* for *Loch Bec, I nUbih Tuitre* (O'Donovan 1864, 238).

The walls of the roofless Medieval church still stand. The building is oriented east-west and measures 52 feet by 21 feet with a door on the south side and windows at both ends and at the sides. The walls, built from local stone, are about three feet thick. The church lies in the middle of a graveyard with about 50 known graves and a number of gravestones on both the north and south sides of the church. The graves include that of Michael Keenan, the builder of the steeple.

In the late 1700s the eccentric Anglican bishop of Derry, Frederick Hervey (who was also the fourth earl of Bristol), constructed a mansion in Ballyscullion on the County Derry side of Lough Beg. To improve his view of Church Island and Lough Beg, in 1788 he commissioned builder Michael Keenan to add a spire to the church ruins. This spire, known locally as Hervey's Folly, still stands and has become an iconic part of the Lough Beg landscape. Like Heaney, Hervey too was interested in the view of Church Island from afar. During World War II an

FIG. 22.4
Church Island headstones.

American aircraft based at the nearby Creagh airbase put a pronounced kink in the steeple when it hit it with its wing tip, though this is disputed by some.

The 'Strand' on the west shore of Lough Beg is a large expanse of wet grassland that is flooded each winter and which has never been agriculturally improved.

> *… Across that strand of yours the cattle graze*
> *Up to their bellies in an early mist …*
>
> SEAMUS HEANEY, *The Strand at Lough Beg*

Lough Beg and its associated aquatic vegetation form part of the internationally important site. The open water and surrounding wetland habitats around the loughs have a range of designations (Ramsar, SPA, ASSI, ASI, NNR), both jointly and separately, indicating their importance to the region's environment and biodiversity. This nature reserve, with Church Island as its focal point, comprises 300 acres of this habitat. In spring and autumn, migrating birds on their way through may pause on their journey to rest and feed. Black-tailed Godwit, Green Sandpiper, Wood Sandpiper, Greenshank and Knot are seen every year. In early summer, the sky above the nature reserve is alive with the calls of breeding waders. It is possible to hear the drumming of snipe, the piping whistles of redshank and the peewit calls of lapwing, all of which depend on this soft, wet ground to rear their families. Many rare plants including pennyroyal and the Irish lady's-tresses orchid share this habitat with the birds. Winter brings floods and with them hundreds of wildfowl to feed on the inundated grasslands.

The area is also of special scientific interest because of its deposits of diatomite and associated materials. The diatomite (also known as Kieselguhr or Bann Clay) deposits in this area were one of the most extensive freshwater diatomite sequences of post-glacial age in the world (see Chapter 3 of this book). The coming together of the natural, built and cultural aspects of heritage has never been stronger than in this area and the view from Ballyscullion or the Strand, as seen by St Patrick, Bishop Hervey and Seamus Heaney still enchants like no other.

FIG. 22.5
Church Island tower.

Fig. 22.7
Lough Beg from a map of
Lough Neagh, 1785
(PRONI, D604/1).
PUBLIC RECORD OFFICE OF
NORTHERN IRELAND

Bibliography

Seamus Heaney, *New Selected Poems 1966–1987* (London, 1990).

Martyrology of Donegal: a Calendar of the Saints of Ireland, trans. John
O'Donovan, ed. James H. Todd and William Reeves (Dublin, 1864).

William Pinkerton, 'Unpublished poems relating to Ulster in 1642–43',
UJA, 1st series, 8 (1860), pp 153–71.

*Acts of Archbishop Colton in his Metropolitan Visitation to the Diocese
of Derry, AD 1397*, ed. William Reeves (Dublin, 1850).

Gregory Toner, *Places-names of Northern Ireland, Volume Five.
County Derry I: the Moyola Valley* (Belfast, 1996).

The Maine Sea

The Cuntie of Antrim

Part of Lough N

Part of the Countie of Tyrone.

23 Salterstown

William Roulston

In the early seventeenth century the Salters' Company was one of the
12 major London livery companies to receive a substantial estate as part
of the Londonderry Plantation.

The company initially developed two settlements, one at Magherafelt and the
other on the shores of Lough Neagh in the townland of Ballymultrea. The latter
was named for the company and by 1622 included more than a dozen mainly
timber-framed houses laid out on either side of a wide street. The 'castle' was
positioned at one end of the village of Salterstown and comprised a rectangular
bawn with two circular flankers at opposite corners; a small house occupied one
of the remaining corners. An early attempt to establish a glassworks here proved
unsuccessful, though an ironworks was more durable. At this time Salterstown

FIG. 23.1

'A generall plat of the
lands belonging to the
Cittie of London as they
are devided and let out to
the 12 Companies',
Thomas Raven, 1622
(PRONI, T510/1/5).

PUBLIC RECORD OFFICE OF
NORTHERN IRELAND AND
LAMBETH PALACE LIBRARY

was a more substantial place than Magherafelt, but in the decades that followed the former faded into obscurity, while Magherafelt became the most important town in this part of South Derry.

The village and castle were burned as a result of the events following the 1641 uprising, but Salterstown recovered to some degree in the second half of the seventeenth century. Archaeological excavations undertaken in the late 1980s revealed numerous artefacts providing evidence for the continued existence of a settlement after 1641. Furthermore, the original house within the bawn was rebuilt on a grander scale; the ruins of the Salters' castle that we see today represent this reconstruction. However, the castle and village were again burned during the Williamite war of 1688–91.

In 1725 a Londoner named Isaac Pyke visited the Salters' estate and left an interesting account of what he found by the loughshore. He wrote that the settlement was 'in a pleasant situation', but had now fragmented into three small clusters: Salterstown, which contained only 12 'very small mean cottages'; Mill Town, where there was a corn mill and a few poor houses; and Forge Town, which was the location of an iron foundry and a small number of cottages. Pyke described the Salters' castle as a 'very fine mansion house' and noted that it had been the summer residence of the company's chief tenant. He also observed that there were 200 tons of timber at the site in preparation for rebuilding the castle. However, there is no evidence that this work was ever undertaken. In a survey of the estate in 1845 it was observed, 'The castle ruin has more the aspect of an ecclesiastical building.' The remains of the castle adjoin a farmyard on private land, but are easily viewable from the side of Salterstown Road.

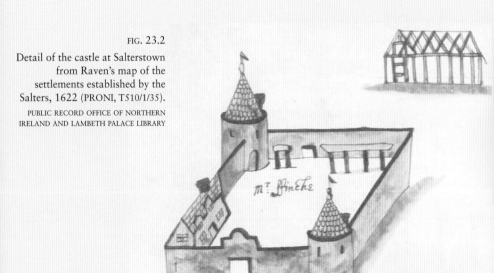

FIG. 23.2

Detail of the castle at Salterstown from Raven's map of the settlements established by the Salters, 1622 (PRONI, T510/1/35).

PUBLIC RECORD OFFICE OF NORTHERN IRELAND AND LAMBETH PALACE LIBRARY

Bibliography

The Irish estate papers of the Salters' Company of London are in the Public Record
Office of Northern Ireland (D4108).
Notes Relating to the Manor of Sal Explanatory of the Terrier of 1845 (London,
1846).
James Stevens Curl, *The Londonderry Plantation* (Chichester, 1986).
Audrey Horning, *Ireland in the Virginian Sea* (Chapel Hill, NC, 2013).

FIG. 23.3
Ruins of the castle
at Salterstown.

24 Mills on the western shore

Sebastian Graham

The many rivers and streams around Lough Neagh provide the essential basis for the development of waterpower. Mills can also be powered by other variables such as wind, animal power or indeed human power. Ever wonder where the term treadmill came from! How and when did mills start appearing around Lough Neagh? The answer, like most things in history, is obscure.

Early utilisation of waterpower occurred throughout Ireland. In fact, Ulster boasts Europe's earliest dated tide mill located at Nendrum, County Down, dated to AD 619 using dendrochronology. Many early mills were located near monastic settlements. In the townland of Ballinderry, just east of Tobermore, a possible eighth-century horizontal mill was discovered during drainage work.[1] These primitive sites, sometimes called Danish or Norse mills, utilised streams to power horizontal paddles, thus providing power to a set of millstones. It is possible, therefore, that in the fields across Northern Ireland there are the remains of hundreds of horizontal mills. Sadly, there are relatively few clues as to where these sites could be. Townland names sometimes hold answers (or raise more questions) in regard to mills. For example, the townland of Mawillian (*Maigh Mhuilinn*), south-east of Moneymore, translates as 'plain of the mill'. In this townland there are the remains of a flax mill from the mid-1800s, but no positive historical data before this. Archaeology and these chance discoveries are the best way to understand our early history.

Manual milling of grain took the form of quern stones. They were small circular or saddle-shaped stones that could grind down the grain. The advantage of querns is that they could be used on the move. Armies brought querns with them to sustain them through campaigns. When he landed in Ireland in 1171, Henry II brought 'canvas to cover the corn and hand mills to grind it'.[2] Of local interest, excavations at Brocagh in 2018 uncovered part of a rotary quern dating to the Medieval period (see Chapter 20 of this book). Querns, however, were cumbersome and required hard labour for little reward.

The answer to the tedious nature of milling by quern stone was the water-powered mill. Mills were an essential ingredient in establishing a settled society, providing sustenance, employment and security. As well as that, they were a source of authority, being the property of the overlord. It is difficult to know exactly how many mills existed around Lough Neagh during the Medieval period. The Anglo-Norman incursions into east Ulster resulted in mill building; among others, mills at Carrickfergus, Ballyeaston and Dundonald are mentioned in 1333.[3] As the western shores of Lough Neagh were not settled by the Anglo-Normans very few records exist which refer to mills. It is also difficult to know the extent to which Gaelic society actively utilised mills. It is likely that the hand quern was used predominantly.

It was during the Plantation of Ulster that mills started to be built on a more widespread scale than before. Mills were promoted by the English and Scottish grantees of plantation land and we find sites such as Bellaghy, Moneymore and Salterstown utilising waterpower. While most of these plantation sites were corn mills, several sawmills also existed. Pynnar, in his survey of 1619, referred to a 'sawing mill for timber' in Salterstown[4] and another was mentioned on the Mercers' lands at Movanagher. Waterpower was also utilised in the production of iron on the western shore of Lough Neagh. The Civil Survey of 1654–5 noted: 'Observable the ruins of a blloomery Iron worke in the possession of Mr Avery in Anno 1640.'[5] This site is in the townland of Ballymultrea, very close to the settlement of Salterstown. There are remains of the structure, but they are overgrown and show little sign of industrial activity. Locals refer to this site as a spade mill so it may well have been used for that purpose in the 1700s. It is

FIG. 24.1

Remains of structure in Ballymultrea on site marked 'Old Furnace' on Ordnance Survey map.

also noteworthy that on the first edition of the Ordnance Survey map (1832–46) the bridge adjacent to the site is called 'Furnace bridge'.

The ironworks at Lissan also date to the early 1600s and were operated by waterpower. The site was requisitioned by Irish forces in 1641 and local tradition maintains that the iron chain or boom across the River Foyle during the siege of Derry was cast at Lissan.[6] The unsustainable practices carried out by these ironworks, sawmills and tanners resulted in a major reduction in the size of the great forest of Glenconkeyne. A letter to the Governors of Derry and Magherafelt in 1658 references the destruction of timber in Londonderry and Tyrone by the ironworks near the River Bann belonging to a Mr Ellison:

> There hath especially of late, been a very great destruction made in the counties of Tyrone and Londonderry and other places thereabouts both of small and great timber upon bishops' and other lands in dispose of his Highness and the Commonwealth ...[7]

It is also recorded that Mr Rainey in Magherafelt moved his ironworks to different sites close to the raw materials he needed to keep the furnaces going.[8] The sites of some ironworks were located beside rivers or streams, with water-powered bellows blowing air into the fire to increase the temperature of the furnace. By the mid-1700s the ironworks and sawmills had mostly exhausted themselves and the skills and heritage associated with them gone.

Most corn mills were built at the behest of the local landowner. The corn mill in Moneymore is well documented. It was built in 1615 by the Drapers

FIG. 24.2
Millstones in Ballynenagh Mill, built 1860–70 by Hutchinson family; later known as Flack's Mill.

FIG. 24.3
Gearing at Ballygurk
Mill; this site dates
back to 1724.

Company, the miller being William Bignell. The millstones were sourced locally and the building was roofed with shingles.[9] The mill was burned in 1641 and again in 1689. The mill was described as a 'double mill', due to the presence of two waterwheels, which powered two separate parts of the corn milling process. The grain needed to be cracked open first using the shelling or shillin stones. The name Shelling Hill or Shillin Hill refers to the fact that after the grain was shelled it was brought up to a high point and wind would separate the chaff from the grain. The grain was then brought to the grinding stones.

To cement control over an area, legal documents were created to ensure that farmers and tenants had no choice but to visit their local mill. Inhabitants or clients of these 'bound' townlands had to pay service to the mill or else face exorbitant fines for having their grain milled elsewhere. Mulcture refers to the toll to which the miller was entitled. In most cases this was based on the amount of grain brought to the mill. The corn mill in the townland of Killyfad, in Drummaul parish, was called the 'Staffordstown mill' and a deed of 1791 stipulated that 'Charles Hamilton has rights to the accustomed 25th toll and mulcture of the eleven townlands of Staffordstown.'[10] On similar lines the

> two water corn mills of Salterstown and Ballygurk ... [were] to enjoy the
> grist, toll, succor and mulcture of the townlands of Ballymultrea,
> Ballydonnell, Ballygurk, Ballyronan more and beg, Belagherty, Ballylifford,

Ballygillen more and beg, Ballyrogully, Ballyeglish, Ballymulligan, Ballyriff, Ballynenagh, Ballymulderg, Druminard and Mawillian.[11]

The Staffordstown deed noted that the owner had rights to the 25th toll, i.e. one in every 25 grains. Other examples refer to one in every 18 grains. Grain was weighed before and after milling and then a portion was allowed to the miller. The miller in turn paid rent to the lord of the manor. This system had started to disintegrate by the 1800s as newer independent mills established themselves without the onerous feudal exactions.

When the grain was brought to the mill it had to be dried sufficiently to go through the millstones. Many corn mills had kilns attached or nearby. A kiln man worked on the top floor on top of tiles or a perforated metal sheet while a fire was lit from below. The fuel could vary from turf, husks from the grain or possibly even coal in some places. The kiln men worked amongst the heat turning the grain often to avoid it being burned. The heat of such a place made it a landmark for locals. The Salterstown corn mill had a kiln and it was noted for being the place where *cèilidhs* took place.[12] This was especially common in rural areas.

FIG. 24.4
The windmill stump at Mullaghwotragh.

The source of power was not always water. Wind was also harnessed, though only a handful of sites exist to the west of Lough Neagh. One possible site is at Springhill, Moneymore. The tower was constructed in 1731 and clues to its former past exist in a map in which it is listed as a corn mill.[13] It has been argued that it was a folly feature added to enhance the landscape. Not far from Springhill, in the townland of Mullaghwotragh, near Coagh, is a windmill stump. The building dates to the late 1700s and worked until the early 1800s. After its functional use the name stayed, being the Windmill farm, and even a local GAA football club was named after it. Locals refer to this landmark as the 'winemill', which may cause confusion to outside industrial archaeologists. It would be interesting to know who the builder of this mill was and why this site was chosen. Is it possible that the Springhill and Mullaghwotragh sites were connected?

By the mid-1800s rural corn mills faced ever increasing competition from modern mills based in ports, compounded by the fact that communications and infrastructure negatively affected these sites. In addition, rural mills found it difficult to grind imported Indian maize due to the toughness of the grain. The saviour at this time was flax. Many corn mills were fitted out with flax scutching machinery. By 1869 a total of 1,411 scutching mills were servicing over 300,000 acres of flax in Ulster.[14]

Conditions in the scutching mills were poor. The air was thick with dust, hours were long and the machinery was very dangerous. The flax had to be brought to the rollers or breaker first. The long stalks went through one end of the fluted rollers and out the other. The scutchers stood in a stand or berth and held the flax beside the upright board. There was a small gap where the flax was inserted so that the scutching handles or arms could hit the flax and beat off the wooden core. The scutcher then grabbed more flax stricks and inserted the flax, repeating the process until a handful of fibre was created. This was then twisted and set above the worker in a box and later weighed at the end of the day. Scutchers often worked in pairs, one being a buffer and the other a cleaner or finisher. The buffer took the raw broken flax and gave it a quick beat in the handles before passing it to the cleaner who finished it off.

FIG. 24.5
Scutching mill handles near Magherafelt.

Scutchers were relatively well paid (compared with other agricultural work) during the 1900s. They were free to move from mill to mill in search of better pay and conditions. Some mills had good reputations, while others did not, and some had strict rules designed to increase production and efficiency. The scutching mill in Ballyronan had a number of rules, one of which was:

> Rule X. That any scutcher or other worker that causes any disturbance or interferes unnecessarily with the other workers, or is guilty of swearing, or scandalous talking, shall be liable to a fine of 1 shilling for each offence, or instant dismissal if persisted in, and forfeiture of any wages or bounty that may be due.[15]

Occasionally farmers would bribe scutchers with whiskey to have their flax scutched first and made ready for the market. The two main markets in the area were King Street, Magherafelt, and Union Street, Cookstown. The flax acreage declined considerably from the 1870s onwards. In 1911 just over 111,000 acres of flax were grown, but by 1939 this had fallen to only 20,000 acres. The western side of Lough Neagh retained a strong flax-growing tradition. Some mills were modernised with the scutching carried out by efficient turbine scutchers. The site above Kingsmill, near Coagh, was the location of one of the turbine mills and Hardy's mill in Ardagh also operated under an automatic scutching machine.[16]

FIG. 24.6
Salterstown: rudimentary datestone on flax mill boiler house dated 1916. It was built by a man named O'Neill.

There is still much to discover regarding the milling history of this district. Local place-names provide clues these industries. In Coagh a land deed of 1750 refers to 'Bark Mill Bog'. Bark mills ground bark or roots of trees to extract tannin used in the tanning industry. Mills need not be water-powered or wind-powered. Some sites were powered by animals such as threshing mills. Horses walked around in a circular horse walk which were connected to a series of shafting and gears to the threshing

FIG. 24.7

Flax mill chimney at Salterstown, built to make use of steam power to increase the productivity of the mill.

machinery. The location of these sites remains obscure as they were in most cases not worthy of recording on the Ordnance Survey maps. Some farms still retain the machinery.

The recent lockdown has led to an appreciation of our local landscapes. The next step is to question the buildings, industries and place-names to understand their history and processes. There is still much to discover regarding our early milling activities. Ballyronan, Salterstown, Coagh and Coalisland all have early industrial activities. The need to feed the inhabitants of these industrial sites expanded corn milling in the area, while the later demand for linen created a boom in flax production and manufacturing. Sadly, the relatively recent memories of our corn and flax scutching industries are fading. It is now more important than ever to ask around and record the memories of those who either worked in or can recall the numerous mills in this district.[17]

Notes

1 https://apps.communities-ni.gov.uk/NISMR-PUBLIC/Details.aspx?MonID=13012, LDY–041–038.

2 G.H. Orpen, *Ireland under the Normans, 1169–1333* (4 vols, Oxford, 1911–20), vol. 1, p. 95.

3 G.H. Orpen, 'The Earldom of Ulster', published in four parts in *JRSAI*, vols 43–5 (1913–15).

4 George Hill, *An Historical Account of the Plantation in Ulster* (Belfast, 1877), p. 588.

5 R.C. Simington (ed.), *The Civil Survey III* (Dublin, 1937), p. 283.

6 For Lissan House, see Hazel Dolling, *The Staples Inheritance* (Cookstown, 2000).

7 Robert Dunlop, *Ireland under the Commonwealth* (2 vols, Manchester, 1913), vol. 2, p. 679.

8 Eileen McCracken, 'Charcoal-burning ironworks in seventeenth and eighteenth century Ireland', UJA, 3rd series, 20 (1957), p. 132.

9 For more information, see James Stevens Curl, *The Honourable the Irish Society and the Plantation of Ulster, 1608–2000* (Chichester, 2000).

10 Registry of Deeds, Dublin, 22 May 1791, Walter Graham to Mulligan, memorial no. 317366.

11 Registry of Deeds, Dublin, 17 Nov. 1780, Samuel Strain to James Given, memorial no. 225671.

12 Interview with Sam McMaster, 25 Feb. 2020.

13 PRONI, T3793/3/321. Although dated to 1862, this is an annotated map with overwriting. Beech walk is mentioned leading to the 'Corn Mill'. The author of this overwriting is not known.

14 *Linen Trade Circular Review* (1870), available in Belfast Central Library.

15 *The Shores of Traad* (St Trea's GFC, 1985), p. 111, in reference to Gaussen's mill, Ballyronan.

16 *Ballinderry Faces and Places: a Photographic History* (2009), p. 147.

17 For more on mills in Northern Ireland, see the author's website: www.millsofnorthernireland.com.

FIG. 24.8

Brookend Mill, started as a corn mill and later utilised for flax scutching in 1855; known as McCormick's Mill.

25 'Lowerings'
engineering water and land around Lough Neagh

Liam Campbell

There is a great deal of civil engineering around the Bann and Lough Neagh. Indeed, the same is true of Lough Erne and Lough Foyle. Today, the shoreline of Lough Neagh is quite different from what originally existed before human intervention. It has a very dynamic and changed coast (though, as earlier essays in this volume indicate, Lough Neagh was very much larger in prehistoric times). Nowhere is this more evident in two places very much associated with the culture of the region, Rams Island and Brocagh/Mountjoy.

Rams Island, site of an early Irish monastery with its associated round tower, one mile off Sandy Bay Point, is the largest island in Lough Neagh. However, it originally measured only six acres and subsequent lowerings of the lough have increased it in size to *c*. 25 acres. In fact the Ordnance Survey map of 1833 shows two islands, the other called Duck Island which is now joined to Rams Island. Walking over the island it is easy to make out the old shoreline from 1833. The now heavily wooded island is viewed clearly when landing at or leaving the Belfast International Airport runway at nearby Aldergrove. (See Chapter 29 for more on Rams Island.)

FIG. 25.1
Flood gates on the River Bann at Toome.

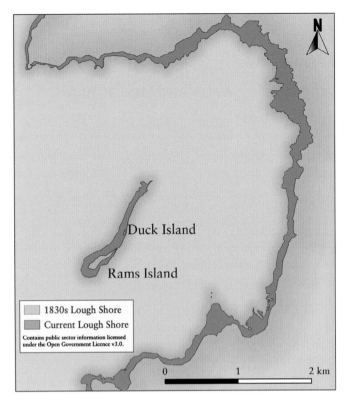

FIG. 25.2
The changing outline of
Rams Island.

Likewise, standing in the hamlet of Brocagh on the western shore of Lough Neagh at the site of one of the castle's built by Charles Blount, Lord Mountjoy, and looking at the map of the area by his cartographer Richard Bartlett from 1602, we realise that the location of the fort was on a rocky shoreline but is now some few hundred metres inland. This was evidenced by the results of a major archaeological investigation and dig carried out by Lough Neagh Partnership and the Centre for Community Archaeology at QUB in 2018. (See Chapter 20 for more on this site.) Indeed between the site of the fort and the new shoreline, when left to nature, the area has been colonised by alder trees and other wetland species. These two sites are evidence of the engineering of water, whether to reduce the problem of flooding, provide power or aid navigation.

In 1795, Oliver Goldsmith wrote:

> God has endowed us with abilities to turn this great extent of water to our own advantage. He has made these things, perhaps for other uses; but he has given is the faculties to convert them to our own. ... Let us then boldly affirm, that the earth, and all its wonders, are ours; since we are furnished with the powers to force then into our service.

We have made the earth simply a subject of our control and are reaping the consequences of this. History shows that the great empires, such as China and Egypt, were built upon central control of the waters of major rivers and even in modern democracies the control of this vital resource is a powerful political position.

Lough Neagh is the largest freshwater lake in Britain and Ireland and draws water from five counties in Northern Ireland and one in the Republic of Ireland. The lough contains over 800 billion gallons of water. It is on average 15 miles wide and 20 miles long, covering some 153 sq. miles The catchment area for which the lough acts as a central reservoir is over 1,500 sq. miles and it receives the flow of many rivers, including the Blackwater, Ballinderry, Moyola, Upper Bann, Six Mile Water and Main. The only outlet is by the Lower River Bann entering the sea below Coleraine. It has always been a holder of these waters but despite its size it is relatively shallow and therefore its capacity is not as great as might be expected.

The Lower Bann valley especially is given to flooding. Prior to the mid-nineteenth-century 'lowerings' some 25,000 acres was subject to regular intuition. Shoals or submerged banks along the riverbed, especially at Toome, slow down the river's flow. In prehistoric times flooding was good as it enriched the land for the hunters and gatherers. However, as people settled and started farming it has been seen as a threat. From the 1700s several schemes were proposed to deal with flooding and navigation, but with little success. One advocate of improvements was the Anglican bishop of Down and Connor, Francis Hutchinson (d. 1739), who argued:

> ... the waters which flow from so many sources can not possibly be discharged by the single outlet of the Bann but must, unless steps are taken to discharge the waters by clearing the obstruction of the river, be annually accumulated to the great detriment of the lands around.

In 1812 Thomas Townsend, an engineer with the Bog Commissioners in Ireland, suggested that river navigation could be improved by building canals and removing the shoals along the river. Seasonal flooding before any changes were made is described in the Ordnance Survey Memoirs of the 1830s, especially in the memoir for Lough Neagh by Lieut. Thomas Graves, in 1832:

Fig. 25.3

The changing shoreline of Lough Neagh near Brocagh.

> ... the water of the lough usually rises from 6–9 feet perpendicularly and spreads over about 10,000 acres of land more than it does when it is at its lowest ... A very considerable tract of land lying between Toome and Castledawson called The Creagh, is annually inundated, besides many other places adjoining the lough ... (*OSM*, vol. 21, 94).

Danny Donnelly discusses 'the shore most liable to flooding' in his book *On Lough Neagh's Shores*:

> for example, Ballymaguigan, Moortown, Derrylaughin, Milltown, Derrytrasna, Aghagallon, the area around and between Portmore Lough and Lough Neagh and in the south-west corner of the northern shore known as Doss ... In Moortown the land bordering the lough was subject to heavy flooding in winter for almost half a mile inland (Donnelly 1986, 126).

In 1822 the famous engineer Alexander Nimmo suggested a scheme joining the Newry Navigation with Lough Neagh to alleviate flooding and 'the value of such a power in seaport, and in the midst of a rich, populous and busily manufacturing country, is not to be easily calculated – indeed, the like is not to be found in Europe.' The Drainage Act of 1842 was passed by the government to ease flooding, improve navigation and mill power of the Lough Neagh basin and the Lower Bann corridor.

McMahon's scheme

In 1844 the canal engineer John McMahon was commissioned to create a navigation scheme for the Lower Bann. His challenge was to help drainage, improve navigation and support fishing. McMahon estimated the cost of the scheme at £163,486. He proposed to build locks and weirs to lower winter flood levels and also store water to help with navigation. Nevertheless, in the degree of flood control and water storage existing in the Lough Neagh basin, even in its natural state, McMahon recognised the great benefits bestowed by a large expanse of inland sea:

> ... placed by nature at a point of convergence of several powerful and turbulent rivers and streams, it receives and calms the impetuosity of these waters, rendering them fit for man's use, and is almost without a parallel as to value amongst his industrial resources.

In 1845, a memorial was signed by the Protestant and Roman Catholic Primates, along with numerous clergy and magistrates, who urged that in view of the failure of the potato crop as much employment as possible should be given to the labouring population. The most glowing anticipations of the benefits to be derived from the scheme in 1846 were conjured up, as W.A. McCutcheon, author of *The Industrial Archaeology of Northern Ireland* (1980), noted:

> Doctors reported that there would be probable benefits in abating epidemics of fever; professors of geology discoursed on the economic value of the deposits of clay which would be exposed near Toomebridge, and further south between Ardboe Point and Portadown – diatomite, peat, lignite and coal, sulphate of lime and sulphate of iron. The Drainage Commissioner, Robert Harding, envisaged a vast improvement of the land that was liable to flooding.

The Board of Works approved the scheme, known as the Lower Bann Navigation, which was implemented over 11 years (1847–58). Locks were created at Toome, Movanagher, Portna, Carnroe and the Cutts. They all had standard sized chambers, 130 feet long by 20 feet 6 inches wide (39.6 m by 6.2 m). Stone used for the various weirs, locks and banks came from excavated material and nearby quarries at Tamlaght, Movanagher and Toome. Brick from Coalisland was used for the lock and lock-keeper's house at Toome. Over 1,500 men worked on the scheme at any one time. The total cost came to £264,000 – over £100,000 more than the original estimate.

The scheme lowered the level of Lough Neagh by approximately 6 feet (1.8 m). It reclaimed up to 30,000 acres of land round the shoreline for agriculture and opened up river traffic between Lough Neagh and Coleraine. However, railways had started to overtake river traffic. Belfast and Newry were also better placed for the shipment of goods along the canals to cross channel ships. In 1862 the Lower Bann Steamship Company started a service along the Lower Bann. The Harland & Wolff-built steamer, *Kitty of Coleraine*, offered a twice-weekly passenger and goods service between Coleraine and Toome. But the service never took off and ceased in 1869.

Shepherd's scheme

In 1929 the Ministry of Finance took over responsibility for the Lower Bann. They employed Major Percy Shepherd to address the issue of flooding along the Bann. Work on Shepherd's scheme began in March 1930. Almost four million cubic metres of non-rock material was dredged. Sluice gates were installed at Toome, Portna and the Cutts to regulate the flow of the river and control the water level of Lough Neagh. There were five gates at Toome with a fish pass in the centre. A footbridge was also built to access them from the County Antrim side. The level of the river was monitored at water gauge stations at Toome and Camus. Three sets of floodgates and five sets of locks on the Lower Bann control the water level of Lough Neagh. Today, Lough Neagh is 3.6 m lower than it was in 1847. A consequence of the schemes was the creation of several new townlands in the parish of Ballyscullion, each of which is named Intake, adjoining the townlands of Ballyscullion West, Church Island and Leitrim.

Returning to the concept of 'controlling nature', one wonders if, or could, these engineering changes happen today? There are many debates about flooding and flood defences. Is it good to try and culvert, control and embank water?

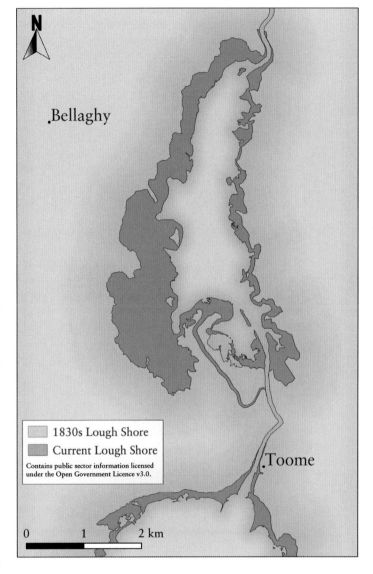

FIG. 25.4

The changing shoreline of Lough Beg and near Toome.

It is not easy if you live by a coast, a river or a lough that is prone to flooding, but what are the long term answers? Is hard engineering and 'controlling nature' the answer? In the Netherlands, *Ruimte voor de Rivier* ('Room for the River') is a government designed plan intended to address flood protection, master landscaping and the improvement of environmental conditions in the areas surrounding the Netherlands' rivers. We might have to make way again too and make room for the water!

Bibliography

Daniel J. Donnelly, *On Lough Neagh's Shores* (Galbally, Co. Tyrone, 1986).

Oliver Goldsmith, *An History of the Earth and Animated Nature*, vol. 1 (London, 1774).

W.A. McCutcheon, *The Industrial Archaeology of Northern Ireland* (Belfast, 1980).

Ordnance Survey Memoirs of Ireland ... South Antrim, Vol. 21, ed. Angélique Day and Patrick McWilliams (Belfast, 1993).

Gregory Toner, *Places-names of Northern Ireland, Volume Five. County Derry I: the Moyola Valley* (Belfast, 1996).

26 Hub of transport

Liam Campbell

I have a very solid image in my memory of a green Raleigh bicycle owned by my grandfather. What amazed me most about it was the Sturmey-Archer dynohub, a powerhouse at the centre of the rear wheel that gave power for the lights. It also housed an ingenious braking system, so if you back peddled it would work as a very effective brake. The hub is the most important part of the wheel, connecting to all the spokes and keeping them in line.

FIG. 26.1
Toome Canal.

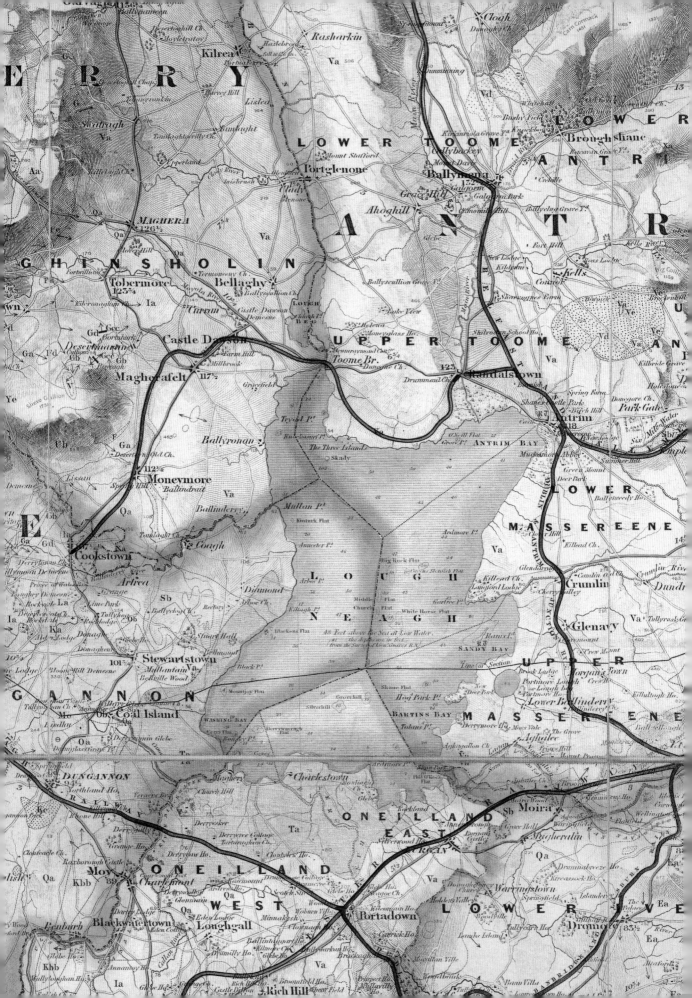

It is a fine metaphor for Lough Neagh, especially in terms of transport. From the earliest Mesolithic peoples who came up the Bann in logboats, to the Vikings in the ninth century, to the larger sail vessels of the Nine Years' War depicted on Bartlett's maps, to the canals of the eighteenth century, the water has been a great connector not a divider. One could travel anywhere on the island of Ireland by canal from Lough Neagh. Topography was again to play its part in the development of the canals as it was with all the forms of transport around the lough. Lough Neagh is some 50 feet above sea level and canal engineers in the early eighteenth century saw the potential for navigational development to the north using the existing Lower Bann, to the north-east using the Lagan corridor and to the south-east to Newry using the naturally flat corridor. Finally in 1841 the Ulster Canal opened, linking Lough Neagh with Lough Erne in the west. This then had links into the Shannon and on to Dublin and the south-east of Ireland.

The demise of the canal network began with the arrival of the railway, ironically almost at the time of the completion of the Ulster Canal. Railways impacted dramatically on waterway traffic, with passenger conveyancing ceasing and the transport of freight declining sharply. They may still have a future and moves are afoot to reinstate the Ulster Canal. It is fair to say that with the arrival of the rail network in the 1860s to its zenith in 1923 you could travel anywhere from around Lough Neagh to almost any location in Ireland. However, like the canals, the railways too 'had their day' and the intricate transport infrastructure would face disintegration. The nature of this 'rationalisation' was strongly influenced by the arrival of the internal combustion engine and its use in mechanically-propelled vehicles, especially the car. This was also facilitated by the Beeching Report of the early 1960s recommending the closure of many railways. The year 1968 saw the opening of the M1 motorway to the south of Lough Neagh and the M2 opened in 1975 to the north. Again, the flat topography around the lough makes all this possible. You either go around the lough by road, cross over it by boat or indeed fly over it.

This vast body of water and surrounding flat land were to make the entire area an efficient hub for aviation and with the onset of World War II, Lough Neagh once again became a major transport asset for the war effort. Military airfields at Aldergrove, Nutt's Corner, Langford Lodge, Sandy Bay, Blaris, Maghaberry, Long Kesh, Toome and Cluntoe/Ardboe serve as reminders of the part that Northern Ireland played in the Allied campaign and subsequent victory. However, it is so important to remember that humans are neither the earth's original nor its foremost route or spoke makers. Think of the eel and the elvers returning from the Sargasso Sea off the Gulf of Mexico or the Tufted Duck blazing a trail between Iceland and here. The swifts and swallows arrive from Africa each summer (though they may spend the night in Belfast!).

OPPOSITE
FIG.26.2

Detail from a map of Ireland to accompany the report of the Railway Commissioners, 1855, showing how Lough Neagh was almost encircled by railway lines.

THE DAVID RUMSEY MAP COLLECTION

Where does this leave us humans and the great hub and spokes of Lough Neagh? Who invented all the routes around Lough Neagh? Humans? The salmon or the eel? The deer? I think no one can claim credit because the essential route, a path of least resistance, is predetermined by the topography of the landscape, the hub of Lough Neagh and its spokes the river valley, and the needs of all the inhabitants, human and non-human. The simple lessons of the history of transport for a schoolchild are so evident around the lough shore. From the logboats of Mesolithic era to the cars of today, we can see the increase in the speed of travel. And the faster we travel, the more intensely we feel our lack of relationship with the land and water we traverse and the disconnect with our fellow travellers.

FIG.26.3
The Toome bypass
bridge over the
River Bann.

27 The early history of the port of Ballyronan

William Roulston

Although a number of sources have attributed the development, even founding, of Ballyronan to the Gaussens, a family of French Huguenot origin, in actual fact there was significant commercial activity here prior to their arrival around 1790. Of crucial importance for its rise as a port was the construction of the Newry Canal and later the Lagan Canal, which opened up trading opportunities far beyond Lough Neagh itself. The *Belfast Newsletter* of 14 September 1764 carried an advertisement for a property in Ballyronan, which proclaimed that by the side of the lough there was a 'good quay for shipping … the best and deepest quay on said shore' and asserted that Ballyronan was 'well known as an ancient place of trade'. By 1758 Messrs Arthur Maxwell and Robert Thompson had established a business at Ballyronan, dealing in a range of commodities including soap and oatmeal. Following Maxwell's death in 1765, his widow Ann continued the business with Thompson.

FIG.27.1
Ballyronan marina in the snow.

FIG. 27.2
Detail showing
Ballyronan from a map of
Lough Neagh, 1785
(PRONI, D604/1).
PUBLIC RECORD OFFICE OF
NORTHERN IRELAND

In late 1767 Thompson used the *Belfast Newsletter* (15 December 1767) to announce that he had erected a 'plateing-Mill' at Ballyronan, where he 'manufactures shovels, spades, pot-lids, coal-boxes, and dripping-pans of as good quality and shape as any in Ireland.' Thompson intended selling and delivering his wares in Derry, Newry, Belfast, Coleraine and Ballycastle, as well as 'at all places contiguous to the Newry Navigation.' The same notice also advertised the broad range of goods that were for sale in the stores of Thompson and Ann Maxwell in Ballyronan:

> first, second and third smalts; black soap, German steel, and Liquorice-ball; which are of their own importation from Rotterdam; Scotch and Galway kelp, barilla and Dantzick ashes, Swedish and Russian iron, deals, rum, brandy and Geneva, sugar and molloses [sic], pots and gridles, English and Irish tobacco, dyeing-stuff or all sorts. Likewise bleachers soap and candles of their own manufacture.

Based on a subsequent advertisement, from 1781, for the 'plating mill', McCutcheon, unaware of the 1767 reference, commented that this was the earliest documented reference to a spade mill in the north of Ireland (McCutcheon 1981, 279).

Around 1790 David Gaussen of Newry established a business, or took over the earlier enterprises, at Ballyronan. The *Belfast Newsletter* of 15–18 February 1791 carried the following notice:

> David Gaussen junr with the utmost respect begs leave to return his most sincere thanks to his friends and the publick, for the very great encouragement he has met with since his commencement in business at Port Ballyronan; takes this method of acquainting them, that he is now largely supplied at his stores with best Dantzig and Memel timber, Dronthon deals, slating and cieling laths, slates, train oil, oak bark, Swedish, Siberia, Nail rod, and hoop iron, blister and German steel, Swansa and Kilkenny coals, Portaferry kelp, old jamica rum, Cogniac Brandy, Gineva, old spirits, whiskey, Bordeaux vinegar, with every other article in the grocery line; and at his place-mill, a large quantity of spades and shovels, equal to any in Ireland, all which he is determined to sell on the very lowest terms, for good payments.

(A subsequent advertisement corrected Portaferry kelp to Pollecheny kelp.)

At the beginning of the nineteenth century, however, trade remained principally in one direction – import – though there were hopes that this would change. In 1802, George Vaughan Sampson observed:

> This port lies on the north-west corner of Lough Neagh; at present sloops of sixty tons can load and unload here. There is little export; the import consists in timber, iron, slates, coal, fax-seed, and sometimes oatmeal. The trade is all in the hands of one merchant, who has the merit of creating both the port and the trade. When the adjacent country shall arrive at the improvement, of which it is susceptible, it is easy to foresee, that this embryo port will then become a place of consequence (Sampson, 1802, 126).

FIG. 27.3
Ballyronan House.

The Ordnance Survey Memoir of Artrea parish of 1836 attributed (incorrectly) the origin of Ballyronan to the Messrs Gaussen and credited them with the construction of the pier, which curved some 257 feet into the lough and was 15 feet in breadth. At this time trade was increasing considerably at Ballyronan, which, as the memoir noted, was 'in fact, the port of Magherafelt'. Grain was the principal commodity exported through the port, from where it was shipped to Newry or Belfast (principally the latter). At this time seven or eight lighters of 40–60 tons made the journey regularly to these places, with others on a more occasional basis. The round trip took ten days. The imported goods were principally supplied to shopkeepers in the neighbouring towns (*OSM*, vol. 6, 6–7, 15).

The Gaussens were also responsible for building a distillery and a brewery in the vicinity of Ballyronan. However, although a great deal of trade passed through Ballyronan, the village itself remained small. In the mid-1830s it comprised 17 two-storey and three one-storey houses, 'most of which are dirty and irregular and inhabited by 1 baker, 1 spirit dealer, a shoemaker, some excise officers and a few labourers' (*OSM*, vol. 6, 6). Possibly built by the Gaussens in the late eighteenth century (though perhaps the dwelling advertised for letting in 1764), Ballyronan House is a substantial and handsome residence and is the principal link with the village's mercantile past.

There is no doubt that under the Gaussens Ballyronan experienced a new and significant period of development. However, it is also clear that this was built on earlier foundations. Ballyronan's commercial importance could not be sustained, however, principally due to the superseding of the canal system by the

FIG. 27.4
Looking south over
Ballyronan marina.

railway network, which never reached Ballyronan. Today, Ballyronan is a popular destination for locals and visitors alike who wish to spend time beside the lough in this beautiful setting.

FIG. 27.5

A late summer evening at Ballyronan marina.

Bibliography

Belfast Newsletter.

W.A. McCutcheon, *The Industrial Archaeology of Northern Ireland* (Belfast, 1980).

Ordnance Survey Memoirs of Ireland... Vol. 6, ed. Angélique Day and Patrick McWilliams (Belfast, 1990).

George Vaughan Sampson, *Statistical Survey of the County of Londonderry* (Dublin, 1802).

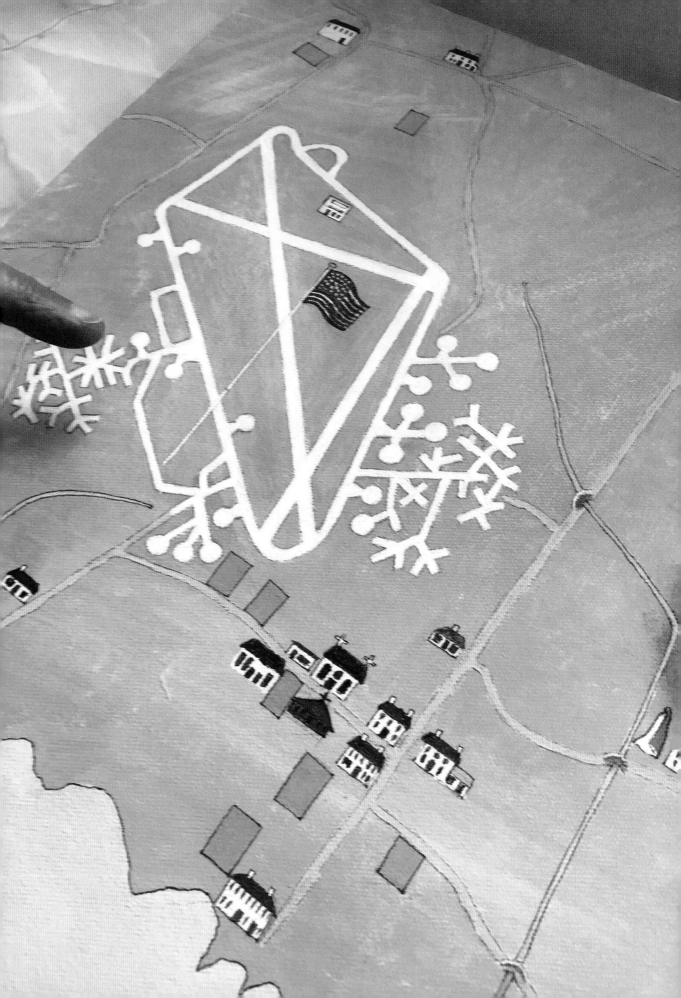

28 World War II and the lough
Cluntoe and Toome airfields

James O'Neill

Storm clouds of war had been gathering across Europe throughout the 1930s. The belligerence of the Axis powers had convinced many that war against Germany and Italy was becoming inevitable. However, at the outbreak of World War II there was little to suggest that the events unfolding in Europe would alter dramatically the peaceful rural districts around Lough Neagh. Indeed, when France and the United Kingdom declared war on Germany after the invasion of Poland, most assumed the effects of the conflict would be confined to Continental Europe.

All that changed after the blitzkrieg advance of the German armies across the Netherlands, Belgium and France during May-June 1940 resulted in the capitulation of France and the evacuation of the British Expeditionary Force from Dunkirk. Though protected for centuries by the English Channel, the United Kingdom faced a real threat of invasion. The UK urgently needed to expand its capacity to wage war and every acre that could be spared was required for the war effort, but Toome and Ardboe must have seemed a world away from events unfolding elsewhere.

The parishes of Ardtrea and Ardboe were a quiet rural idyll on the shores of Lough Neagh. But momentous events globally transformed the peaceful fields and wetlands. Generations of farmers had tilled the land but this was all swept aside to meet the needs of the war in the air over Europe. One key aspect of both parishes met the needs of war – they were flat. Each airfield needed three runways set at 60 degrees with the longest almost 2,000 yards long, surrounded by miles of perimeter tracks. These needed to be as flat as possible for safe take-off and landing. Irrespective of the wishes of the locals, dozens of families were forced to leave their farms. Paid £50 per acre, their cattle and machinery were auctioned off. Forced to start new lives elsewhere, many would never return to their old lives after the war. Construction began at Cluntoe in December 1941, and at Toome in January 1942. The demands of construction brought levels of employment to the region as never before.

Hundreds of buildings were erected, with technical buildings such as the control towers and hangars. Dispersals were built to store aircraft around the airfields, as to keep them together only invited air attack. Synthetic trainers were

FIG. 28.2
Norden bombsight
vault at Toome.

built, such as bombing trainers, link trainers, turret trainers and airmanship halls to instruct crews on operating their aircraft without leaving the safety of the ground and without risking the lives of crew or damage to airframes.

The entry of the United States of America into the war in 1941 led to an influx of American airmen and ground crews. The calls of native birds were drowned out by the roar of warbirds such as the B-17 Flying Fortress, B-26 Marauder and the A-20 Havoc, made in their thousands on production lines in Seattle, Baltimore, and Santa Monica. The early morning rumble of dozens of engines warming up for operations filled the air, and the smell of aviation fuel would have permeated the atmosphere across the district.

Toome and Cluntoe were renamed AAF Stations 236 and 238, respectively, by the USAAF. With the establishment of the US Eighth Air Force in England, it became apparent that the training of aircrews in the blue skies of the US had not prepared them for the practicalities of flight operations in a war zone, nor the challenging flying conditions and poor weather prevalent in the European theatre. Consequently, the priority for USAAF in Northern Ireland was training. Both Toome and Cluntoe became Combat Crew Replacement Centres, where crews were trained in gunnery, bombing procedures, navigation and other skills needed to operate effectively under combat conditions. They were also brought together to train on their assigned aircraft under the supervision of veteran pilots. Cluntoe trained crews for B-17 Flying Fortresses and later B-24 Liberators. Ten miles to the north, crews stationed at Toome trained on A-20 Havocs and B-26 Marauders. New crews were taught how to operate as a team in the aircraft they would fly in combat. It would be their last stop before flying combat missions. For many who never made it home, Toome and Cluntoe would be their last experience of relative safety and peace.

Training with military hardware was not risk-free and there were many accidents. There were air-crashes on and off the airfields, some of which resulted in the loss of flight crews. The roads around the lough also became hazardous as the small rural roads were filled with military traffic. The influx of thousands of young men driving jeeps and lorries made the roads a dangerous place for drivers and pedestrians.

As the Allies began to get the upper hand in the war, training began to be run down at both airfields, with flying operations ending by the end of 1944. The thousands of American personnel and aircraft disappeared as quickly as they had arrived, with quiet descending once more to the region, no doubt eerily to those who had got used to the incessant noise and bustle of the busy aerodromes. The bomber crews were gone but the district's wartime experiences did not end in 1945. More strangers appeared in the area in 1946 as German prisoners-of-war were quartered near Toome. They interacted well with the community with many skilfully crafted toys and ornaments making their way into local homes.

FIG. 28.3
Control tower at Cluntoe.

The airfield at Cluntoe got a second wind after the war as flying briefly returned. The site remained a reserve airfield for the Royal Navy Fleet Air Arm after the war and for a while was renamed HMS Gannet. It was reactivated and refurbished by the RAF during the Korean War (1950–53) when on 1 February 1953, 2 Flight Training School opened. The school operated until June 1954, when it returned to England. The airfield remained as a reserve station but was finally closed in 1957.

Though the flight crews, ground maintenance personnel and flight instructors have passed into history, the many miles of runways, perimeter tracks, aircraft dispersals and training structures survive as physical reminders of wartime – the past made manifest in brick, concrete and steel. Some are derelict, others reused as byres or warehousing. Others have been turned into homes, such as the structure known as a bombing teacher at Cluntoe, remodelled into a home, perhaps few guessing at its original purpose.

FIG. 28.4
Armament classroom at Toome.

Both airfields have small buildings that were unique to the US presence. Often mistaken for jails due to the bars on the windows, these two buildings were secure vaults for storing the top-secret Norden bombsight. This technologically advanced sight enabled precision daylight bombing. The device was so secret it was kept in these specially constructed secure stores when not on missions. There

are also a few examples of wall art to show that these sites were once home to part of the 'Mighty' Eighth Air Force.

Life goes on and redevelopment has obscured many features at Toome, as manufacturing fills in the gaps, but at Cluntoe the network of runways and perimeter tracks remain intact. Their age makes structures merge with the background as the needs of agriculture reclaimed the land, but sites such as the operations block and control tower at Cluntoe and the three hangars at Toome are unmistakable in their origins during World War II. The crews and aircraft are long gone but the airfields remain. They loom so large in the landscape they are almost invisible, hidden in plain sight almost, but if you look closely you can find them and imagine what it was like over 80 years ago when war came to the lough.

29 Rams Island

Liam Campbell

Rams Island is the largest island on Lough Neagh and has been a source of refuge and solace down through the centuries. It is first mentioned in the Annals of Ulster in 1056 as the site of an early Irish monastery, now marked by the remains of a round tower, where a chief's *anam cara*, soul friend or confessor, was commemorated. It has had many famous visitors for various reasons. Jeremy Taylor, the famous seventeenth-century theologian and Anglican bishop of Down and Connor, is said to have retreated there for study and prayer. In the eighteenth century Theobold Wolfe Tone, in the company of Henry Joy McCracken, Thomas Russell and other United Irishmen leaders, paid a visit there on 11 June 1795. Tone described the beauty and romance of the place, adding that they agreed that '… whatever quarter we find ourselves, respectively, to commemorate the anniversary of that day.' The island also was to provide refuge of a different sort in 1679 for the infamous highwayman, Redmond O'Hanlon, who hid there to recuperate after being wounded by mercenaries hunting him down.

FIG. 29.1
Rams Island.

The Rams Island of today is not as it has always been. Now measuring some 25 acres, it was originally only six acres before successive lowerings of the lough (see Chapter 25). The Ordnance Survey Memoir of the 1830s describes 'a narrow tongue which extends northward being often all under water except a small portion of it known by the name of Duck Island'. This little island, formerly lay off the north shore of the Rams Island. Comparing the 1833 Ordnance Survey map of Rams Island with the 1858 map shows clearly how the two islands merged after the lowering of the lough.

As regards the place-name, the final element of it appears to be a rare personal name, according to Pat McKay and Kay Muhr in *Lough Neagh Places: Their Names and Origins* (2007). It seems to derive from *Dar Cairgreann*, i.e. daughter of *Cairgiu*. However, the name may have been anglicised as Rams Island due to the perceived similarity between the word 'ram' and the final syllable – *reann* – of the place-name. The Ordnance Survey Memoir of 1836 claims that the modern name comes 'from its resemblance in form to a ram's horn', another very plausible explanation.

As noted already, the Annals of Ulster refer to a monastery on the island, while Speed's map of Ulster in 1610 shows a church here and Taylor and Skinner's map of 1777 has an illustration of a round tower. In his contribution to Shaw Mason's *Statistical Account or Parochial Survey of Ireland* (vol. 2, 1816), Rev. Edward Cupples described the round tower as standing some 43 feet high and noted the discovery of bones on the island. This convinced Cupples to follow the theory that round towers were ecclesiastical. He also thought that churches on the island were unlikely, and took seriously the suggestion of a causeway to the island from Gartree Point in Killead.

As well as the round tower, the ruins of Lord O'Neill's nineteenth-century summer house may be found on the island. This was described in the *Dublin Penny Journal* of 17 August 1833:

> This beautiful little cottage is situated on one of the small islands of Lough Neagh, at a distance of three miles from Crumlin, and about one mile and two-thirds from the shore, from which the traveller can easily procure a boat for the purpose of visiting the island. The cottage which is extremely pretty, and furnished in the most tasteful manner, was some time since erected by Earl O'Neill, to whom it belongs. The only object of antiquity here is a round tower of which: "Time, with assailing arm / Hath smote the summit, but the solid base / Derides the lapse of ages."

The island was last permanently occupied in the 1930s by the Cardwell family who were the caretakers for Lord O'Neill. Now derelict, contemporary photographs of the house show a very ornate, thatched building covered in multi-coloured pebbles with the O'Neill coat of arms set into the front wall. Robert Cardwell passed away in 1929 when he was in his nineties and his wife Jane passed away three years later aged 102. Jane's funeral cortege from the

FIG. 29.2
The round tower.

FIG. 29.3
The ruins of Lord
O'Neill's summer
house.

island was widely covered in the local press with the final tribute of a procession of some eight Lough Neagh fishing boats leading her remains to the mainland. One daughter lived permanently in the cottage until 1937. Since then, no-one has lived on Rams Island, though Lord O'Neill leases the island to the River Bann and Lough Neagh Association which runs a heritage project there. Rams Island is now very heavily wooded, but can easily be seen from flights as one approaches Belfast International Airport. It continues to be a source of refuge and solace from the 'modern' world.

30 Mud-walled buildings

Philip Smith

FIG 30.1
Former Derrykeevan
Post Office, 134
Dungannon Rd,
Portadown.

The vernacular buildings in the lands immediately south of Lough Neagh, in common with their counterparts throughout the globe, owe their form in large respect to their physical environment, most being defined by the fact that they were crafted from materials gathered close to hand. As the frequency of townlands with 'Derry' (Ir. 'Oak wood') prefixes attests, this area was heavily wooded during the Medieval period, and as such many of its dwellings would have been of timber construction, evidence suggesting cruck structures with wattle and daub walling, and perhaps – in some higher status cases – shingled roofs.

Like many other parts of Ireland, the deforestation of much of this landscape in the late sixteenth and seventeenth centuries meant that vernacular construction was forced to shift from the use of timber as the main structural component to one of mass load-bearing walls. With the relative abundance and accessibility of rubble stone throughout the island, stone buildings thus became the norm for much of rural Ireland from the later 1600s onwards. But in some locations, such as the flat, low-lying plains of northern edge of County Armagh, readily available stone was a less common commodity and many local builders had to rely on earthen, that is mud-walled, construction.

The prevalence of the use of mud-walling as a traditional building method south of the lough has long been known, but as a heritage asset it has perhaps been somewhat under-appreciated. In some respects, this has probably in part stemmed from a view of mud buildings as poor cousins of their stone equivalents, crude, cheaply built structures with greater associations with poverty than the vernacular in general, a long-held perception articulated by Thomas McIlroy in the 1837 Ordnance Survey Memoirs, who felt it was 'scarcely possible to conceive of anything more miserable' than the 'mud, thatched and 1-storey high' cottages of Tartaraghan parish. In addition to this, 'mud' as a construction material has tended to conjure up notions of impermanence, such buildings (so the logic goes) being more susceptible to the decaying effects of our perennially damp and frequently windy climate. And so, it has perhaps been easy to dismiss local earthen buildings as both a subject not worthy of study, but also one whose examples have probably not survived in enough numbers – or in decent enough condition – to warrant serious attention anyhow. In more recent years, however, a realisation of what we have lost in terms of our built heritage combined with the broader question of sustainability has helped lead to a more widespread recognition of the importance of all aspects of the vernacular. Nonetheless, in spite of some academic interest in mud-walling, our knowledge of these buildings in the Lough Neagh hinterland, and elsewhere, remains comparatively low.

Amongst other things, a chance to gauge the extent of survival of mud-walled structures in the area was offered to my Historic Environment Division (HED) colleagues and I in spring and early summer 2018, when as part of HED's ongoing Second Survey of Historic Buildings in Northern Ireland, we undertook a survey of a cluster of townlands around The Birches and Maghery – covering much of the north and east of Tartaraghan. Our initial task, as with much of our work, was at the desktop, comparing the various historic and modern maps and aerial photography (as well as Google Streetview) in order to compile a list of sites of possible interest. In doing so we were immediately struck by the continuity in terms of sites, many of the buildings marked on the 1835 and 1862 Ordnance Survey sheets having been retained in some form (many of them, incidentally, easily identifiable from aerial views due to their red corrugated-iron roofs!) Of those sites of pre-1835 origin, a comparison with John Rocque's highly detailed and seemingly accurate County Armagh map of 1760 suggested that the majority of these had been developed in the late eighteenth or early nineteenth centuries, the older map showing the area covered in large tracts of bog with very little places of habitation in evidence. Clearly the general increase in population throughout Ireland in the late 1700s through until the Great Famine, aided by the growth in the (increasingly linen-centred) economy within north Armagh in general, and improved land reclamation techniques in this area in particular, all had a hand in this.

At the end of this desktop part of the exercise around 90 vernacular structures were earmarked for further examination on the ground and of these 81 were eventually recorded. Most had been abandoned or appeared to be so, but in spite of this the majority were in relatively good condition. In terms of their construction, 11 were either positively observed and/or were confirmed by their owners to be wholly mud-walled. Due to the fact that the owners of most of the 70 or so others could not be readily traced – which also of course ruled out access to the interiors – and that their walls were so heavily coated in thick render (early to mid-twentieth century cement render, frequently 'pebble-dashed' with small chips of coloured glass and crockery, with smooth bands to the openings is a particular characteristic of the vernacular in this area), meant that their composition could not be determined accurately. I personally believe there is little to reason to doubt, however, that a good percentage of the buildings that we identified are indeed of earthen construction, and that remarks such as the aforementioned Ordnance Survey Memoirs that 'the cottages of the area are in general of mud', remain valid as far as the remaining pre-1900 building stock is concerned.

But whilst it may have been difficult to assess numbers, one thing that our survey did attest to is the durability of the earthen buildings themselves, our observations indicating that given the upkeep of both roofing and render, that mud walls display a resilience that would seem to rival rubble. This hardiness did have an ironic drawback for us, in that it inhibited any study of the actual make-up of the mud itself, examples of walls in the process of decomposition being difficult to find. On one particularly isolated and long-vacated house, however, serious damage to the roof had resulted in the shearing of part of the render exposing of the fabric of a gable end. Here, the subtle differences in the colour of the various layers of the mud could be seen, revealing that the walls of this particular property had probably been built up in 'brick' form rather than shuttered. This supports Thomas McIlroy's 1837 statement that walls were 'built up with sods placed upon the bare bog'.

A testament to the quality (and state of preservation) of mud-walled buildings in this area is the fact that of the six vernacular dwellings currently listed by HED in this area, only one is rubble-built. Two of these – 36 Derrycush Road (ref. HB14/01/001) and 57 Derrycarne Road (HB14/01/033) – were listed in 1977 and 2002 respectively, with remaining three – 40 Derrylileagh Road (HB14/01/053), 125 Dungannon Road (HB14/01/106) and 134 Dungannon Road (HB14/01/104) – gathered in the 2018 survey. All three of the newer listings are pre-1833 structures, single-storey, with tin over thatch roofs, and, in common with most vernacular houses in this part of the world, 'lobby-entry' with the entrance directly in line with the main hearth.

Of the three, that at 134 Dungannon Road in Derrykeevan townland is perhaps the most interesting. Located on the western side of what is a very straight busy road between Portadown and the M1, the house is immediately noticeable as one speeds along not only because it remains an attractive well-preserved example of the vernacular, but also because successive re-surfacing of

the road has left the property noticeably below the level of the carriageway itself. Having been in the ownership of the same family since at least 1863, it served as the local post office from at least 1907, being superseded in recent decades with the transfer of its functions to the large neighbouring garage. Despite the loss of this role, however, it has been carefully maintained by its owners, who in common with the holders of other mud-walled buildings that I have encountered in recent years, take a certain pride in possessing such a building and in playing the role of custodians.

As the attitude of such owners shows, the stigma that may have been attached by some to these 'miserable' structures in the past is disappearing. Hopefully, future surveys and further studies of our earthen buildings in both the Lough Neagh area and beyond will ensure that they find even more adherents, and for those buildings that have been abandoned, re-uses.

FIG 30.2
125 Dungannon Road, Portadown.

31 Expressions of faith in the built heritage of Antrim town

William Roulston

Like other towns and villages across Northern Ireland, the built heritage of the town of Antrim includes places of worship of a variety of different religious denominations, as well as reminders of a much deeper Christian heritage. One of Antrim's best known landmarks is the well preserved round tower, all that remains of an important monastery founded nearly 1,500 years ago. The monastery had a strong association with St Comgall, the founder and first abbot of the monastery in Bangor in the sixth century. It is possible that Comgall established the monastic site in Antrim – certainly the religious houses at Bangor and Antrim were closely connected.

The earliest mention of the name Antrim is from the year 612 when, according to the Annals of the Four Masters, '*Fiontain Oentreibh, abb Bendchair, décc*' – 'Fintan of Antrim, abbot of Bangor died'. The original Irish word for Antrim, *Aontreibh*, means 'single house or habitation', and it is believed that it this refers to the ecclesiastical settlement. Following the destruction of the monastery at Bangor in Viking raids in the early ninth century, the relics of Comgall were transferred to Antrim.

Archaeological excavations carried out in 2008 uncovered possible evidence for the ditch enclosing the early monastic settlement, which seems to have been considerable in extent. In the early nineteenth century the site was extensively landscaped, with the result that wall foundations, a substantial quantity of building stones and human remains, which had been uncovered during the works, were removed. However, the round tower was retained and stabilised, and is now one of the best two preserved examples of its type in Northern Ireland, the other being on Devenish Island. The Antrim round tower is known as The Steeple, with the name

FIG. 31.1
The Steeple.

documented in the seventeenth century (e.g. the place-name 'Steeple Towne' appears in the 1669 hearth money roll of Antrim parish). The tower probably dates from the tenth or eleventh century. It rises from a low mound and is 28 m (92 feet) in height and 5.5 m in diameter externally at the base. The doorway is 2.85 m above the level of the mound and faces north, possibly providing an indication of where the monastic church was located. Above the lintel of the doorway is a stone displaying a carving of a ringed cross. The tower is topped by a pointed conical cap, though the present appearance of this feature may be due to the works carried out in the early 1800s to stabilise the structure.

Near the round tower is the 'Witch's Stone', a basalt boulder with two oval depressions cut into the top of the stone, which, according to a tradition recorded in the 1830s, were the result of a witch jumping from the tower and landing on her knees on the stone. The feature has been categorised as a bullaun stone and while the function of these is not known for certain, they are often found at monastic sites and may have been used as fonts. A short distance to the north of The Steeple is Holywell or Holy Well, which, as the name suggests, is the location of a well with religious significance. In 1838 James Boyle, an official with the Ordnance Survey, wrote 'there is also a tradition of charms or miracles were wrought at it and that stations were made from it to the Witches Stone near the tower. ... It is used for domestic purposes and has lately been cleared and faced inside with stones. There are neither old thorns, stones, paths or anything about it, which could indicate its former use.'

Little is known of the subsequent history of the monastic site, though Antrim appears periodically in the annals and there is a record in the Annals of the Four Masters of Antrim being burned, though by whom is not stated. The monastery's early importance seems to have been due to its association with the main lineage within the Dál nAraide, one of the principal people groups of the Ulaid, whose seat of power was at nearby Rathmore. The site appears to have continued to be a significant religious centre under the Anglo-Normans under whom Antrim became the headquarters of an important bailiwick within the earldom of Ulster. A large motte was constructed, and possibly a bailey also, within what are now the grounds of Antrim Castle Gardens. A few further references to the Medieval church can be found and 'Eccl. de Antoria [Antrim]' is mentioned c. 1542 in the Register of Primate George Dowdall.

In the late sixth century a monastery was founded at Muckamore near Antrim by Colmán Elo (or Colman-Eala), a nephew of Columcille. The name derives from the Irish *Maigh Chomair*, meaning 'the plain of the confluence', i.e. the confluence of the Six Mile Water with Lough Neagh. Records show that the monastery suffered at the hands of the Vikings in the ninth century. An early account of the monastic settlement described it as 'a great and fair monastery in a place in the middle of the wood, watered with many streams and beautiful with fields'. In the late twelfth century, under the Norman knight, John de

Courcey, Muckamore was refounded as an Augustinian priory dedicated to the Virgin Mary and Colmán Elo. Muckamore was a wealthy priory, with extensive lands attached to it. It was dissolved following the Reformation and in the early seventeenth century came into the possession of Roger Langford and then the Clotworthys of Antrim. According to local tradition, the priory stood on the site of the walled garden of Muckamore Abbey House. This was confirmed through archaeological excavations in the 1970s, which revealed the foundations of a number of buildings, including the priory church.

Under the patronage of the O'Neills of Clandeboy, a Franciscan friary was built on the southern shores of the Six Mile Water at Massereene sometime around 1500. A Kingdom Hall of Jehovah's Witnesses stands alongside the site today. Excavations in the 1970s uncovered a small rectangular church along with a curving ditch, measuring some 2–3 m wide and 2 m deep. A hoard of coins, dating to 1500–05, were found within the ditch. In 1601, during the Nine Years' War, Sir Arthur Chichester took possession of the friary buildings, constructing earthworks around it and making it a key base in the campaign against the forces of Hugh O'Neill, earl of Tyrone. In the aftermath of the war, Hugh Clotworthy, one of Chichester's captains, was granted a sizeable estate in this area, beginning a new chapter in Antrim's history.

Of today's places of worship in Antrim, the most prominent, due to its positioning near the centre of the town and its tall and elegant early nineteenth-century tower and spire, is All Saints Church of Ireland, an Anglican parish

FIG. 31.2
All Saints Parish Church.

church. The main body of the church is much older, dating back over 400 years, and is in the Late Perpendicular Gothic style. The construction of this church signified a change in the religious centre of gravity in the parish away from the earlier site at The Steeple. The new church was built as a place of worship for a new religious expression – Protestantism – which the Clotworthys and most of the English and Scottish settlers arriving in Antrim in the early seventeenth century espoused. The south transept of All Saints includes the burial vault of the Clotworthy-Skeffington family, ennobled as Lords Massereene. Within the church there are several high quality monuments to members of this family. The churchyard adjoining All Saints is the oldest burial ground in the town of Antrim and those whose earthly remains are interred here represent the full spectrum of the local community. The church was caught up in the events of the Battle of Antrim during the 1798 Rebellion, with some of the United Irishmen taking up positions in the churchyard, before eventually being forced to withdraw.

In the course of the seventeenth century Presbyterianism emerged as a distinct religious denomination in Ireland and several current and former Presbyterian meeting houses can be found in Antrim. The first specifically Presbyterian meeting house in Antrim is believed to have been built on the road to The Steeple around 1680 or so. In 1699 Antrim's Presbyterians acquired a site on what is now Church Street where they would build a church which still stands today, though much altered from when it was first erected. A date-stone on the present building states that it was erected in 1700 and renovated in 1891. Following the first major dispute within Irish Presbyterianism over the issue of subscription to the Westminster Confession of Faith, the congregation divided in the mid-1720s

FIG. 31.3
Former Non-Subscribing
Presbyterian Church.

with the 'New Lights' or 'Non-Subscribers' retaining possession of the meeting house. In the twentieth century the membership of the congregation declined sharply to the point where services ceased. The church is now empty, but some years ago was used as a boxing club. A small area at the front of the church has been used for burials, with a much larger graveyard to the rear of the church. There are several memorials from the late eighteenth century and this is one of the earliest Presbyterian graveyards in Ireland. Those interred here include victims of the Battle of Antrim.

In the late 1720s, in the aftermath of the abovementioned split, Presbyterians in Antrim in favour of subscription built a new meeting house in Millrow. Later this church was enlarged with the addition of a wing, transforming it into the traditional T-plan structure so associated with Presbyterian places of worship. The congregation grew substantially in the early 1800s, necessitating a new meeting house. This was built on a different site, one that was set back about 90 yards from Church Street. Though the year 1834 appears in the pediment on the entrance front, the church – a handsome Greek-inspired edifice – was not opened until 1837. In fact, the building we see today was subject to a major work of restoration if not rebuilding following a disastrous fire in 1862 (though

FIG. 31.4
First Antrim
Presbyterian Church.

apparently replicating the original design). The congregation is known as First Antrim. A further Presbyterian congregation was established in Antrim in the mid-1800s. Now used as commercial premises, the former meeting house of High Street Presbyterian Church stands close to All Saints. Designed in the Gothic Revival style and constructed of black basalt, this meeting house opened in 1853. In 1974 the congregation moved – 'ported' in Presbyterian terminology – to a new building near The Steeple in Antrim.

The founder of Methodism, John Wesley, preached in Antrim on three occasions, including on his final tour of Ireland in 1789. For much of the nineteenth century there were two Methodist chapels in Antrim. The Primitive Methodist Church of 1823 was located on the south side of Church Street. It still stands and is now used as commercial premises, though its ecclesiastical origins are unmistakable. There was another early nineteenth-century Methodist meeting house in Kiln Entry, which was replaced by a new church on an adjoining site in the 1860s. Following the union of the two main branches of Irish Methodism in 1878, this meeting house served as the place of worship for the united congregation. In 1977 Antrim's Methodists moved into a new suite

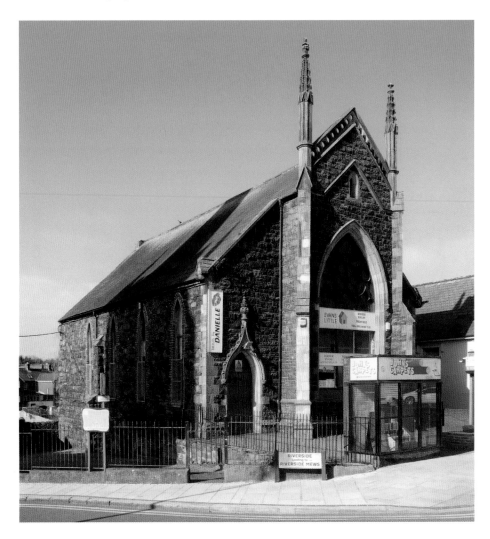

FIG. 31.5
Former High Street Presbyterian Church.

of building on Greystone Road. For a time the former Methodist church was used as a library; it is now a funeral parlour. Other Protestant denominations with a presence in the town today include the Baptists, Elim and Free Presbyterians, meeting in buildings in a range of modern styles.

St Comgall's Catholic Church, completed in 1870, is a prominent landmark at the junction of the roads leading from Ballymena and Randalstown into Antrim. It is not the first church to stand on this site for an earlier place of worship was erected here in 1818–20. Before this Antrim's Catholics attended worship in Randalstown and previous to that, during the era of the Penal Laws, Catholics around Antrim met for worship at a number of places and in a variety of settings. The church completed in 1820 was a cruciform building and one of the arms (the eastern) was used exclusively as a school. Moves towards building a new Catholic church in Antrim began in the mid-1860s. The new place of worship was built around the old church until it reached roof level when the stonework of the original building was removed. The new church was built of basalt with white dressings. Like its predecessor, it is a cruciform structure and in style can be described as Italianate.

FIG. 31.6
St Comgall's Catholic Church.

The final religious denomination to be mentioned here is the Society of Friends, whose adherents are popularly known as Quakers. The founder of the Society of Friends in Ireland, William Edmundson, lived for a time in Antrim, though it was in Lurgan that he established the first Quaker meeting on this island. A Quaker meeting house was built close to Church Street in the early eighteenth century. Antrim's Quakers also opened a separate burial ground of their own at Moylinny, which can be found on the south side of the Belfast Road leading from Antrim to Templepatrick, not far from the junction with the Oldstone Road. The Quaker cause in Antrim does not seem to have been particularly strong, certainly in the latter part of the eighteenth century, and ceased altogether by the middle of the nineteenth century.

FIG 31.7

Entrance to the Quaker burial ground, Moylinny.

Bibliography

C.E.B. Brett, *Buildings of County Antrim* (Belfast, 1996).

David Butler, *The Quaker Meeting Houses of Ireland* (Dublin, 2004).

Maurice H. Collis, 'Antrim Parish Church for three hundred years', *UJA*, 2nd series, 3 (1896–7).

Peter Gates, Mervyn Kidd and John Wallace, *Celebrating 400 Years, All Saints Parish Church, Antrim* (Antrim, 1996).

H.L. Henry and W.J. Canning, *A Church for the People: a History of High Street Presbyterian Church, Antrim* (Antrim, 1999).

George Hughes, *Hewn from the Rock: the Story of First Antrim Presbyterian Church* (Antrim, 1996).

Alastair Smyth, *The Story of Antrim* (Antrim, 1984).

FIG. 31.8
Former Antrim Methodist Church.

Floating glamping pods at Ballyronan.

Cultural heritage
Folklore
Community
Place

32 Lough Neagh, upwelling and other origin stories

Sharon Arbuthnot

It has a virtue that hardens wood to stone.
There is a town sunk beneath its water.
It is the scar left by the Isle of Man.

A Lough Neagh Sequence: Coda
SEAMUS HEANEY

In three simple statements, originally published in 1969, Seamus Heaney captured the essence of the stories of Lough Neagh which have emerged and grown over more than a millennium. A text in Latin, often attributed to a ninth-century Welsh monk, is one of the first to mention the 'virtue that hardens wood to stone'. The legend of the sunken city was recorded in the twelfth century by a Cambro-Norman archdeacon, traveller and historian. That the waters of Lough Neagh fill a gap left by the Isle of Man is a tradition which flourished especially amongst English-speaking communities of the post-Plantation era. The Medieval story of the origins and naming of Ireland's largest lake did not make Heaney's list, but is fittingly preserved in the oldest surviving manuscript written (almost) entirely in Irish. Throughout the centuries, tales of wells and wonders associated with the lough, of strange creatures and cures, have attracted the attention of diverse peoples, who wrote and spoke of these matters in diverse languages.

How the lough was formed and named

In the literature of Medieval Ireland, the landscape is everywhere portrayed as both evolving of its own accord and continually affected by the human and Otherworld peoples who inhabit the island. Loughs, rivers and bays often were understood as the effects of water bursting through formerly dry ground.

Tomaidm is the Old Irish word for the eruption of a body of water from underground. Many such events are mentioned in early Irish literature and history. Lough Neagh is depicted as a relative newcomer. Irish place-lore puts the eruption of Lough Neagh in the first century after the birth of Christ; the Annals of Inisfallen are particularly precise, dating the event before the death of Emperor Nero, so before the year AD 68.

Despite its supposed late arrival on the scene, Lough Neagh came to occupy a position of utmost importance amongst the natural features of the island. Around the ninth century, a text best known in English as 'The Triads of Ireland' identified 'the three loughs of Ireland' – in other words, the three most significant loughs – as Lough Neagh, Lough Ree, in the midlands, and Lough Erne, County Fermanagh. Perhaps around the tenth century, scholars began to arrange tales into categories and relate these to levels of attainment in learning. 'Eruptions' are listed alongside tales of deaths, feasts, battles, cattle-raids and visions as *prímscéla* or 'principal tales' which all poets were expected to know. The first *tomaidm* to be cited in these lists is the eruption of Lough Neagh.

Lough Neagh is an anglicised form of the original Irish name. In Modern Irish, the lough is called Loch nEathach or Loch nEachach; in Old Irish it was Loch nEchach. There are two parts: *loch* 'a lough' and Echach, which means 'of Echu', Echu being a common Medieval Irish name for a man.

The Annals of Ulster provide a year-by-year account of the most significant events in Ireland and further afield from AD 431 onwards. In the entry for the year 684, Lough Neagh is referred to as Loch Echach. Throughout the seventeenth century, a great variety of forms with and without the n- can be found in English-language documents: Loughneigh, Loughneah and Lough Neaghe stand in contrast to Lough Eaugh, Lougheagh and Lougheaugh. Late sixteenth- and early seventeenth-century attempts to rebrand the lough as Lough Sidney and Lough Chichester, after two lord deputies of Ireland, Sir Henry Sidney and Sir Arthur Chichester, respectively, never really gained ground, and instances of these names are largely confined to the Irish Patent Rolls, administrative records kept by the British Chancery.

In the narratives of Lough Neagh, Echu is generally depicted as a native of Munster who eventually became a king of the Ulaid. In its modern spelling of Ulaidh, this is now the Irish name of the province of Ulster, but in the Middle Ages Ulaid comprised a much smaller area in present-day counties Antrim and Down.

Tomaidm Locha Echach

Although the title *Tomaidm Locha Echach* 'The Eruption of Lough Neagh' appears in an early list of tales, no story with that title has come down to us. We do, however, have accounts of the eruption of the lough embedded in other Medieval Irish literary works. One of these is *Dindshenchas Érenn* 'Traditions

of Ireland's Notable Places'. There are some differences in how the many manuscript versions of *Dindshenchas Érenn* describe the chain of events which lead to the formation of Lough Neagh, but the basic narrative is as follows. Echu mac Maireda travelled with a thousand followers towards the Boyne. Around the area known today as Newgrange, he encountered Óengus In Mac Óc, a figure from the Otherworld. Óengus instructed Echu's company to move on. When they did not, he killed their cattle, then he killed their horses. Only when Óengus threatened to kill Echu's people did the group agree to leave. Because he had destroyed their horses, Óengus lent Echu a 'wonderful horse' (*ech ingnad*) which was able to carry the belongings of the entire group. Echu was warned, however, to send the horse back before it was allowed to urinate or they would all suffer sudden death.

Echu moved on to a place called Líathmuine, arriving on a Sunday in September. Almost inevitably, the horse wandered off and urinated, generating so much water that a well was formed. Echu built a house over the well, now named Linnmuine, and left a woman to guard it. That is how the situation remained for 19 years, during which time Echu became joint-king of the Ulaid. Eventually, however, the woman allowed the well to overflow and Lough Neagh was formed. In keeping with Óengus' prediction, Echu, most of his family, and the inhabitants of the local area all drowned. The story of the eruption of Lough Neagh might strike us today as both comedy and tragedy; at this distance, it is impossible to know what a Medieval audience would have made of it. We might assume, at any rate, that the purpose was not only to recount an entertaining story but also to explain the names of numerous places mentioned in the tale and known to those who might hear or read it. The main focus, of course, is the lough itself.

The overflowing well

The original story of the formation and naming of Lough Neagh was probably more or less confined to the information given in *Dindshenchas Érenn*. There is reason to think that it was already in existence in some form as early as the seventh century. The core details concerning the woman and the overflowing well are still circulating, though, and oral versions have been collected throughout Ireland in recent times.

The Ordnance Survey Memoirs offer a glimpse into the story as it might have been shared amongst the people of Antrim in the 1830s. According to the summary incorporated into the volume for 1832–8, the well was 'under the influence of the fairies or, as they term them, "gentle spirits"'. It was guarded by an old woman, 'probably a witch', who neglected her duties, having 'made too free with the "crathur"'. In this telling, the water overflowed and followed the woman as far as Toome, where she was thrown into the emergent lough by the local residents as punishment for her misdemeanour. With that, allegedly, the overflowing ceased. It hardly needs saying that 'crathur' here is an allusion to home-made whiskey. The earliest documented reference to whiskey in Ireland is from 1405 and, although the Irish had probably been brewing the spirit for several centuries by that time, the account given in the Ordnance Survey Memoirs is obviously more attuned to the social norms of the 1830s than to those of the time in which the eruption of Lough Neagh was originally set.

In a twelfth-century Latin adaptation of the origin-tale, Giraldus Cambrensis, otherwise known as Gerald of Wales, who was a Cambro-Norman archdeacon, wrote of his travels and experiences in Ireland in a book entitled *Topographia Hiberniae* 'The Topography of Ireland', completed around 1187. Gerald was not particularly well-disposed towards the Irish and at times he seems to cast them in a deliberately negative light. In his reworking of the Lough Neagh story, he states that the people of this region were given to beastiality and so God drowned them all by causing the well to erupt. In detailing how the eruption happened, Gerald mentions that a woman came to draw water from the well but left the cover off as she attended to a child who was crying. It is from Gerald of Wales too that we get an early reference to the submerged city which is said to lie under the lough. His book claims that the tops of church towers, 'tall, slender and rounded', were visible under the surface of the water in calm weather. These towers reappeared in the nineteenth century, in Thomas Moore's *Irish Melodies*, which was issued as ten separate volumes between 1808 and 1834. In this work, Moore supplied English lyrics for a series of popular Irish tunes. One of the pieces, entitled 'Let Erin Remember the Days of Old', conjures up an evocative image of a Lough Neagh fisherman as he observes:

> the round towers of other days,
> in the waves beneath him shining.

While many Irish scholars were content to drop occasional references to the eruption of Lough Neagh into their texts, sometime around the end of the eleventh or start of the twelfth century, an industrious scholar took strands of tradition concerning the lough, wove them together and added material to the narrative. In this new production, entitled *Aided Echach maic Maireda* 'The Death of Echu mac Maireda', there were additions to the cast of characters and a development in the plot which brought the action forward to the sixth century and the time of St Comgall of Bangor. *Aided Echach* occupies under three pages of the 67 leaves which have been preserved of this Medieval book. Although the title given to the text in the manuscript itself focuses on Echu, the most important character in the tale is Echu's daughter, Lí Ban or Lí Bán. She deserves a chapter on her own and will be dealt with in the next one.

Other origin-tales

Ask the people of Ireland today about the legend of how Lough Neagh was formed and many will recount a tradition centred not on the character of Echu mac Maireda but on Fionn mac Cumhaill or Finn McCool, as he is better-known in English-language contexts. This version of the lough's origins tells how Fionn, a giant, scooped up a sod of earth and hurled it at an opponent on the other side of the Irish Sea. The hollow left in Ireland filled with water and became Lough Neagh, while the sod itself fell into the sea to create the land-mass we know as the Isle of Man. Fionn mac Cumhaill has been featuring in Irish literature since at least the eighth century, but it was not until the later Medieval period, especially from the twelfth century onwards, that he became a central and popular figure. In stories from the Middle Ages, he is portrayed as the leader of a band of followers, many of whom seem to be in a transitional life-stage, between boyhood and manhood. Living mainly on the margins of society, constantly on the move, and occupied with hunting, fighting and abducting women, these bands were known as *fianna*. Fionn's followers actually seem to have been modelled on groups of trouble-makers which really existed in Ireland. Under the year 847, the Annals of Ulster report that a large band of *fianna* had been 'invading kingdoms like heathens'. Clearly, this band was not a literary figment but a serious, real-world threat. The Annals refer to its members ominously as 'the sons of death' (*maic báis*).

Lough Neagh is said to have been made by a single scoop of Fionn's hand. All of these traditions obviously assume that Fionn mac Cumhaill was of enormous size. This idea that Fionn mac Cumhaill was a giant has come to the fore, however, only in relatively recent times. Two trends are particularly prominent in modern folklore, neither of which was strongly felt in the earlier, written tradition: Fionn is characterised as a giant and he is associated with great feats of leaping and throwing. In Ireland, folklore began to be collected seriously only in the nineteenth century and some of the earliest activity took place in the north of the country. It was, in the main, middle-class antiquarians and language enthusiasts who began the work of documenting cultural heritage. They gathered and preserved examples of Irish vocabulary, stories, cures, sayings, customs, beliefs, explanations of place-names and other material deemed to be of significance to particular communities.

Also, the Ordnance Survey fieldworkers were first active in Ulster around the same time. They recorded a substantial amount of folklore centred on Fionn and his fianna, and the article in the Ordnance Survey Memoirs of 1832–8 which records the tale of the overflowing well and the neglectful old woman who partook of 'crathur', includes also an account of the formation of Lough Neagh by 'Fin McCool', who is described as a 'great favourite among the lower orders'. This account tells how Fionn being exasperated at some act of indiscretion, or to show his great power; is said to have seized a handful of such size that the hollow caused by its removal formed the basin of the present lough. The earth being thrown into the Irish Channel formed the Isle of Man, which is gravely stated to be of exactly the same shape and size as the outline of the lake. It is also a prevalent belief that if a fire is not continually kept burning on the island, it would return to its former situation.

A violent earthquake had thrown up the rock at Toome ...

In the nineteenth century, those not inclined to repeat tales of overflowing wells and squabbling giants could turn to another explanation for the existence of this huge body of water in the north of Ireland. Many accounts written around that time link the creation of Lough Neagh to an earthquake. The extract below is taken from the edition of the *Dublin Penny Journal* which appeared on 17 August 1833. On the subject of Lough Neagh, the anonymous writer says:

> we are informed, on the authority of the late Lord Bristol, Bishop of Derry, that, 'in a Monastery on the Continent, a manuscript existed, which mentions, that in the sixth century, a violent earthquake had thrown up the rock at Toome, which, by obstructing the discharge of the rivers, had formed this body of water ...'.

The authority to whom this information is attributed is, presumably, Frederick Hervey, fourth earl of Bristol, who was Anglican bishop of Derry until his death in 1803. And that is all that can be established with any degree of certainty about this strange claim. No surviving manuscript is known to contain an account of an earthquake which deposited a rock at Toome and no trace of a substantial rock impeding the progress of the Bann can be found in the area today. There is, however, a trace of an actual event which might have inspired the 'violent earthquake' of this account of the origins of Lough Neagh.

Ireland is not generally noted for its seismic activity, but the land-mass which now makes up the island was once in two different continents, with the area around modern Donegal and Mayo on a separate plate. As a result, tremors are occasionally felt. Activity of various kinds is recorded from earlier centuries also. Notes in Latin in the Annals of Ulster allude to a terra motus around the year 600, and two similar events in the north of Ireland are logged in the space of a single week in the early eighth century. The latter may represent an earthquake and its aftershock, but Latin terra motus means simply 'movement of the earth' and the phrase can refer also to landslides, rockfalls, bog-bursts and other sudden shifts in the ground. It is difficult to know, then, whether any of these events were actually earthquakes.

Even if it could be shown that the popular nineteenth-century tradition linking Lough Neagh to a sixth-century earthquake was inspired by an actual seismic event, the fact remains that the lough itself is much, much older than the sixth century. It is generally thought that the Lough Neagh area covers an early

Cenozoic pull-apart basin. In other words, the lough is assumed to be underlain by a fault-line which parted as the crustal plates slid past one another, causing the basin to sink and fill with water from feeder rivers. In the 1820s and '30s, when the information attributed to the bishop of Derry was being reproduced in print time and again, this scientific explanation was yet to be formulated, but clearly many of those interested in the origins of the lough were already seeking answers in the geological domain.

This essay is derived from the author's book Wonders and Legends of Lough Neagh, *published by the Ulster Historical Foundation in association with Lough Neagh Partnership in 2021.*
Illustrations are by Matthew Donnelly.

33

Lí Ban
a Lough Neagh enigma

Sharon Arbuthnot

While many Irish scholars were content to drop occasional references to the eruption of Lough Neagh into their texts, sometime around the end of the eleventh or start of the twelfth century, an industrious scholar took strands of tradition concerning the lough, wove them together and added material to the narrative. In this new production, entitled *Aided Echach maic Maireda* 'The Death of Echu mac Maireda', there were additions to the cast of characters and a development in the plot of the origins of Lough Neagh and one character in particular.

The introduction of Lí Ban

According to *Dindshenchas Érenn*, Conaing and Dairiu or Airiu, a son and a daughter of Echu, survive the flooding of the plain of Líathmuine. In *Aided Echach*, Airiu drowns and another daughter survives the flood with her lap-dog, Conbroc. The name of this second daughter of Echu can be understood in different ways. Medieval Irish scribes often omitted the length-marks over vowels which distinguish *bán* from *ban* and *lí* from *li*, so the name might represent early Irish *lí ban* 'appearance of women' or, if it includes the adjective *bán* 'white, fair, pure', it may mean roughly 'fair appearance'. There will always be an element of doubt and the name may have had different connotations at different times, but as it is tempting to suggest that in the original she was called Lí Ban and that the audience of the tale would have understood from the first mention of her name that this daughter of Echu might turn out to be more complex than she seems initially.

Having retold the story of the overflowing well, *Aided Echach* goes on to describe how, for the first year after the flood, Lí Ban (as we shall call her) and her lap-dog lived in a *grianán* under Lough Neagh. Based on the word *grían* 'the sun', *grianán* usually denotes a place or structure open to the sun; it is well-known from the place-name Grianán Ailigh or Grianan of Aileach in County Donegal. In the Medieval tale of *Fled Bricrenn* 'Bricriu's Feast', the word *grianán*

is used also of a separate area behind glass, where trouble-maker Bricriu can safely observe activities at the feast of the title without being able to cause any havoc himself. So, perhaps we are to imagine Lí Ban protected in a kind of glass bubble under the lough. She seems to be able to see the fish swimming around at any rate, for one day she speaks to the Lord and expresses how good it would be to swim with them. The Lord obliges; she is partially turned into a fish and her dog is turned into an otter. They remain like that for three hundred years.

What does Lí Ban look like?

Internet and press articles on Lí Ban are often illustrated with an image of the fish-woman from Clonfert Cathedral, County Galway. The fish-woman in question, carved in stone on a pier of the chancel arch, is thought to date from the fifteenth century, though, so the image is several centuries later than the tale of *Aided Echach*, for which the figure of Lí Ban was conceived. An egg tempera and gold-leaf icon produced by Betsy Porter in 2010 has accompanied work written about Lí Ban also, but this illustration owes more to modern perceptions of mermaids and to the artist's experience of working on sacred icons in the Byzantine style than to Medieval descriptions of Lí Ban.

How, then, are we to imagine Lí Ban in her transformed state? The descriptions provided in the prose and poetry of *Aided Echach* are not entirely consistent. When Lí Ban's metamorphosis is mentioned in the prose narrative, she is said to be 'in the form of a *bratán*' (*i richt bratáin*) or 'half a *bratán* and half a person' (*a leth 'na bratán ocus a lleth n-aill 'na duni*). In early Irish, *bratán* was a general word for a fish; deriving from *brat* 'a captive', it was probably applied to any commonly caught fish. In Modern Irish, however, *bradán* refers to a salmon, and sometimes Lí Ban is described in ways which make clear that the fish-like part of her body is, specifically, salmon-like. Using a different word for 'salmon', she even declares herself to be 'in the form of a salmon except my head' (*i rricht íaich acht mo cheann*)!

In contrast to all of this, the poems which constitute a significant proportion of *Aided Echach* suggest that the salmon of Lough Neagh actually served as a food-source for Lí Ban. In one poem, she mentions how she tastes salmon in the early morning, and she says that she is a *muc mara* and a *bled*. The former term continues in Modern Irish as *muc mhara* 'a porpoise'. English porpoise comes from Old French *porpais*, which is based on the words for 'pig' and 'fish'. This name was probably inspired by the creature's snout-like nose and Modern Irish *muc mhara* similarly translates as 'pig of the sea'. *Bled* is not so easily explained. Sometimes, it seems to mean 'whale' (it is given as an Old Irish equivalent of Latin *ballena* 'whale' and *belua marina* 'sea-beast'); on other occasions, *bled* seems to be used for a fictional beast rather than a real-world organism.

It seems, then, that the different strands of Lí Ban tradition which were brought together in the tale of *Aided Echach* did not entirely agree on the physical appearance of the woman after she had been partially transformed. That said, it is obviously not appropriate to perceive her in terms of images produced in the fifteenth or twenty-first centuries. Bizarrely, though, Lí Ban seems also to have little in common with other fish-women and sea-women of Medieval Irish tradition.

Medieval Irish water-women

Tellers of tales in Medieval Ireland often seem fascinated by the possibilities of what lived and lurked under the sea and in other deep waters. Just as 'eruptions' explain how certain enclosed bays and loughs came into being, so turbulence on the surface of water was sometimes attributed to the movement of water-monsters. Predictably, then, monsters were most closely associated with areas of extreme and dangerous waves and white-water. Where early Irish water-creatures are envisaged as being partly human, they are almost always female

The Annals of Ulster record that, in the year 1118, a *murdúchann* was caught by the fishermen of Listerlin, County Kilkenny, and another was caught near Waterford. No description of the creatures is given in either of these sources, but they were obviously considered sufficiently strange for their capture to be worth registering in the annals.

None of various water-women tales take us much further forward in our search for the inspiration for Lough Neagh's Lí Ban, who seems utterly unthreatening in nature, has a special relationship of some kind with salmon and sings only to attract the attention of messengers from St Comgall. When Lí Ban sings, the action is compared in the Irish text to *celebrad aingel*. *Celebrad* comes from Latin *celebro* 'I celebrate (in song)' and the Irish word is almost always used in a religious context. *Celebrad aingel* means 'the celebration of angels'.

Lí Bán in the Acallam

The tale of *Aided Echach* says nothing about Lí Ban's life in the three hundred years between her transformation into a fish-woman and her meeting with messengers from St Comgall. There is, however, a possible glimpse of her in *Acallam na Senórach* 'The Conversation of the Elders'. The *Acallam* is a lengthy text, in prose and verse, which probably dates from the early thirteenth century. In it, a party of warrior-hunters, who had been followers of Fionn mac Cumhaill (or Finn McCool, to whom we shall return shortly), travel around Ireland with St Patrick and recount their past adventures. As this unlikely group journeys through the area of present-day County Down, St Patrick hears about 'The Hunt of Slieve Donard and the Exchange with Lí Bán'. The Irish for 'The Exchange with Lí Bán' is here *Imacallam Lí Báine*, so the author of this short narrative obviously took the name to be Lí Bán 'fair appearance'. She introduces herself as a daughter of Echu mac Eogainn maic Ailella rather than a daughter of Echu

mac Maireda. Nevertheless, this woman bears a suspicious resemblance to the Lough Neagh character: she is placed in the same general geographical area, she claims to have been in the water for three hundred years in one manuscript (for one hundred years in others) and she can sit on a wave just as well as she sits on a hill or on a rock.

The main purpose of the short story about Lí Bán in the *Acallam* is to enhance the reputation of Fionn mac Cumhaill – the water-woman says that the last time she chose to reveal herself to anyone it was to Fionn and she lifts her head above the water now only because she recognises his former companion. Apart from that, Lí Bán merely assists the group in hunting animals which have run into the water and, while she is clearly portrayed as a long-term resident of the sea, she is never said to be anything other than 'a young woman' (*ingen*). Indeed, at one point, she is described as swimming on her back, swimming on her side and 'foot-swimming' (*traigirsnám*); the last of these is a particularly interesting choice as the fish-tailed woman of Lough Neagh presumably did not have any feet! It may be, though, that *traigirsnám* was such a common way of referring to treading water that the author of the story did not think too much about the literal meaning of *traig* 'foot'.

Lí Ban in the annals

A short passage in the *Acallam*, then, is the sole possible sighting of Lí Ban/Lí Bán from the time of her metamorphosis, a year after the eruption of Lough Neagh, until the sixth century when St Comgall was installed in Bangor. Otherwise, *Aided Echach* states only that she went 'under the water and under the seas … in every direction' until she chose to reveal herself to Béoán mac Innle, who was on his way to Rome when he heard her angelic singing. Lí Ban does not rejoin humanity at this stage but arranges to meet members of St Comgall's community at Larne in a year to the day. At the appointed time and place, she is caught in the net of Fergus of Mulleague and taken to land.

The capture of Lí Ban is actually mentioned in the chronicles of Ireland – but only as a result of what seems to be a Medieval muddle. The Annals of Ulster record the capture of a *muirgeilt* in the year 572. To what this refers is not certain; it may have been taken to be a supernatural creature, but *geilt* was a name for some species of bird and, as *muir* means 'sea', the *muirgeilt* may have been simply a rare seabird. Whoever composed one of the poems incorporated into *Aided Echach* must have known the tradition of the *muirgeilt* which was supposedly caught in the sixth century, because in that poem Lí Ban distinguishes herself from it, saying 'I was not the famous *muirgeilt*'. In spite of this, later prose passages in the tale assert that Lí Ban *is* the *muirgeilt* and what may have begun as a simple error took on a life of its own. The Annals of Roscrea, Boyle and the Four Masters all add details about Lí Ban to the statement announcing the capture of the *muirgeilt*. The entry in the Annals of Boyle for the year 565 nicely illustrates how these two pieces of information have been brought together: the main text of the manuscript states, in a mixture of Latin and Irish, 'in this year the *muirgeilt* was caught', and then in the margin of the manuscript, a scribe has written in Irish 'i.e. Lí Ban, daughter of Echu mac Maireda, on the strand at Larne in a net, i.e. of Beonán mac Innle, a fisherman of Comgall of Bangor'.

Merging originally separate statements is not particularly unusual in Medieval Irish texts. When scribes thought they knew of additional facts and traditions which could shed light on particular points in a narrative or on events mentioned in chronicles, they often took the opportunity to insert them into the texts they were writing. As well as adding useful and relevant details, occasionally they supplied also mistaken and misleading information – and some of their additions have been interpreted in ways which the scribes themselves could not have foreseen. All of this is worth bearing in mind as we come to examine how Lí Ban's tale ends and how she is remembered today.

Lí Ban's salvation

The final section of *Aided Echach* recounts how, after being caught in Fergus' net, Lí Ban was put on display in a vessel of water and crowds of people came to look at her. A dispute over ownership of her then arose: St Comgall asserted that she belonged to him as she had been found on his territory, Fergus claimed her as she had been caught in his net and Béoán argued that she was his as she had promised to be buried with him when they first met. The debate was settled by an angel, who advised that the chariot which carried Lí Ban should be yoked to two stags which would arrive the following day from the place which is now Carnearny, County Antrim. Wherever the stags pulled the chariot, Lí Ban should remain. Events turned out as the angel predicted and the stags carried Lí Ban to Tech Da Beóc, possibly Saints' Island in Lough Derg. There, the fish-woman was given a choice: to be baptised and go immediately to Heaven or to live another three hundred years before entering Heaven. She chose the first option and St Comgall baptised her with the name Muirgein before she died. The tale of *Aided Echach* ends by stating that wonders and miracles were performed through Lí Ban at Tech Da Beóc and that, like every holy young woman, she is honoured and revered, just as God honours her in Heaven.

Clearly, this closing part of the story of Lí Ban has a very different purpose from the legend of the eruption of the lough: it is less concerned with landscapes and names and more focused on Lí Ban's contact with and acceptance into the Christian faith. The arrival of Christianity in Ireland around the fifth century is directly linked to the introduction of literacy. The Latin alphabet was quickly adapted for writing in the Irish language and the Irish went on to develop the most extensive surviving vernacular literature in Early Medieval Europe. This close relationship between Christianity and literacy meant, of course, that for several centuries, stories were preserved, modified and probably made up in monasteries by scholars who were also ecclesiastics. Understanding something about the people behind the stories, and about their interests and concerns, can help explain developments in the plot of the tales themselves.

A number of tales found in Lebor na hUidre involve characters from pre-Christian times who are either seen to be converted by representatives of God or made to endorse the benefits of Christianity and emphasise the hardships of those who continue to live unbaptised. In *Siaburcharpat Con Culainn* 'The Phantom-Chariot of Cú Chulainn', the most famous hero from the Ulster Cycle of tales is raised from Hell by St Patrick in order to urge Lóegaire mac Néill to 'believe in God and in blessed Patrick … lest the earth swallow you'. In *Scél Tuáin meic Cairill* 'The Story of Tuán mac Cairill', the Tuán of title survives from the time of Partholón to tell a history of Ireland and declare 'I am with God'. In a poem embedded in the tale, Tuán says that God has 'put me … in many shapes', and we can deduce that he has been turned into a stag, a boar and a hawk to help him survive through the centuries.

Set against this background, certain aspects of the story of Lí Ban are seen to be purposefully managed. She hails from a time before the arrival of Christianity in Ireland, her transformation into a part-fish has enabled her to exist beyond a normal human lifetime so that she can come into contact with the early saints. She chooses to be baptised and die rather than to continue to live in an unbaptised state. She receives divine reward for that decision. Like Cú Chulainn and Tuán mac Cairill, she is being used as a vehicle for the promotion of Christianity and baptism. It may be significant also that Lí Ban is received into the faith and dies while still part-fish and that her baptismal name, Muirgein, means 'person of the sea'. Amongst learned Irish ecclesiastics, there seems to have been some curiosity about how those who suffer from deformities and disabilities and those whose bodies have been altered in the process of dying – such as by fire – will appear on Judgement Day. Lí Ban's fish-like form may have acted as an assurance that physical perfection at least was not a requirement for salvation or for honour and reverence in Heaven.

Saint Lí Ban?

The person who shaped *Aided Echach* was obviously concerned with Lí Ban's salvation and sought to use her story to promote the message of baptism, but that tale never claims that Lí Ban became a saint. The concept of the 'mermaid saint', which has become popular in recent years, can be traced mainly to a calendar of saints and their feast-days called *Félire Óengusso* 'The Martyrology of Óengus'. Lí Ban is only one of three options put forward in comments on *Félire Óengusso*. According to 'The Martyrology of Tallaght', on which *Félire Óengusso* may have been based, the male abbot of Glenn Uissen is the Muirgein commemorated on 27 January. Could more than one saint called Muirgein have their feast on that day? In 'The Martyrology of Donegal', 27 January is given as the feast-day of both Muirgein, abbot of Glenn Uissen, and Muirgein 'whom the books call Libán, daughter of Eochaid'. 'The Martyrology of Donegal' was produced by Mícheál Ó Cléirigh, though, in the early part of seventeenth century, and Ó Cléirigh's treatment of the *múrduchainn* in *Lebor Gabála Érenn* – which seem to be freely adapted to the mermaids of his own day – suggests that we should be wary of placing too much trust in Ó Cléirigh adhering closely to Medieval sources.

Having said all of that, there is reason to think that some Medieval scholars did, indeed, regard Lí Ban as a saint. Genealogies of saints are recorded in numerous manuscripts. Amongst these long lists of saints and their ancestors, we find references to '*Libáin*' and '*Liban*, i.e. Muirgein, a daughter of Echu mac Maireda'. It may be that the character from the Lough Neagh legend has become confused here with a saint called Liban or Libanus, who was a man and whose feast-day is 18 December. The various references to individuals called Muirgein, Lí Ban, Liban, and so on, are difficult to disentangle. It seems significant, though, that none of the texts which deal with saints mentions anything about Lí Ban being part-fish and that the main point made by the author of *Aided Echach* is simply that any 'holy young women' can attain salvation by baptism just as Lí Ban did.

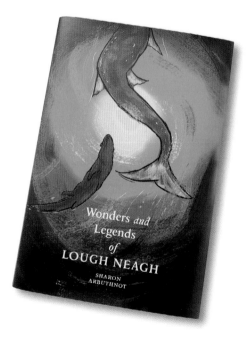

This essay is derived from the author's book Wonders and Legends of Lough Neagh, *published by the Ulster Historical Foundation in association with Lough Neagh Partnership in 2021.*
Illustrations are by Matthew Donnelly.

34

Ardboe Cross
memories, legends and folklore

Pat Grimes

Inevitably many stories and legends have been passed down through the years concerning the monastery and cross at Ardboe, not least those that link Colman's abbey and Lough Neagh. These are set down here – in no particular order – just as they appeared in print, or were recorded.

Francis Quinn (The Pin) interview, 1948

Collected in the summer of 1948 from the parish of Ardboe

By Henry Devlin, Clunto-quin, County Tyrone
[later Fr Henry Devlin PP, Cloghogue, Upper Killeavy (1923–93)]

Collector's note

The parish of Arboe, or Ardboe, is situated in the north-east corner of County Tyrone. It lies along Lough Neagh and so is noted for its lakeshore scenery. In the parish is the remains of an ancient monastery, which is said to have been founded by St Colman in AD 590 and to have been destroyed in 1166. Near the monastery is the far-famed Celtic Cross, of tenth-century workmanship. This High Cross is one of the finest in Ireland and is elaborately carved with twenty-two scriptural scenes. As will be seen, most of the folklore centres round these geographical and historical facts. Special foot-notes will be given re: particular places and object material.

The remarkable thing about the people of the parish is the number called Devlin or Quinn. In fact the electoral division is called Muintirevlin. To overcome this difficulty – many people of the same name – different families

FIG. 34.2
The cow mawed 'Ardboe'. Pin's Frank Quinn, long-time caretaker of the cross and graveyard, pictured on the abbey shore in 1952 with Nancy Ann McConville.

were given different nicknames as: Devlin (Dhu); Devlin (Ban); Devlin (Mor) etc. For further information about the people of the district, see the recent publication by Joseph Chubb Devlin, under the title of: *The Story of an Irish Sept* or *The Devlins of Tyrone*.

The following information was recorded on the 27 July 1948. The informant, who is 65 years of age, lives quite close to the Old Celtic Cross, of which mention was made at the beginning. He got most of his knowledge from an old man, who died recently, named Mick Donnelly. This Mick Donnelly was recognised as the leading authority in folklore yet my informant – Mr Francis Quinn – is the number one authority in folklore of the Old Cross district. Mr Francis Quinn's address is Farsnagh, Coagh, County Tyrone.

Informant: Mr Francis Quinn

They say this chapel was built from the milk of a cow. The mortar is hard to chip and it is supposed to be made with the milk of a cow that came in out of the lough. She left her track on the flat stones – every place she put her foot, she left the track of her hoof.

There is a stone up at Eglish's place – they were Devlins lived there, but Eglish was a nickname – with the track of the cow, and the calf's hoof, and the end of a staff where a man pointed down.

When the church was finished building, as far as we can hear, the cow and calf went out to the lough again and mawed "Ardboe" – they said the place got its name from that: Ard, height, and Bo, the cow – height of the cow – and that's how Ardboe derived its name. There are some stones still with the cow's track on them.

There were only sheep-walks in Ireland at that time and the cow was coveted and taken away because she was that great a milker. But the men that were building the church traced the cow, with the tracks on the stones, along the shore, on to the Blackwater, County Armagh, on up to Benburb. They took her back here and they kept a better watch on her. That's the reason of the tracks on the stones along the lough.

Collector's note

The word 'mawed', used in the information given above, is a common word meaning 'roared loudly'. The reference to the stones with the marks of the cow, etc evidently has much to support it because there are two of these, which I have seen, and the marks on them are very clear. Indeed it is a great pity that these stones are not preserved because at the moment they are lying in the grass and will be lost. One of these stones – with markings most pronounced – is lying near an old house belonging to Thomas Devlin, Sessiagh, Coagh, County Tyrone. The other one is in the possession of Mrs Treanor, Farsnagh, Coagh, and she is quite willing to give the stone to anyone. In fact Mrs Treanor has a number of other stones, which formerly belonged to the old Abbey, and she would be willing to give them to any interested person.

Informant: Mr Francis Quinn

There are many funny [*odd*] headstones in this old graveyard. It is a funny, interesting thing that about twenty stones show that the wife always took her maiden name to the death. It is still the custom in Ardboe, when the people are talking among themselves, that wives are called after their maiden names.

There would be twenty of these stones in this graveyard. One of them has the name of Bernard Lappin, deceased January 3rd 1712; also of Grace Kelly his wife who dyed 1727. Also, another stone has – "Sacred to the memory of Peggy Devlin, spouse of Dominick O'Farrell, who departed this life August 16th 1720". There is a stone there over three brothers and one of them was Bernard Devlin, late Guardian of Dungannon Convent, and if we could get the date we would have everything correct. "He paid the great debt due to nature" – that is what is on the stone. This stone is over three brothers, and they were priests. One of them, Barney Devlin PP of Kilmore, and the other Rev. Pat Devlin. There are other names, fathers or brothers, all of Kinross, but it was or is Kinrush. That was the name of Kinrush in 1727.

There is a stone called the Friar's stone. It is one of the most important in the graveyard. It is supposed to be that the last friar was the name of Lappin and in the bad times the church and monastery were destroyed. He darned be seen as there was a price on his head. Well, he had to live in an oul mud house with people called Doorish. The ancestors of this friar were buried on the other side of the stone in 1712 – they are called Lappin too. They buried on the east side – the ordinary people are buried facing the rising sun and the clergy are buried facing the setting sun. The two faces on the arms of the stone are oul monks. These people – Lappin – occupied it in 1712 and they must have been some ancestors of the monk. The monk was in banishment because the monastery was destroyed in the 17th century – 1645 or 1646. Two stones in this graveyard have raised printing on them. They were erected in 1743. The writing is in English and there is a V for U.

One of the tombstones has a coat of arms which includes the Red Hand and a sword, and a bird – a very strange bird. An oul officer, an Englishman, told me that the bird represents a bird which lives on blood. The O'Neills lived for blood. There are some interesting things on this tombstone:

Sacred to the memory of the aftermentioned viz Captain Lewis Gordon
O'Neill, who died at the Cape of Good Hope 16th Jany 1808 aged 37 years
Also Adjutant St John O'Neill who died at Bombay 4th Octr 1814
aged 30 years
Also their mother Elizabeth O'Neill, late of Killygonlan, who depart'd
this life 1st July 1818 aged 66 years

Another headstone has the following on it, which seems very strange as I don't know what JVGY means: IHS JVGY MULLOY DIED THE 2 DAY OF JUNE 1707.

About the 17th or 18th century they did not put crosses on the headstones, for fear of them being demolished at that time. This was a mixed burying ground up to 100 years ago. Kinrush school, like this graveyard, was under the rector. So if the people put crosses on the headstones it showed they were Catholics and then the stones would be destroyed. This oul tree, filled with pins, pennies, nails, buttons, and such things, is called the wishing tree or pin tree. It was there in my father's and grandfather's time. Everybody that comes here puts in a pin or a nail or any such thing and makes a wish. I heard them saying – my father and other people – that a man once went into a hole in the face of a bank near here. This hole is supposed to lead to the Cove at the parochial house in Mullinahoe. This man went in playing on his bagpipes and the people outside listened and they heard him playing the tune:

> *I doubt, I doubt, I never will get out*
> *The farther in the deeper O!*

That used to be a well-known tune at the time. The man never came out of the hole, and anything that ever went in, never came out. The hole is now called the

FIG. 34.3
The tradition of the wishing tree, or 'Pin Tree' as it was known, being explained by local historian Pat Grimes in June 1986.

piper's hole and you can see it up at Crosswiggy; that is an oul Irish name, I suppose.

If there had been a history attached to the old Abbey, it would have been very big. There was a tunnel from the monastery to the church. The hole in the graveyard here is supposed to be the roof of the tunnel caved in. There is a cellar beyond the Abbey and with a roof it must have been some kind of a cave. I think they boated in their stuff and the boats went up into the cellar from the lough.

Master O'Neill – oul Master O'Neill, who might be twenty years dead – told the craic that the sacred vessels passed from Ardboe to Ardmore. Some say it was to Anavore drain. He said it was Ardmore but it was Anavore. They never crossed the lough to Ardmore but they went to Anavore which is near here. There is a difference in the two places.

They say the lough was formed this way: a mother went for a can of water and she left her child in the creddle. The child started to cry or the house went on fire and the woman ran to her child. She left the well uncovered and it overflowed and she could not get back to cover it. So the whole valley was filled with water and made Lough Neagh.

On May day the people used to gather the dew of one farm and bring it to their own, or else milk a cow belonging to someone else, and so take their luck away. This lasted up to about fifteen years ago. It is supposed to be that the borrowing days mean that they borrowed two days off April to skin the oul cow. This means they made March a long month and April a short one.

Lammas used to be a day for pilgrimage to Ardboe. It started on the 24th of June and ended on the second day of August. There is a verse of a song about this –

> *They do assemble from every part*
> *For to petition the King of Heaven*
> *To pardon sinners of a contrite heart*

That is a couple of lines of Oul Ardboe – a song about Ardboe. The man that made it was hung in '98. His name was Garland – a Lurgan man. Lammas has faded away a number of years now. The oul people say there used to be upwards of 50 or 60 in their day. Now only a few stands come, but the children around gather here on Lammas Day. There is a custom in this parish to this very day for New Year's Day. The people look to see who comes into their house first. If a black-haired person comes in first it is all right, but if a red-haired person comes in first: "Fare ye well, Killeavy!"

The high cross of Ardboe

Collector's note

This high cross of Ardboe is one of the finest in Ireland and it is carved with 24 scenes from Scripture. These are not as sharp as they used to be but most of them are still quite clear.

Informant: Mr Francis Quinn

We start at the east side with the bottom panel:

1 This shows Adam and Eve in the Garden of Eden
2 Here Abraham is seen offering up his son as a sacrifice
3 Daniel in the lions' den
4 This shows the children in the fiery furnace – the flames are easily seen
5 Here there are fourteen faces and they represent Joseph and his brethren
6 This shows Christ in judgement with beam and scales at his feet. The heads around represent people

Next we go to the south side:

1 Cain slays Abel
2 David rescuing the lamb from the lion
3 This is David and Goliath the Great
4 Here you see David and Saul reigning under one crown
5 This one is uncertain but might represent implements used at the crucifixion

Now for the west side:

1 This one represents the nativity
2 Angels adoring our Lord
3 Christ driving the money-changers out of the temple
4 Triumphal entry into Jerusalem
5 Christ taken prisoner
6 The crucifixion: on the two arms is portrayed Christ's visit to Caiaphas and from Caiaphas to Pilate

FIG. 34.3

East face of Ardboe Cross, 1857.

Drawing by Henry O'Neill; published in 1859 in his book *Illustrations of Some of the Most Interesting Sculptured Crosses of Ancient Ireland.*

The north side:

1 Here John is seen baptising Our Lord in the Jordan
2 Moses is supported in prayer
3 Here the two mothers are seen holding the leg of a child each
4 Solomon is here sitting in judgement – prepared to cut the child in two
5 Nails used at the crucifixion

Collector's note

It may be interesting to you to know that since I collected the folklore from Mr Quinn, the BBC recording car has visited him. His reading of the Old Cross was recorded and has already been broadcast some time before Christmas 1948.

Mick 'Robin' Devlin interview, 1948

Mick Devlin (1868–1957) was a Lough Neagh fisherman who grew up just 300 yards from the cross and Colman's abbey. He was nicknamed Robin on account of his flaming red hair. In the summer of 1948 he was interviewed by Henry Devlin, a clerical student at Maynooth, who was from the townland of Cluntoquin in Ardboe parish.

I was born in Sessia in 1868 and reared a short distance from the old Abbey and Celtic Cross. Most of my knowledge about the lough and the local area I got from my parents and other old people.

How Lough Neagh came to be. There is a story which says that the oul woman went to the well for a pail of water and everybody was supposed to shut the well. She did not shut the well with the result that the well overflowed and the water overtook her and she nearly drowned, and the water was supposed to enlarge so much that it turned into a big lake called Lough Neagh.

"When you see the round towers of other days in the waves beneath them shining" – that is, of a nice day you will see the walls shining in the water, like the oul castle in County Derry. The round tower, you will see it also shining in the water.

There was a boat one night and she went close past us and we could see nobody in her. She went round us until she disappeared out of our sight. That would have been sixty-five years ago. That boat was talked about previous to this, and she has even been seen again since that, but nobody has ever seen anything further than that.

On the lough, at a place called the White House Flat, there were men one time lifting more nets than they set, and a monstrous animal of some sort rose beside the boat. It scared them so much that they made off for the shore as quickly as possible.

Some people hold that before you go out on the lough fishing you

FIG. 34.5

Francis Quinn, universally known as 'The Pin',
Lough Neagh fisherman and caretaker of the
Old Cross and graveyard, pictured in
1959 with his granddaughter,
Elizabeth Crowley of New
Jersey, USA.

should turn the boat with the sun, that is, you should turn towards the south, for luck.

There is a small lough in County Antrim and they call it Feumore and this Squire Dobbs got a lot of men to drain it, by making a big drain to empty this wee lake into Lough Neagh. Well, he kept them working for years and years and at the latter end he failed in all his work which reduced him to poverty. He came round when he had failed in his job; he came round to see the oul place and a song gives us how he felt:

> He formed a windmill to drain the wee lough
> But the wee lough is there still
> He wrought by the perch and he wrought by the yard
> And he wrought by the hour when work had grown hard
> But their working and toiling it was all in vain
> For the lake of Feumore could never be drained.
> Bonny Port Mor you shine where you stand
> The more I look at you the more I think long
> But if I had you now as I once had before
> All the money in Europe wouldn't purchase Port Mor
> Your door is of ivy and your door is of ash
> Where lords used to dine now farmers do thresh.

There is a point up the Banks in Farsnagh called Gollomon, and there used to come out on this point from Lough Neagh a horse. It fed for one hour on this point and then went back into the lough and they never seen it more. It came once a year about the same time.

There is a place in the townland of Farsnagh called the Street. There were eight houses in it with a family in each house but the landlords in days gone by racked the houses and put the people on the road. In the houses they worked at fishing, weaving, and spinning. They carried away their webs to Portadown – a distance of eighteen miles. Here they sold them and got weft. Weft was the thread the buyers gave the people. They did not pay for the weft but sold their webs to the man who gave the weft. I mind the time that some of these houses were there, but there is not wan of them there now.

The Bridge Fight was a famous event. The Orangemen held a meeting in Coagh and they decided to cross the Ballinderry Bridge and rack Ballinderry Chapel, but the Catholics all gathered under Father McGeough. When the Protestants came marching against the Bridge, the Catholics turned them, and beat them so much that they never came back. That was in the year 1879. It is still called the year of the Bridge Fight.

On Lammas Day, which means the first day of the harvest, that is the first of August and then on the second of August, there were six or seven counties gathered round the Old Cross to celebrate the beginning of the harvest. They all knelt down and recited the rosary and then went down to the lough and washed their feet and hands and head. Then they came up and recited the rosary again. After that they all retired as best they could for their own homes.

I mind when I was fifteen or sixteen years of age that they did these things but they naturally died away. The self-same thing happened on the twenty-third of June, that is, Midsummer Day. They also called it Bonfire Night because they lit the fires in the evening, at different points. After midnight some of the smart fellows would take what they called the flour of the fire and run away with it, to take the luck from that place. This carried on until about forty years ago. At that time if you had stood at Ardboe Point you could have seen these fires all round Lough Neagh.

The fog on the cross used to be took by people from every direction, to cure whooping cough and it is done yet. There used to be holy water around this cross. The rainwater filled holes that were at the foot of the cross and when it lay there it became holy water. The people emigrating from around here to America and elsewhere took chisels and hammers and broke edges off the cross to bring with them to their destination, wherever they were going. They took it for luck, lest anything should happen, as an oul relic. The Rural District Council got railings put round it to safeguard the cross and from that time there was no more taken off it. This Old Cross stands eighteen feet high and a small distance from this cross is an ancient abbey where in days gone by new-born children, if they were dead-born or died after birth, were buried. That would be over one hundred years ago. There is a stone at the Old Cross where St Patrick was supposed to bend his knee on. The track of the knee is still there.

The Pin Tree at the Old Cross is a wishing tree. Warts and lumps can be cured by sticking a pin into the lump and then putting it into the tree. The lump is supposed to disappear.

The Cove on Mullinahoe Hill, Ardboe, in 1880 was opened. In getting into the cove, previous to it being opened, you had to go into an oul well and creep on your hands and knees till you got by a big stone that was in this cove and then, when you got by this big stone, you could have walked with a little bend right round it. In the cove there was charred sticks or burned sticks and it was supposed that these sticks were burned by the Danes in years gone by. Father McElvogue took charge of the opening.

On May Eve you dare not go to any neighbour's house for milk, water, or a loan of any class, because if you got it you were supposed to take away their luck.

I heard an oul custom about marrying:

Monday for health
Tuesday for wealth
Wednesday the best day of all
Thursday for losses
Friday for crosses
Saturday no day at all!

On May Eve the children gather mayflowers and rowan trees and put them right round the houses, at the door and windows, and stick the rowan trees in every field lest any man should blink it. This custom is still kept.

The women used to tie a red rag on the door and put the tongs on the creddle, where the child was, in order to keep the fairies away. They did this when they were going out of the house.

There used to be an oul custom about burying. If there were two funerals on the same day then both parties tried to be at the chapel first, because it was thought that the last person through the gate remained at the gate until the next funeral came. Indeed it is related that many a time there was a race to the chapel with the coffin in order to get there first.

FIG. 34.6
Some people believed that the rainwater which filled these holes on the base of the cross became holy.

Joe Mallaghan of Clunto-quin

Joe Mallaghan (1891–1981) was a small farmer who had spent some years in USA in the 1920s and '30s, where he worked with teams of horses on farms. He had a retentive memory and was often sought out to answer queries about the olden days.

Interviewed in 1970 about the Old Cross of Ardboe, he stated matter-of-factly that the stones for the cross were quarried in Carland [*north-east of Donaghmore*] and were transported from the quarry to Ardboe by water. The stones were loaded onto rafts which were launched into the Torrent River. The Torrent meanders here and there, eventually joining the Blackwater shortly before that river flows into Lough Neagh. The rafts then followed the shoreline down to Ardboe Point. Joe also remarked that in the winter months in earlier days, funerals from the Moortown district of Ardboe parish on their way to the graveyard at the Old Cross, left the road at the top of the Moor Hill and cut across the fields, keeping to the higher ground to avoid the flooded bogs. This route was known as the Coffin Pad. He stated that Moortown chapel was built in 1846. The original intention was to erect it at the Kiln Corner in Clunto-quin townland but the landlord refused to give a site. However, Robert Alexander of Portglenone, the landlord of the adjoining townland, Clunto-richardson, gave a half-acre field to the Ardboe parish priest, Fr Thomas McKenna. The field was part of the small farm of John Quinn, known as Jessie. "That's how Moortown graveyard got the name Jessie's Garden," explained Joe. "The first person to be buried in Jessie's Garden was Michael Mallaghan. He was 20 years old and he was buried there in 1855."

Nailly Coney of Killygonland

Nailly (1918–88) was a Lough Neagh fisherman, songwriter and raconteur.

We called the month of July on Lough Neagh the good month. The water temperature was high in July. The old fishermen also referred to the worm month. This would have been roughly from the fifteenth of July to the fifteenth of August. You would have took a poison very easy during that month. There was what we call the Lammas Fair held on the second day of August beside the Old Cross of Ardboe. For many years people went down to the Lammas Fair and bought yella man and maybe had a bottle of Guinness or two in the pub. They had their lines set on that particular day before they came down and right enough some of them wasn't in a hundred per cent shape for lifting them lines the next morning but they tried anyway. Lammas is an old custom.

FIG. 34.7

Old cross woodcut: the lines from Tom Moore's song refer to the fable of how Lough Neagh was created.

"On Lough Neagh's bank, as the fisherman strays, When the clear cold eve's declining;

He sees the Round Towers of other days In the wave beneath him shining."

I used to listen to the old fishermen who fished in the past. Especially the fishermen from the far shore of Lough Neagh. I used to listen to them – and I remember thinking back, about these stories I heard them telling about what they had seen on the lough. It might have been fancy, it might have been superstition, you never know. But I composed a little poem about it anyway. The title is *The Lough Neagh Queen*. It's about a mermaid. It starts off:

> *One night I stood in a sally grove by the side of a lonely bay*
> *Where a fisherman had ceased his toil and homeward made his way*

and it goes to tell the story of the Lough Neagh Queen, who had a spell cast on her by a Druid and who can come back just the one day every thousand years to roam on the west shore of Lough Neagh and she can only be seen by the lonely fisherfolk.

Patrick T. Tobin of Moortown, Ardboe

Patrick T. Tobin (1894–1961) hailed from Kilbrien, County Waterford. He became principal of Moortown Boys' School, Ardboe, in 1914. A man with a keen interest in a multitude of subjects, he lost his eyesight 1940 and had to retire from teaching. He mastered Braille and began writing articles for magazines on his Braille typewriter. The following article was first published in The Irish Weekly and Ulster Examiner *on Saturday, 27 June 1953.*

Pilgrimage to an Ancient Abbey

> *On the twenty-fourth of June and the second of August*
> *They do assemble from every part*
> *For to petition the Queen of Heaven*
> *To pardon sinners with contrite heart.*

This is a stanza from a local ballad. The ballad itself, lengthy, and a strange mixture of much doggerel and some good poetry, is wedded to a beautiful air, and is sung in praise of the ancient Abbey of Ardboe and its Celtic Cross which are to be found at the end of a cul-de-sac on the west shore of Lough Neagh, in the parish of Ardboe, in the district of Munterevlin, County Tyrone, about ten miles south-east of Cookstown.

The extract quoted above indicates that the Abbey and its surrounds had for long been a place of pilgrimage on the feasts of St John the Baptist and of Lammas respectively; and this was so until the creeping in of abuse caused the suppression of the religious ceremonies altogether, sometime during the first half of the nineteenth century.

The custom of holding a fiesta at Lammas, as far as the laity was concerned, persisted through the years right up to the end of the first quarter of the present century; since then the feast is commemorated only by the children who come early with their savings on the morning of Lammas. These savings they rapidly exchange for cakes and yellow-man, lemonade and dates, toy whistles, mouth-organs, bugles, and other musical instruments.

Having gorged themselves to the full on the sweetmeats and washed them down with copious draughts of lemonade, the youngsters then proceed expertly to convert the instruments of melody into instruments of torture; and for the rest of the afternoon the quiet Abbey re-echoes the happy laughter of the children, accompanied by the fearful din made by the continuous blaring of the aforementioned instruments.

This goes on until late afternoon or until the children are exhausted and then, out of breath and out of pocket, they reluctantly turn towards home – unless it has happened that anxious parents had been impelled to go in search of their offspring and had driven them home.

Despite ecclesiastical proscription of public processions, small groups and individuals made their way every year to examine the ruins and to worship at the cross. They included Parnell, Joe Devlin, John Dillon, Mr de Valera, Sean McDermott, Liam Lynch, Dr George Sigerson, Dr Lloyd Praeger, and Francis Joseph Bigger.

At one time or another they have all made their way to the Abbey in an endeavour to make it yield up its secrets for, apart from the fact that it is there and that the Celtic Cross is one of the best examples extant, there is only a small body of knowledge of the history of this foundation, and much of that knowledge is legendary and very little is perhaps accurate.

There are those who come from near and far on cycles and on foot to visit the graves of their dead, and the town folk who come to the lough shore for a bathe and a breather and include a visit to the Cross as part of their itinerary. Others spend every possible moment of leisure around its grounds, scanning the tombstones, discovering the last resting place of priest or monk; looking at the Cross. Looking and learning, learning and remembering, remembering and praying – and thus, as in the cloister, finding in prayer, peace.

There has always been in the hearts of the people a desire to revive this ancient pilgrimage. Some thirty years ago the present parish priest, Very Rev. Arthur Rogers, then acting as curate at Ardboe, received permission to recite the Rosary in Irish at the Cross one summer afternoon. The crowd was large and their conduct exemplary, and they impressed him so much that last year, as parish priest, he sought and obtained permission to hold evening devotions within the Abbey grounds. The response was so satisfactory and so stimulating that arrangements were recently made for open-air devotions on the twenty-first of June.

During the previous week evenings many willing helpers, boys and girls, bearing names such as O'Neill, Quinn, Devlin, and others, that left one in no doubt as to their descent from Tyrone's princely stock, under the guidance of that indefatigable doyen of parochial workers, Mr Thomas O Neill, trimmed and furbished, festooned and garlanded the whole Abbey area, whose grass had been shorn to a billiard-table smoothness by the caretaker Mr Francis Quinn. He spends his whole time cleaning and working amongst the ruins, and his readings of the sculptured figures are familiar to many a sightseer, while his broadcasts on his beloved Abbey have stirred the hearts of many an exile and turned their thoughts towards home.

Mid-summer Day dawned most unpropitiously cold and wet but the afternoon cleared up and towards evening the people of the district began to make their way to the Old Cross. The early arrivals visited the graves of their forebears, pausing here and there to look at the inscriptions on the tombstones; to read anew the writings on the old; to discuss the adventures of the O'Neill who died soldiering at the Cape of Good Hope; to talk about the local soldier whom the Americans brought home for interment at the end of the first world war; to pray for those who have come to rest here since their last visit; to enjoy the scenery, and to examine the altar from which Benediction was to be given.

There was a hush when Father McKeever CC began to preach. He was standing where Colman stood, and in front of him were the same people who received the good news from Colman. There was a group bearing the very same surname as that borne by the chieftain of Brocagh, who alternately protected the monastery from the attacks of marauders from Tullyhogue, Lecale, and elsewhere, only to plunder it himself and let his soldiers loose on the district to exact coigne and livery when the Brocagh treasury was empty. It was an O'Hagan who razed the Abbey in the 12th century.

There was a group of young men whose surname (Quinn) proclaimed that they were of the lineage of Conn of the Hundred Battles. Many others of the family of Conn were there – the Conways, the Conlons, the O'Neills, the Devlins – the Devlins of Munterevlin, the Devlins who were the standard-bearers of the O'Neills, the Devlins who were his bodyguard, the Devlins of his household gallowglasses, the Devlins who were his ostlers and horse-boys, and Devlins who … But this is not a history lesson.

A tall lone figure quivers with pride whenever the preacher mentions the name of Colman, for he is a Colman – Big Frank – born and reared within a stone's throw of the Abbey in the home that has been the Colmans' home for centuries.

Here they all stand listening to the sermon; standing on the hallowed dust of their forefathers – the dust of soldier, saint, and savant; of fisherman, friar, and farmer – dust that is distributed only to receive the departed relatives of each succeeding generation, and then only to enshroud and embrace them protectively until the day when they are to be called to receive the reward promised to those who persevere until the end.

In the line of vision of the preacher is the Church of Our Lady at Moneyglass, from whose tall spire, silhouetted in the evening sun against the Antrim hills, is wafted across the lough the peal of the vesper bell calling Duneane to prayer. With them, as Father McKeever finishes, those at the Abbey join with their own parish priest, Father Rogers, in the public recital of Mary's Rosary and await on suppliant knee the blessing in solemn Benediction of Mary's Son and their God.

The lusty singing of *Faith of our Fathers* at the close suggests a compelling thought. During the centuries that have passed since this Abbey was founded, great empires have risen and fallen, nations which were in their time great champions of Christendom have abandoned the faith or apostatised; yet here through all the years in this little strip of territory the loyalty of the people has never wavered and the faith of Patrick is as strong here today as it was when Colman preached it thirteen hundred years ago. Perhaps the rhymer had something of this in mind when he wrote:

> *I've travelled France and I've travelled Flanders,*
> *And all the countries beyond the Rhine,*
> *And in all my rakings and undertakings*
> *Ardboe your aiqual I ne'er could fin'.*

35

Attitudes towards place and place-names in the Lough Neagh basin

Roddy Hegarty

'the record shows a lake notable in legend and in history, with a coast made famous by warrior, saint and chieftain'[1]

In 2009 Dr Brian Turner, writing in the journal of the Federation for Ulster Local Studies, *Due North*, stated, 'Ulster local historians know the fundamental importance of townlands and their names. We know that all documentation referring to rural location and landholding, stretching back for hundreds of years, depends on the townland identification.'[2]

FIG. 35.1
Richard Bartlett's map of south-east Ulster, *c*. 1602, showing Gaelic territories adjoining the southern shoreline of Lough Neagh.

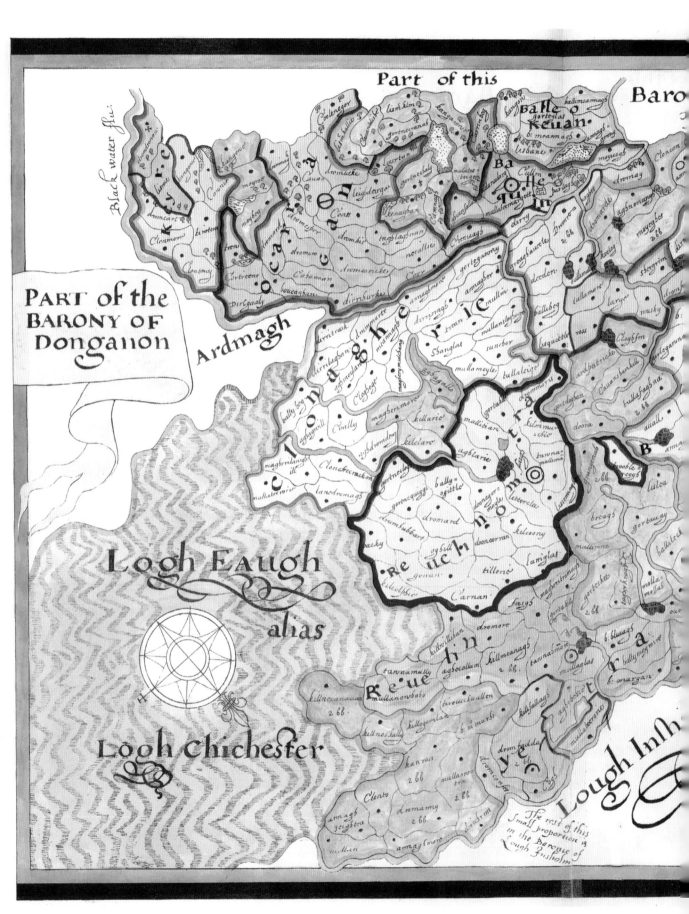

Part of this   Baro

Balle o Keuan

Ba Offe tin

o Carrid gan on

PART of the BARONY OF Donganon

Ardmagh

Clonaghe ... rie

... noma ... tra

Reuch

Logh Eaugh

alias

Reue tin

tra

yeu

Logh Chichester

Lough Insh

The rest of this
Small proportion is
in the Barony of
Lough Insholm

Black water flu:

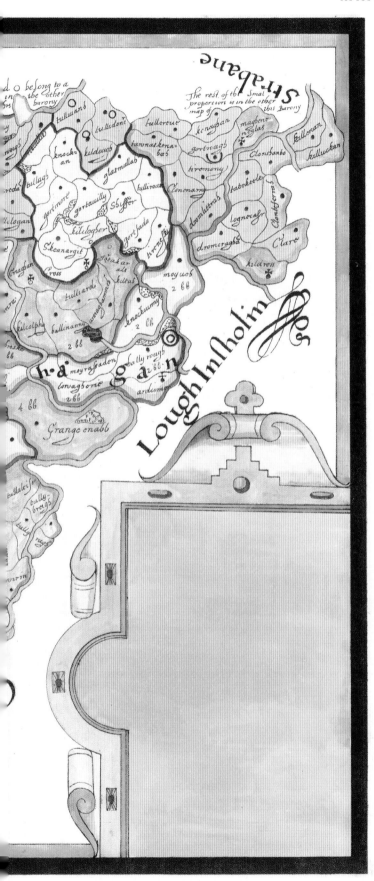

Turner was writing at a point in time when despite the concerted efforts of campaigners for the best part of 30 years, townland names were still perceived as being under threat. That threat, it was argued, came from the imposition of road names and house numbers where none had existed for hundreds of years. Furthermore, many of the road names were either erroneous or misleading and often recorded names of places several miles away from the area through which they ran.

The Federation's response to this perceived threat in 1991 had been to publish *Every Stoney Acre has a Name* as an encouragement to people to celebrate their townlands. Seven years later, still faced with the dual challenges of officialdom's need for conformity and the apathy of town dwellers, Dr Bill Crawford wrote, 'Only when their own personal traditions come under attack do they begin to realise the vital part that tradition plays in our emotional life.'[3]

More than a decade after Turner's commentary there are still rumblings of discontent and a genuine fear in many rural areas that this important aspect of local identity is being eroded by a need to conform to the needs of government bodies and large corporations. There remains a commonly held belief that local place-names are under threat in spite of the fact that many local councils have adopted the inclusion of townland markers on signage, and many community and voluntary groups have placed boundary markers at the mearing of townlands in their own locality.

FIG. 35.2

Bodley map of part of the barony of Dungannon, 1609.

CARDINAL TOMÁS Ó FIAICH MEMORIAL LIBRARY AND ARCHIVE

Much of the evidence of discontent has been anecdotal with little empirical research carried out on attitudes towards place-names and identity. In the spring of 2021 the Lough Neagh Landscape Partnership commissioned a short survey to explore attitudes around the lough, the results of which provide one of the first focused pieces of research in this field at a local level. The online survey was conducted over a three-week period and gathered the opinions of 107 people over the age of 18 from almost 70 locations across 21 parishes around Lough Neagh. The survey drew responses from across the age range and also looked at the potential for variation in attitudes between those who had left their home place to attend university and those who had not. It also sought to determine if there was any variation between those of differing religious backgrounds.

The survey confirmed that there was a genuine perception that local names were at risk of being lost and that the reason for that loss was the replacement of traditional townland names with postcodes, road names and house numbers. However, the survey also shed light on some additional interesting trends and attitudes. The survey was interested in how townland names were being used and therefore asked a number of questions relating to these. On the question of how many townlands each respondent was familiar with almost half stated that they knew of ten or more, while only two were unable to say that they knew any.

It was unsurprising to find a reasonably high level of knowledge in relation to townlands given the various campaigns promoted by local historians to preserve these and in recent years a strong focus on academic surveys led by Northern Ireland Place Names Project. The publication, in 2007, of *Lough Neagh Places: Their Names and Origins* by Patrick McKay and Kay Muhr has no doubt contributed to a more acute awareness of townlands in the area. Indeed, the section of the survey covering place-names and identity confirmed that townlands remain an important element in local culture and identity.

Despite this deeply held emotional attachment more than one in five of those surveyed never use the townland name in correspondence, with 31% stating that they always did so. It could reasonably be concluded that the work of the Federation and the historically central administrative role of this land division, as outlined by Turner, has embedded its place in the rural psyche and that even if not universally employed there are sufficient historical sources to ensure the survival of these names.

What was of greater significance arising from the survey was the potential reservoir of names that could be described as sub-denominations. These are often portions of townlands, names for parts of roads or rivers, landings spots on the loughshore, or fishing stands and fields. The majority of these names are undocumented. They are of no real administrative purpose and are often known only to a small cohort. Some, however, may appear in land transactions and estate agent's records.

FIG. 35.3

Learning more about
local place-names at the
Lock Keeper's Cottage,
Toome.

Recent work in other parts of Ireland has proven invaluable in rescuing thousands of such names. Major collection projects have been undertaken in Galway, Kilkenny, Louth, Meath and Westmeath as well as in Donegal. The Louth project has given rise to a major publication which states: 'Place names are one of the most intangible but vital layers of this landscape. They tell us about those who have gone before us and how they interacted with and understood their surroundings.'[4]

The survey of Lough Neagh clearly demonstrated that there currently exists a good level of knowledge. However, the experience elsewhere would indicate that this is a finite resource. Much of this knowledge is confined to older generations and changes in agricultural practice over the last half century has led to a decrease in communal, co-operative farming in favour of single family enterprises. Fields are as likely to be recorded by a number as they are to have retained their unique name. There is an urgency required to collect and record these names, perhaps much greater than the urgency that sought to preserve the names of townlands a generation ago.

In conclusion, the Lough Neagh survey has provided an important measure both of knowledge and identity that if used in conjunction with the experience elsewhere provides a strong rationale for future heritage projects in the locality focusing on minor and erstwhile undocumented place-names. The methodology has already been developed and with the possible exception of access to the 1937–8 Schools Folklore Scheme (this did not include Northern Ireland) all other major sources are extant and accessible. The principle resource, however, resides in the local community and it is only with the engagement of that community that such a vital project can succeed.

Notes

1 John J. Marshall, *Lough Neagh in Legend and History* (Dungannon, 1934).
2 *Due North*, 2:3 (Autumn/Winter, 2009), p. 3.
3 *Townlands in Ulster: Local History Studies*, ed. W.H. Crawford and R.H. Foy (Belfast, 1998).
4 *The Field Names of County Louth* (Louth Field Name Project, 2014) p. 1.

36 *Briseann an dúchas trí shúile an chait*
Heredity breaks through the eyes of the cat

Malachy Ó Néill

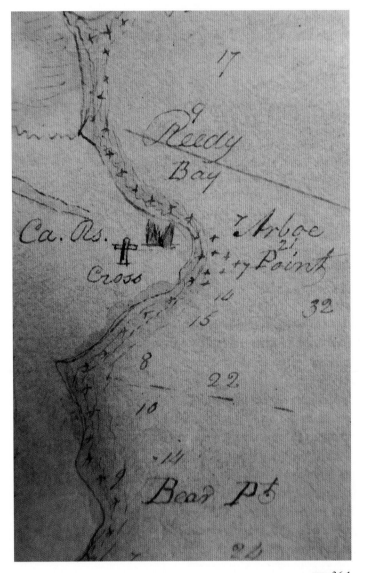

FIG. 36.1
Detail showing Ardboe Point
from a map of Lough Neagh, 1785
(PRONI, D604/1).
PUBLIC RECORD OFFICE OF NORTHERN IRELAND

A direct translation of the English word 'heritage' in Irish is often a source of some conjecture. The fantastic new *Concise English-Irish Dictionary* (Ó Mianáin 2020) offers the two most prevalent options: *oidhreacht* (from *oidhre* meaning 'heir') and *dúchas* (from *dú*, an archaism for 'a place'). Both are equally plausible equivalencies and each term articulates a certain sense of the privileged position we enjoy as the current custodians of the rich tapestry of language, culture and landscape, which is the rightful inheritance of all those fortunate enough to call the loughshore home.

Dinnseanchas, the traditional Irish lore and topography of famous places, remains central to our makeup and the sense of identity with its indelible association with place. Therefore, a comprehension and appreciation of the etymology and toponymy that surrounds us is imperative in understanding and valuing our surroundings. This is particularly apparent in the loughshore community in which I grew up in the parish of Ardboe.

The omnipresent role of Irish in this identification of place and in articulating its value has inspired my personal engagement with the language. An initial classroom investigation of the words, sounds, myths and legends that have moulded this loughshore linguistic landscape ever since primary school days. Back then the discovery of the genesis of familiar townland names of Ardboe whetted the appetite and demanded further analysis. Pat McKay and Kay Muhr have gone further, providing a scholarly examination of *Lough Neagh Places: Their Names and Origins* (2007) which serves as a reference for loughshore inhabitants and a great many further afield.

Diarmuid Ó Giolláin (2013) has discussed this 'valorisation of vernacular' language and tradition as 'a product of a dialogue between universalism and particularism'. He identifies 'the inherent quality of belonging to a specific place' and language is central to this sense of affinity and association with location. As is the case in parishes the length and breadth of Ireland, the Irish language is fundamental therein and it is worth considering local attitudes and actions with regard to language in the post-famine Ireland as English emerges as the dominant linguistic force, particularly following the initiation of the National School system.

A fleeting reference to the prominent role of an Ardboe native in the Gaelic revival movement of the late nineteenth century is an interesting place to start. Listed amongst the key contributors to a meeting of the Society for the Preservation of the Irish Language at No. 9 Kildare Street, Dublin, 'Felix O'Neill, Ardboe' is mentioned in 'The Irish Language' feature in *The Freeman's Journal* of 23 August 1882 with the following commentary:

> The delegates who attended and spoke in Irish, gave a great satisfaction. The congress was considered a great success, about fifty delegates attending each of the five sittings.

While a 'National School teacher' of the same name is listed in the townland of Annaghmore in the census return for both 1901 (aged 54) and 1911 (aged 64), it is noteworthy that no reference is made to linguistic capacity in Irish in either case, the 'Irish language' column left blank on each occasion. Given his age profile and professional credentials, however, it is plausible that this individual is the language activist of the 1882 report.

Ardboe and the Irish language revival also feature in the national press some years later. Writing under the pseudonym of *Lamh Dhearg* ('Red Hand'), this contribution to *An Claidheamh Soluis* (the newspaper established by Pádraig Pearse) from Saturday, 22 May 1909 refers to the passion of local people in relation to language preservation and acquisition:

> "Lamh Dhearg" writes us: –
> "Early in the present year a branch of the Gaelic League (Craobh Lamh Dearg) was formed in Ardbo, County Tyrone, and an Aeridheacht under the

auspices of this Branch will be held at the "Battery," Ardbo, on 29th June. Ardbo is one of the most beautiful districts in Tir Eoghain, and the "Battery," as well as the Old Cross which is beside it on the banks of Lough Neagh, is famous as a tourists' resort. It is expected that the Aeridheacht will be a big success and contribute largely to encourage old Irish games and sports in that part of Tir Eoghain.

"Though very few people in Ardbo understand the Gaelic language they are all most anxious to have it taught in their schools, and at least one Irish teacher will reside in the parish."

Rev. Patrick S. Dinneen in his *Irish-English Dictionary* defines *aeridheacht* as: walking for pleasure or health; an entertainment in the open; lightmindedness, vanity. No doubt, this 1909 occasion at The Battery was part of a series of events which sought to revive interest in native language, culture and sport in the years that followed the inception of Conradh na Gaeilge (the Gaelic League) in 1893, following the establishment of the Gaelic Athletic Association (GAA) in 1884.

Ardboe has been celebrated in poetry, prose and song for centuries – the verse of John Canavan, the songs of Geordie Hanna, and the novels of Polly Devlin each capturing in their own way this 'valorisation of the vernacular'. Seamus Heaney too found inspiration in the native parish of his wife Marie, who has published with distinction in her own right on key aspects of Irish heritage.

My own mentor, Dr Diarmaid Ó Doibhlin, a native of The Loup and an inspirational literary scholar and teacher for generations of Irish language students at Ulster University, found a muse in the familiar motif of the milch-cow which emerged from 'the lough's lush meadow' in his Irish language poem which bears the parish name, *Ard Bó*:

> Shiúil loilíoch amach
> As móinéar méith an locha,
> Balláin lána
> Ag líonadh
> Bhearna an ghátair,
> Blianta sin an ghorta,
> Gur bheathaigh lucht ocrach do thí,
> Gur nasc le chéile
> Garbhchlocha do mhuintearais.
> Tearmann na naomh, na laoch is na saoithe.
> Fothrach inniu,
> Seanbhallóg spíonta,
> Sniogtha,
> Gan doras, gan díon, gan teallach beo na scéalta.
> Reilig inniu,
> Cillín fionnfuar an dearmaid,
> Doibhlinigh is Crúiséaraigh ina luí
> Ag feitheamh le buabhall an aiséirí.

Cuardóidh mé carn mo mhuintire.
Cá bhfios nach dtréiginnse seal
Bainne forgaí an tsaoil?
Cá bhfios nach bhfeicinn
Géimneach ard na bó?

His lyrics portray an iconic 'high cow', nourishing the hungry inhabitants of every homestead, providing shelter to saints, heroes and scholars, and enshrining a final resting-place for his own kinsfolk who bear the quintessential loughshore surnames of Devlin and Crozier. This magnificient beast also provides the poet with a means to escape the concerns of the modern world and renew his acquaintance with his own sense of heredity by the loughshore.

This work of a scholarly son of *Muintir Dhoibhlin* ('Munterevlin', or 'the people of Devlin', synonymous with Ardboe and this loughshore patrimony) is testament to the relationship between people and place, language and landscape, which embodies loughshore heritage. It also evokes the words Heaney when he reflected on the role of language, and Irish in particular, in appreciating fully the virtues of this part of world past, present and future:

> Not to learn Irish is to miss the opportunity of understanding what life in this country has meant and could mean in a better future; it is to cut oneself off from ways of being at home.

Our sense of belonging, our innate appreciation of place, and the role of language in our unique loughshore identity will ensure that heredity (with or without the help of the cat!) will continue to resonate as a key factor in the vernacular of the people for many generations to come.

Bibliography

P. Dinneen, *Irish-English Dictionary* (Irish Texts Society, Dublin, 1927).

P. McKay and K. Muhr, *Lough Neagh Places: Their Names and Origins* (Belfast, 2007).

D. Ó Giolláin, 'Myths of Nation? Vernacular traditions in modernity', *Nordic Irish Studies*, 12 (2013), pp 79–94.

D. Ó Doibhlin, *Briseadh na Cora* (Dublin, 1981).

P. Ó Mianáin, *Concise English-Irish Dictionary / Foclóir Béarla-Gaeilge* (Dublin, 2020).

Aspects of a Shared Heritage – Essays on Linguistic and Cultural Crossover in Ulster (Gael Linn, Dublin/Armagh, 2015).

An Claidheamh Soluis, 22 May 1909.

The Freeman's Journal, 23 August 1882.

1901 and 1911 censuses, National Archives of Ireland: http://www.census.nationalarchives.ie.

Parish

Bay

Muckamore

Grange

Ballyoo

Shanogestown

Ballygannel

Ballyaway

Killowly

LOWER

Killead

Dungonnells

Crookedstone

Tully

OF

H

Moore Esq

Britsh

Ballyquelan

Parish

Moore Esq

Siaish

Killead Church

Handoe

MASSARENE

W Moore Esq

Ballyoran

Ballina

Galnagolton

Crumlin River

Ballygowariff

Ballynomary

Cherry Valley

McGoman

Crumlin

B. macoften

Ballygorlgay

Cobb

B. staroshill

Parish

McMullin

B. macimor

Tullyewbar

Ighnaslavagh

Tullyewbar

Glenavy Waterfoot

Ballyollan

Glenavy River

Glenavy

Black Shore

Glenavy

Tullyewtruck

Rams Sound

Glenavey Parish

Sandy Bay

Arbadelvan

Glenavey

UPPER

Ballynacat

37

The north-east Lough Neagh region
an area of cultural transition

William Roulston

The propensity for characterising an area by the way of life and origins of its inhabitants has a long pedigree in Ireland. This short essay considers how the people living along north-east shoreline of Lough Neagh were described in the Ordnance Survey Memoirs drafted in the 1830s, and in particular how the authors of the Memoirs observed an area of cultural transition in this region. For the most part, the transition documented in the Memoirs for these districts was not a change from British to Irish (or vice versa), but rather a move from Scottish characteristics to English. To begin with, a brief overview is given of the migration of families from Britain into the area.

The movement of British families into the region

In the early seventeenth century significant numbers of families from Britain began to settle in the north-east Lough Neagh region. Families from the Scottish Lowlands predominated in the Six Mile Water valley, with the muster roll of *c.* 1630 showing that Scots formed a majority of the British inhabitants on the Clotworthy estate at Antrim and the Upton estate at Templepatrick, both owned by English Presbyterian families. These settlements continued to expand over the rest of the 1600s and into the 1700s, with a 'Scotch Quarter' developing in the vicinity of the Presbyterian meeting house in the town of Antrim. In the south of County Antrim the major estate was owned by the Conways (later ennobled with the title Hertford) and here British settlement was seems to have been mainly English in character, though in the absence of a muster roll for the estate we cannot be certain of the precise ratio of Englishmen to Scots in the early 1600s.

FIG. 37.2

Street sign in Antrim incorporating the place-name Scotch Quarter.

OPPOSITE
FIG. 37.1

Section showing the eastern shoreline from a map of Lough Neagh, 1785 (PRONI, D604/1).

PUBLIC RECORD OFFICE OF NORTHERN IRELAND

Between the Clotworthy and Conway estates, encompassing the parish of Killead, were two territories, or tuoghs, named Killelagh and Kilmakevet (spelled variously), which were granted in 1606–07 to two O'Neill brothers, respectively Neal Oge and Hugh. Roughly speaking, Killelagh, the larger of the two, occupied the northern portion of Killead and Kilmakevet the southern. Neal Oge's son was Henry O'Neill, whose lands were confiscated by the Cromwellians in the 1650s, but restored to him in the 1660s; in 1666 Henry was created a baronet. His son Sir Neill O'Neill died of wounds received at the Battle of the Boyne and afterwards the estate was forfeited and sold in 1701. Prior to 1636 the other branch of the O'Neills in Killead sold a portion of Kilmakevet and the remainder of this territory seems to have been confiscated in the 1650s and passed into the possession of the Langfords, another English Presbyterian family. The extent to which British families had penetrated this district prior to 1640 is impossible to say. Nonetheless, it is probable that at least some English and Scottish families had settled there in the early decades of the seventeenth century. The changes in landownership and the opening up of the area to settlement in the mid-1600s certainly resulted in numbers of families from Britain moving there.

Firmer evidence for the extent of British settlement can be found in the hearth money rolls, two of which are available for County Antrim – one for 1666 and a more detailed roll for 1669. These have been carefully edited and analysed by Trevor Carleton in his book *Heads and Hearths* (1991). The hearth money rolls reveal that by the late 1660s the parish of Killead had been quite heavily settled by families from England and Scotland, especially from the latter. Focusing on the townlands bordering on the eastern shore of Lough Neagh, we find that Gartree, which may have included Ballymacmary, seems to have been exclusively Irish, with several Mulhollands among the hearth tax payers. Ardmore seems also to have been entirely Irish and possibly only one of the hearth tax payers in Ballynageeragh – a Mr Humphrey – was British. Ballyginniff was the home of Sir Henry O'Neill, whose house – taxed on five hearths – was larger than any of the others in the parish.

Other Killead townlands along the shoreline of Lough Neagh were more ethnically mixed. The hearth tax payers in Gortnagallon included householders named Hamilton and Hunter, as well as Mulholland and O'Hamell. Likewise in Ballyclan the names Adair (Adeare), Crawford (Crafford) and Delap (Dunlop) appear alongside more Mulhollands and householders named O'Cleary and O'Dornan, among others. On the other hand, the other shoreline townlands in the parish, Corbally and Dungonnell, were predominantly British. In fact the only Irish hearth tax payer in either townland seems to be a Mulholland in Corbally. A number of the families that were to rise to prominence in the parish in later years, had already settled in Killead by the 1660s. These include the Barbers in the townland of British and the Cunninghams in Crookedstone. Another prominent Scottish family in Killead was that of Montgomery of Boltnaconnell.

The author of an 1875 biography of Rev. Henry Montgomery (1788–1865), a leading liberal Presbyterian minister who was born at Boltnaconnell, described the district in which the young Montgomery was raised in the late eighteenth and early nineteenth centuries in the following terms:

> The land here, as over most of the flat reaches of Killead, is strong and fertile; and the fields, through nearly the entire district, are laid out with a regularity of square and rectangle rarely to be found in Irish farming, and strikingly contrasting with the irregularity of adjoining districts and counties. These, with the general prevalence of well-grown hedge-rows, the long vistas of straight-lined roads between, the large farms and farm-steads, and the better-class farming everywhere observable, resemble so much more the agricultural parts of England and Scotland than the rest of Ireland generally, that one is led to conclude that the district must have been formerly colonised almost exclusively by English and Scotch settlers – a conclusion abundantly verified by the appearance, manners and habits, the names, descent and history of its people.

The Ordnance Survey Memoirs

The compilers of the Ordnance Survey Memoirs, written in the 1830s to accompany the first large-scale mapping of the island of Ireland, regularly included details on the everyday habits of the people they came across, as they listened to their speech patterns and scrutinised their way of life. One of the principal authors of the Memoirs in County Antrim was James Boyle, a senior civil assistant with the Ordnance Survey and possibly a minor landowner in the

FIG. 37.3

Headstone to Nathaniel Waugh (d. 1751) in Muckamore graveyard, featuring the coat of arms and motto (*Industria ditat*) of the Waugh family of Larkhall, Roxburghshire, Scotland.

mid-Antrim area (*OSM*, vol. 19, xi). He was, therefore, not an outsider to the Lough Neagh region in the way that some of the officers of the Ordnance Survey had been in the early days of collecting the information for the Memoirs. Boyle's keen observational skills come through time and again in his writings as he commented on the personality of the region and its people. In particular, he was intrigued by the change from districts where characteristics derived from Scotland predominated and those where Englishness came through more strongly.

In 1838 Boyle noted that the inhabitants of the Grange of Muckamore were 'chiefly' of Scottish origin:

> The grange of Muckamore is the first district in which, proceeding southwards through the county, a change is found in the accent and customs of the people, as it forms, as it were, the line of boundary between the English settlers of the southern and Scottish settlers in the northern districts of the county (*OSM*, vol. 35, 69).

With regard to their patterns of speech, he noted that the residents of Muckamore 'have much less of the Scotch customs or habits and more of the English than the people of the adjoining northern and eastern parishes. Their accent is more agreeable and they are more civil and courteous in their manners than the latter.' Immediately south of the Grange of Muckamore is the parish of Killead. Boyle made similar comments about it:

> Killead is, as it were, the link between the purely Scottish districts immediately north of it and those as purely English immediately south of it. In it, in proceeding southward, the traveller first notices the disappearance of the strong Scottish accent of the more northern parishes, and in it he first perceives in their orchards, gardens and taste for planting (particularly the elms in the hedgerows along the roadside) the characteristics of an English colony (*OSM*, vol. 35, 17).

Later on in his memoir for Killead he remarked, 'The Scottish accent almost disappears in Killead; many of their idioms are, however, Scottish, but it is only occasionally that that dialect is heard' (*OSM*, vol. 35, 23).

The parish of Camlin lies to the south of Killead and Boyle had the following to say about its inhabitants:

> The people are partly of English and partly of Scottish extraction, the latter being principally found along the northern side of the parish, which may be termed as the link of connection between the 2 races, those to the south being almost exclusively English and those to the north of the county of Scottish descent (*OSM*, vol. 21, 68).

From other details that he recorded, it is clear that Camlin was overall more English than Scottish in character:

FIG. 37.4
Crumlin Presbyterian Church, 1839. The Latin inscription in the panel above the doorway was probably intended to emphasise the congregation's doctrinal orthodoxy and Scottish roots.

> ... the people along the western side of the parish are much the most independent, have the largest farms and the best houses but here they would seem to be almost exclusively English in their extraction, from their taste for gardens and orchards, there being scarce a house that has not an orchard attached, and these are in general very profitable (*OSM*, vol. 21, 68).

To the south of Camlin lay the parish of Glenavy. The compilers of the Ordnance Survey Memoirs considered it as much more English in character. It had, for example, the 'appearance of a rich English district' and 'freedom from the Scottish accent' (*OSM*, vol. 21, 87). Other nineteenth-century commentators made similar observations about this region. For example, Abraham Hume, writing in the late 1850s, noted that Crumlin lay 'on the borders of the Scottish district'. The influence of Scottish agricultural practices was also discernible in certain areas. The Ordnance Survey Memoir for Killead noted that 'the farmyards and homesteads are after the Scotch plan'. Lewis's *Topographical Dictionary* of 1837 included the following comments on Killead: 'The land is in a high state of cultivation, and there is neither bog nor waste land; the whole surface is drained, fenced, and managed on the Scottish system'.

Moving west from Antrim town along northern shore of Lough Neagh there were also contrasts. Here, however, the differences tended to be between the Scots and the Irish, rather than the Scots and the English. The inhabitants of Drummaul, with the exception of the detached portions of the parish bordering on Lough Neagh, were 'almost exclusively of Scottish descent.' It was stated that while there had been settlements of Scottish families in the early 1600s and again in the 1640s, the principal one occurred between 1680 and 1695 due to the encouragement of Rose O'Neill, marchioness of Antrim (*OSM*, vol. 19, 52–3). It was also noted that: 'Their dialect, idioms and phraseology are strictly Scottish, but rather less so immediately along the south west side of the parish' (*OSM*, vol. 19, 61). In actual fact, the hearth money rolls reveal that British, and especially Scottish, settlement was already well established in the vicinity of Randalstown in Drummaul by the 1660s. The Ordnance Survey Memoir for the Grange of Ballyscullion recorded that the eastern half of the grange was almost exclusively peopled by the descendants of families from Scotland, while the west was predominantly Irish. The former retained 'much of the custom and dialect of their forefathers' (*OSM*, vol. 19, 4–6).

The tendency to delineate English from Scottish districts on the basis of certain characteristics continued long after the Ordnance Survey Memoirs. At the beginning of the twentieth century the editor of the *Ulster Journal of Archaeology*, the well-known antiquarian F.J. Bigger, concluded a short article on 'Ulster gardening in the seventeenth century' with the following pithy observations:

> The English-planted districts in Ulster are still fragrant with fruits and flowers, no parishes being more noticeable in this respect that those in the Moira,

Downshire and Hertford Estates, in South Antrim and Down. The Scotch-planted districts are the very opposite, there no gardens as a rule are to be found, and the filth of the cattle surrounds the dwellings. The most casual observer notices the changes at once when passing from one to the other, say from Carnmoney or Ballynure to Glenavy or Ballinderry.

Bibliography

[F.J. Bigger], 'Ulster gardening in the seventeenth century', *UJA*, 2nd series, 8 (1902), pp 95–6.

S.T. Carleton, *Heads and Hearths* (Belfast, 1991).

John Armstrong Crozier, *The Life of the Rev. Henry Montgomery*, vol. 1 (London, 1875).

Abraham Hume, 'The elements of population in Down and Antrim, illustrated by the statistics of religious belief', *UJA*, 1st series, 7 (1859), pp 116–30.

Samuel Lewis, *Topographical Dictionary of Ireland* (2 vols, London, 1837).

Ordnance Survey Memoirs of Ireland, ed. Angélique Day and Patrick McWilliams (40 vols, Belfast 1990–98): *South-West Antrim* (vol. 19); *South Antrim* (vol. 21), *Templepatrick and District* (vol. 35).

38 Mental mapping and traditional ecological knowledge on Lough Neagh

John McKenna, Rory J. Quinn, Daniel J. Donnelly
and J. Andrew G. Cooper

In recent decades, there has been an increasing interest in, and respect for, traditional systems of resource exploitation (Folke et al. 2007). In the area of common property resources, for example, many workers have emphasised the fact that traditional methods of exploitation have produced long-term sustainability – in some cases over millennia (Berkes and Farvar 1989; Larson and Bromley 1990; Ostrom et al. 1999). This shift in attitude is also well illustrated in the case of fishing (Acheson 1989; Ruddle 1989). The long-term sustainability of some traditional fisheries is contrasted with the ecological, economic, and social misfortunes caused by non-sustainable 'industrial' exploitation, e.g. the catastrophic collapse of important fisheries such as those in the North Sea and on the Grand Banks off Newfoundland (Finlayson and McCay 1998). Interest in traditional systems of resource use is also evident in other fields, e.g. Shipman and Stojanovic (2007) criticise an over-reliance on technical approaches in coastal management. They believe that this ignores the value of indigenous knowledge, both 'traditional' as in the case of fishermen, and also empirical, local knowledge held by modern commercial and recreational users of coastal resources.

This essay looks at the communal knowledge bank of the fishermen in a traditional fishery in Lough Neagh. The paper explicitly sets out to rigorously assess the objective accuracy of one aspect of the fishermen's LEK (local ecological knowledge), their mental (cognitive) map of the geography of the habitat. This map does not have a hardcopy graphical representation, but it represents the accumulated knowledge of generations of fishermen and is passed down to new generations as they learn the fishermen's craft.

The genesis of the paper owes little to either fishing or LEK. In 1996–7, three of the four authors were part of a University of Ulster team commissioned by a government department to carry out a side-scan sonar survey of the bed of Lough Neagh. This information was required because of concerns that the scale of ongoing sand extraction by licensed suction dredges might be negatively

FIG. 38.1
Lough Neagh fisherman
Gerry McNally.

FIG. 38.2

Location map and two-dimensional contour plot (bathymetric variation) of Lough Neagh. Place-names and geographical features cited in the main text are plotted around the shoreline of the lough.

impacting the lough. Almost ten years later, the university team became aware of the existence of a mental map of the lough's substrate in a book by a social geographer, D.J. Donnelly, published a decade before the side-scan sonar survey was carried out. The close resemblance between the mental map and the side-scan sonar map prompted us to check the accuracy of the mental image against two technically acquired images – the sonograph described above and a published Admiralty chart. This seemed to us the logical approach to take, as

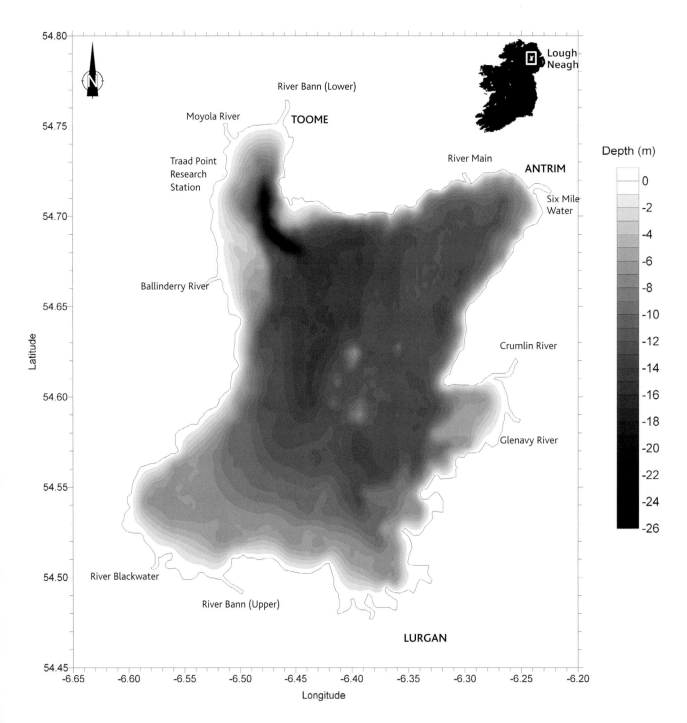

we were already familiar with the accuracy standards of the technical sources, but did not have equivalent information for the mental map. In the latter case, we had no more than a general qualitative impression of accuracy. The claim to originality and innovation in this paper lies in the comparison of existing sources of data. The side-scan sonar map of Lough Neagh is our own work and has not previously been published, but we do not regard that as the significant contribution of the paper. What was new was the semi-quantitative comparison of a 'traditional' mental map with two science-based maps, after careful assessment of the error margins of the latter. To our knowledge this had not been done before in such an objective manner.

The Lough Neagh fishery

Lough Neagh is the largest freshwater lake in the British Isles. Its physical, hydrological, and ecological characteristics are described in detail in the text edited by Wood and Smith (1993). The lough is aligned in a general north-south direction, and has an almost rectangular plan. Maximum length is *c.* 30 km along a south-west to north-east axis, whereas width varies from *c.* 12 km to 16 km west to east. The lough has a maximum depth of just over 30 m in the north-west corner, but only 3% is below 20 m and the average depth is only *c.* 9 m. The fishery is centuries old, and is carried on by a distinctive community. Donnelly (1986) gives a detailed description of the fishery as it was around 35 years ago. There were then around 250 fishing families, totalling approximately 1,550 persons. There were 500 active fishermen, operating 226 fishing boats out of around 50 small inlets or 'coves'; 60% of the fishermen worked from the western shore. In order of commercial importance, the main fisheries on Lough Neagh were eel (*Anguilla anguilla*), perch (*Perca fluviatilis*), pollan (*Coregonus pollan*) (a freshwater herring), and trout (*Salmo trutta*). The main fishing methods used were draft net, trammel net, and long line. The most widely practised method was draft netting, which was used to catch eels (the main catch), perch, and occasionally trout and pollan. The draft is a long, bag-shaped net pulled in a semi-circular sweep by a boat. The trammel net is a vertically orientated gill net *c.* 2 m deep and *c.* 40 m long, used variously as a floating surface net, in mid-water, or sunk to the bottom. It was used to catch perch, trout, and pollan. Baited long lines extending for *c.* 10 km, with up to 2,000 hooks on the line and weighted to lie on the bed of the lough, have been traditionally used for catching eels.

Detailed knowledge of the lough's bathymetry and surficial sediments was, and is, essential for the fishermen. For reasons relating to food supply and life cycle, species migrate to different bottom types and water depths at different times (Crozier and Ferguson 1993; Wilson 1993; Winfield et al. 1993). Drafting is effective on the muddy bottom (the net is often drawn through the surface layer of bottom mud) and along the sloping sandy shores of the lough's larger embayments, but it is relatively less successful along the western and northern shores, which have a stony or rocky bottom. In the latter areas, it is still used, but only by experienced, highly skilled fishermen with detailed local knowledge of selected areas. Long-line fishing demands detailed bottom knowledge over long distances. In places, shallow stony or rocky 'flats' interrupt the uniformly flat muds that characterise about 75% of the lough bed. The wide muddy corridors between the flats are known as 'gulfs' and they are prime long-line fishing sites for eel. However, the proximity of the hazardous stony bottom that might snag lines demands precise knowledge of the bed. Bottom relief and substrate also have an important influence on the direction and velocity of the 'swimmeries', i.e. the bottom currents. Knowledge of these is fundamental to the use of both nets and lines.

In a master's thesis (Donnelly 1981), and in a subsequent book based on the thesis (Donnelly 1986), the author included a mental map captioned, 'The bed of the lough as perceived by local fishermen.' This map is reproduced here in Fig. 38.3 (p. 7 in the 1986 book). The mental map is, in essence, a substrate map, that is a portrayal of the lateral variation of surficial sediment type on the lake bed. The map identifies seven bottom types, augmented by spot depths in feet. Specific areas of the lough bed are named. The mental map exercise was carried out over the period October 1980 to March 1981, and was compiled using the collective perceptions of 12 experienced fishermen.

The mental map of Lough Neagh

Comparison with the science-based sources confirms that the mental maps held by Lough Neagh fishermen are highly accurate. The accuracy standards are even more impressive in light of the fact that the interviewees were asked only to produce a map at the scale of the entire lough. They could have easily produced highly accurate and detailed substrate maps of much smaller areas, at nested scales, with correspondingly enhanced definition. The broad pattern is that, on all shores, fishermen with many years of experience have a comprehensive knowledge of the lough. Younger long-line fishermen also demonstrate impressive familiarity. However, in general, fishermen from the western shore tend to have the most complete knowledge, because traditionally they travelled further across Lough Neagh than fishermen from the other shores. The main reason for this was that western shore fishermen specialised in long-line fishing for eels, and the best eel fishing grounds lie near the eastern shore. Another factor was that the greater concentration of fishermen on the western shore made it

FIG.38.3

Mental map of the substrate of Lough Neagh as perceived by local fishermen (after Donnelly 1986).

necessary for some to travel longer distances to find fishing space. The technique itself demands detailed knowledge of bottom characteristics over long distances.

At the time the mental map exercise was carried out, the fishermen used no position-fixing equipment, nor did they use echosounders to ascertain water depth. Indeed, most boats did not even have compasses. Echosounders appeared

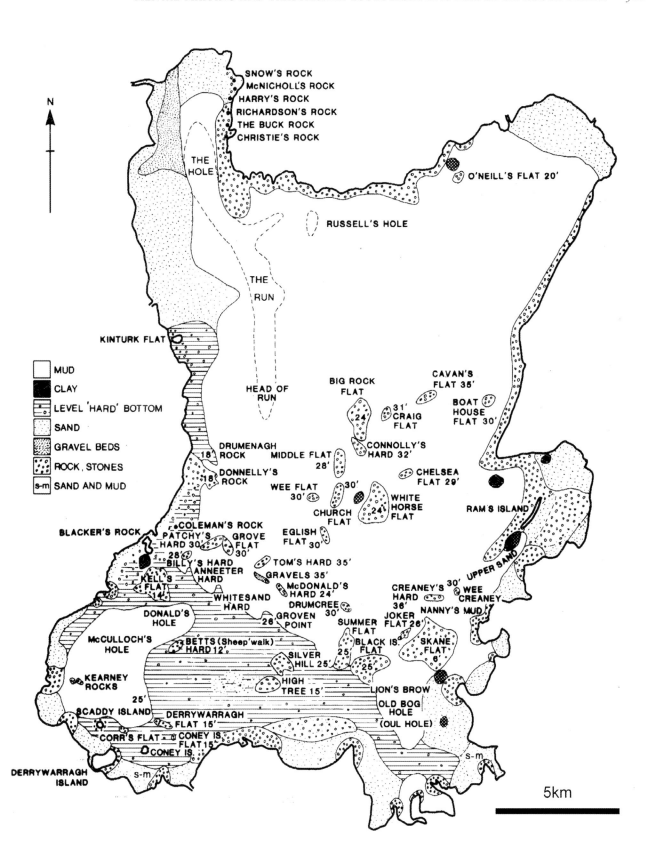

for the first time in the early 1980s, but none of the elderly men asked to compile the mental map would ever have used one. GPS technology was introduced in the late 1990s, but even now it is used only to fix the positions of buoys, not for general point-to-point navigation. The mental map is a product of an era when fishermen established locational fixes for water depth and substrate type using various shore landmarks such as isolated trees, distinctive houses, hills, woodland, and high buildings such as church spires. The conjunction of two easily identifiable features on the shore would indicate that the boat had reached a known point.

In the early years of the twentieth century, fishermen used a method akin to leadline soundings, but to establish substrate character rather than water depth. A stone tied to a line was dropped over the side, and when the stone hit bottom the nature of the tension transmitted up the line enabled the experienced man holding it to distinguish the full range of bottom types. This method was used as a precaution where a sandy area suitable for drafting was surrounded by gravelly flats that would 'rag' nets and lines. In discussing location, fishermen describe the lough bed as a farmer might describe individual fields, with each area given a specific name. They do use the cardinal compass points, but they also make extensive use of a 'secular' terminology, using expressions such as 'beside', 'beyond', 'over beyond' and so on. Donnelly (1981; 1986) also noted that the fishermen have little sense of scale in the conventional sense. He had to precede the mental map exercise by carefully explaining the 1:63,360 scale of the outline map at a very basic conceptual level. As they have no tradition of using hardcopy maps, the fishermen's mental world is experienced essentially at a 1:1 ratio.

The accuracy of the Lough Neagh mental map stands in sharp contrast to the characteristic distortion of the classic mental map, developed almost exclusively in urban environments. For example, Bell et al. (1978, 267) state that 'compared to "reality" the cognitive map is sketchy, incomplete and distorted. In a sense, it is highly impressionistic ...'. Indeed, it is this very divergence from reality that gives the mental map its general and academic interest, as researchers try to elucidate the personal cognitive, emotional, and lifestyle factors that lie behind errors and distortion. Fishermen could not obtain an overview of the lough bed in an era predating echosounders and side-scan sonar. The accuracy of the Lough Neagh map is even more noteworthy because, in this environment, there can be no question of 'inferential structuring', a term that describes the anticipation or prediction of the spatial organisation of a given environment from experience elsewhere. For example, urban dwellers can anticipate elements of city structure from previous experience of block patterns in another city.

The environment presented by the bed of Lough Neagh is a huge challenge to accurate mental mapping because it scores so low on 'legibility', a concept introduced by Kevin Lynch (1960, 2–6) in his ground-breaking work on the mental maps of American cities. Legibility describes the ease with which a subject can form a cognitive map of an environment. It is promoted where an environment has elements that enhance human ability to impose a pattern, an organising structure that assists learning. Lynch identified five groups of such elements: paths, edges, districts, nodes and landmarks. A high degree of visual access to these various elements improves legibility. Although equivalents of Lynch's elements do exist on the bed of Lough Neagh, they are visually inaccessible from the surface. The lough bed is much more difficult to visualise than its closest urban 'equivalent', the city subway, an environment regarded by Bell et al. (1978, 275) as particularly challenging to accurate mental mapping because of its lack of visual cues and overview opportunities. There are a number of factors that, taken together, may explain why the fishermen's mental map of Lough Neagh is so remarkably free of distortion.

In the literature, the mental maps under discussion are invariably those of individuals rather than groups. Indeed, Gould and White (1974) see individuality as fundamental to the very concept of the mental map. However, they go on to outline communal or group concepts that help to throw light on the genesis of the Lough Neagh map, 'While every view is unique … there may be considerable overlap between the mental maps of people. The more homogeneous the group in terms of age and experience, the more overlap we might expect between the mental images' (Gould and White 1974, 52). This leads them to the concept of the 'homomorphic map', which is a single, representative mental map constructed from the many individual viewpoints of people in a group. Even though each Lough Neagh fisherman has his own mental map, the map is a communal rather than an individual construct, because it is a compendium of the knowledge of many individual fishermen from several generations.

At various times in the past, individual distortions undoubtedly existed because relative inexperience, or an untypical or chance event, may well skew a given fisherman's perception of his working environment. However, the process of mental map construction is self-correcting as in the event of disagreement between the accepted version and a new perception, it is almost inevitable that the traditional perception will prevail. Thus, the essential conservatism of the process acts to filter out errors by laying the onus of persuasion overwhelmingly on those advocating change. It could be argued that conservatism should militate against improvement of accuracy, because it prevents acceptance of corrections and additions to the communal knowledge bank. However, economic self-interest will serve to counterbalance conservatism by acting continuously to prevent errors from becoming institutionalised. Even at the individual level, economic interest acts as a constraint on distortion, and emotional factors are unlikely to play much part. This contrasts with the urban mental maps portrayed in Lynch's study (Lynch 1960).

A change in the accepted view will be gradually incorporated in the fishermen's collective perception of their environment, but only when the change has long-term sanction by majority opinion, and in particular where it has the authority of the most experienced and most respected fishermen. Over time, individual distortions are counterbalanced and corrected by other influences, and significant inaccuracies are filtered out of the folk record. This process of gradual adjustment and refinement may be greatly aided by the fact that the map is a mental map, rather than a hardcopy chart. The latter is a fixed 'official' representation, and accordingly is more likely to be defended against change. On this point, Turnbull (2003, 148) observes that 'arguably there is a greater requirement for conservatism in an oral tradition to ensure effective transmission, but that conservatism or closedness does not of necessity preclude change any more than it does in Western science.' The Lough Neagh mental map may be seen as the ultimate homomorphic map generated by the combined perceptions of a relatively homogeneous community reliant on a specific resource, but with a vital additional self-correcting dimension created by economic self-interest acting over a long period of time.

It should be noted here that self-interest in a more immediate sense is also served by accuracy. The lough is dangerous, and over the years, many lives have been lost in boating accidents. The transmission of this collective knowledge through the medium of the relatively few fishermen interviewed in depth by Donnelly brings no risk of distortion, because to these fishermen the communal knowledge bank of their community and their own personal knowledge are identical. The notion that this knowledge is communal, rather than personal, property is illustrated by the fact that the fishermen exhibit no reluctance in sharing their knowledge of the lough. This is in sharp contrast to the attitudes of inshore fishermen on many open ocean coasts. In areas as far apart as the coast of Maine in the USA and the north Irish coast, lobster and crab fishermen zealously protect their specialist knowledge of areas that they regard as historically 'theirs', and they strongly resent any encroachment by others on their territory. In contrast, in Lough Neagh, there is no sense that particular areas of the water body are the exclusive property of any individual or group.

On Lough Neagh, fishing is very much a family affair, often with three generations represented. Kinship groupings are of central importance, e.g. the artificially excavated coves the boats use as bases were originally dug by family groupings. As the coves are still family owned, an unrelated outsider cannot break into the family-based fishing circle (and in any case a newcomer could not get a licence from the co-operative that controls the fishery). The fishermen themselves acknowledge that the vital key to transmission of all aspects of their fishing knowledge is the tradition of fishing in family groups. Fishermen usually operate in two-man partnerships with a friend or relation but there are also three-man partnerships. It is almost unheard of for two or three young (teenagers or twenties) men to form a fishing partnership. The usual mix is a younger man with his father, uncle, or even grandfather. This type of organisation is ideal for the transmission of traditional oral knowledge.

Transmission of the fishermen's knowledge is also facilitated by the fact that the fishing community is historically very closely knit. Donnelly (1986, xx) observes that 'The Lough Neagh fishing community is notoriously difficult to penetrate; its members do not communicate easily with outsiders.' In 1986, 35% of western shore marriages were within the local fishing families; in the early decades of the twentieth century, the proportion was 55% or higher. Donnelly (1986, 171, 173) presents maps showing the alongshore and cross-lough marriage and kinship patterns that have developed over the years. Many of these were established in the days of sail when, up until about 1940, it was common for fishermen to spend at least one night and often up to a week on the opposite shore. Fishermen also migrated across and alongshore to live in new areas. In modern times, day-to-day contacts continue to take place across a wide range of age groups and fishing experience. Fishermen regularly meet out on the lough, and it is common for two boats to lie alongside for some time as the men talk and exchange opinions and news. Some fishermen are also small farmers, and they meet in that context, e.g. at markets and through co-operative farm work. Fishermen have regular cross-generational contact at social occasions such as sporting events, where they habitually 'talk shop'.

Accurate mental mapping in Lough Neagh is certainly a challenge because fishermen cannot see the bottom, but in the longer term, it is facilitated by the fact that the lough substrate, particularly in the gravel flats, which are analogous to 'islands' in a sea of mud, is an essentially fixed morphology unlike, for example, the constantly changing bedforms often found in tidal estuaries and on some open coasts. The finer sediments, sand and mud, do move under the influence of currents, but the gross geometry of the bed remains unchanged. Importantly, Lough Neagh is small enough to be known in its entirety. Consequently, repeated fishing experience over many years will aggregate, confirm, correct, and refine environmental knowledge. This combination of substrate stability, relatively limited extent, and extended fishing experience over generations means that, in practice, the fishermen's mental map is already at optimal accuracy at the scale required for use, and so is not open to revision or 'updating.' (For example, in practical terms, there is no improvement when traditional knowledge of water depths in units of feet (30.5 cm) is replaced by echosounder data using units of 5 cm.) An individual fisherman will accept that his own knowledge has limitations, but the collective knowledge of the fishermen as a group is regarded as exhaustive. If a young fisherman using an echosounder calls out a water depth reading to his father, it merely confirms what the older man already knows. Indeed, older fishermen perceive their knowledge of the lough bed as the 'gold standard' that can be used to confirm the accuracy of the echosounder, rather than vice versa.

The Lough Neagh fishermen certainly have a strong sense of separate identity. Historically, their relative isolation over long periods of time has produced a community of fisher families that kept much to themselves, e.g. marriage was predominantly within the community. These influences helped to produce what Donnelly (1986, 243) calls 'a remarkable homogeneity of cultural background.' There was also a perception that the fishermen were socially inferior to the neighbouring farmers, due to relatively poor economic returns from fishing during extended periods, such as the 1920s. However, their distinctiveness must not be overstated. The fisher families feel that they are part of a wider society, and share its prevailing cultural norms. All the fishing families have kinship relations and friends who have no fishing tradition. There have been periods, e.g. the 1980s, when good prices for their catches left them financially better off than neighbouring non-fishing families. They are also pragmatic: they adopt new technologies perceived to be useful as and when they become available, and they welcome any innovation that makes their work easier. Their mental map was generated by experience and simple position-fixing methods, not because they valued this traditional approach, nor because they accorded it any spiritual significance, but simply because that was the optimum method available to them.

This paper is one of very few that has attempted to compare LEK with scientifically acquired data. If such accuracy is indeed typical of the mental maps held by other resource users, the lesson for academic researchers and resource managers may be that they should reconsider any scepticism about the value of so called anecdotal knowledge. It is unwise to disregard LEK just because it is not acquired by high-technology, scientific methods. The process by which mental maps of a resource are generated may not be 'scientific' in the usual sense, but it has an inherent rigor and quality control at least equal in efficiency to those associated with technology.

A pessimistic scenario is that continuing failure to recruit young men will ultimately lead to the end of the fishery, and with it the mental map of the lough that has been transmitted down through the generations. This outlook may be unnecessarily gloomy. The mental map will survive as long as the occupation it serves survives. Although numbers of fishermen may decline still further, there will probably always be a market for eels, and consequently fishing will continue on Lough Neagh. It seems likely that for the foreseeable future the fishermen will continue to rely heavily on the mental map of the lough handed down to them from the past.

*This is an abridged version of the following article: John McKenna,
Rory J. Quinn, Daniel J. Donnelly and J. Andrew G. Cooper, 'Accurate mental
maps as an aspect of local ecological knowledge (LEK): a case study from
Lough Neagh, Northern Ireland', Ecology and Society 13:1 (2008): 13,
available online at: https://digitalcommons.usu.edu/unf_research/34.
We are grateful to the authors for permission to publish it here.*

Bibliography

J.M. Acheson, 'Where have all the exploiters gone? Co-management of the Maine lobster industry' in Berkes (ed.), *Common Property Resources* (1989), pp 199–217.

P.A. Bell, J.D. Fisher and R.J. Loomis, *Environmental Psychology* (Philadelphia, 1978).

F. Berkes (ed.), *Common Property Resources: Ecology and Community-based Sustainable Development* (London, 1989)

F. Berkes and M.T. Farvar, 'Introduction and overview' in Berkes (ed.), *Common Property Resources* (1989), pp 1–17.

W.W. Crozier and A. Ferguson, 'The fish of Lough Neagh, part C. Investigations on the brown trout (*Salmo trutta* L.)' in Wood and Smith (eds), *Lough Neagh*, pp 419–37.

D.J. Donnelly, 'A study of the Lough Neagh fishing community', thesis, Queen's University Belfast (1981).

D.J. Donnelly, *On Lough Neagh's Shores: a Study of the Lough Neagh Fishing Community* (Galbally, Co. Tyrone, 1986).

A.C. Finlayson and B.J. McCay, 'Crossing the threshold of ecosystem resilience: the commercial extinction of northern cod' in F. Berkes and C. Folke (eds), *Linking Social and Ecological Systems: Management Practices and Social Mechanisms for Building Resilience* (Cambridge, 1998), pp 311–37.

C. Folke, L. Pritchard, F. Berkes, J. Colding, and U. Svedin, 'The problem of fit between ecosystems and institutions: ten years later', *Ecology and Society*, 12:1 (2007): 30, available online at: www.ecologyandsociety.org/vol12/iss1/art30.

P. Gould and R. White, *Mental Maps* (Harmondsworth, 1974).

B.A. Larson and D.W. Bromley, 'Property rights, externalities and resource degradation: locating the tragedy', *Journal of Development Economics*, 33 (1990), pp 235–62.

K. Lynch, *The Image of the City* (Cambridge, MA, 1960).

E. Ostrom, J. Burger, C.B. Field, R.B. Norgaard and D. Policansky, 'Revisiting the commons: local lessons, global challenges', *Science*, 284:5412 (1999), pp 278–82.

K. Ruddle, 'Solving the common-property dilemma: village fisheries rights in Japanese coastal waters' in Berkes (ed.), *Common Property Resources* (1989), pp 168–84.

B. Shipman and T. Stojanovic, 'Facts, fictions and failures of integrated coastal management in Europe', *Coastal Management*, 35 (2007), pp 375–98.

D. Turnbull, *Masons, Tricksters and Cartographers: Comparative Studies in the Sociology of Scientific and Indigenous Knowledge* (2nd edition, Amsterdam, 2003).

J.P.F. Wilson, 'The fish of Lough Neagh, part D. Investigations on pollan (Coregonus autumnalis pollan Thompson)' in Wood and Smith (eds), *Lough Neagh*, pp 439–50.

I.J. Winfield, C.M. Tobin and C.R. Montgomery, 'The fish of Lough Neagh, part E. Ecological studies of the fish community' in Wood and Smith (eds), *Lough Neagh*, pp 451–71.

R.B. Wood and R.V. Smith (eds), *Lough Neagh: the Ecology of a Multipurpose Water Resource* (Dordrecht, 1993).

39 'On Lough Neagh's banks as the fisherman strays ...'
aspects of folklore collecting in the North of Ireland in the twentieth century

Patricia Lysaght

Shortly after the publication of his first book, *At Slieve Gullion's Foot* (1940), describing the life and traditions of his native South Armagh, Michael J. Murphy, Dromintee, was approached by the Director of the Irish Folklore Commission (1935–70), Séamus Ó Duilearga, a Glens of Antrim man, to collect folklore in County Armagh and neighbouring County Down on behalf of the Commission. Many years later, having collected folklore across much of the North of Ireland, Murphy wrote that this work had enabled him to give his undivided attention to the interest that lay closest to his heart.[1]

Appointed a part-time collector by the Irish Folklore Commission in late October 1941, Murphy worked as such until 1 November 1949 when, having traversed large areas of counties Armagh and Down as a folklore collector, he was employed full-time by the Commission. He continued in that capacity for the Commission's successor, the Department of Irish Folklore, from 1971 until his retirement at the age of 70 in 1983. Ó Duilearga described him as a countryman, whose understanding of the people among whom he was collecting was reflected in his work. During his long career as a folklore collector he worked in counties Antrim (including Rathlin Island), Armagh, Down, Fermanagh and Tyrone in Northern Ireland, and also in the border counties of Cavan, Louth and Sligo in the Republic of Ireland. His first posting as a full-time collector was to the Glenhull area of County Tyrone where he spent two years (late 1949–51). His journey to Glenhull, settling down in a new environment with his family, and his experiences there as a collector, are vividly set out in his book, *Tyrone Folk Quest* (1973). He and his family then moved to north-eastern County Antrim where he collected successfully for four years (1952–6), residing first in Layd, Cushendall, and then in the Glenarrif area. During this period he made two trips to Rathlin Island (August 1954 and June-July 1955). The diaries which he kept for the Commission about his Rathlin visits include details of his sea-journeys back and forth to the island, his initial sense of isolation in unfamiliar surroundings, the people whom he met and vividly remembered, and his collecting strategies. A representative sample of the lore collected by him on Rathlin, and a selection of his photographic documentation of people, places, and travel and trade by sea between the island and Ballycastle on the County Antrim mainland, feature in his 1987 publication: *Rathlin: Island of Blood and Enchantment. The Folklore of Rathlin.*

Murphy had concluded his work in north-east County Antrim by December 1956 and by then he was residing in the Warrenpoint area of County Down. He continued to collect in the North and in the border counties, and in later years returned to his native Dromintee, before retiring after more than three decades as a full-time collector in 1983. His extensive documentation of the folk culture of the North of Ireland ranging from folk narratives, beliefs, customs, social organisation, and livelihood on land and sea, to material culture, is clearly evident in the bound volumes of the material collected by him, preserved in the National Folklore Collection, University College Dublin. It is also reflected in other publications of his, including, *Now You're Talking... Folktales from the North of Ireland* (1975), *Ulster Folk of Field and Fireside* (1983), *My Man Jack. Bawdy Tales from Irish Folklore* (1989), *Songs and Stories from Slieve Gullion* (1990), as well as in his many journal and newspaper articles and contributions to radio and television programmes over the years.

FIG. 39.1
Lough Neagh fishermen
Brian and Mark Conlon.

While Murphy was the most important collector for the Irish Folklore Commission in the North of Ireland, others also contributed. Liam Mac Reachtain (1921–76), (Portaferry, County Down), worked as a part-time collector for the Commission in counties Antrim and Down from 1947 to 1948, as did Jeanne Cooper Foster (Belfast), also in a part-time capacity, from 1939 to 1944. Her comprehensive *Ulster Folklore* appeared in 1971.

In addition, respondents scattered throughout the North of Ireland replied to the Irish Folklore Commission's (and subsequent institutions') frequent questionnaires issued over the years. Included among the Commission's early questionnaire respondents was Dr Francis McPolin, Ballymaghery School, Hilltown, County Down. McPolin also contributed to the collecting work organised in the North of Ireland itself from the early 1950s, as a result of the setting up of the Committee on Ulster Folklife and Traditions, which worked fruitfully with volunteer contributors across the region.[2] The schools' scheme, organised by the Committee in 1955–7, led to the successful collecting of folklore by primary-school children, and extracts of material submitted by schools across Northern Ireland were published in *Ulster Folklife* in 1957.[3]

A guidebook, *Ulster Folklife and Tradition. Collectors' Guide*, listing topics and instructions for collecting, was issued by the Committee on Ulster Folklife and Traditions to volunteer contributors in 1957, and, from 1958 to 1962, extracts of material received as a result of this initiative were published in *Ulster Folklife*.[4] The first ten volumes of this journal, first published by the Committee (re-formed as the Ulster Folklife Society in 1961[5]), were issued between 1955 and 1965.[6] The Ulster Folk and Transport Museum (founded by Act of Parliament in 1958 as the Ulster Folk Museum, opening officially to the public on 2 July 1964[7] and becoming the Ulster Folk and Transport Museum from 1967) continued publication thereafter. The holdings of the Ulster Folklife Society, incorporating the Committee on Ulster Folklife and Traditions, including the results of the 1955–7 schools' collection scheme, were transferred to the Museum, where they form part of the paper archive in the institution's library. That the Museum itself continued with the issuing of questionnaires on a wide range of topics is evident from the annual reports of its activities. Focused on intangible, as well as tangible cultural heritage, the formal recognition of a Department of Non-Material Culture in 1975–6, and the appointment of research assistants, served to widen the scope of, and add momentum to 'the coverage of the non-material aspects of Ulster folklife' by the Museum.[8] That this dimension of the Museum's activities, involving extensive fieldwork, has continued over the years in many parts of Northern Ireland and beyond, is also evident from its annual reports and staff publications.

Among the intensive field studies carried out by the Ulster Folk and Transport Museum was a survey conducted by Linda-May Ballard in 2007–08, in the context of curating intangible cultural heritage. Focused on the eel fishermen operating on the County Tyrone shore of Lough Neagh,[9] the study demonstrated the importance of intangible, as well as tangible cultural heritage in this connection. Thus, not only fishing processes, techniques and skills, formally or orally transmitted, were dealt with, but also the beliefs and narratives of the fishermen themselves. These reflected both those connected with the fishermen's own work practices and worldview and also those of the surrounding community. These aspects will be dealt with later. First it is of interest to consider some other Lough Neagh traditions appearing in different oral and literary contexts over time. These concern, for example, the lake's origin, and the cry of the banshee said to be heard on its Antrim shore prior to a death in a prominent local family.

Lough Neagh

In his 1937/8 study of the Irish language of Rathlin Island, County Antrim, the Swedish linguist, Nils M. Holmer, stated: 'Irish traditions are not less familiar to the Rathlin people than are Scottish stories and songs, as appears from the following version of the story about Lough Neagh.'[10] The story in question, included among the specimens of Rathlin Irish taken down by Holmer, tells about the inundation of Lough Neagh in mainland County Antrim. According to Annie Black, Kinramer, Upper End, Rathlin Island, the lake originated because a woman visiting a particular spring well at evening time did not replace the board (cover) on the well, which was locked every night. As a result, the water came forth, flowed on, and flooded the land, drowning buildings, including a city, a large castle, many houses, and all the inhabitants, thus leaving only a large lake in its wake.[11]

This oral account of the origin of Lough Neagh – caused by the overflowing of a well left uncovered by a woman – echoes a scenario found in the early literature of Ireland, which also seeks to explain the nomenclature of the lake – 'Loch nEchach'[12] – as 'the lake of Eochu'.[13] Another common origin story about Lough Neagh, found throughout Ireland, is that it came into existence because of a contest between the mythical Fionn Mac Cumhail, the leader of the Fianna of Ireland, and a Scottish giant. As Fionn pursued the retreating giant across east Ulster, he scooped up a large piece of earth with his hand and flung it after him. It fell into the sea to create the Isle of Man, while the depression left in the ground from whence the earth had been taken, filled with water, thus forming Lough Neagh.[14]

Shane's Castle of the Clandeboy O'Neill sept of the Northern Uí Néill, on the north-eastern shore of Lough Neagh, featured prominently in nineteenth-century accounts of the manifestation of the banshee (*an bhean sí*). Well known in Irish oral tradition, this supernatural female messenger of death is said to be attached to certain Gaelic families, particularly to the male head of those of noble and illustrious lineage. Regarded as an ancestress of the family she 'follows' from

generation to generation, the cry of the banshee is usually heard shortly before the demise of a family member, near the seat or 'old family home' of the person about to die, even if nothing is left but its ruins, as in the case of Shane's Castle on Lough Neagh's Antrim shore in later times. Here, echoing a tradition known throughout Ireland, her cry, heard at night, is said to be 'peculiarly mournful' resembling the 'melancholy sough of the wind', but having 'the tone of a human voice', and being 'distinctly audible to a great distance'.[15] It was regarded as an inevitable sign of death for the Clandeboy O'Neills down through generations.

When discussing the beliefs and practices of the Lough Neagh eel fishermen, the role of fish in the diet and economy of the Lough Neagh shore communities requires consideration. The Ordnance Survey Memoirs (1832–8) for the counties and parishes bordering on the lake, offer an historical perspective in this connection. In Aghagallon parish, for example, the people were said to fish to 'satisfy their own wants', especially for 'pullens' (pollan) as this fish when salted was 'a good winter's provision for the cotters', and when 'champed up with potato' made 'an excellent dish'.[16] The memoir of Lough Neagh itself provides much information on fish varieties, fisheries, including eel fisheries, and associated beliefs and practices, in the nineteenth century. Thus we are told that eel fishing took place between June and February, with August, September and October being the best months in terms of quantity and quality 'for as the season advances, the eels become strongly flavoured and tough'.[17] Traditional fishing practices at the time are said to have included fishing in the dark of night with the wind to the south-west, these being regarded as the most favourable conditions for taking eels. The period towards the end of September, with 'the decline of the moon after Michaelmas' (29 September), termed by the eel fishermen 'the Michaelmas dark', was considered 'the most propitious part of the season'.[18]

These early nineteenth-century fishing ideas and practices are not without some contemporary resonance. Ballard, as part of her work with the County Tyrone eel fisherman in 2007 and 2008, found that 'Counting the Moon' (forecasting the moon's phases) featured among the traditional skills of Lough Neagh eel fishermen at the time. She noted: 'It is difficult to establish how widespread this tradition is, but at least some fishermen share with previous generations a belief or environmental observation that eels may be more plentiful at "the Dark of the Moon".' She further noted that knowledge of the moon's phases might also be applied to land-based subsistence activities, such as the planting of crops in small land holdings, and added: 'Knowing a formula for forecasting the moon's phases is therefore of great value.'[19] Ballard recorded further customary habits and ideas of the Lough Neagh eel fishermen, knowledge of which also existed in the wider local community and further afield. The use of an eel skin, for example, as a binding for a sprain by the fisherman whom Ballard recorded, was also practised in South Armagh.[20] The widespread

FIG. 39.2
The late Eamon Moore at the eel factory in Toome.

changeling belief, involving the idea that the fairies might abduct a healthy human child leaving a sickly substitute in its place, known on Lough Neagh's shores, has been recorded throughout the North of Ireland, including Rathlin Island.[21] Belief in the practice of 'blinking' or 'overlooking' by people of jealous or evil disposition in situations of limited or unpredictable means of livelihood, was, according to Ballard (2008) 'still very strong in the eel fishing community in the 1930s and traces of this belief system still survive today'. Found in a variety of different contexts throughout Ireland, 'blinking' was also often regarded as a May Eve or a May morning magical practice among the farming community in the North of Ireland. Traditionally heralding the summer and dairying season in Ireland, the May festival was viewed as a temporal juncture during which evil-minded persons could 'steal' their neighbours' milk-luck by 'blinking' their cows in the fresh green pastures at that time of the year.[22]

These ideas, beliefs, and habits associated with Lough Neagh fishermen, and with local and wider communities, provide a glimpse of an immensely rich tapestry of intangible cultural heritage in the North of Ireland, documented in literature, practice, archival repositories, and studies, north and south on the island of Ireland.

Notes

1 Michael J. Murphy, *Now You're Talking...* (Belfast, 1975), p. ix.

2 *Ulster Folklife*, 1 (1955), p. 7.

3 K.M. Harris, 'The Schools' Collection', *Ulster Folklife*, 3 (1957), pp 8–13.

4 *Ulster Folklife*, 4 (1958), pp 37–49; 5 (1959), pp 35–53; 6 (1960), pp 18–31; 7 (1961), pp 23–32; 8 (1962), pp 35–42.

5 Alan Gailey, 'Emyr Estyn Evans: an appreciation', *Ulster Folk & Transport Museum. Annual Report for the Year 1989–90* (1991), p. 7.

6 Vols 1–6, 1955–60, published by the Committee on Ulster Folklife and Traditions; vols 7–10 (1961–5), published by the Ulster Folklife Society; vols thereafter published by the Ulster Folk and Transport Museum.

7 Alan Gailey, 'George Barton Thompson, Director, Ulster Folk and Transport Museum, 1959–1986', *Ulster Folk & Transport Museum Year Book 1986–87* (1988), p. 4.

8 *Ulster Folk & Transport Museum Year Book 1975–76* (1977), pp 33–4.

9 Linda-May Ballard, 'Curating Intangible Cultural Heritage', *Anthropological Journal of European Cultures*, 17:1 (2008), pp 74–95. Survey 'undertaken as part of the preparations to represent Northern Ireland in the 41st Smithsonian Folklife Festival held in Washington DC in the summer of 2007', (ibid., p. 77). For Lower Bann eel fishing (mid-1960s), see N.C. Mitchell, 'The Lower Bann fisheries', *Ulster Folklife*, 11 (1965), pp 1–18, 22–4, 25–8. See also Daniel J. Donnelly, *On Lough Neagh's Shores: a Study of the Lough Neagh Fishing Community* (Galbally, Co. Tyrone, 1986).

10 Nils M. Holmer, *The Irish Language in Rathlin Island, Co. Antrim* (Dublin, 1942), p. 148 (no. 36). Here 'Irish traditions' refer to those of mainland County Antrim.

11 Ibid., pp 148–9. Annie Black, 'aged about 72', was 'of a family descended from the old stock of Irish settlers in Rathlin' and was then living in Ballycastle, County Antrim (ibid., p. 3). For legends and descriptions of an underwater world in Lough Camlough, South Armagh (said to include horses, cattle, and an inhabited castle), collected by Michael J. Murphy in the 1940s, see National Folklore Collection (NFC) 974: 7–8.

12 Now 'Loch nEathach', according to *Logainm.ie*.

13 Eóin Mac Néill, 'The mythology of Lough Neagh', *Béaloideas*, 2:2 (1929), pp 115–21; Osborn Bergin, 'Observations on "The mythology of Lough Neagh", *Béaloideas*, 2:3 (1930), pp 246–52; E. J. Gwynn, *The Metrical Dindshenchas*, Part IV, (Dublin, 1991), p. 66, lines 121–8; 67, lines 137–40.

14 Much favoured by schoolchildren, this was a popular origin story for Lough Neagh in the 1937–8 School's Scheme conducted by the Irish Folklore Commission in conjunction with the Primary/National Schools throughout the Republic of Ireland (Dúchas.ie, Schools' Collection, 'Lough Neagh'); see also 'Lough Neagh', *Ordnance Survey Memoirs of Ireland ... Vol. 21: South Antrim*, ed. Angélique Day and Patrick McWilliams (Belfast, 1993), p. 93.

15 Mr and Mrs S.C. Hall, *Ireland: Its Scenery, Character, &c.*, vol. 3 (London, 1843), pp 104–06; Patricia Lysaght, *The Banshee. The Irish Supernatural Death-Messenger* (Dublin, 1996); Patricia Lysaght, *A Pocket Book of the Banshee* (Dublin, 1998).

16 *Ordnance Survey Memoirs of Ireland ... Vol. 21*, p. 4.

17 Ibid., p. 95.

18 Ibid., p. 96.

19 Linda-May Ballard, 'Curating intangible cultural heritage', *Anthropological Journal of European Cultures*, 17:1 (2008), p. 89.

20 Ibid., p. 88, Fig. 14; Linda-May Ballard, 'An approach to traditional cures in Ulster', *Ulster Medical Journal*, 78:1 (2009), p. 26, Fig. 1; 31; Michael J. Murphy, *At Slieve Gullion's Foot* (Dundalk, 1940), p. 87.

21 Michael J. Murphy, *Rathlin: Island of Blood and Enchantment* (Dundalk, 1987), pp 39–40; NFC 1390: 43–4 (Rathlin Island); NFC 1365, 218–19 (Glenshesk, County Antrim); NFC 1363: 177, 183–4 (Glens of Antrim); also Séamas Mac Philib, 'The changeling (ML 5085). Irish versions of a migratory legend in their international context', *Béaloideas* 59 (1991), pp 121–31, and works mentioned there.

22 For a County Antrim charm for the recovery of 'blinked' milk or milk 'profit', see *Ulster Folklife*, 7 (1961), pp 29–30; see also NFC 1019: 73–6 (Glenravel, County Antrim, 1947).

40 The eel co-operative

Pat Close

FIG. 40.1
Fishing by draft net for eels.

The history of Lough Neagh Fishermen's Co-operative Society Ltd ('the Society') dates from the early 1960s. It was established to represent the interests of local fishermen and to lobby on their behalf in an effort to gain access to fishing rights on Lough Neagh. At that time, the exclusive right to the commercial eel fishery on Lough Neagh and the Lower River Bann was owned by Toome Eel Fishery (NI) Ltd ('the Company'). The Company's title was traced back to a Crown grant made in 1661. It also relied upon the assertion under common law that there is no public right to fish in non-tidal, inland lakes which I am informed and believe was established in the nineteenth century arising, coincidently, from two cases concerned with Lough Neagh.

The Company's title was challenged in 1962–3 when it brought proceedings against named local fishermen for unlawful fishing on Lough Neagh. The case was lost by the fishermen in both the High Court and the Court of Appeal. With

the title of the Company so confirmed, fishermen reorganised and began negotiating in an effort to secure enhanced fishing rights and to establish procedures for the granting of eel fishing licences.

In 1965, one of the five companies which owned shares in the Company decided to sell its 20% shareholding. After negotiation, this was acquired on behalf of Lough Neagh fishermen by the Society. The purchase was financed through the subscription of its members and by bank loan. As part of that process, the Society was registered under the Industrial and Provident Societies Act (NI) on 24 May 1966 with a view to administering the shareholding. It was given a formal constitution and its rules were registered with the Registrar of Friendly Societies on that date. (The Rules were revised in 1995 and the revision duly registered.)

Shares in the Society were distributed among its members, while initially profits were devoted to the repayment of bank loans. Once this had been achieved, profits were shared with members as and when finances permitted. From 1967 onwards, the Society undertook its own marketing of 'brown' eels (that is, the maturing eels harvested from the lough) and used a proportion of the profits to build sufficient reserves to purchase the remaining 80% shareholding in the Company. This was ultimately achieved in January 1972.

The Society has control over the granting of licences for eel fishing on Lough Neagh to the extent that it has legal ownership of the relevant fishing rights. It has, through its Management Committee and Board of Directors, developed policies and procedures for the grant of those licences, taking account of elver recruitment levels, long-term assessments of stock levels and marketing considerations. In 1992 the Society purchased the fishing rights to what are commonly known as the scale fish rights but it was not until 2016 that it took an interest in managing that sector. The Society's aim is to exploit the lough only in a sustainable manner and thereby protect it for succeeding generations. Scale fishing peaks during the winter months thereby presenting an extension to the season for those who previously concentrated on eel fishing from May to October in any given year.

FIG. 40.2

Fisherman Matthew Quinn.

The lough is a finite resource and therefore requires careful management including the control of fishing intensity. The Society operates a number of important control mechanisms through which it can regulate this. These include the following:

a A defined fishing season – the open season by law is from 1 May to 10 January with the highest fishing intensity occurring in the spring and summer months. (In practice the yellow eel season effectively winds to a close by mid-November as the weather, length of day and water temperatures become less favourable).

b Placing a numerical limit upon the number of eel fishing licences issued each season.

c Placing a daily limit (quota) upon the weight of eels which any one boat owner may market.

Governance

The Society has just over 600 shareholding members, the majority of whom are fishermen, retired fishermen or members of their extended families. The management of Lough Neagh Fishermen's Co-operative Society Ltd is the responsibility of the Committee of Management and the Board of Directors who meet on a regular basis throughout the year. The Committee of Management, elected by shareholders, consists of 20 shareholding members, representing a number of geographical districts around the loughshore who in turn appoint five Directors from amongst their own number.

The Society is owned and run by its members and it exists for the benefit of its members. It is, therefore, required to ensure that licence holders are able to make a reasonable living from fishing while endeavouring to secure the industry for future generations. Therefore, since the lough is currently only to some extent a replenishing natural resource, its policies are driven by an attempt to balance the competing interests of livelihood and conservation. Going back 25 or more years, there were more boats fishing on the lake, with up to 180 boat owner's licences issued in the early 1990s, compared to fewer than 110 in more recent years.

Modern-day fishermen are generally much better equipped, having access to more powerful boats which facilitate travel over greater distances in less time. Technological advances in navigation aids, fish-finders, depth-sounders, hydraulic winches and communications equipment have all contributed to higher average output per unit effort. These developments have coincided with the widely publicised crash in elver recruitment, experienced not only on Lough Neagh but across Europe, and the inevitable resulting decline in stock levels of juvenile and mature fish within the Neagh/Bann system.

The harsh reality is that the commercial eel fishing industry on Lough Neagh can no longer accommodate all those who wish to fish and if not managed responsibly will be depleted very quickly, leaving little or no return for those who fish its waters and most certainly little prospect of future generations being able to earn their livelihood from it. Therefore, it continues to be necessary for the Society to impose constraints, for example: on the number of boats licensed to fish; on the intensity of fishing (by way of daily quotas); on permissible fishing gear; and by way of self-imposed fishing regulations. The Society is custodian of one of the few indigenous industries left on these islands. The industry is also of huge importance to European efforts to aid the recovery of the stock of the European eel. The Society has worked closely with DCAL (now DAERA) and the Agri-Food & Bioscience Institute for many years in an open and transparent manner, including access to extensive data collated over more than five decades.

The award of PGI status to 'Lough Neagh Eels' (2011) is regarded by the local industry as a significant accolade, recognising the heritage, tradition and authenticity of what are regarded as the best quality eels available in Europe. The Society has marketed its produce in Continental Europe for more than 50 years and has developed a reputation for quality and reliability of supply. The main markets are in the Netherlands, Germany and England.

FIG. 40.3

Matthew Quinn and Kevin Johnston grading eels before sending them to the co-operative.

The eel industry on Lough Neagh received approval for its EU Eel Management Plan in 2010. This was testament to the unique management regime employed by the Society over many decades, particularly with regard to its approach to conservation, restocking and viability. In view of the much documented decline in elver recruitment right across Europe the Society is more conscious than ever that it is dealing with a limited natural resource which must be protected and managed in such a way as to secure a viable future. The EU Management Plan identifies the eel industry on Lough Neagh as sustainable and as making a significant contribution to conservation, while PGI status identifies the produce as authentic eel from Lough Neagh. The discerning customer can, therefore, identify with the brand on a number of fronts: quality, sustainability and tradition. We are keenly aware of the importance to modern consumers of the provenance of their food purchases and see the award of PGI status as an opportunity to affirm the profile of the unique brand that is 'Lough Neagh Eels'.

Some recent research

For all respondents to a recent survey, the fishery is a central part of their lives. Many expressed having started in the fishery by helping their fathers or grandfathers as young children with tasks like running lines and then, as they entered their teenage years, they were able to participate in the fishing itself. It is widely acknowledged by fishers that the work can be gruelling and the hours unsociable. At a minimum, a typical day's work with longline fishing involves several hours of running (preparing lines), before going out in the late afternoon or evening to set the lines by boat, then waking up the following morning around 3 or 4am to pull in the lines, grade the eels by size, return to shore, and wait for the lorry to collect them.

Draft netting involves less preparation time, but is more energy intensive during the active moments of fishing. The use of modern technologies, such as fish-finders and hydraulic pulley systems has greatly increased the ease and success of this method; however, it is still used by fewer fishers than longlines, with some fishers switching between the two methods. When fishers were asked on the questionnaire why they fish, they cited a number of reasons, with money being the most universally motivating factor.

While this study provides only a glimpse into the lives of the people involved in the Lough Neagh eel fishery, it demonstrates that the industry is economically essential to both the fishers and other employees and contractors. Over the years, it has developed into a model of co-management that has wider benefits for the local economy and community cohesion, as well as contributing to conservation goals. The economic benefits, in particular, extend beyond the geographic limitations of the region and all along the supply chain.

Lough Neagh Fishermen's Co-operative Society faces specific challenges in maintaining its viability into the future, namely enticing more young people to enter the fishery and negotiating post-Brexit regulations governing management and trade. For the time being, and for those involved in the daily activities of keeping the fishery going as it has throughout living memory, it remains deeply significant. As one 70-year-old fisherman emphasised when asked if he would ever retire, "When I'm three days dead." Fishers also described deeply personal feelings that kept them fishing:

"It's in the blood. There's something there that just keeps you going."

"It's a disease. It's a challenge. Every day is a school day out there. There's no two days the same."

"You always get a buzz. It's not a mundane job. There's naught as good as getting a catch of eels. Good quality eels."

"The only reason why I do it is because I've been here from a child. My dad died at 56 and I'll never forget his words to me. He was down at the hospital and he says, 'Keep an eye on that boat because if that boat's there you'll not starve.' So, I've been here ever since and that sticks in my head."

While the fishery is financially important for those who fish and are otherwise employed in the fishery, it also provides an economic foundation for the surrounding local communities as it has throughout its history. Over the last several decades, with the arrival of other industries in the area, including construction, food manufacturing and sand dredging, the fishery appears to have become less prominent; yet it is still acknowledged for its beneficial effect on the regional economy. Upon being asked what would happen if the fishery were to close, one interviewee responded:

FIG. 40.4

The eel fishery at Toome.

"The majority of people around here are all fishermen. So, it would be a big blow to the area. A local chap was saying to me that they depend on the fishermen. If there are no fishermen, if they have no money, then we have no money."

Besides the multiplier effect of those involved in the fishery spending their income in the local area, the economic benefits of the fishery extend throughout the supply chain. Up to a quarter of the glass eel catch in England and Wales is transferred to the lough for restocking each year, supplemented during low-catch years with glass eels caught in France (P. Wood, pers. comm., April 2018). With prices paid to glass eel fishers typically ranging between £100–200 per kg, restocking in Lough Neagh represents a substantial portion of the income generated for the UK glass eel fishery.

At the other end of the supply chain, the wholesale buyers of Lough Neagh eels also generate economic benefits for their local and regional economies. Among the six main buyers of Lough Neagh brown and silver eels, only one is located within the UK, with the others in Germany and the Netherlands. Approximately 20% of the Lough Neagh catch is sold to Mick's Eels housed at Billingsgate Market in London, which supplies retailers and consumers in Continental Europe and in the UK, including the traditional jellied eel trade in

FIG. 40.5
Grading eels in the
co-operative.

London. Supplementary observation and interviews were conducted with two staff members of Mick's Eels, as well as with the owners of five shops in London selling jellied eels to consumers. Four out of five of these relied exclusively on supply from Mick's Eels. The Lough Neagh eels are sought after by certain discerning customers who prefer the 'wild' flavour, as opposed to the eels raised in farms.

A concern frequently mentioned by interviewees was the decline in young people entering the fishery. However, during interviews and participant observation it was noted that several individuals under the age of 30 were actively participating in fishing, assisting older family members or friends. One interviewee estimated the current number of young people involved at around ten, although he would prefer 20–30 to maintain the future viability of the fishery. Barriers to young people entering the fishery mentioned by interviewees included the 'unsociable' hours of fishing, the inconsistent and seasonal nature of fishing income, the arrival of other industry in the region and the improvement in childhood education that has opened up other career opportunities for local youths.

One fisherman described the changes like this:

> "Years ago, you were a family around the lough and you had six or seven in the family and it was a hard life. There was no work anywhere else. You took to the lough. The young ones from seven to ten years of age they were learning to tie a hook on, learning to run a line, maybe for a couple of pounds, for pocket money. Now the young ones go to Tesco, pack shelves. So, it's a dying thing. It wouldn't be very nice to see it dying out."

Even for younger people who would like to continue the tradition, there are obstacles. One interviewee, aged 36, had started fishing at an early age, assisting his father and grandfather. As a teenager he worked in a local sausage factory and then returned to fishing aged 21. He had fished throughout his twenties and early thirties, first with his brother and then with a cousin. For personal reasons, neither the brother nor cousin are now able to fish. This interviewee has been unable to find another fishing partner and while he continues to be a member of Lough Neagh Fishermen's Co-operative Society and would prefer to fish full-time, he has been forced to find other work.

FIG. 40.6
Bagged eels ready for transporting to London.

41 Traditional boat-building

Kieran Breen

Lough Neagh Heritage Boating Association is a small group of traditional boat builders based at Maghery on the south-west shore of Lough Neagh. We are carrying on a tradition of wooden boat-building around the lough that stretches back into the mists of time.

Some of the evidence of the earliest people recorded in Ireland can be found along the banks of the Lower Bann and the shores of the lough. They were attracted to the rich food source and in places like Mount Sandel and Toome remains can be found of their diet of eels, salmon, trout, char, water birds, boar, deer and an abundance of wild plants, seeds and nuts. The early people of course arrived here by boat and it was natural that over time they would adopt their style of boat to suit their new environment.

The oldest type of boats found here were logboats or coti, a hollowed out tree trunk usually of oak or alder, that would be paddled rowed or even sailed. The flat bottomed craft of the lough are still called cots and carry on the history of logboats in their name. One of our members found the remains of an ancient logboat that was dated by experts as being 6,440 years old. Later examples have been found, such as one at Portadown, which were dated much later to the seventeenth century. Here was an ongoing tradition of boat-building in the area that we are trying to keep alive.

OPPOSITE
FIG. 41.1
Boat-building at Traad.

FIG. 41.2
Lough Neagh cot.

We as a community group were started 20 years ago as part of a development project initiated by Holger Lonze, a German artist. Our first builds were Donegal currachs from around Dunfanaghy and Sheephaven Bay. The enthusiasm for the project led us to keep going as a group and we became passionate about recording and building other types of currachs and then traditional wooden fishing boats of Lough Neagh, Lough Foyle and the South Down coast.

The Lough Neagh fishing boats come in a variety of styles and sizes. Along the south shore the craft ranged from 16 to 19/20 feet. They were clinker-built of overlapping planks, roved together with cooper nails and rowed with a single set of oars. The oars were the Irish type with wooden clogs or bulls attached to the oars and set over pins attached to outriggers on the outside of the boat. On the northern shores a bigger boat of 21–4 feet was used probably because of the prevailing southerly winds creating bigger waves and rougher conditions along that coast. The boats were rowed or sailed to the fishing grounds where long

lines of baited hooks or nets were used to catch salmon, eels, pollan and dollaghan (a large trout native to Lough Neagh).

Inshore fishing was carried out using the flat bottom cots. Larger cots were used for transporting people and goods. At Toome these were used to transport diatomite clay from where it was mined along the Lower Bann to drying sheds in Toome. Small cots were made all around the lough. An interesting double-ended cot called a drimmin was used from Bartin's Bay in the south to Doss and Annaghmore in the north, and we have managed to gather photographs and measurements from fishermen and build a replica of this old type that has pride of place in our collection of boats.

The continuing fishing tradition here is a testament to the skill and tenacity of the generations who called the lough their home and worked the dark waters to provide for their families. Our boat-building helps to keep an ancient tradition alive, remembering those that went before and hopefully introduce new people to the wonders of Lough Neagh.

FIG. 41.3
View from Maghery slip, looking towards the church at Milltown.

42 Mud, peat and brick
resourceful loughshore culture

Liam Campbell

In my job at Lough Neagh Landscape Partnership I have spent many nights near Ardboe in a little house known locally as Coyle's Cottage. It was built in the early 1700s. Although now some 1 km from the lough, the previous owner Ned Coyle (now deceased) claimed it was originally on the loughshore, accounting for the various lowerings of the lough over the years. The cottage however has changed little over the years. It measures internally 5.95 m in length, 4.15 m in breadth and 1.8 m for the wall head. Sampson, writing about the houses in County Derry at the beginning of the nineteenth century, tells us that where stone was not available, such as the boggy areas, that exist especially around the southern shores of Lough Neagh, mud with straw or rushes, called provincially 'cat and clay' was used (Sampson 1802, 298).

Fig. 42.1
Coyle's Cottage at Moortown is a good example of an early eighteenth-century mud-walled house. Now situated about 1 km from Lough Neagh's edge, it was originally on the shoreline prior to various 'lowerings' and drainage schemes.

Evans puts it wonderfully when he writes: 'the use of local building materials meant that they fitted into landscapes of which they were literally a part, their clay or stone walls gathered from the earth on the spot, their timbers dug from the bogs, their thatch harvested from the fields' (Evans 1957, 40). These vernacular treasures are often deeply hidden, as tin often covers thatch, in this case cement render covers mud (and usually thatch under tin too). Staff of the Historic Environment Division have recently completed a survey of some of these buildings in The Birches ward of south Lough Neagh and uncovered a wealth of heritage as Philip Smith's essay in this book attests.

Past

Tempered earth is a more technical name for what is often locally just known as mud. There is some debate as to the date of origin of this in Ireland with the Early Christian period being most cited, but Evans and Ó Dannachair suggest that the concept was introduced by the Anglo-Normans (Evans 1969, 80–81). There seems to be general agreement that tempering the mud for building involved mixing the earth with water in a pit and trampling with animal or human feet (like mud or baked turf of the lough shore area), adding straw, rushes or other fibres for binding and leaving for some time to sour Gailey's research indicates that the houses were of walls *c.* 55–62 cm in width, built in layers 45–60 cm deep and covered with straw of other organic material for binding (Gailey 1976, 56–7). The layer was then allowed to dry to become load-bearing before adding the next layer. Ó Gruagain mentions the oral tradition of the Carrickmore area of using mud since the early 1700s:

> In the Carrickmore area wet blue clay was dug, rushers were trampled through the clay and the mixture was left to 'sour' for approximately one year. Wall foundations were generally of stone upon which the mixture of clay and rushes was placed in layers. Each layer was approximately 0.5 m in depth which was left to dry before the next layer was applied. Sometimes shutters were used to contain the wet mud and prevent slippage. The triangular upper parts of the gable were built of stones, mud bricks, sods or mud while the internal gable tops were often topped with sods and turf (Ó Gruagain 1982, 16).

Before building work started, the site would be marked out by placing large flat stones at the corners, each with a smaller stone on top, to be left there overnight. If they were still in place on the following day, it was a taken as a sign that the prospective dwelling was not being built across a path used by the 'good people', or *slua si* of Irish mythology. Making a clay house began by mixing the marly sub-soil excavated from the earth. Chopped straw was added to the mix as it was turned over and sprinkled with water, then it was left to 'sour' for a few days until it was sufficiently firm to use as a building material; the test was whether it could stand 18 inches wide and a foot deep without bulging. By then the stone foundations, usually nine inches deep and rising another nine inches above ground level, would have been laid before the mud walls were raised using a graip or sprong – a long-handled implement with four flat metal prongs at the end – to manipulate the clay, patting it down to improve its adhesive properties.

Mud walls were built up with a fork in layers 12 to 18 inches deep of a mixture of damp clay and cut rushes which had been left to sour. A stone foundation layer sunk into the ground was usually built first, and sometimes the gable ends, especially if the flue was to be included, were built entirely of stone. They were afterwards trimmed with a sharp spade to a thickness which averages about 20 inches but may be as much as 30. They have to be of massive construction for stability, and the doors which were cut out subsequently were kept narrow. Similarly the window openings were narrow and placed high in the walls, coming directly under the thatch, so that they resemble eyes glinting below shaggy eyebrows. Thick coats of limewash renewed annually gave protection from the weather and it was essential that the thatch should overhang the eaves (Donnelly 2010).

Evans makes particular reference to

> an interesting variant of the mud house occurs around Lough Neagh, where the main weight of the roof is carried on three massive purlins the ends of which can be seen projecting outside the upright gables. I suspect that these houses were built to take tall looms, for the use of the purlins means that there are no couple-ties crossing the room, but the distinction between the purlin and the couple-rafter roof may be fundamental. The purlin-roof may go back to the log house with which it is associated, for example, in Scandinavia ... (Evans 1969, 80).

Local distinctiveness and evidence of Vikings! And at the end of it all, though made from clay, the builder would have a house that was 'neat, cleanly and commodious', as the *Irish Farmers' Journal* noted in 1814. The late Dr Alan Gailey noted that many older folk considered the mud-walled hoses to be warmer than modern constructions and having spent many a night in Coyle's Cottage, I can attest to that from my experiences at the hearth.

Earth building methods are arguably the oldest known to man; the technique varies from region to region as each has been tailored to the type of soil available locally. Mixes were either applied in situ or dried in the shape of bricks and blocks, from the common clay brick to CEBs (compressed earth blocks, essentially rammed earth bricks). The production of brick around Lough Neagh and along the Bann is in a sense a natural follow on to the use of mud.

Unlike the rest of Europe and indeed the world, brick production and use in Ireland appears to be a mostly Post-Medieval phenomenon with little record of bricks used in Irish buildings before the sixteenth century. By the latter part of the 1500s, the use of brick in Ireland seems to be associated with high status buildings such as country houses and fortifications but towards the end of the seventeenth century it was also being employed in a limited way in vernacular housing in parts of Ulster. We are very fortunate around the lough shore in having many examples of this skill intact. In fact, Mountjoy Castle at Brocagh is an excellent example of early brick. Archaeological evidence shows the proliferation of brick kilns in the wider area. Brick 'clay' is found around especially the southern and western shores and along the river banks. The location beside water is not only useful in providing a water source but also a means of transporting the finished product, which by its very nature is bulky. Whether it is the vernacular Coyle's Cottage or the imposing Mountjoy Castle, the building material was literally on the doorstep.

The clay was generally manually dug out of pits and usually left to sour. The few stones were then picked out by hand, and traditionally the clay was worked to the right consistency for moulding, by watering it and trampling underfoot, a process known as tempering. (A project in brick-making was completed with school children in Brocagh in 2018 and what child doesn't like playing with mud!). Once tempered the bricks were moulded and left to harden prior to firing. Names like 'brick hole' and 'brickfield' are very common in the general south-west Lough Neagh and Lower Bann areas.

Fig. 42.2

Mountjoy Castle with its early seventeenth-century brickwork.

Fig. 42.3
Eddie Brogan (on right), a traditional brick-maker from Arney, County Fermanagh, giving a demonstration of the skill to locals at Brocagh as part of a Lough Neagh Partnership project in 2018.

At most brickfields the clay was normally dug out during the first four months of the year to allow it to weather. Brick-making was generally a seasonal activity on the smaller brickfields, such as that at Mountjoy/Brocagh, where the brick-makers could be seasonal workers or even farmers, the main period of production being around April to September. In many parts of Ireland from the seventeenth century to the early twentieth century bricks were traditionally fired in a clamp kiln, a rectangular arrangement consisting of alternate courses of bricks. The construction of the clamp could take up to two weeks, and involved the building of a series of pillars with unfired brick, which was generally formed into a series of arches. The arches, which were at right angles to the clamp, served as fire settings, into which either coal and or turf (ready supplies were available in this area around the lough shore) were placed and ignited. Clamp kilns were almost universally on Irish brickfields in the mid-nineteenth century but by the early 1850s more permanent kiln structures were beginning to be built. This was to culminate in this area of Tyrone with the establishment of a major brick industry, such as Tyrone Brick.

Earth and subsequently brick when used as a building material is fireproof, contributes to the regulation of the indoor environment (temperature and humidity levels), and when correctly specified and built, is sufficiently strong for buildings up to ten storeys high. It is estimated that, even today, earth buildings house some 30% of the world's population. Rammed earth is stronger than cob and less prone to shrinkage as the mix is compacted and requires less water, shrinkage and subsequent cracks being caused by water evaporation.

And yet mud and turf have a long history of being demonised in colonial writing though this dates back to Anglo-Norman times.

The inhabitants of Ireland do not have affinity with castles as a means of defence; instead they make the woods their stronghold and the bogs their stinking trenches.

Giraldus Cambrensis/Gerald of Wales (1185)

> Ireland is a wasteland in need of improvement that is flat, empty and
> inscribab full of wolf and woodkerne.
>
> Edmund Spenser, *A View of Ireland* (1595)

In 1685 William King – later to become bishop of Derry and then archbishop of Dublin – published 'Of the bogs and loughs of Ireland' in *Philosophical Transactions*, in which he calls Irish bogs 'infamous' and equates extensive bogland with barbarity. The bogs offered an advantage to resistant natives, who, King believed, deliberately built near them: they were

> a shelter and a refuge to tories [dispossessed natives turned outlaws], and thieves, who can hardly live without them. They take advantage then to them to have the country unpassable, and the fewer strangers came near them, they lived the easier. The bogs are very inconvenient to us.

The census of 1841 estimated that nearly half of the families of the rural population of Ireland, then some 84% of the total, were living in one room cabins. Evans refers to the bog-strewn areas where stone is not readily available and transport of materials is difficult, the clay-walled house remains typical. But he cautions as to how we should view them: 'At its best the mud-walled house could be both durable and comfortable and many observers warn us not to assume the poverty of their builders' (Evans 1957, 46). He also quotes Arthur Young's observation made in 1780: 'Before we can attribute such deficiencies to absolute poverty we must take into account the customs and inclinations of the people.'

Whilst the eighteenth- and nineteenth-century period of 'Improvement' – during which many of these structures were destroyed, repurposed, or left to decay – has received extensive attention by historians, there exists little serious study of the human and environmental dimensions. Through analysis of the material aspects of landscape resource use and analysis of the historical perceptions of such use, we emphasise the national significance of this undervalued aspect of our built and cultural heritage, increasingly at risk of being lost completely, highlighting the prior ubiquity of mud-wall structures.

The reasons why such a drastic decline in the use of both turf and mud-wall took place in Ireland over a period covering three centuries from the mid-1700s have typically been seen as part of the narrative of Improvement. Agricultural revolution is seen to be followed by industrial advancement, the emergence of a more all-encompassing economy and increasing availability of cheaper imported building materials following the advent of extensive railway networks. This meant that local context, climatic conditions, and the lifestyles of the rural population were no longer the underlying rationale for building methods or, indeed, materials utilised. Ulster's landscape today is a product of these developments with stone-built buildings and clachan settlements typically viewed as romantic remnants of past times. The reality, however, is that the many stone

farmhouses, with their homogenised appearances across the regions of Ireland, are generally part of a relatively modern eighteenth- and nineteenth-century aesthetic that severed links to traditional vernacular buildings and the methods of their erection.

The instincts of many present-day heritage organisations appear to remain focused on evocative buildings. Consequently, such organisations may overlook 'lowly' constructions unless in dramatic or romanticised settings. However, it is in vernacular buildings within rural settings that the experiences of the vast majority of Ulster's past population are found. Perceptions of materials used also change; stone, which was deemed a necessary means of improving the building stock by the later eighteenth century, was often used earlier as a vernacular material.

During the Emergency (1939–45), Dublin architect Frank Gibney suggested that people should be encouraged to build with clay because of its widespread availability. He also argued that clay-built houses, in terms of their design, construction and insulation properties, were 'superior to many of our modern, standardised thin-walled cottages'. The only impediment to reviving the ancient art that he could see was 'a psychological one, for public opinion may appear hesitant in considering an idea associated with "mud cabins", peasantry and poverty.' And indeed, the prejudice against this most vernacular of Irish building types was so entrenched that his plea fell on deaf ears.

It would be impossible to exaggerate the pervasive nature of this prejudice; it is part of our cultural baggage. As long ago as 1878, the *Irish Builder* lamented that mud cabins were 'still, alas!, too plentiful' and sought to have these 'barbarous relics' replaced by 'a better class of human dwellings in stone, brick and concrete materials'.

Present

According to Hugo Houben, a French architect based in Grenoble, building with earth is also the most efficient way to produce housing in the developing world. The material is widely available, it is economical to use and also has the advantage of being both culturally and climatically suitable; it is the essence of 'sustainable development'. Britain has tens of thousands of mud-walled, or cob, buildings – mostly in the south-west of England. 'After cob was dismissed earlier this century in favour of mass-produced bricks and concrete, this most green of building methods is coming back into favour,' the London *Times* reported, in a 1995 article on the Devon Earth Building Society.

Historic England lists five reasons 'Why You Should Love Them':

1 Mud or earth building is one of the oldest methods of construction in the world.

2 They're energy efficient, carbon neutral and good for wildlife. The only energy you need to make a mud wall is a hearty breakfast for the labourers who are building them. The mud was usually dug from the ground close to the building site, so it was and remains a very sustainable material. If, as was often the case, the walls were covered with a protective layer of lime wash, they absorb carbon dioxide, rendering them carbon neutral. Also, because the walls are usually thick and strong, they are great at insulating the buildings they were used for, keeping buildings warm in winter and cool in summer.

3 They were a tax avoidance scheme. The Brick Tax was introduced in 1784 to help pay for the costs of fighting the revolutionary war in the Thirteen Colonies. The tax was, unsurprisingly, unpopular, and there were many ways in which people tried to avoid paying. Building walls and buildings using the clay lump blocks avoided firing the clay to make normal bricks, and therefore was not subject to the tax.

4 Mud walls are quick and dirty.

5 There are still a lot of places where buildings and walls using this traditional method of construction can be found.

It is important to emphasise that historic earth-built vernacular structures could be made entirely permanent when appropriately maintained with regular new thatch and lime harl. Therefore, the propagation of negative perceptions of vernacular mud-wall dwellings must be partly explained by disparities in the quality of build and suitability of external finish. It may thus be assumed that many mud-wall buildings of 'lower' status were left unrendered upon completion, leaving them unprotected from water infiltration and wind erosion and so liable to be lost. A further qualification is that the relative ratios of cost and maintenance, rather than longevity of a building's life-cycle, can determine perceptions of permanence. Thus, the notion follows that true permanence is determined by high initial and low maintenance costs, whilst semi-permanence is defined through low building cost with a need for frequent repair. This defines the essential nature of historic earth-built structures that a disconnection to such regimes within modern Western society likely influences the perception of vernacular tradition.

Future

We need to look at new uses for the existing buildings due to their unique nature – uses such as a bothy, etc, could be useful. We need to look at planning laws to see how these can be adapted and we need further research at our universities and other institutions as to how we can look at these building processes anew in this time of dramatic climate change and sustainability challenges. We have to look at how the past informed many negative attitudes to this type of vernacular building and how we can turn these around to provide a positive future value for us all.

FIG. 42.5
Coney Island.

Acknowledgement

I am indebted to Barney Devine from the Cuilcah to Cleenish project at Arney in County Fermanagh for advising on the manufacture of brick.

Bibliography

Danny Donnelly, *Foothills of the Sperrins* (Galbally, Co. Tyrone, 2010).

E.E. Evans, *Irish Folk Ways* (London, 1957).

E.E. Evans, 'Sod and turf houses in Ireland' in Geraint Jenkins (ed.), *Studies in Folk Life: Essays in Honour of Iorwerth C. Peate* (London, 1969), pp 79–90.

Alan Gailey, 'The housing of the rural poor in nineteenth-century Ulster', *Ulster Folklife*, 22 (1976), pp 34–58.

C. Ó Dannachair, 'The bed-outshot in Ireland', *Folk-Living*, 20 (1956), pp 26–31.

O.P. Ó Gruagain, 'House and hearth', *An Tearmann*, 3 (1982), pp 14–17.

G.V. Sampson, *Statistical Survey of the County of Londonderry with Observations on the Means of Improvement* (Dublin, 1802).

43

'One direction of travel'

Barry Devlin

The land

A big red corrugated hayshed stood in the haggard below our house in Sessia, the townland that sits furthest out on Ardboe Point on the east side of the lough.

It was made by a manufacturer in Laois (probably while Ireland still had no internal border): in late autumn it was packed to the girders with bales of hay that dropped from the back end of a static thresher during the fifties and then from a mobile baler pulled behind Paddy Quinn's big blue Fordson Major as the fifties turned into the sixties.

That hayshed – set square in its haggard yard below the stables and the duck house – was the scene of what I can only describe as a pageant at threshing time. That was the time (always blindingly sunny, it seemed, with the motes dancing in the heat)

FIG. 43.1
Lough Neagh fishing boat,
Doss Bay.

when the grass seed that my father grew on Motty's Hill and the bottom meadow was hefted up onto the big faded-pink Marshall thresher and fed into its rumbling innards by what seemed to my ten-year-old self to be an army of men armed with pitchforks and wearing a uniform of striped collarless shirts and caps to keep the stour out of their eyes and hair.

Reconnaissance and light duties best described my presence there. I was one of at least a dozen children – the Devlins and the Croziers together mustered that number easily – all 'helping': checking the paddles at the back of the thresher that shuffled the grain into sacks, bringing tea for the thirsty men to drink, fetching and carrying ropes, rakes, tools. In reality, the men did all the jobs and that our presence – or mine anyway, for I was imaginative and inept, a daydreaming menace to myself and others – was anything other than a danger (what would health and safety and indeed common sense make of it today?) was a kindly fiction on the part of all concerned.

Every second of the threshing day was magic to me: the tractors arriving early along the back loaning, past the linthole, a modern Fordson Major followed by a scary, rust streaked Fordson pachyderm from the thirties that snorted and boiled merrily as it powered the belt of the thresher; the ricks in the haggard being dismantled in minutes and the mice that had been foolish enough to build nests underneath scattering to the winds, prey to the many cats that were enjoying the occasion just as much as us; dinner – held, properly, in the middle of the day, at 12 o'clock – with a menu of stew and floury potatoes from our own drills, the men putting their caps on the table and falling to, the familiar kitchen full of strange and unfamiliar faces and stories and gossip and much laughter and then after the tea at the end, the chorus of "We're goin' on" as the caps were set back on and readjusted; the more relaxed rhythm of the late afternoon and the sense of winding down as the working day edged to a close – the working day in the haggard that is, for there were cattle to be brought in and milked and things to be redd up.

But not by us.

For us, children of the lesser god, the best bit of the day was just about to begin.

The lough

The lough, blue and hazy-warm and echoing with faint bird calls from Golloman's Point and The Battery and the ash and alder clad bays beyond was half a mile away by the tarmac road that led down to the Old Cross. But as the crow flew (and our house had a notable rookery in the pines that surrounded it) the nearest inlet was only three scrubby fields away.

So, it was that when the last of the day's threshing was done, at maybe 7 or 8 o'clock, the climax of the day arrived.

By then every bit of us was sun blasted and itchy – all that white skin to burn, all those bodices and vests for chaff to get under and itch – and we couldn't wait to get into the shallow cooling water of the lough.

But there was a protocol to be observed, time honoured and enforced by the older children, my sister Marie and Moya Crozier. This was to be no rabble's rout: there was to be a race with a winner, a *one two three go*! and a leaping, laughing, stumbling headlong charge along Creaney's bank and across Martin's shore into the cool waters of the quay at the Wee Rock.

The heat of the haggard – the land – splashed away by the shock of the shallow water – the lough (which soon revealed itself as comfortingly tepid) – that was the revelatory moment for us, the bit that made us joyfully certain about who we really were and what our life really was.

Because though we were farm children who did farm things (not too strenuously in my case, idle boy) we had another dimension to our lives: a dimension that when we look back at as a family clearly declares itself to have been the important one. Though we grew up as farmers' children it was not the land that defined and shaped and enclosed and opened out our lives, not the fields but the lough.

There was only one direction to travel from Ardboe Point, (a direction enforced by the lough itself) and that was west, away from the shore. East and you were in the water in minutes. Any other direction, due north or south would lead you back to the water's edge, at Blacker's Rock or Kinturk Flat.

That is why we define ourselves now as lough children: we see clearly that we lived on the edge – literally, a scalloped line, limned, on misty mornings, between the flat alluvial land and the mirror – still water, a border apprised by the distant cries of Common Gulls and Little Terns.

For me, though, there was a more direct and practical link to the lough, one that made it not just a place for sport and pleasure but – however briefly – a workplace.

FIG. 43.1
Sailing on Lough Neagh.

My father as well as being a farmer and publican and a grocer was a fish merchant. So, in my final year at primary school and first years at college, I came with him on his daily rounds to pick up eels at Eglish quay.

Those days still live on in my memory with a vividness and clarity no photo could match (photos were rare, in any case); I still see the big quay with its raw, recently excavated jetty lined with half a dozen high-prowed, clinker-built boats, (hewn to a newer, less elegant pattern than the dainty boats that lay upturned on the shore); the bikes piled untidily inside the gap; the tin hut where the lines were run; the fishermen about their business, burnt teak brown by the summer sun and the lough's breezes.

Their names come back to me now, phonetically, as they were shouted across the shore, Lodilly and The Rong and Pat Hagan and Big Jack, a roll call of the dead.

When my father drove in to these men to weigh and box their catch, the eels would be lifted from the submerged wire cages where they were kept alive: they surfaced in a roiling, boiling, glittering mass, powerful and packed – like a single muscle flexed and pumping, ready for the work of survival.

Packing them in ice in their wooden packing cases gave me a huge regard for their will to stay alive, their determination to escape, their ability to slither free leaving the loop of your thumb and index finger coated in – *slime* is a harsh term for its tenderness – their warm, life preserving coating.

They would slither yards through the scutch grass and into the lough if you were not quick enough and I have to confess to being tardy on purpose on a couple of occasions … and getting bawled out for my pains.

I became so used to their sine wave unfolding process through the water and the grass that it came as a shock to me when I saw them, a lifetime later, asleep

in an aquarium, not sinuous and graceful but blocky and awkward, bent in an inverted L-shape.

Once a fortnight, that daily routine of weighing and packing was interrupted by a longer trip to Belfast docks, to pick up and haul away huge blocks of ice to pack the eels in on their journey to Billingsgate. (I still have some of the labels that guided them to their destination, Salmonsen and Bremmer & Morck.)

We had an Austin pickup, based on a Devon chassis and it was hard work for her with the big chunks of ice in the back. We laboured the 40 miles home trailing a melancholy streel of melting ice and secreted it in one of the stables under bales of straw brought down from the hayshed: lough and field, water and land in a metaphorical embrace, not that I was precious enough to think of it like that, (though growing old has worn down the whimsy alarm).

The eels are in trouble these days, the red hayshed has collapsed and mouldered and the lough I grew up around has changed entirely, not least in the huge decline in its fishing population.

The boats have sonar now and little cabins in the prow, but there are far, far fewer of them – "Young fellas would rather be electricians than keep hard hours," one fisherman explained. But he said it without bitterness, with a resigned acceptance that this was the way of the world.

And so it is.

There was a time and a place 'joining the edge of Lough Neagh's bright waters' as the song 'Old Ardboe' has it.

That time is past … but the land and the lough live on.

FIG. 43.3
Boat wake on Lough Neagh.

44 A view from my place of mind

Seamus Burns

Lough Neagh and its hinterland is the place I call home. I grew up three miles from its north-west shore and I have lived in this area for over 50 years. Lough Neagh has been a central part of my life, my reference point when describing where I come from. Like many who live here, I am fiercely proud of my home place, and feel very fortunate to have never had to move away from the area in search of work or a home life elsewhere.

Born in 1969, to parents Jim and Martina Burns, I was the eldest of five, with my brother Paul, and my sisters Ursula, Nuala and Annette. Our mother grew up in Magherafelt where she lived out her life. My father was from the nearby Glenullin (Eagle's Glen) and came to Magherafelt where he too lived out the rest of his life. Childhood visits to our grandparents, uncles and aunts included regular trips to Glenullin. Lasting memories include the smell of burning turf that hung in the air on a Sunday afternoon as we made our way

FIG. 44.1
Maghery slip.

through the glen to see our granny. As with many families living among the rural peatlands of Ireland, homes around Glenullin were kept warm in this traditional way. We would often go fishing for trout on the Agivey river in summer. There was always an excitement about going fishing on a fresh run of water following a spell of rain in the Sperrins. The waters of the Agivey ran dark into the Lower Bann, stained by the surrounding peatlands. The fresh run of water was said to have made for good salmon and trout fishing. The rural landscape of Glenullin brought the beauty of nature to my attention through my father from a very early age.

I grew up on the edge of the rural town of Magherafelt, surrounded by a landscape where we could go exploring for tadpoles in pools of an old flax dam, hunt under stones for stone loach in the Coppies river, and watch out for brightly coloured male bullfinches in the surrounding hedgerows. The waters of Lough Neagh could be seen in the distance when we were at the top of the hill near our home. We would venture to the shores of Lough Neagh, occasionally on foot or by bike, but most often by car when someone could take us. As children we went there to paddle in the water at Ballyronan or at Traad Point, or to walk through the woodland on the shoreline. As a child, the wooded shoreline felt fairy-like and mystical, where marsh marigold flowers would grow in spring.

We grew up hearing our father recall the sound of corncrakes and curlews that called from the meadows and the peatlands around his home in Glenullin, or the song of the linnet (whin grey) as it sang from the whin bushes where they had built their nest. We would hear our mother recall memories of days on the beach at Traad Point on the north-west shore of Lough Neagh. When she was young, she would travel there by horse and cart, with my grandfather Jimmy Campbell, a general merchant in the town. Granda and Granny Campbell raised their family in a big house on Meeting Street beside the police and army barracks in Magherafelt. The house has gone now, demolished in the mid-1970s when a bomb exploded in a bin lorry. Out of the rubble of that explosion came the first pair of binoculars I would ever see through to look at birds up close. The bomb-damaged binoculars had double vision, which meant closing one eye to see properly. They belonged to my uncle Michael. Uncle Micky bought me my first ever bird identification book when it became clear how keen I was on watching birds. This was closely followed by a second book bought for me by my brother Paul, brought home from a school trip he was on from primary school.

I started visiting Traad Point, Lough Neagh in the late 1980s, but people were no longer visiting the beach in the way that my mother did. I found a very different world to enjoy. The place was secluded and peaceful, and the beach was now a great big reedbed, where great crested grebes and the coots had made their home. Traad Point became a very special place for me. I would spend countless hours alone with nature here all the way through the 1990s. I got to meet many interesting and knowledgeable people, from the scientists and

students who were based at the University of Ulster Freshwater Lab
that was there when I first arrived on the scene, to the local fishermen
who went fishing for eels and pollan on boats from the nearby quays,
to the fathers and sons who traditionally hunted for wild duck with gun
and dog along its shores between September and January.

Traad Point became my spiritual home on Lough Neagh, my outdoor
learning space, the place where I taught myself about the lough, its wildlife,
and its community. I left school at 16. Going to University was never part
of the plan when I was at school. Apart from a few teachers who
encouraged me in the subjects that interested me, I found most subjects at
school too difficult to deal with, and instead spent most of my teenage years
playing the classroom clown. At primary school I recall with fondness having
to attend Mrs Heaney's class. These lessons could best be described as extra

FIG. 44.2
Storm shore at Brookend.

support with my reading and writing. I was born with spina bifida and hydrocephalus. Hydrocephalus causes, among other things, a build-up of fluid in the brain which usually leads to some level of damage. It is clear to me now that this was a factor contributing to why I found learning at school difficult. The fortunate thing about this is that I got to attend Mrs Heaney's class for extra help, and the change that made in my life. Mrs Heaney would help us learn in a number of very practical ways, including showing us television programmes. It was while in this class that I watched a programme called Sky Hunter that featured the RSPB, part of the Look and Learn series at the time. The programme was shown over several weeks and followed the story of three children on holiday on a canal who got involved in catching a man who had been stealing wild birds' eggs. It is the earliest memory I have of being inspired towards volunteering and working with the RSPB to protect birds.

My experience of Lough Neagh and Lough Beg was enhanced by time spent around the Toome Canal, while staying with my Aunt Bridie and Uncle Tommy in Toome in the late 1970s. It was while staying there I discovered Lough Beg (the wee lough) for the first time. The Lower Bann leaves Lough Neagh at Toome, on its way to the North Atlantic. Two miles north of Toome, the river spreads out across the floodplain grazing marshes of Lough Beg, about a mile east of Bellaghy. I recall leaving Toome with my uncle and aunt in their boat, travelling downstream along the Lower Bann, and entering the wide open waters of Lough Beg. We landed on the shore at Church Island, where I discovered the remains of an old graveyard with its aged headstones and dominated by the shadow of the church spire. We visited the wishing well – I was told that St Patrick knelt on a stone and left an impression that filled with water that now has healing powers. There was a mute swan nest by the shore. I lifted an egg from the nest and was given a stiff telling off for doing so, learning a valuable

FIG. 44.3

View of Church Island, Lough Beg, with flag iris (*Iris pseudacorus*) in the foreground.

lesson on how to behave and respect nature. This experience was life-changing, and so it was inevitable that I would go back in search of the place again alone when I was old enough to do so in the late 1980s.

I left primary school and started secondary school in 1980. Up until that point, Mrs Heaney had discovered my passion for nature, and my ability to draw and paint. Her kindness encouraged me to look at nature, and to draw and paint the subject as a way of learning about it. At secondary school, I was drawn towards the more practical subjects of art and woodwork. My experiences of reading and writing with Mrs Heaney carried through to secondary school where I continued to develop a fondness for writing lessons in my English class. I was fortunate that my form teacher for the majority of my time at secondary school was Mrs McMahon. She was also my English teacher. Mrs McMahon had a kindness similar to Mrs Heaney, and I felt encouraged. I recall Mrs McMahon paying me the ultimate tribute when she discovered the birds that I had drawn for my CSE art coursework. I believe I actually gifted her some of these at the time, as a result of the positive interest coming from her.

Having left school in 1985, I got a job through a youth training programme, working for the Hughes family in a furniture factory in Castledawson. I worked there for 13 years, while spending every spare moment I had in evenings and weekends engrossed in the conservation of wildlife around my home in South Derry. In the late 1980s I joined the RSPB as a member and started to volunteer as a youth leader, to run a Young Ornithologists' Club for children at my former primary school. Volunteering quickly became a part of my education having left school. I joined the British Trust for Ornithology (BTO) and volunteered to carry out surveys of birds. I then started co-ordinating and organising surveys for other volunteers and became the BTO representative for County Derry in the late 1980s. I married Jean Darragh, a local girl from Eden, near Bellaghy, in 1989, and with her by my side, continued my volunteering, while working in the factory. In the early 1990s I was a founding member of the Moyola Conservation Group, a voluntary group of local people with a passion for nature conservation. This group of people became a central part of my life outside work and family life for several years through the '90s. I joined the Ulster Wildlife Trust in the early '90s, and started volunteering as a warden on their nature reserve in the area. By the mid-1990s, I was volunteering for several nature conservation charities, while holding down my full time job.

In 1995, Jean and I had our first child. Our daughter Orla was born in April that year. Our second child, our son Ciarán, was born four years later in June 1999. Having had all of these achievements, I started to believe that I could achieve a university degree after all. The Open University was the route I took, a pace of learning that suited my learning abilities. I eventually graduated through the Open University with a degree in 2008. By that stage though, I had left the furniture factory job to take up jobs with the RSPB, Ulster Wildlife Trust and Lough Neagh Partnership. I was a fieldworker for the RSPB, doing bird surveys across the west area of Northern Ireland, then moved to the Ulster Wildlife Trust to deliver educational events with schools and communities across Northern Ireland, and then to Lough Neagh Partnership to become the Lough Neagh Wetlands Biodiversity Officer.

My job as Lough Neagh Wetlands Biodiversity Officer started in 2005, and brought me full circle to where it all began for me at Lough Neagh. I was fortunate to have been given the opportunity by Lough Neagh Advisory Committee, and the Lough Neagh Partnership, and for the next five years I would develop a Local Biodiversity Action Plan in partnership with the community around Lough Neagh. My main goal was to understand the concerns of the Lough Neagh community from the outset, so I held stakeholder engagement meetings with several hundred people around Lough Neagh during my first year – starting in Bellaghy, then moving anti-clockwise to Ardboe, Washingbay, Peatlands Park, Lough Neagh Discovery Centre, Glenavy and finishing off in Antrim town. It was while listening to the concerns of the people and understanding how communities wanted to play their part in nature conservation that allowed me to develop plans with them for a range of species and habitats around Lough Neagh. This culminated in the launch of the Lough Neagh Wetlands Local Biodiversity Action Plan on World Wetlands Day, 2 February 2008.

The launch of the Biodiversity Action Plan took place in Toome. I had recently returned from a trip to Iceland, where I had been part of a group of people who were there working on a conservation programme for the Whooper Swans that visit Lough Neagh from Iceland each winter. While in Iceland, I met BBC *Autumnwatch* presenter Kate Humble, who was there to film with us for the programme, as we worked with scientists to fit GPS technology on six birds so that they could be tracked on their migration journey back to Ireland and the UK. Kate Humble paid us ultimate tribute by agreeing to come to Toome in February 2008 to help us launch the Lough Neagh Biodiversity Action Plan, alongside over one hundred stakeholders/members of the Lough Neagh community who had helped put the plan together. Many of these stakeholders/community would go on to deliver the actions from the biodiversity plan.

Among the stakeholders/partners who were part of the production of the plan, was RSPB Northern Ireland. RSPB NI had played a key role in the development of a plan for the breeding waders – Lapwings, Redshanks, Snipe and Curlews, of the Lough Neagh Wetlands. In 2009 I would go on to join RSPB NI as their Restoration Officer, to deliver the restoration of wet grassland at Lough Beg for breeding waders. This led to the development of the Lough Beg Management Plan in partnership with the farmers/landowners who had been involved in the stakeholder meetings in Bellaghy in 2006, right through to the launch of the Biodiversity Action Plan in 2008. By 2010, the Lough Beg farmers/landowners, in partnership with RSPB NI, Northern Ireland Environment Agency and others, agreed a five-year plan to restore the area. This plan had the support of the poet Seamus Heaney, who grew up in the area. By 2015, the Lough Beg Area of Special Scientific Interest had been restored for its breeding waders, as a result of the collaboration of so many people. In 2015, the Lough Neagh Partnership built upon this and led further work for the wet grassland and peatlands of south-west Lough Neagh, which focused primarily on breeding Curlews. By then, curlews were disappearing from all over Ireland, and the south-west corner of Lough Neagh was one of the very few places away from Lough Erne in Fermanagh, or the Antrim Plateau, where a number of birds still bred.

The large numbers of wildfowl that once occurred on Lough Neagh up until the late 1980s, have declined now to half of what was there then. Factors such as climate change and habitat quality point towards their decline. As a result of climate change, wetlands further north into Europe no longer freeze in the way the once did, so science indicates that birds are going there in preference to making the extra journey south to us here at Lough Neagh. However, the quality of the open water habitat, and the co-ordinated management of activities to provide safe and secure refuge areas for wildfowl on Lough Neagh, needs to continue for those birds that are here, and that will on occasions be joined by many more when they are forced to come here during the harshest of winters further north.

The future for nature all around Lough Neagh looks as good as I've ever known it. The community-led approach through the efforts of Lough Neagh Partnership and others, has the ability to really target conservation work into the places where nature needs it most. Curlews, Lapwings Redshanks, Snipe and Irish lady's tresses orchids can do really well if given space to live on large expanses of species-rich wet grasslands in places like south-west Lough Neagh, Portmore Lough and at Lough Beg. Common terns and gulls can thrive through targeted conservation of the islands on Lough Neagh, and great crested grebes will continue to breed along the reedbed shoreline through careful and targeted attention on these habitats. Space can be made for the iconic Whooper Swan to live alongside farming around Lough Neagh and along the Bann valley. Rare species like marsh fritillary butterfly and Irish damselfly will benefit from targeted conservation of peatlands in south Lough Neagh. Space too for wet woodlands to expend and grow along the traditionally wooded shorelines along the north of the lough, from Ballyronan/Traad Point, all the way round to places like Rea's Wood in Antrim. A well balanced approach to conserving Lough Neagh and its shoreline opens up the opportunity for new species to arrive from southern Europe – to follow the little egrets that came here in the early 1990s and have since enhanced our experience of the Lough. If we create the space, they will come. Lough Neagh and its community has an exciting future when we think like that.

45 Robert Cinnamond
the Ballinderry Balladeer

Róisín White

In my young days growing up in south County Down during the 1950s and '60s, the loughshore and surrounding area was a far-away place. We were not fisher folk, but mountain farmers on hilly, rocky ground, with a few cattle, about 50 sheep, chickens, and a small patch for growing our vegetables. Self-sufficiency was the normal practice for everyone. Our entertainment was the radio, house-visiting, story-telling, playing outside from morning till night, helping on the small farm. This was the pre-electricity era and there was no traffic chaos! My mother sang all day, while doing her work around the house and farm. Some of the songs she sang include 'Moonlight in Mayo', 'Rathfriland on the hill', 'John Mitchel', 'The three flowers'. Many of these songs are with my siblings still, even though we don't get opportunities to sing them very often. They have remained in the memory simply by being repeated often.

We learned about Lough Neagh at school, its location, formation and mythology. Our teacher Miss Campbell taught us 'Tis pretty to be in Ballinderry' and little did I think then that song, and place-name, would bring me on a trip, many years later, to Glenavy and Ballymacrickett, County Antrim, not far off the loughshore. I moved to teach in Armagh in the mid-1970s and had the blessed fortune to meet my dearest friend Sarah Anne O'Neill (Hanna), who, along with my mother, was the greatest influence on me as a singer.

Sarah Anne had a large store of local songs, e.g. 'Fisher's cot', and she introduced me to many songs and singers around the loughshore, Tyrone side, and further afield. She had a very infectious nature and was a favourite at sessions throughout Ireland, often in the company of her brother Geordie. They both preserved a rich store of song during their lives and singing was the very fabric of who they were. They knew the famous song, 'You rambling boys of pleasure', and I had heard the name Robert Cinnamond mentioned in relation to this song. I remember Sarah Anne saying she had heard his name also. The name Cinnamond attracted me and I decided I would find out more about Robert. I went to see his daughter Vera Kennedy, who lived in Belfast, in the early 1990s, and she 'introduced' me to her father. He was born in Tullyballydonnell, near Ballinderry. The area is rich in Gaelic place-names, e.g. Moygarriff, Aghadavy, Aghalee, Derynaseer, Portmore, Legatiriff, Aghadolgan, and Ballymacrickett, near Glenavy, where Robert and his wife Elizabeth are laid to rest. A brief timeline for Robert is presented below:

1884	Born Tullyballydonnell.
1889–96	Educated at St Mary's School.
1912	Won a silver medal, perhaps for piping or fiddle.
1913	Married Elizabeth Murphy, Cloghogue, Newry; lived at Aghadolgan.
1936	Elizabeth died aged 42; Robert continued raising his large family.
1940s	During WWII Robert worked at Langford Lodge.
1950s	Recorded by collectors from the BBC in the early 1950s.
1950s	Moved to the USA to live with family members after 1955–6(?).
1960s	Returned to Ireland in the early 1960s.
1960s	RTE collectors recorded him on his return from America.
1968	Died.

The recorded material resulted in the LP, *You Rambling Boys of Pleasure* (Topic Records, 1975).

Robert played a fiddle and was a tremendous singer with his own unique style, ornamented and high-pitched. He answered a letter in the local paper which requested readers to send in any songs they might have. Robert replied saying he had 'an odd song here and there'. Collectors from the BBC and RTE recorded over 100 songs from him in early 1950s and again in early 1960s. His handwritten notes, scribbles, lists of songs and recordings are stored in the Irish Traditional Music Archive (ITMA) in Dublin.[1]

Robert and his siblings attended the local St Mary's School, located at the front of St Mary's Chapel in Tullyballydonnell. His parents William and Sarah Anne were married in 1866 and William may have worked as a farmhand. Both of Robert's parents were singers and he said in an interview that his father got songs from his own father before him. House dances and céilithe were held in the area and anyone who sang or played a tune was welcome to attend. Robert tells of his father and a friend called Roddy going to Lisburn to a fair with cattle. They sold the animals, and had a few drinks with their earnings. They came out on to a street and met a ballad sheet seller. They bought a few sheets and went around the town entertaining the people with the ballads.

Robert remembers his mother singing. "She was a sweet singer – I can remember as a little boy when she'd be putting me to bed at night, she'd put her arms around me, hold me up to her – even yet I can feel the heat of her breast on my head. She'd croon airs." He mentioned 'Maid of 17' as one of the songs he got from his mother. When asked by the collector Seán Ó Boyle, "Where did you get these songs?" Robert replied:

> "The house I was born in, way back in those early days, 70 years ago and more – there were 4 looms in our house. There's an old saying, 'the weaver sings a merry song sitting on his loom.' In wintertime when they'd light the lamps around 4 o'clock – get their tea, and then on to the loom, they'd sing from that till 10 o clock, and weave their best. That's where I learned a good lot of my songs, a lad standing behind the loom."

He continued, describing the way bobbins were wound, "and you daren't wind the bobbin too large or it wouldn't fit into the shuttle. The weavers all sang and the beautiful old airs made an impression on my memory that was never erased."

Robert was a keen gardener all his life. His daughter Vera told me she would often hear him singing loudly while working in the garden of her house in Belfast. Robert referred to singing while working: "I remember if a man was digging the garden I'd peep to see him working, and he'd be singing and digging – and digging's no easy job!!" "Did the fishermen sing?" he was asked. His reply was:

> "Yes, as a rule the fishermen were musical. The rolling waves coming in on the shore, that's music in itself. When they were making the nets, they'd be singing all the time – a treat to hear. When they'd be coming in off the lough with a boat-load of pollans, they were shining like silver, and you'd hear those boys singing songs – it'd do your heart good."

Robert's memory was clear and he recounted many events to his collectors. He held a strong affinity with his local area, its people, its stories and songs, its terrain and traditions associated with the lough. He often referred to the local entertainment scene as in this account.

> "There might have been a céilí in someone's house – they got the web done – it taken to Lurgan – and before they commenced another web there'd be a cup of tea – maybe a wee drop of something stronger. Mary Ann, Kitty – we'll have a verse of a song; maybe the old fella would get up and dance a bit of a step – and so the evening's entertainment would proceed."

Robert sang a couple of verses of a song called 'Noble Tom Campbell', who was drowned in the Blackwater (no date is mentioned). Robert said, "A very good man and there was great sorrow at the loss of his life."

> Come all you good people I pray you take heed
> The sad lamentation would make your heart bleed
> For the loss of Tom Campbell we all sigh and moan
> Who lately was lost off the banks of Tyrone.
> 'Twas the 3rd August on the Sabbath day
> From his loving lady he was called away to Omagh assizes—.

Robert said about Glenavy, "It's a lovely village, well-situated with groves of trees, and friendly kindly people." He sang a few verses of 'Glenavy dear' written by the poet Hugh McWilliams (1783–1831), who lived at Dillon's Hill, Ballymote. It goes to the tune of 'Ye banks and braes o'bonny Doon':

> Glenavy dear my native soil where I spent my youthful days
> Though distant from you many a mile I'm still inclined for to sing your praise.
> Your fine green hills and meadows broad, your walks and groves and streamlets
>   clear
> Where many a pleasant hour I played unknown to cares, Glenavy dear.

Robert wrote among his notes a piece about the weaver.

> The young man has now made himself familiar with all the many gadgets which are so necessary to the weaving of linen cloth. His watchful eye must glance over all the equipment, ever on the alert to see all is right. His employer sits alongside – to direct him in what he is doing – the cloth must be even, not too tight or slack – he pulls the shuttle – watches it travel across.

Robert added that his time spent weaving was brief! He did not relish it too much. He wrote an interesting account on a quilting dance at Brady's. It must have been a local family, whose members were very industrious:

> The dance was long talked of, and looked forward to. There were 6 girls and 4 boys, and all great dancers. The quilting dance was held now and then and all the locals attended. Andy Brady was a carpenter and his wife Mary was thrifty and bought lots of coloured material suitable for quilting and she received orders for quilts. Andy knew the local singers, musicians and dancers which made the quilting dance a great success. The first dance was the Lancers, followed by a polka-style dance. Then came the 3 and 4 hand reel. The timing and intricate steps were excellent. The 'Blackbird' was danced by the 6 Brady sisters – and all had a night full of fun and laughter.

Robert mentioned in his notes at some point, 'It is very much regrettable that the trend of dancing has gone away from the old style'.

I learned quite a number of the songs handed down by Robert, as I have done from many other singers in Ulster and beyond. Some of these songs include 'Willie Brennan', 'The bleacher', 'Banks of sweet Loughrea', 'Van Diemen's land', 'Dobbin's flowery vale', and many others. His style always appeals to me and his is a delivery not heard today. Folk traditions, customs, styles of singing, accents all are part of everyday living. They evolve, live on, change, adapt, some are lost along the way. Robert's accounts and songs link us to his era, over 100 years ago. He paints a vivid picture of life in County Antrim around Lough Neagh and through his interviews we learn about fishing, weaving, basket-making, and ways of life that are gone, to a great degree. It is often said that all the songs and traditions have been collected, and we are 50 years too late to gather anything of value from people. This was said in 1950 when BBC collectors were starting their work of collecting songs in Ireland. It is very heartening, in that light, to learn of a new collection of songs published in December 2020 by CCE Clanbrassil, 'Songs from Clanbrassil, Killultagh and Kilwarlin, around the southern and eastern shores of Lough Neagh'. The list includes ''Tis pretty to be in Ballinderry', 'Down by the canal', 'Drowning of young Robinson', 'Bonny Portmore', and many more echoes from the repertoire of Robert Cinnamond. He would have been familiar with the place-names mentioned in many of the songs in this collection, e.g. the River Bann, Lurgan, Ardmore Bay, Aghagallon, Gawley's Gate, Derrymore, Derrytagh, and the name McGarry. A Felix McGarry was a good fiddle-player friend of Robert.

The year 2018 was the fiftieth anniversary of Robert's death and it was very appropriate to have a song gathering in his memory. The weekend events include the launch of a tribute booklet, ''Tis pretty to be in Ballinderry', plus two CDs of songs. The first CD is a reissue of the Topic LP, *You Rambling Boys of Pleasure*. On the second CD there are 14 songs from Robert's repertoire, sung by local people. I would like to thank the Lough Neagh Partnership for their valuable support with this project.

Robert is a key part of the circle of song transmission, in my opinion a circle which continues to move, develop and enrich itself. Robert displays his love of the soul of the song, his respect for a song and its story. The information he gave in his interviews reflects how his life was; how the singing was woven into everyday life through storytelling, work, socialising, the rural landscape and labouring folk. We sing for enjoyment, to share with others, to hand on to the younger generation, following in Robert's footsteps. We draw from the deep well of song and story left to us by Robert. Let us cherish his memory and rich legacy by singing out with heart and soul.

OPPOSITE
Mute Swans amongst reeds
at Washingbay.

Note

1 Irish Traditional Music Archive, 73 Merrion Square, Dublin 2, info@itma.ie, www.itma.ie.

46 Geordie Hanna
a man, a place and the songs

Ailish Hanna

Geordie Hanna was born on 18 February 1925 in the townland of Derryvarne, Coalisland, County Tyrone. His father was named Joe Hanna and his mother Elizabeth (formerly Hughes). When Geordie was a young boy his family moved from Derryvarne to Derrylaughan, an area called the Ferry, which was separated from Maghery, County Armagh, by the River Blackwater. In later years, when Geordie was being interviewed by Séamus Mac Mathúna about his singing background, he was asked, "Could your mother sing?" Geordie replied, "She could sing none. She hadn't a note." So, it was Joe Hanna, then who was the first musical influence on Geordie. His father Joe was a good singer and played the fiddle. He would sing around the house. As a young boy, Geordie had not much interest in singing, much to his regret in later years. He recalled that the only song he got from his father was 'On Yonder Hill there sits a Hare'. Geordie also had two uncles who were renowned singers, especially his Uncle Peter, who left Derrylaughan for America in the 1920s and never returned.

For Geordie throughout his adolescence and as a young man there was no doubt that certain musical seeds were sown both through nature and nurture. Geordie went to a primary school called Kingsisland, where he sang in the school choir, and then in his early twenties joined the local church choir, Kingsisland – apparently the numbers attending Mass increased just to hear Geordie sing (Latin melodies were sung in those days). When it came to marrying, Geordie didn't stray too far. He travelled next door to the townland of Derrytresk to marry Anne Mae Fitzgerald and eventually settled in Derrytresk. Geordie worked in the coal mines in Coalisland and as a fisherman on Lough Neagh as well as cutting turf in the moss/bog. He enjoyed hunting and playing football as a pastime.

Geordie became particularly interested in traditional singing in his early thirties. He was drawn to songs of the local area and when he heard a song that

FIG. 46.1
Geordie Hanna.

he really liked he just had to get it. One such song was 'The Lisburn Lass', which he got from Jimmy Robinson, a fisherman from Maghery. Back in the fifties, *céilí* was the main entertainment for most young men in the area and Geordie was no different. One of the *céilí*-houses in the area which Geordie frequented was McCann's – by all accounts the brothers Dan and Matt McCann were wonderful characters and very witty men. This was another forum for Geordie to hear and collect songs and stories and he learned songs such as 'Old Ardboe' from Dan. Other sources of songs Geordie collected were his neighbours Paddy McCann ('big house Paddy' or 'Paddy from the big house'), Paddy McMahon and Jimmy McGurk.

Wherever Geordie sang, or recorded the songs he always acknowledged and recalled a story about the source of his songs. He did not feel that he needed the limelight: he saw himself as a member of the community. The songs were a celebration of who he was and where he came from. There was an authenticity about his singing that was truly wonderful; he made you part of the song – it was so natural, so interwoven into the culture and identity of the area and its people of whom Geordie had a deep affection for. His love of Lough Neagh and the Moss – the land spoke to him – was evident in his singing. His songs were about love, emigration and recalled history. Some of his best known and best loved songs celebrated the beauty of the local area and often give warning about the allure of faraway fields, songs such as 'The Fisher Cot' and 'The Emigrant'. It was a local song 'Brocagh Brae' which brought him success in the prestigious John Player Trophy in 1967.

Apart from being a gifted singer, Geordie had a great ability to communicate with others and he had a great presence. The singer and song collector David Hammond interviewed him and remarked, "When you were in company with Geordie Hanna, you knew that he was giving you all his time and attention for he could put his intensity into an encounter as well as into a song or story." Up until the late sixties Geordie sang mainly at community gatherings or local parish concerts. Geordie and his late sister Sarah Anne O'Neill, who was also a very fine singer attended a 'big night' at the Ferry when a man named John McCann recorded them on a reel to reel recorder and sent the tape to Seán Ó Boyle, who was quite taken by Geordie's singing and style. Seán Ó Boyle was a school teacher from Armagh and a collector of songs from the cultural tradition.

Geordie and Sarah Anne were now officially recognised as 'traditional singers' with a distinctive style of their own. Geordie went on to record *Geordie Hanna Sings*, which featured songs and stories and was produced by Manus Ó Boyle (son of Seán) and Daithi Connaughton. On the sleeve notes Seán óg Ó Boyle wrote:

> We feel that these stories capture something of the atmosphere surrounding Geordie's home on the shores of Lough Neagh. They bring to life some of the

characters who influenced Geordie's style of singing and provide an insight into some of the events that have shaped the lives of people in that area.

From the early seventies onwards the home of Geordie's sister's Sarah Anne was a focal point for singers and lovers of music to meet and exchange songs and stories. On one occasion Sarah Anne met the well known Antrim singer Len Graham at a *fleadh* in Clones. Len was telling Sarah Anne about this great singer called Geordie Hanna that he had heard to which she replied very proudly, "That's a brother of mine." So it was not long to a singing session was organised in Sarah Anne's home so the two could met. Many other singers attended these gathering including Joe Holmes, Cathal McConnell and Jeannie McGrath, musicians such as John Hayden and a young Cathal Hayden, and local singers and musicians.

It was probably a trip to the All-Ireland Fleadh Cheoil in Buncrana, County Donegal, in 1976 that made Geordie known in traditional singing circles throughout Ireland. There a young Séamus Mac Mathúna, who was an accomplished singer and musician credited with preserving traditional heritage, heard Geordie sing. Séamus ran to a fellow musician and said, "You must come and hear this wonderful singer." It was Geordie's style of singing that was different, but it was upon meeting Geordie that an even deeper impression was made on Séamus. Geordie was now an established Irish traditional singer of high renown. Television and radio appearances followed and he recorded another record with his sister Sarah Anne called *On the Banks of Sweet Lough Neagh*. He also toured America and Canada with Comhaltas Ceoltóirí Éireann and was a regular guest at singing festivals. Geordie never really warmed to the formalities of concert stage being most content singing in a session or at the fireside.

Geordie Hanna died suddenly on 23 July 1987 at the age of 62. His untimely death was a great loss to the community as well as the traditional singing fraternity. The late Paddy Tunney, a renowned traditional singer from Fermanagh, wrote in his book about Geordie, *Where Songs do Thunder* (1991), 'Next to my mother, Brigid Tunney, God Rest her, he gives me more listening pleasure than any other traditional singer I ever hear.' Bernadette McAliskey, a close friend of Geordie, penned a tribute which best sums up what Geordie was all about:

> Geordie Hanna was a rare breed of a man. If you ever met him you'd remember him. If you didn't, you missed an opportunity to know in all its 'wonderment', to use a word he might have used himself, a plain ordinary decent man, the essence of whose being embodied generations of the tradition of his people, which he carried with ease and confronted you with it for what it was, no more, no less.
>
> Geordie came out of the moss, from the Lough shore. He worked hard all his life. He never aspired to, and never obtained, any great material wealth. He was an intelligent man without formal qualifications or ambitions.

Geordie's reputation as one of the finest traditional singers of our time is beyond dispute. The wealth of the knowledge he possessed is well known, yet he never forgot how he came by a song, he never resented passing it on from him to whoever would use it on again. "He can sing none the best" was as much criticism as the least musical rendering you would get from Geordie.

I thought it was music to hear him talking. The way he used language was a gift. And it was a gift he never abused. Geordie could tell you yarns, relate everyday events with a phrase or saying that was never said before and nobody could repeat to the same effect.

FIG. 46.2
The published biography of Geordie Hanna.

The Geordie Hanna Traditional Singing Weekend

The inaugural Geordie Hanna Traditional Singing Weekend was born out of a desire for the Coalisland/Clonoe Comhaltas Ceoltóirí Éireann branch to mark the passing of their valued member. A singing night was held in the local Derrytresk GAC in the autumn of 1987 spearheaded by Martin Fox (secretary of CCÉ). Geordie's close friend, the singer Róisín White, immediately saw the potential for an entire weekend of traditional singing devoted to Geordie's legacy. With financial support from the Arts Council of Northern Ireland and help from myself, she organised a magical event in April 1988. Singers from all corners of Ireland came together to sing over three days, as well as musicians on the Friday night. Geordie was also a great lover of the music despite not playing a musical instrument. The stage was now set for what would become an annual gathering and Róisín would remain instrumental in its organisation and promotion for another decade. In 2000 the Hanna family formed the Geordie Hanna Traditional Singing Society.

For 30 years, the Geordie Hanna Traditional Singing Weekend was a strong part of the arts and cultural infrastructure of the loughshore area and over its three decades was a focal point in the calendar of traditional singing and music events both locally and nationally. The name of Derrytresk became synonymous with traditional song and music, and the events contributed to creating a platform for young singers and musicians from the area who have gone on to great success, including All-Ireland Fleadh titles and professional musical endeavours. Niall Wall from County Wexford was the guest speaker at our singing weekend held in November 2016, in which the theme was 'Crossing Borders'. Niall observed:

> We are all connected through song, through shared experiences of singing –
> we are all part of the circle of song … we all are indeed kin: It is some kindred
> rooted in shared history; it is rooted in shared identity; it is rooted in shared
> culture; and we are grateful for it and is has great value.

We approached the Lough Neagh Partnership for support to produce a book and in 2019 the Geordie Hanna Traditional Singing Society identified Martin J. McGuinness, nephew of Geordie, as the author and along with Geordie's family, relatives and friends a wonderful book was produced entitled, *Geordie Hanna: the Man and the Songs*. This book of traditional songs and narrative highlights the wonderful contribution Geordie Hanna has made to his community and the world of traditional singing. The book is a great educational resource for young people and also provides a legacy for older generations and recognition for the people of the area no longer living amongst us. It is a source of great pride for the Hanna family and the people of the loughshore.

47 Lough Neagh Rescue

Conor Corr and Gerard McVeigh
(in conversation with Liam Campbell)

Between the two of us we have over 50 years' service with Lough Neagh Rescue (LNR) on this great inland sea. Nobody ever knows anything about the lough really. Don't let anyone say otherwise – no matter how many years you are on it, you learn every day and can easily be caught out no matter how well you think you know the lough. We have a massive coastline with lots of centres of population. It is a beautiful place but can be treacherous and wicked too. The establishment of Lough Neagh Rescue was a result of a crucial need and was created following the tragic drowning of a local man while on his passage home across the lough. That man, David Gray, now has our rescue craft named after him. Indeed, all our boats are named after people deeply associated with the place who have died.

We started in summer of '89 after David's drowning. He was one of three young men who were heading from Ballyronan marina to Kinnego. At the White Horse Flat their boat took on water and sank quickly; two of the men were rescued but the third lost his life. There were no lifeboats at all on the lough at that time. Prior to this, the fishermen did all the rescue work. If anyone was in trouble, all fishermen ceased work and went out to search. All they had were CB radios – no VHF radio or similar at all. The army used to help out and we would listen in on searches. We remember going out in 1981 and lost a man and were left wondering, "How do you organise 20 to 30 fishing boats to get together to do a sweep search of the lough?" It was a gale force 8 and very wicked. Some boats split in half. The waves on the lough are very different from the open sea, in that they are short and very sharp with no long rolling waves that you get at sea.

Paddy Prunty, who was the harbour master in Kinnego, and a few others began a search for David Gray. His father started a discussion about a search and rescue service and put up money from his own pocket to buy the first lifeboat. In response to David's death £20,000 was raised to supply the first lifeboat and a crew of local volunteers was raised and trained to deal with the various scenarios encountered on the UK and Ireland's largest inland waterway.

When the crew was recruited in 1991, it was quickly recognised that there was a need for a secondary rescue base on the west shore. Pat Grimes and many other locals set up at The Battery in Ardboe. The Coastguard had established a communication station on Black Mountain and classed Lough Neagh as an inland sea. They then looked for the area where the most recruits were and about 60 came along to The Battery at Ardboe. It was the best place on the west shore as we can go out quickly in any direction. It was a long fight to get a boat on the western shore, with many, many meetings. The RNLI did not want to entertain a freshwater rescue service, so we had to go independently. We built an underground station first, all through local fundraising and labour. Lots of the crew were originally fishermen but now the men and women come from all backgrounds. Folk move on too and circumstances change but most stay 10–15 years.

This boat, *The David Gray*, has saved many lives – if it only saved one life then it's all worth it. The recovery of a body is such an important thing for a family. On one occasion we spent 30 days in a recovery operation. You get to know the family and they you – but you can only get involved to a degree as we have a job to do. If it was one of your own, you would like to think that someone would do it for you. It has to be done. We have seen families desperate for someone to help them find their loved one. And if we can help in any way to bring some closure – it may not bring the person back, but it means that family has a grave to go to. It's very difficult.

FIG. 47.2
The David Gray.

So, in 1991, a second lifeboat station was developed at The Battery Harbour, Ardboe. A third station was developed at Antrim in 2014 to provide a faster response time as over 30% of call-outs were originating from that area. HM Coastguard has worked closely with LNR over the last 29 years and during this time the organisation has been deemed a 'Declared facility' for the Maritime and Coastguard Agency, which co-ordinates rescues on Lough Neagh. LNR is now a fully registered charity and a company limited by guarantee. Its mission statement says that it is committed to 'preserving and saving life on Lough Neagh and its associated waters and rivers' and actively 'works in partnership with other agencies to achieve this'. We now have brand new buildings in Kinnego and Antrim.

The four corners of the lough are covered and we are in a triangle of stations. Most problems are close to the shores as there are few obstructions out in the middle of the lough. We have all the nasty waypoints in the GPS. It takes us 15 minutes to be out on the lough and a maximum of 20 minutes to get to the furthest point. We can travel at up to 40–45 knots in optimum conditions. The nasty parts are about half a mile from the shore. But you must remember that six miles is a long time to travel on water and the lough has 100 miles of shoreline.

Lough Neagh Rescue adopted an ILU competency-based training programme in 1999. The LNR Training Team set out to manage effectively its operational remit and duty of care responsibilities to its 70 volunteers, each of whom undergo a foundation programme of internal assessment, practical learning, skills and knowledge acquisition. This is supplemented by external qualification validation, which includes RYA 2 Powerboat certification, Boat Safety, VHF DSC, Radar, First Aid/Defibrillator, Sea Survival and SAR Techniques, RYA Advanced/Day skipper level and Instructor levels, First Responder Flood and Technician rescue – some 40 categories in all.

We do the same training as the RNLI and are fully recognised by the coastguard and other external agencies. We have to train in all conditions and have to be fit to take on the roughest that the lough can throw at you. We have never come across a time when we couldn't go out. We also stand on the street to shake a collection box and that is often forgotten about too and it's our volunteers who do that also.

Since we are a declared facility by the Coastguard, we are part and parcel of NISAR and could be deployed anywhere, including the likes of Mourne Rescue and Foyle Search and Rescue. We are swift water trained too. The training is very tough. We train every Tuesday night and Sunday mornings and we are all on call 24 hours. The boat takes a crew of a minimum of three and maximum of five, including a fully trained coxswain. All the volunteers are paged to an incident but they could be anywhere. There are always enough of us close to home to respond. The first three or five go ahead. After being out on the water the boats have to be readied again. Indeed, our engines are serviced every 50 hours, such is the level of professionalism needed.

Fishermen didn't generally use charts and we had so much learning to do. We traditionally used landmarks on the shore. Indeed, when we are training, we still at times turn off all the technology to see how we can navigate without it. Taking the marks off the land is part of the lough's heritage. The traditional ecological knowledge and the fishermen's mental maps are still very important and that knowledge is passed down. Even if the volunteers do not have a fishing background they benefit from the inherited collective wisdom.

The north-westerly and north wind can be nasty on the western shore but if you are up by Antrim the south-westerly can be nasty there too. The predominant wind would be south-west, but if you are in Antrim you then have 20 miles of water behind that. The waves can be wicked. The sea has long rolling waves, but they are short and sharp here – very close together and they hammer the boats. You are battered the whole time. You get very squally wicked showers out there too and they can bring a breeze. The old fishermen said that you always have to watch the wind shifting from a south-west into a north-west. It can change or brew up very quickly and you can get caught out. Leisure craft pose more risks generally than fishing boats. People on the likes of jet-skis, etc, think it's calm and not going to change. The fishermen tend to look after themselves and we have few call-outs for them.

By 2014, LNR had developed its first swift and flood water response teams to proactively contribute to waters beyond Lough Neagh, under the jurisdiction of both the Coastguard and the PSNI (under what became Northern Ireland Search and Rescue (NISAR)). In 2010, Lough Neagh Rescue joined the NISAR forum, which was facilitated by PSNI Search and Rescue, and where LNR ensures awareness and assimilation with all Civil Contingencies, Defra's Flood Rescue National Enhancement Project, Water Safety and Rescue Training, other related training and guidance as well as where cross-organisational practical activity and skills sustainability training is achieved. In July 2014, Lough Neagh Rescue reached four important milestones in its history: 25 years of voluntary service; its one thousandth team tasking to service call-outs; the establishment of its third base; and the formation of two type D flood water response teams and technicians.

In support of the voluntary service required to man the lifeboats, members have also spent many thousands of hours dealing with the administration and management of Lough Neagh Rescue. This has included accessing European, local authority and statutory funding for: the building of a state-of-the-art rescue station in 2003; to allow for the replacement of its two 'operational duty' vessels in 2008 and 2009; the setting up of a new rapid response station with vessel in 2014; the establishment of new swift/flood water response teams in 2014; and the maintenance of all assets and capabilities to date. This has all been achieved on a voluntary basis. Previous funding for LNR included grant-aid through the Northern Ireland Rural Development Programme and the Department for Transport 'Inshore and inland lifeboat grant scheme'.

To date, LNR's inland lifeboats have rescued over 446 people, assisted 744 people in distress and recovered 19 people for return to their grieving families. LNR has over 70 trained water rescue power-boat operational volunteers detailed to three inland lifeboat teams. They are dedicated to search and rescue for Lough Neagh and its tributaries as well as swift and flood rescue throughout Northern Ireland and beyond. Each team is based in its own boat station located at key strategic water access points, and provides 24/7, 365 days per year response coverage through a pager system operated by HMCG Belfast. LNR is also as concerned with recovery as much as search. Thankfully most recoveries are close to the shore. There are many more on the lough now and this increases every year and will be even more so since Covid 19.

FIG. 47.3
Hunter's Point.

In LNR we have a great bonds of friendship and though Covid has brought many challenges, such as not meeting up as a group as often, we have been able

to keep running safe and well. People are out and about again and engaging with the local landscape and especially the lough. You cannot trust the lough and you are always learning. It always changes and sandbars change, the weather changes – don't believe the man or woman who say they know the lough. The waves can be very crabbit and hard hitting. On the morning of the opening of Antrim a 17-year-old volunteer was spotted in one corner of the room and in another corner there was a 72-year-old volunteer. That's a team – we have all ages and backgrounds.

The reason I [Conor Corr] joined is that my son and I got caught in a rip tide abroad some years ago and we were saved by a local man. When I returned home, I came straight down here to the station and joined. That was 20 years ago and if I was here for another 20 years I couldn't repay that man for saving my life. I'd never have enough thanks. The lough is beautiful and we love it but we respect it as it be very treacherous. Lough Neagh Rescue may not always be seen until something goes wrong and then we are really needed.

48 The sand industry

Conor Jordan and Liam Campbell

Sand extraction is intimately connected with Lough Neagh today, providing the raw material necessary for a range of products within the glass, tile and concrete industries. The lough bed and shoreline are rich in sand deposits. But where did this all begin?

In the geological Caledonian period, some 225 million years ago, massive tectonic shifts took place which began the formation of Lough Neagh as we

know it. This was followed by a period of intense volcanic activity and in turn some 1.8 million years ago the various ice ages commenced. With the ice receding some 10,000 years ago, the larger lake emerged into which was deposited vast amounts of sand, possibly from as far away as Scotland. It literally became a pit for sand. Due to the various meltings and flow waters after the Ice Age most of the sand beds were along the northern side of the lough. These are divided into three types relating to the typography; the beaches such as at Ballyronan, the beds above the current water line (mostly under bogs at 9–10 feet deep) and deposits under the lough waters.

It is not known exactly how long man has been extracting sand from the lough but a glassworks was established at Salterstown, on the western shore near Ballyronan, following a patent issued to William Robson in 1611. A considerable amount of goods were exported to London from here by 1614, but in 1618 production had ceased, possibly due to a problem with the patent rights. It is assumed that sand for the glassworks was extracted from the nearby shore and it must be pointed out that the sand banks located offshore in this area are well known by the present sandmen for both the quantity and quality of the sand. Medieval glass has been unearthed during recent archaeological excavations around the shore.

FIG. 48.1
Sand barges on Lough Neagh.

FIG. 48.2

Plaque on fountain in Toome.

The earliest accounts of someone seeing the potential for commercial marketing of Lough Neagh sand are mentioned in *Quiet Places of the Lower Bann* (1998). John Cary (1800–91), a former Presbyterian minister from Duneane, had a rather colourful life: he disappeared totally from public life for some seven years after being accused of shooting a fellow clergyman, only to reappear in Toome in 1850 to set up a sand business. Toome become quite famous for sand extraction at this time. *Bassett's Guide and Directory for County Antrim* of 1888 states:

> A growing industry in Toomebridge is the collection of sand on the shore of Lough Neagh, a quarter of a mile from the village. Mr William Ellis is an extensive shipper of it chiefly to Belfast, for building purposes. Mr Henry Catherwood is also engaged in the trade.

The *Ulster Directory* of 1910 lists a Mr Henry Catherwood as being a 'grocer and general merchant' from the Creagh, Toomebridge. The arrival of the Belfast to Ballymena railway line in 1856 with a branch from Toome to Belfast, with the ready supply of sand close to the station, brought a burgeoning market and local entrepreneurial skills together and a modern sand industry was born.

In the early days sand could only be extracted from the beaches and shallow water using manual labour with horses and carts. Cement became an important building material and locally based companies such as Scotts, Emersons, Turkingtons, Irwins and Walls were established in the following decades. The onset of World War II and the construction of the new airfields around the loughshore created a strong demand for concrete runways, taxiways and aircraft stands as is still evidenced today, especially at Toome and Ardboe/Cluntoe airfields (which, ironically, are now industrial estates). The next step in sand extraction was the idea that a slurry of sand and water could be pumped by centrifugal pumping techniques, which enabled underwater extraction with the use of barges. The industry expanded exponentially after WWII, to the point that by the 1950s there were not enough barges in use to meet demand.

For this purpose a fleet of decommissioned Guinness barges was purchased by Scotts, Emersons and others in the late 1950s and early 1960s and refitted for sand extraction; these were the *Castleknock*, the *Killiney*, the *Boyne*, the *Chapelizod*, the *Clonsilla*, the *Foyle*, and the *Lagan*. Other barges converted to sand extraction were the dumb barges formerly owned by John Kelly and used on the River Lagan to transport imported coal to the Belfast Gasworks. Barges were also manufactured by the Portadown Foundry. Unfortunately, the majority of these barges were sunk when decommissioned, with some, such as the *Lagan* at Sandy Bay and the *Boyne* at Toome, forming new quays for the sandmen. However, two barges the *Enterprize* and *JK 16*, now called *Sandmartin*, have been recovered from the lough to be used as interpretation centres. The *Sandmartin* has recently been repaired and refitted by the Rams Island Heritage

FIG. 48.3
Barge at Sandy Bay.

Project and is now stationed on the island. The second barge, the *Enterprize*, is currently under repair by Armagh, Banbridge and Craigavon Borough Council and was moved in February 2010 to its new location beside Waterside House, Oxford Island.

Sand quays were built at the Creagh outside Toomebridge (northern shore), Ballyginniff and Sandy Bay (eastern shore), and Derryadd (southern shore) and here the sand was processed prior to sale. These sites are still in use. Northstone, Breedon, Emerson, Mulholland and Walls are currently the five companies licensed to extract sand from the lough. The barges they employ are largely imported from the Netherlands.

With regard to the ownership of the sand and bed of Lough Neagh, much has been written and indeed contested about the issue. During the Nine Years'

War (1593–1603), Lough Neagh was very important strategically. As a recompense for his part in the campaign to subdue the native Ulster lords, one of Elizabeth I's commanders, Sir Arthur Chichester, was granted control of the lough. Some of these rights have now passed down to the current holder, Lord Shaftesbury, whose company, the Shaftesbury Estates of Lough Neagh Ltd, collects a royalty on each ton of sand extracted from the lough bed.

FIG. 48.4
Scrubland at Killycoply.

Bibliography

John Hughes and Donal Barton, *Quiet Places of the Lower Bann* (Belfast, 1998).
Noel Quinn, *The Toome Sand Industry* (Belfast, 2012).

49 Lough Neagh and food

Eimear Kearney and William Burke

History of food availability around Lough Neagh

An examination of the prehistoric record would suggest that Lough Neagh and its shorelands has maintained settlements for much, if not all, of the span of Irish prehistory, that is, from 7000 BC until the fifth century AD. Settlements tend to develop in areas where resources, especially food availability, are plentiful and Lough Neagh provides one of the best examples of this. As Ireland was an isolated island from perhaps the very beginning of the Holocene, it has a very restricted animal population – in particular there were relatively few native mammals and freshwater fish. This restricted the range of food which hunter-gatherers could procure. The large mammals usually played an essential role as the major source of food for early Boreal hunters. However after the ice melted, two of the largest mammals, elk and wild cattle, were absent from Ireland, in contrast with the Early Mesolithic of Europe where these species along with red deer played a major role.

With the restricted potential of the mammals, different food strategies had to be developed by the settlers. For example, finds of carbonised remains of plant foods at Mount Sandel, consisting mostly of hazel nut shells with a few water-lily seeds, suggest they were collected in the autumn and late summer and were not only consumed at that time but may have been stored as an extra winter resource. Fish on the other hand were a major source of food. Archaeological evidence from around the lough has produced a range of salmonid bones as well as eels. Both salmon and eels have the advantage of running in large numbers at differing times of year and could be captured with traps, nets or spears, all of which are known from the European Mesolithic. The main crisis for these hunter-gatherers would come in late winter when fish were less plentiful. This hunter-gatherer lifestyle seems to have been replaced by a farming economy during the fourth millennium BC with the residents' dietary changes being led by the introduction of two large domesticated animals, cattle and sheep, and a range of domesticated plants, in particular cereals.

Since historic times, the main crops grown around the lough were potatoes, wheat and oats. Since their introduction to Ireland in the sixteenth century, potatoes had become the staple diet of the Irish. An important attribute was that a small area of land could yield a large crop and thus the potato became indispensable amongst the small tenant farmers. A succession of famines caused by potato blight in the eighteenth and early nineteenth centuries culminated in the Great Famine of 1845–9 when malnutrition led to widespread disease and death. It must be noted, however, that those living around the shores of Lough Neagh were not as badly affected as elsewhere in Ireland as fish from the lough provided a much needed source of food.

Potato crops were cultivated in hand-dug ridges, known as lazy-beds, and harvested by spade. The use of drill ridges became more common in the later nineteenth century; drills could be ploughed instead of being hand-dug and therefore took less time with fewer labourers, saving time and money for the farmers. The introduction of the mechanical digger was embraced on large farms as a much welcomed labour saving device. However, the small tenant farmers of Lough Neagh and elsewhere continued to harvest by hand, their yields being smaller. Potatoes continue to be cultivated around Lough Neagh but in small quantities which are mainly consumed on the farm.

Prior to mechanisation, grain crops such as wheat and oats were harvested by hand with a reaping hook. Sheaves were divided into individual bundles or 'stooks' and left to dry in the fields before being threshed, i.e. removing the grain from the sheaf. Again this work was done by hand with sheaves being beaten with a flail to remove the grain. Wheat grain was brought to corn mills where it was ground into flour and sold on at market. Oats were ground into a coarse and fine meal both of which were popular with the weaving class who made 'stirabout' (a type of porridge) with the coarse meal and thin oatcakes with the fine. Unlike today nothing was left to waste: oats and the stalks left over from threshing made a healthy animal fodder, and unused, undamaged wheat stalks were used for thatching.

Space does not permit more than a brief mention of the history and methods of fishing on the lough. For eels, the two main catch methods are long lines and draft nets, each of which has a long ancestry and whose relative importance has varied at different times. Long lines may be up to six miles in length, each with as many as 2,000 hooks which must be baited, a laborious task not in much favour with the younger fishermen. They are used most often by fishermen along the western and northern shores, especially in Ardboe parish, where there is much 'hard bottom', which is unsuitable for draft nets unless used with skill. These nets are best suited to sandy bottom which is most widespread in the south and east of the lough. Fishermen in the Sandy Bay, Derrytrasna and Maghery areas are their main exponents. But both methods are interchangeable and in the course of time have spread over the lough from their source areas.

Lough Neagh produce in the twenty-first century

If the public were to be asked today, "What food produce would you associated with Lough Neagh?" their almost immediate response is likely to be the Lough Neagh Eel. This response is to be welcomed and is a positive indicator of the promotional and marketing work carried out by Lough Neagh Fishermen's Co-operative and others. The European Union award of 'Protected Geographical Indication' (PGI) to the Lough Neagh Eel is regarded by the local industry as a significant accolade recognising the heritage, tradition and authenticity of what are regarded as the best quality eel available in Europe. It distinguishes Lough Neagh Eel as a unique food item alongside the food elite of Europe, such as Parma Ham, Champagne and Feta Cheese. Other Northern Irish produce to have been awarded PGI are Comber Early Potatoes and Armagh Bramley Apples. Lough Neagh Eel is renowned for its texture and flavour, a direct result of the eel's natural diet that includes invertebrates, which are indigenous to the lough. The Fishermen's Co-operative are keenly aware of the importance to modern consumers of the credentials and traceability of their food purchases and the PGI status is a valuable asset in the promotion of the product.

Another indigenous species, Lough Neagh Pollan, was registered as a Protected Designation of Origin (PDO) in 2018. Lough Neagh Pollan are produced, processed and prepared in Lough Neagh using traditional production methods. The quality and characteristics of Lough Neagh Pollan are due exclusively to Lough Neagh. Pollan are the only European vertebrate found uniquely in Ireland and their distribution is restricted to only five Irish loughs. They are only commercially available from Lough Neagh. Lough Neagh Pollan are a genetically unique variant of Irish Pollan. The listing of Lough Neagh Pollan as a unique food item, from one single source is fitting for this very distinctive fish species. The accolade is just reward for the fishermen of

Traditional fried Lough Neagh Eel

What you need:

> 20 cuts of eel approximately 8 cm
> 1 tsp Harnett's rapeseed oil
> 1 tsp fine salt

How to cook:

> Heat a heavy based frying pan until it is quite hot.
> Brush a very little amount of the rapeseed oil over the pan.
> The eel produces a lot of oil, so a lot of other oil is not necessary.
> Sprinkle salt over the pan, this will also reduce sticking.
> Place the eel cuts onto the hot pan.
> Cook the first side for up to 30 minutes without moving it, until golden and crispy.
> After turning, cook the other side for 20 minutes.
> The result will be golden and crispy on the outside with white fluffy flesh on the inside.

FIG. 49.1
Traditional fried
Lough Neagh Eel

Lough Neagh, They work diligently, using sustainable, traditional fishing methods to maintain a viable future for both the species and the industry.

In 2019, Lough Neagh Artisans was established when Lough Neagh Partnership brought together a group of likeminded creatives who appreciated the diverse heritage and culture captured around the shoreline. Members of the Lough Neagh Artisans live within ten miles of the lough and operate as a collective, believing that there is a strong need to collaborate among Lough Neagh businesses which complement each other and inspire people from around the world with their crafts, food and drink, hospitality and experiential initiatives which are unique to this part of the world. Lough Neagh Artisans includes Lough Neagh Tours – a unique range of food and cultural tours which can be enjoyed on the lough and on its shoreline; they produce whiskey from the oldest thatched pub in Ireland; bake bread to be savoured with homemade chutneys; they produce gin and offer distillery tours; they create bespoke afternoon teas; grow and produce rapeseed oils; sell finest meat products from a farm shop; produce a range of nettle based products; mix history and tea at the north shore heritage centre and offer immersive B&B accommodation.

In essence, this brief account of food sourced in and around Lough Neagh is very much a story of resource utilisation from the Mesolithic period to the present day. Changing circumstances, among which advances in technology figure prominently, mark its progress. It is increasingly apparent that the lough needs coordinated protection and careful management. No longer is fishing the only primary food source involved, and it is clear that its future can be affected by other developments. Fortunately, there is now growing awareness of the interdependence of economic activities. It is encouraging to find that an umbrella organisation like Lough Neagh Partnership exists to coordinate efforts to safeguard and promote the lough and its resources.

FIG. 49.2
Duneane Pollan
Fishcakes.

Duneane Pollan Fishcakes

What you need:

Potato base

> 500g potatoes
> 2 tbsp scallions chopped finely
> Salt and pepper
> 1 tbsp butter
> 3 tbsp milk

Fish

> 250g fresh Lough Neagh Pollan (deboned)
> Juice and zest of 1 lemon
> 1 tbsp Harnett's rapeseed oil and extra for frying
> 3 tbsp plain flour
> 3 eggs beaten
> 300g breadcrumbs

How to cook:

> Peel the potatoes and cut into even sized chunks and place into a pan of lightly salted water.
> Bring the potatoes to the boil and simmer until tender.
> Place the fish into a baking tray, drizzle with the rapeseed oil, season with the salt and pepper and squeeze on half the lemon juice.
> Cook the fish in the oven at 180°C for 30 minutes until opaque.
> When the potatoes are cooked, drain in a colander to remove all excess water.
> Return the potatoes to the pan and turn the heat on low.
> Add the milk and butter and allow to warm and melt.
> Mash the potatoes well into the milk and butter before adding the seasoning and chopped scallions and stirring well through.
> When the fish is cooked, remove the skin and gently flake it into the potatoes.
> Add the fish cooking juices into the potatoes along with the lemon zest and the rest of the juice, stir everything well through and check for seasoning.
> To assemble the fishcakes gather the potato and fish mixture into golf ball sized portions and set aside.
> Place the flour, the eggs and the breadcrumbs into three separate dishes.
> Roll the fishcakes first in the flour, then the egg and finally the breadcrumbs.
> Fry them in rapeseed oil, turning regularly until completely golden brown all over.

50

Lough Neagh
management and sustainability

Gerry Darby

Introduction

In Northern Ireland, environmental resource management has traditionally been directed on a 'top down' approach, that is, statutory organisations give direction to landowners, businesses and others on how to ensure their actions have no negative impact on natural resources, heritage assets, habitats and species. Examples of this can be observed across a range of government departments including the Department of Agriculture, Environment and Rural Affairs (DAERA), which is currently promoting an Environmental Farming Scheme (EFS) directed at farmers, and aims to promote the management of wet grassland systems for breeding waders; the Northern Ireland Environment Agency (NIEA), which legislates for the management of designated sites such as ASSIs; and the Planning Service, which through consultation with other departments ensures development proposals reflect conditions set out in various Planning Policy Statements (PPS).

FIG. 50.1
Looking across the lough from Brookend.

However, in recent years it has become evident that this top down approach has failed to fully address issues of public concern that are widely understood to have a high probability of negatively impacting on our built, cultural and natural heritage. There is currently a widespread public dissatisfaction with the current governance, management and sustainability arrangements for Lough Neagh. Lough Neagh Partnership has consulted with stakeholders of the lough who claim that its heritage and wider resource significance is not being recognised and that change is needed to ensure the long term sustainability of the system.

Lough Neagh is the largest shallow freshwater body in the UK and Ireland covering an area of 383 km². Historically, the lough has influenced the location of settlements and has functioned as a resource for sustaining livelihoods through the provision of food and employment. Its natural resource has been exploited for drinking water, navigation, coal/lignite, turf, fish, sand and, more recently, recreation. Its rich ecology and biodiversity have been recognised both nationally and internationally, receiving designations including Area of Special Scientific Interest, Special Protection Area and Wetland Ramsar. Over the decades, the freshwater and wetland habitats of the lough have been subject to a downturn in quality, particularly as a result of agricultural intensification within the catchment.

There is direct exploitation of the natural resource assets (sand, fish and fossil fuels) in and around the water body itself, resulting in a decline in species numbers especially birds and water quality. Attempts to resolve these issues have been fragmented, led by policy from statutory agencies, but the overall integrated nature of the use of the lough and wider concerns of considering sustainability have been largely neglected. The aim of this paper is to reflect on the historical value and use of Lough Neagh as a public resource, review what is happening today and provide a road map for future sustainable management and governance of the freshwater system.

Historical exploitation of Lough Neagh as a resource

Lough Neagh had been geographically at the heart of the north of Ireland since its formation four hundred million years ago. However, politically it has always been on the periphery in both pre- and post partition Ireland. Even though it is the biggest lough in the United Kingdom, Ireland, and Northern Ireland, it has been a place ignored by government and in recent times somewhat abandoned. It is often viewed simply as a major natural resource to be used and people's relationships with it have, in general, been somewhat transactional. It was, and still is, to a certain extent, seen as a place to be exploited and its resources of sand, peat, fish, and water to be extracted and sold.

From the earliest times, Mesolithic hunter-gatherers travelled along the River Bann and settled by its shores primarily because of its abundance of fresh water, fish, and eels. The lough was from the very onset seen by its early inhabitants as

FIG. 50.2
Washingbay.

a resource to be obtained. Later Neolithic people settled along its alluvial river plains and began to farm its surrounding land, but also started the early deforestation of its shores and indeed the deforestation of the rest of Ireland. This does not mean to say that the lough did not have other relevance, purpose or meaning to ancient people's lives. Iron Age Celtic Ireland placed great emphasis on the spirituality of water and the 'other world' that lived within its depths. We know of the huge folklore and pantheistic spirituality associated with the water and animals who lived on and within its depths, including Lí Ban and Echu (see Chapters 32 and 33 of this book).

Cranfield holy well on the northern shores of the lough and the Holy river at Washingbay on the southern shores, provides a modern-day glimpse into this ancient pre-Christian world of water gods and connectivity to the other side. This tradition continued within Medieval Christian Ireland, where many early monasteries and churches were built near its shore, including one at Rams Island and Antrim town, both of which have round towers. However, the fact remains, that these sites were also built, not just because of their spiritual connection, but again because of their provision of basic resources such as water, food and shelter.

The use of its natural resources was advanced to a more modern and systematic level with the coming of the Plantation of Ulster in the early seventeenth century and it should be of no real surprise that many of the early Plantation bawns and villages were built near or along the lough's shores, including at Bellaghy and Salterstown. As part of the Londonderry Plantation, Bellaghy was built on land transferred to the Vintners' Company and Salterstown on land allocated to the Salters' Company (see Chapter 23). In Medieval Ireland, the lough's resources were used primarily for local use, but under the Plantation commodities were now traded within a wider British geography and in a more commercial context, with a new political connectivity and power relationships with Great Britain and between the native Irish and the new English and Scottish settlers. As we know, these new relationships and power structures have not

FIG. 50.3
Rea's Wood.

always been agreeable and have left a legacy of violence, distrust, and resentment to this very day.

The main natural resource targeted was not so much on the water system itself, but the loss of the great woods and forests that surrounded its vast shores. The northern shore of the lough was surrounded by the 'Great Forest of Glenconkeyne', described by Sir John Davys, the Irish attorney-general, in 1607 as having 'the best timber in Ireland'.[1] Flowing into the north-east corner of the lough, the Six Mile Water was called the *Abhainn na bhFiodh*, or the 'River of the Wood', and it was said that people could walk from Newry to Lough Neagh on top of the treetops of the forests to its south. The Glenconkeyne forest seems to have been one of the first main targets of the plantation private companies, with James I permitting the cutting of the Glenconkeyne valley to assist in the building of Derry City. The historian Eileen McCracken commented:

> At the end of the seventeenth century the greater part of Ulster's woods were gone. The adoption of a resolute policy by the Tudors was probably the first step towards the general reduction of the forest-areas, as for the timber it was used up in several ways, apart from clearings deliberately made by the army or for agriculture. Its chief uses were for the building of frame houses for the new settlers.[2]

The coming of the Plantation of Ulster laid the foundations of an agricultural revolution in the eighteenth century and the industrial revolution in the nineteenth century, with new agricultural power and draining technology introduced, together with the building of new mills and factories exploiting the power of water along the main rivers flowing into the lough. A significant impact on the natural environment of the lough was the technology to drain water and enable the lowering of the actual lough level itself. Past drainage schemes lowered the lough by an average of approximately two metres. The McMahon scheme of 1847–58 lowered the water level by 0.76m, while the Shepherd scheme of 1930–42, plus 1952 and 1959 schemes lowered average water levels by 1.26m.

Whilst there is no exact historical data for wetland lost, the environmental impact must have been huge, with most of the lough's wetland flood plains drained with a huge loss of reedbed, wet woodland and of course wild birds and other wetland species. The eighteenth and nineteenth centuries also saw the building of three canals: the Lagan linking to Belfast; the Newry linking Newry and Dublin by sea; and the Ulster connecting to the Lough Erne system and other Irish canals. The Lower Bann was also made navigable to the sea. Through these developments the lough reached its economic peak with the extraction of a greater number of resources and materials, including coal, timber, clay, sand, and agricultural produce now grown on the newly drained lands.

Twentieth-century decline

The continued extraction of resources has continued into the twenty-first century with approximately 1.5 million tonnes of sand a year taken from the lough, vast areas of raised bog exploited for peat along its southern shores, the continued commercial fishing of eels (whose numbers have declined exponentially), and the fact that 45% of Northern Ireland's water supply is sourced from Lough Neagh by Northern Ireland Water. It is important to highlight that the extraction of resources from the lough has created substantial numbers of jobs, providing incomes and wealth for local people who live and work around its shores, and the process has without doubt improved the quality of life of many of them. It has also provided the essential strategic materials of water and sand to the wider Northern Ireland economy and contributed significantly to its regional Gross Domestic Product.

However, there are two fundamental truths that still need to be addressed: that there has been a negative impact on the lough's natural environment (e.g. there has been an 80% fall in wildfowl numbers on the lough, with once common birds like the Curlew now near extinction) and the private sector, whilst creating jobs and wealth, has not taken any significant mitigating action or returned investment to the lough to help address these environmental losses. Furthermore, up until recently the public sector and the Northern Ireland Government have been somewhat remiss in both protecting and sustainably developing the lough in an integrated manner and some feel they have even abandoned the lough altogether, allowing it to decline economically and environmentally.

However, it was not always like this. In pre-partition Ireland, Lough Neagh was one of the economic hubs of the island with canals transporting materials and agricultural produce all over the country and beyond. But with partition the first real signs of its economic decline began. The Ulster Canal was the first to close in 1931, followed by the Newry Canal in 1936 and the Coalisland Canal in 1956. The canals in the Republic of Ireland followed a similar fate, assisted by the development of motorways and lorry freight transport. It was not until the 1980s that the Irish government began to take a new strategic approach with a major restoration programme for its canals and large navigable waterways, targeting tourism and rural village regeneration. A major development was the opening of the Shannon-Erne Waterway in 1994.

As part of the Good Friday Agreement, Waterways Ireland was established as one of six North/South Implementation Bodies under the British-Irish Agreement of 1998. This new body was a cross-border navigational authority responsible for the management, maintenance, development, and promotion of over 1,000 km of inland navigable waterways, principally for recreational purposes. One would think that the largest commercial working navigable lough in the whole of Ireland, Lough Neagh, would obviously be included within the remit of this new body. But unfortunately, here is where the story turns sour and political and government involvement in the integrated protection and management of the lough was abandoned. To this day nobody knows the true reason why this happened, although some plausible suggestions have been made. Lough Erne and the Lower Bann came under the remit of Waterways Ireland within Northern Ireland and the Barrow Navigation, Royal Canal, Shannon-Erne Waterway, Grand Canal, and Shannon Navigation became the responsibility of Waterways Ireland within the Republic of Ireland. The massive navigable water system in the middle of Northern Ireland remained excluded from these arrangements, giving rise to considerable disappointment and frustration.

The economics of Lough Neagh in the twenty-first century

Within Northern Ireland, the mineral products industry is an enabling sector which plays a wider role in overall economic activity in the region. Sand extraction remains the largest commercial enterprise on Lough Neagh, with the Lough Neagh Sand Traders supporting over 340 direct jobs, associated wages of £9 million, and contributing over £20 million to the economy through value-added activities that rely heavily on the sand, such as the manufacture of concrete products. Sand extraction from the lough historically operated without planning consent – due to its longevity, extraction predated planning regulations and environmental designation. The sector applied for planning permission to seek full authorisation and compliance for its operations. This regulatory legacy issue was reassessed through a public inquiry process in June 2018 with the recommendation to approve planning permission in May 2019. Planning consent was granted in January 2021 via a series of conditions that can demonstrate 'no harm' to the environmental designations of Lough Neagh. Lough Neagh sand extraction is now heavily regulated and works to demonstrate full regulatory control on the lough.

By comparison, the Lough Neagh Co-operative that engages in eel fishing, currently has a turnover of £3 million and has 16 employees. The co-operative fishes in the region of 2.5m eels a year, or 400,000 tonnes and is the largest producer of wild eels in Europe. In addition, the co-operative puts into the lough between three and four million baby eels every year. Eighty per cent of the eels that are caught are sent to Holland and Germany, while the remainder go to London for the jellied eel industry. Eel fishing is a seasonal operation. The Lough Neagh Co-operative also owns the rights to scale fish, which includes pollan, trout, bream, pike, roach and perch. The co-operative has secured Protected Geographical Indication for the Lough Neagh eel, which was awarded in 2011. Equally, Lough Neagh pollan has been recognised by the EU as a foodstuff of particular quality and an identity associated with a specific area. According to the regulator statement, Lough Neagh pollan remains an economically important species and over the last 15 years between 50 and 200 tonnes have been harvested annually from the lough.

Both the fishing and sand dredging industry have a strong associated heritage narrative and cultural legacy which contributes to the third economic generator for Lough Neagh – tourism. Tourism on the lough is promoted through the

FIG. 50.4
Oxford Island jetty.

adjoining council authorities and directly marketed as a core function of Lough Neagh Partnership. However, a number of factors have frustrated tourism development at Lough Neagh including underutilisation of the built, cultural and natural heritage, underutilisation of existing activity facilities such as canoeing, walking, and bike trails, underutilisation of existing forestry services and facilities, gaps in marketing and promotion, poor navigation and markers and associated concerns for safety, eutrophication and the absence of an overarching and coherent strategic plan for the lough.

Lough Neagh attracts the majority of its leisure visitors from within Northern Ireland, predominantly day trippers, with less than one in five of all visitors staying overnight in the area. While many are visiting to see a specific attraction, a high proportion make a return visit and in particular to visit a favourite place, reflecting the high proportion of domestic visitors. More so than for any other region, visitors choose Lough Neagh as a destination specifically to be active and take part in activities outdoors. Although Lough Neagh is currently an underperforming tourism asset, it can become one of the major attractors for visitors subject to investment and greater strategic focus by government.

FIG. 50.5
Canoe at Ballyronan.

A way forward

Despite its extent and its widespread use for a range of activities, the lough has ever only had one integrated management plan. This plan was developed by the Lough Neagh Advisory Committee in 2002 and tried to introduce actions that gave consideration to the objectives of all the stakeholders and organisations involved with the lough. Although some of the actions were successfully delivered, the more complex issues around long-term management of resources and addressing negative environmental issues were never progressed mainly due to the absence of a sufficient budget. This essentially sets the context for the future that in a relatively small region such as Northern Ireland, the only organisation to lead from the front to address environmental issues and resolve resource conflict has been a non-governmental organisation (NGO), which takes a bottom up, partnership approach to holistic environmental management.

In 2004, the first part of the lough's slow regeneration occurred, through the creation of a new group of stakeholders. Sand traders, fishermen, farmers, community groups and the main councils around the lough came together to form a stakeholder and management body known as Lough Neagh Partnership (LNP). In some ways, LNP has been remarkably successful in attracting substantial amounts of investment into the lough area through European and Heritage Lottery funding and becoming the environmental management body for the lough, working very closely with the Northern Ireland Environment Agency in maintaining and monitoring the important environmental designations. Likewise, it has collaborated closely with councils to promote and develop important tourism infrastructure. But in another sense, it has not been successful, because it has been unable to persuade the Northern Ireland Government to take greater responsibility to provide greater investment and coordinated management for the lough. Numerous meetings with ministers have been held over the last ten years but the simple truth remains that there is still, in 2021, no navigation authority for Lough Neagh. Not even a simple interdepartmental management group for the lough exists. Twenty-three years after the Good Friday Agreement, Lough Neagh remains outwith the remit of Waterways Ireland.

So just what is the future for Lough Neagh and how can it be better protected and better managed? Well, the answer to this question is quite simple and already bodies like DAERA and the Northern Ireland Environment Agency have stepped up to the mark and developed strong practical working relationship with Lough Neagh Partnership to collaborate closely with farmers, bringing in new environmental farm scheme investment and encouraging farmers who live along the shore to develop new farm practices and create new nature connected areas. In July 2007, the remit of Waterways Ireland was extended by the North South Ministerial Council to include responsibility for the reconstruction of the Ulster Canal from Upper Lough Erne to Clones, and in 2021 funding was allocated to complete the connection to Clones. There is no reason however, why some work on the northern side of the canal, which starts at Lough Neagh, cannot be identified and investment agreed.

In Northern Ireland, the Rathlin model is also a fitting example of how several departments, with a lead department and senior civil servants driving policy, can oversee an integrated government plan for important landscapes like Lough Neagh. The private sector can also recognise the need to take mitigating actions against the loss of species and habitats that may have resulted from natural resource extraction and development, and could come together to provide funding for specific environmental protection and restoration projects. In the long term, investment and ring-fenced income could even come from the public purchase of the bed and soil asset of Shaftesbury Estates and both governments in the south and north could eventually implement the spirit of the Good Friday Agreement and give Lough Neagh a fully functioning navigation authority under the remit of Waterways Ireland. More recent discussions and interest from the Northern Ireland Assembly MLAs now seems to be happening and so let us hope it does not take another 23 years before the management needs of this vast and wonderful body of water are to be fully addressed and its natural resources used in a more sustainable way for the benefit of everyone.

FIG. 50.6
Engaging Lough Neagh stakeholders in the strategic planning process.

Notes

1   'The Plantation of Ulster and its effect on native woodlands'
    (https://meonjournal.com/read/the-plantation-of-ulster-and-its-effect-on-native-woodlands).
2   Eileen McCracken, 'The woodlands of Ulster in the early seventeenth century', *UJA*, 3rd series, vol. 10 (1947), pp 15–25.

Traditional boat race at Ballyronan, 2019.

Index

PERSONAL NAMES

The Six Mile Water at Antrim
Castle Gardens.

Cranfield church ruins.

Mallard duckling.

The Battery Harbour, Ardboe.

The Lough Neagh Partnership

The Lough Neagh Partnership is a not-for-profit organisation that was established in 2003 to help protect and promote Lough Neagh and the interests of the many communities around its shores.

Since its formation the partnership has gone from strength to strength and is heavily involved in a wide range of projects and programmes that cover issues, such as the promotion, protection and rejuvenation of Lough Neagh's built, cultural and natural heritage.

https://loughneaghpartnership.org

PROJECTS

FUNDERS